The School of Libanius in Late Antique Antioch

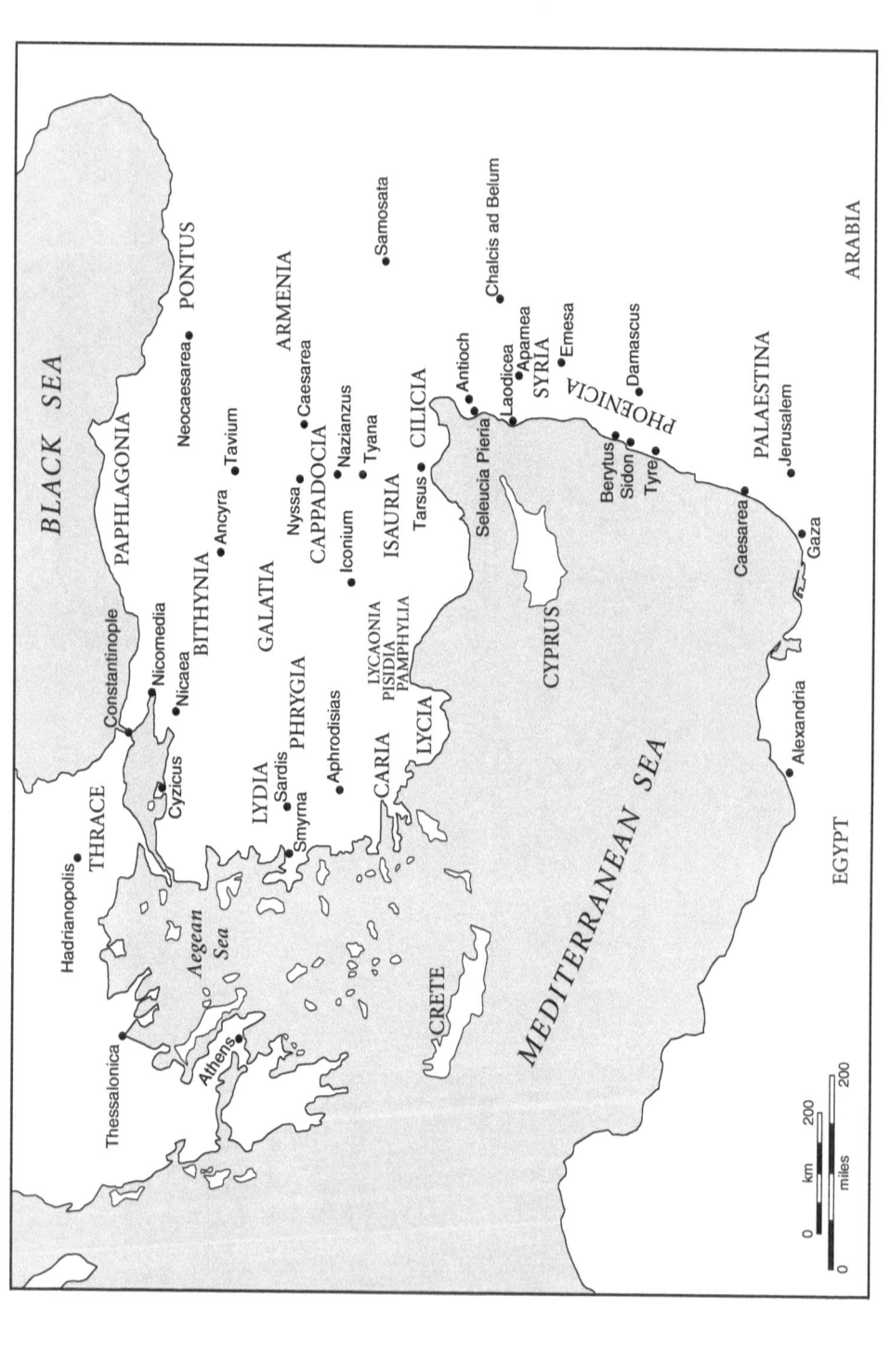

The School of Libanius in Late Antique Antioch

Raffaella Cribiore

PRINCETON UNIVERSITY PRESS
PRINCETON AND OXFORD

Copyright © 2007 by Princeton University Press
Published by Princeton University Press, 41 William Street, Princeton, New Jersey 08540
In the United Kingdom: Princeton University Press, 3 Market Place,
Woodstock, Oxfordshire OX20 1SY

All Rights Reserved

Library of Congress Cataloging-in-Publication Data

Cribiore, Raffaella
The school of Libanius in late antique Antioch / Raffaella Cribiore.
v. cm.
Includes bibliographical references and index.
Contents: Libanius and rhetoric in Antioch—Schools and Sophists in the Roman East—The network—Admission and evaluation—teaching the logoi—The long and the short path to rhetoric—After rhetoric—Conclusion : words and silence—Appendix 1 : the dossiers of students—Appendix 2 : length of students' attendence.
ISBN-13: 978-0-691-17135-7 (hardcover : alk. paper)
ISBN-10: 0-691-17135-7 (hardcover : alk. paper)
1. Libanius. 2. Philosophy—Study and teaching—Turkey—Antioch—History. I. Title.
B577.L44C75 2007
808.0071′03943—dc22   2006013514

British Library Cataloging-in-Publication Data is available

This book has been composed in Sabon

Printed on acid-free paper. ∞

pup.princeton.edu

Printed in the United States of America

10 9 8 7 6 5 4 3 2 1

*Ai miei genitori
tanto amati*

Contents

PREFACE	ix
A NOTE ON REFERENCES AND ABBREVIATIONS	xi
INTRODUCTION	1
CHAPTER ONE Libanius and Rhetoric in Antioch	13
CHAPTER TWO Schools and Sophists in the Roman East	42
CHAPTER THREE The Network	83
CHAPTER FOUR Admission and Evaluation	111
CHAPTER FIVE Teaching the *Logoi*	137
CHAPTER SIX The Long and Short Paths to Rhetoric	174
CHAPTER SEVEN After Rhetoric	197
CONCLUSION Words and Silence	229
APPENDIX ONE Dossiers of Students	233
APPENDIX TWO Length of Students' Attendance	323
APPENDIX THREE Concordance of Letters in Appendix One Translated into English	329
SELECT BIBLIOGRAPHY	331
INDEX LOCORUM	347
GENERAL INDEX	355

Preface

WHEN I WAS writing about Greek education in Egypt in *Gymnastics of the Mind*, I looked for an ancient writer against whom I could test some of the ideas that the papyri suggested. It soon became apparent that Libanius was ideal. The sheer quantity of his writing was daunting at the start, but also tantalizing and promising. When my project reached its end, I was well aware that I had left much behind and that Libanius was still waiting for me. His speeches were extremely useful in helping to trace the story of his famous school in Antioch and of the fluctuating state of rhetoric in the fourth century. His letters captivated me entirely as he truly became part of my life.

I had already written some parts of this book and translated Libanius's letters (many more than this appendix includes) when I was given the opportunity to spend the fall semester of 2004 at the Institute for Advanced Study in Princeton. I spent a blissful and constructive period there, communicating daily with superb scholars in the company of some great mosaics from Antioch. At the Institute, I was finally able to put into perspective some of the issues that still troubled me. I am very grateful to Glen Bowersock for so generously "letting me drink at his spring of excellence in the garden of the Muses" (as Libanius would say). I also warmly thank Heinrich von Staden for being there when I needed help. Several people contributed to this book in various ways, by reading the whole manuscript or parts of it, providing valuable criticism, discussing points in the translations, and helping me check the text. Thus I am grateful to Peter Brown, Alan Cameron, Eleanor Dickey, William Frosh, Iannis Papadoyannakis, Robert Penella, Giovanni Ruffini, and Maria Wenglinsky. To my family, love as always.

A Note on References and Abbreviations

JOURNALS AND WORKS are abbreviated as in *L'Année philologique* and the *American Journal of Archaeology*. Ancient authors and their works are abbreviated according to the third edition of the *Oxford Classical Dictionary*. Modern works that appear in the Select Bibliography are cited in the text by author's name and date of publication.

The numbers in this study that sometimes follow the names of people who appear in Libanius's works refer to the prosopography in *PLRE* I (*The Prosopography of the Later Roman Empire*, vol. 1: Jones et al. 1971) and occasionally in *PLRE* II (Martindale 1980). When only one person by a certain name is included in those lists, I provide the page reference. The vast majority of the students and members of their families were not of such a status as to be included in *PLRE*. It is necessary to refer to them by the numbering used in Seeck 1906, which is the only complete prosopographical work on Libanius's letters. Thus names that are followed by Roman numerals are included in that work. A double citation (according to both *PLRE* and Seeck) is used when both prosopographies contain valuable observations.

In the text, I cite Libanius's letters that appear in Appendix One by the numbering (in bold characters) used there. I refer to other letters of Libanius by citing the numbering in Foerster's edition (1903–27). References to translations in Norman 1992 (N) and Bradbury 2004a (B) are given according to the numbering in these collections.

The School of Libanius in Late Antique Antioch

Introduction

THE SOPHIST LIBANIUS, who was an exponent of the revival of Greek literature that started with the Second Sophistic,[1] taught in Antioch in Syria in the fourth century C.E. In *Oration 55*, he extolled to a student the advantages of a career as a teacher of rhetoric:

> How great it is to rule over wellborn young men and see them improve in rhetoric and proceed to the various paths of life! And what about the honors one receives from them and their fathers, from citizens and foreigners? Teachers of rhetoric are respected by all governors, small and great, and even by emperors. (23)

There are many similar statements in Libanius, as well as fervent commendations of good students. There are an equal number of negative assessments of the condition of rhetoric—a despised and silent discipline—and condemnations of youths indifferent to its charms. In general, Libanius's letters present a different view than the orations. In attempting to understand the reasons for the discrepancy and to unravel other puzzles that the vast corpus of the rhetor's surviving writings presents, this book delves into the workings of the most prominent school of rhetoric in Antioch (the modern Antakya, in south Turkey), where Libanius taught as "official sophist of the city."[2] The school served youths from all provinces of the Roman East. Its curriculum and teaching methods were common to other schools of the Roman Empire, so that the works of Libanius also provide a clear, welcome window on higher education in other times and places. We can apply to Libanius the words of the poet Meleager, who lived centuries before: "If I am a Syrian, what wonder? Stranger, we live in one country, the world."[3]

Libanius kept a vast correspondence to advertise the quality of his teaching and to maintain contacts with the families of his pupils, former students, and a few other teachers. I have included in an appendix translations of about 200 letters that concern his teaching activity.[4] All of the

---

[1] The phrase, which comes from Philostratus (*VS* 481, 507), is commonly applied to Greek culture from mid-first to mid-third century, but much evidence comes from later times. Pernot (1993, 14 n. 9) proposed the term "Third Sophistic" for the fourth century.

[2] These words were uttered bitterly by a former student, John Chrysostom, *In Honor of the Blessed Babylas, Against the Hellenes* 18; Schatkin 1990.

[3] Meleager lived in the first century B.C.E. This quotation comes from an epigram, *Anth. Pal.* 7.417.

[4] See Appendix One. In 1738, J. C. Wolf produced an edition with translations of the 1544 letters, but naturally, he could not take advantage of the magisterial text established in

surviving correspondence of Libanius, which is more than double that of Cicero's, belongs to two separate periods, his first ten years of teaching in Antioch and the last five years of his life.[5] This study, in any case, is based not only on the texts I have translated, but also on all of his correspondence with relevance to education, as well as several of his speeches that pertain to pedagogical issues.

There is more than one Libanius, and this book does not pretend to interpret them all or to solve all the puzzles. The questions I am asking depend on my specific interests and are only tangential to other fundamental questions. By the beginning of the third century, Christianity had gained a hold over the intellectual elite, but Libanius, a major representative of Hellenism when it was starting to break down, was an exponent of paganism, since his fervent belief in classical culture brought with it a religious allegiance.[6] Issues such as Libanius's relationship with the emperor Julian go beyond the teacher-student rapport that I explore; they have been asked before and will continue to be asked.[7] I will only touch upon Libanius's relations with two of his well-renowned students, John Chrysostom and Basil the Great, who followed paths of life different from him but continued to draw on the rhetorical skills they had acquired.[8] In the same way, I will not linger on his interactions with emperors and pivotal figures of the age, with whom he sometimes had

---

1921 by Foerster. Festugière 1959 partly or wholly translated into French some 100 letters regarding education, but his translations are somewhat inadequate. Recent translations of Libanius's letters contain only a handful of letters concerned with education; see Norman 1992; Fatouros and Krischer 1980; Cabouret 2000; and Bradbury 2004a. A concordance of the letters' translations is in Wintjes 2005, 279–91. Gonzales Galvez (2005) has translated into Spanish the first part of the collection of letters, but this translation was not available to me before this book entered production.

[5] About 80 percent of the letters fall in the period 355–65, and the rest mostly cover the years 388–93. In Appendix One, I have not followed a chronological order but have included separate dossiers for each student. I did not include a dossier for those students of Libanius who make only a brief appearance in a letter.

[6] On Hellenism as consciousness of descent from the ancient Greeks and aspiration to linguistic purity, see, e.g., Swain 1996 and 2004; Whitmarsh 2001. On Hellenism and paganism, see Bowersock 1990. The nineteenth-century Greek poet Constantine P. Cavafy, who was born and lived in Alexandria, aptly comments on the feelings of belonging to classical Greece: "Let us finally accept the truth; we too are Greeks—what else are we?—but with loves and emotions of Asia, but with loves and emotions that sometimes astound Hellenism." Dalven 1976, 272, "Return from Greece."

[7] I use the name Julianus for the teachers and students by that name, but I will refer to the emperor as Julian.

[8] I occasionally mention John Chrysostom; on him, see Kelly 1995; Liebeschuetz 1990, 157–227; and Festugière 1959 (pp. 412–14 on his disputed chronology); see also the useful summary of various issues in Wintjes 2005, 177–90. I will dedicate only a little more attention to Basil; see Chapter Three below.

tempestuous relationships, or on his influence on public affairs in Antioch, or on his concern *(philanthrōpia)* for the lower classes and protests about social injustice and against an oppressive system.[9] Libanius (probably rightly) boasted to have written "more than any man alive" and revealed much of himself; much of what the Middle Ages preserved still awaits interpretation.[10]

But even though I concentrate on Libanius as an educator, and the factual claims I make are based on a process of inquiry and the examination of a large body of material, I am aware that I cannot pretend to have captured him fully. Letters manipulate reality no less than do speeches self-consciously composed for public consumption or autobiography. While one should read them (when possible) in conjunction with other writings of an author, it is not always easy to find overall coherence, if that is what one seeks. The farther a reader is from a text, the less competent he is to interpret it,[11] and this is particularly true with letters. Apart from the issue of influence from other texts and trends, letters need to be situated in context in order to reconstruct the meaning they had for their original readers (the recipients principally), the people to whom they showed them, the subsequent readers who had Libanius's collection at their disposal after his death, up to the present readers. A letter not only is a veritable dialogue between two parties, as ancient literary critics maintained, but it also significantly involves the persona of the carrier, who brought it and supplemented its content, and the subsequent audience, which eavesdrops on a distant conversation and enriches its significance. Through a method of historical reception, one is more equipped to reach the original meaning of an epistolary text, but attempts to reconstruct what has been called a "horizon of expectations" may be only partially successful.[12] So, for example, while we can interpret and predict to some degree the impact of the literary and philosophical references of Libanius's letters, something still escapes us with regard to various allusions. Does an obscure expression reproduce an ancient proverb, a colloquial utterance, or a private joke between writer and recipient? We are sometimes inescapably severed from the text's meaning.[13]

---

[9] Harries (1999, 118–34) argues that the evidence from his work cannot be discounted and needs to be reevaluated.

[10] See *Or.* 11.1. In addition to the letters, Libanius's corpus (Foerster 1903–27) includes sixty-four orations, fifty-one declamations, a great number of "preliminary exercises" *(progymnasmata)*, and summaries of the *Arguments of Demosthenes*. The manuscript tradition has mostly preserved speeches that dealt with public affairs and school matters.

[11] See White 1971.

[12] See Jauss 1971.

[13] See, e.g., letter **14** and the allusion to the wine vats.

A literary letter, which is simultaneously the product of both real life and literature, is a text that is far from transparent. As readers, we have to rediscover the subtle balance between letters as functional documents and letters as works of art, a balance that was operative when the writer composed his message, but that has insensibly changed upon reaching us. Libanius's letters lay between private and public and were intended to have a literary and lasting value, as indicated by the reactions of his recipients, who often publicized them or claimed inability to respond with similar art. Libanius kept duplicates of his letters, but it is unclear whether he published a limited collection during his lifetime.[14] We may view a letter as an outpouring more spontaneous than an unquestionably literary text (his orations, for example), but in his correspondence, Libanius constructed a personal view of reality and of himself, just as he did in his other works.

Much distinguishes Libanius's letters from the straightforward correspondence of more-or-less educated people that survives from Roman Egypt and, to some degree, from many other sophisticated epistolary texts.[15] Since they originate from a copybook, introductory and final expressions are not included. It is likely that Libanius dictated most of his letters to his secretary and did not pen them himself. A generally unnoticed remark from a contemporary writer, the Roman rhetor Julius Victor, is enlightening: "As a rule, the ancients wrote in their own hands to those closest to them, or at least frequently appended a subscription."[16] In attributing to the *veteres* (Cicero, for example) the habit of penning their own correspondence to intimate people, Julius Victor appears to note a difference from contemporary writing habits and seems to refer to some change in epistolary etiquette.[17] Libanius continued to subscribe his letters to friends, but it is not certain whether he did the same with all correspondents.[18] His letters plunge *in medias res*, describing a unique moment, a request, a mood, and often include an elegantly crafted and clever ending. Some traditional epistolary topics are transformed in his correspondence. So the customary wish for health is there only when there are realistic questions about the recipient's condition, and this often mutates into an

---

[14] On the question, see Seeck 1906; Silomon 1909; Norman 1992, 1:29–31; and Wintjes 2005, 24–27. The dates and order of all the letters would benefit from some fresh attention.

[15] Cf. the collection in Trapp 2003.

[16] *Ars rhetorica* 27.

[17] Ammianus (15.1.3) says that Constantius subscribed his letters with the words *aeternitas mea* and called himself *orbis totius dominus* when writing in his hand, but it is unclear if the emperor added postscripts in his hand or penned whole letters.

[18] Cf. *Ep.* 1223.1, where he appears to be adding the customary "farewell" to a letter of his friend Acacius 6. In *Ep.* 1456, he shows himself about to write with papyrus and pen in front of him, but it is impossible to tell if the description corresponded to reality.

excursus on Libanius's own welfare. In the same way, the common complaint about not receiving news often includes a reference to an addressee's reluctance to write lest his rhetorical skills not measure up to Libanius's stringent standards, and the lament about lost correspondence (a reality with ancient mail delivery) becomes a colorful description of a letter's vicissitudes.[19]

The letters that pertain to education present some uniformity as a group insofar as they throw into relief Libanius's persona as teacher, illuminate some pedagogic issues, and disclose a world of people connected with his profession. Yet one should not attempt to forcefully pigeonhole them into a well-defined epistolary category. Most often, letters do not serve only a single communicative function, but rather discharge a multiplicity of clear (or hidden) roles.[20] Many voices can be heard in them, in contrast to Byzantine letters, which revolve entirely around the relationship between writer and recipient.[21] Most often, Libanius discusses a certain young man with a member of his family, but this trio of voices can be expanded by the mention of other relatives or friends who know the student or by a brief excursus on the letter carrier.

The letters, orations, and pedagogical works of Libanius reveal both continuity and change in education. I refer frequently (both in the main text and in the notes) to education in other periods and societies and to my previous work on this subject, but I did not think it necessary to write a separate account of the distinctiveness of Libanius's school vis-à-vis others.[22] Libanius himself emphasizes continuity in teaching methods and in the curriculum, but we will see that only a few of his students were able to follow his ideal, taxing program. He was not inclined to acknowledge discontinuity and modifications of a proven system, yet the short attendance and defections of many of his students must have forced him to make some adjustments. It is also possible that, like all great teachers, he introduced some innovations, which are now hidden among the traditional features of his rhetoric. There is a continuous interplay between his role as a representative of the art of rhetoric and his function as a teacher devoted to instilling the same principles in others. Fidelity to tradition gives a recognizable density to his words, so that his work as rhetor and

---

[19] See, e.g., *Ep.* 865.
[20] Even letters that I have identified as reports of progress or recommendation do not fully belong to only one category.
[21] See Mullett 1981, 82, and 1997, 18–19.
[22] In Cribiore 2001, I treated rather exhaustively the comparison of Libanius's methods and curriculum to what we know of other schools. In this book (Chapter Five), I make the picture more complete and ask further questions. Moreover, what emerges from Libanius on school organization, didactic methods, and the relation between schooling and future professions is unique and detailed, and does not find an adequate comparison in antiquity.

sophist may appear to be only the result of sedimentation of things practiced, taught, and learned from the distant past. Yet the issues of his own times, his creativity, and everyday intercourse with his students must have had some impact on his production that we are not able to detect. Though one is tempted to find an uninterrupted discourse that links him to contemporary exponents of Attic oratory, to the Second Sophistic, and in turn to Hermogenes, Aristides, and Demosthenes (among many others), the differences and limitations in the functions of fourth-century rhetoric inevitably shaped his work.

But let us return to the question raised at the beginning concerning the numerous contradictory statements that one encounters in Libanius's work throughout his life and the differing picture that often emerges from his orations and letters. The Libanius most readers know is the old, embittered sophist of the *Autobiography* and his late speeches, the educator who ranted against rival studies and the indifference of his pupils in his old age.[23] The vast majority of the preserved letters, however, is from his early years of teaching in Antioch, when he was still immune from the criticism later leveled against his educational system. This question is intertwined with historical circumstances that valued some studies like shorthand, Roman law, or Latin more than traditional rhetoric, yet one must keep in view that from the first century C.E. to our time, there have been frequent lamentations about the decline of rhetoric as an indicator of the decline of political and societal health.[24] The state of Libanius's mental and physical health, which deteriorated insensibly with the passing of the years and the accumulation of loss and disappointment, also deserves consideration. What place (if any) are we supposed to give to Libanius's personal vicissitudes and temperament? The recourse to a biographical and psychological approach is valuable and sometimes inescapable. One may choose not to raise questions about subjective factors, but they are present in the construction of a text in concomitance with sociocultural components and may help explain internal inconsistencies.[25]

Psychological, biographical, and historical reasons, which are helpful in other respects, do not provide a full answer to the question at hand, since most of the late letters continue to project an image of Libanius's satisfied dedication to teaching and appreciation of his pupils. Audience and genre, however, may account for some of the unevenness. Most of the letters that refer to education (including the later ones) concern individual

---

[23] Most of the orations in Norman 2000 belong to the 380s and later.

[24] See, e.g., Edwards and Reid 2002. For a negative view of the culture of Late Antiquity, see MacMullen 1990.

[25] See Izenberg 1993.

students and usually good students.[26] The late orations, however, denounce a whole group of prevaricating, insolent pupils who cared for other disciplines and did not show a disinterested love for the ideal, consuming rhetoric that Libanius cultivated. Are these "bad" students (or at least the students collectively) completely absent from the correspondence? Very occasionally they do appear, but only as a foil to the young man who is the protagonist of the moment. Thus they may serve to throw into more prominent relief a peaceful student, who does not like to fight in spite of his bodily strength, or they are an ideal backdrop, with their "sleepiness," to the "awakened" commitment of another, or their disinterest may underscore the diligence of a pupil who seeks academic supervision after his departure from Antioch.[27] But these are rare instances. As a rule, a letter is entirely dominated by the portrait of the student whose family Libanius is contacting. The restricted original audience of a private letter is enlarged in an oration, but no generalization is possible. A speech might address Antioch's Council on internal issues or might be delivered in front of the whole school as a performance with a pedagogic aim. It might address the emperor and vividly refer to his actual presence at the delivery without being sent to or pronounced in front of him.[28] Controversial orations were restricted to a limited group of friends with whom Libanius could afford to give vent to his frustrations or might be transmitted to an equally select circle at court. He probably confined to his own file drawers some of the bitterest personal tirades against public figures still in power.[29]

In pointing to the specific characteristics of epistolary versus oratorical texts, I have been relying on generic distinctions. Generic considerations can explain some inconsistencies, but they need to be applied with caution and elasticity. Genres are in a continuous state of mutation, so that adjustments are necessary in order not to create disparity between literature and generic descriptions.[30] We assign a work to a generic type, but not all the embodiments of a type share the same characteristics. Libanius's letters

---

[26] Cf. below, Chapter Four.

[27] See **5, 82,** and **27**. In *Ep.* 444, such students appear as *hoi polloi*, the mass of the students who are worse in rhetoric than a certain boy. In **147**, students (considered as a group) are the joyful friends of a popular young man; and in **75**, they are impressed by the renown of the family of a newcomer.

[28] Cf. *Or.* 45.11 and its denunciation of public policy. This speech was certainly not delivered before Theodosius, in spite of the vivid, "You are weeping, Sire." It is likely that none of the speeches addressed to this emperor were sent directly to him. On their resemblance to Dio's *Kingship Orations,* see Swain 2004, 368.

[29] See Petit 1956b.

[30] On ancient misapprehensions about genres, see Fowler 1982, 20–36. The best genre criticism should be descriptive rather than prescriptive and far from dogmatic; see Hernadi 1972, 1–9.

vary considerably with regard to their practical aims and rhetorical coloring. Even though he was sensitive to his public image every time he wrote, letters touching on educational matters are generally more casual and shorter than the others and abound in references to everyday problems. Libanius's letters, in any case, distinguish themselves from early and late Byzantine epistolary texts, which on the whole are more rhetorical, convoluted, and decorated and appear crystallized into forms that were used for centuries.[31] Libanius's orations also vary greatly in terms of occasion, subject matter, audience, and rhetorical density: a school speech, a panegyric, an invective, and an oration of reproach each have a physiognomy and a tradition of their own.

A generic characteristic of correspondence that contributes to smoothing out a letter's edges is the fact that a letter exists to establish or crown a relationship, most often a friendly one. This feature stands out already in the earliest discussion of epistolary theory in a work from the second century B.C.E., *On Style* by Ps.-Demetrius, who stated that Aristotle considered some topics inappropriate for a letter, and that epistolary writing should aim at communicating warm feelings of friendship.[32] Theoretically, a letter could convey the whole gamut of moods and behaviors inherent in social intercourse and did so occasionally, but generally fourth-century letters are smooth vehicles of friendship.[33] Scholars have remarked with astonishment the apparently duplicitous behavior of Libanius toward some public figures with whom he corresponded with courteous and flattering letters, but to whom he addressed inflamed invectives in his speeches.[34] Psychological and biographical reasons are rightly invoked to explain the flagrant disparity, but generic considerations also need to come into play. As an instrument of meaning serving writers and readers, genre helps establish a system of communication that bridges distance.[35] The process of generic recognition and interpretation helps us to identify some of the limits within which Libanius worked. We will see that generic considerations provide another backdrop against which we can evaluate several problematic stances of this author.

---

[31] See Mullett 1981; Gruenbart 2005.

[32] Demetrius, an otherwise unknown writer, *On Style,* 230–32. The current consensus favors the second century B.C.E as a date for this work (cf., e.g., Kennedy 1972, 285–90).

[33] See Thraede 1970, 125–46; White 1992; and Van Dam 2003a, 136–38. On Christian letters expressing the love of friends and reflecting the love of Christ, see Conybeare 2000, 60–90. See, however, in Libanius's correspondence, four hostile letters from the dossier of twenty-six letters he sent to Anatolius of Berytus, which are quite exceptional: Bradbury 2000, 173–74.

[34] Cf. below, Chapter One.

[35] See Fowler 1982, 256–76. Mullett (1992) gives a clear example of the usefulness of generic characteristics of letters versus those of biography.

I am committed to attempt a reconstruction of the world of Libanius's texts by taking into account not only the unique moment in which he operated, but also, in some measure, the collective, diachronic dimension of a period, the type of society in which he lived, the landscape common to that culture, and the set of traditions that affected him. Other texts that are outside that world, and are even separated from it by many centuries, may provide an additional understanding of patterns of human life, education, and growth. It is the continuity of human experience that justifies some venturing in other directions. With regard to this project, tempting *comparanda* are available with the letters of an anonymous professor who was the head of a school of secondary education in tenth-century Constantinople, a morose man who lived for his books and his students and did some writing of his own in his spare time.[36] The correspondence of Johann Amerbach, who had a successful publishing-printing firm in Basel in the upper Rhine area at the turn of the sixteenth century, can also be illuminating, since he exchanged letters with his children and their teachers.[37] Johann Amerbach had two sons who studied away from home, and I will sometimes refer to their vicissitudes as students abroad and to the frustrations of their father, who worried about their progress and did not want "to send young asses to Paris and get full-grown asses back."[38] Parents of Libanius's students had similar concerns.

In the course of this book, I often argue against aspects of the work of Paul Petit, a historian who produced an invaluable study of Antioch's society, of the complex prosopography of Libanius's writings, and of the identities of the young men who were part of his *chorus*, that is, his school.[39] My debts to his research are many. He provided a basis for my study, and my interpretation became more nuanced and comprehensive because it could rest on his findings.[40] My areas of disagreement are fundamentally two. First, Petit, who believed in isolating facts as irreducible entities, considered Libanius's letters documents that could be interpreted objectively, cobblestones still set in what was once a firmly built road. The framework he constructed and presented as objective (supported by

---

[36] *Anon. Lond.*; see Lemerle 1986, 286–96; and Markopoulos 2000. These 122 letters, 40 percent of which regard education, date to the first quarter of the tenth century. The school in question was a grammar school that probably also reached the rhetorical level.

[37] Johann Amerbach (ca. 1440–1513); see Halporn (2000, 137–206), who collected and studied the letters they sent home during the whole period of their schooling. I thank Therese de Vet for this reference.

[38] Halporn 2000, 152–53 no. 98.

[39] See especially Petit 1955, 1957, and 1956a. I am also very indebted to the accurate research of Otto Seeck (1906). Libanius often calls his school (including the teachers) a *chorus*.

[40] On the benefits of disagreement, see Heath 2002a, 9–11.

minute percentages) is, however, fragile at many points. Exclusive immersion in the "facts" does not lead to a perception of the past that can be said with any certainty to correspond to reality; quite the opposite. I am ultimately concerned with cultural history and, although my account of the past naturally aspires to be a logical reconstruction of it, I am aware that sometimes it may represent only my version of the "story," as I am trying to capture the cultural sedimentation in Libanius's work as well as the subtle shifts that make him unique.[41] Second, Petit, influenced by nineteenth- and twentieth-century European (especially French) educational practice, presumed a rather rigid pattern of schooling, and his conviction strongly shaped the factual claims he made and sometimes blinded him to other realities.

Petit's account, which is mostly not in narrative form, mainly consists of a reconstruction of the list of students, their years of attendance, and their provenance and recruitment, province by province. Compounded with the absence of a translation of the relevant letters, this continually fragments his description of Libanius's school and makes it difficult to follow. My book applies techniques of historical research, but it is in narrative form. Unlike autobiography, letters look forward and recount a series of events in their chronological succession, but I found it more useful to divide the letter collection (in Appendix One) according to dossiers of the various students, to give a clearer idea of their identities, attendance, and subsequent paths in life.

The first chapter of this book gives a preliminary evaluation of the personality of Libanius as a man, rhetor, and sophist, and delineates the contours of the landscape: his school of rhetoric in the city of Antioch. Since several excellent archaeological descriptions of this city are available, I simply attempt to show the type of cultural and physical environment (distractions included) that it offered to visiting students. I focus then on the school, the specific functions of the other teachers who assisted Libanius, and the surviving information concerning the activities of other sophists in Antioch. In the second chapter, I attempt to view Libanius's school against the vast landscape of the teaching of rhetoric in the Roman East.[42] This sketch of rhetorical schools from Athens to Constantinople, to the Anatolian plateau and the Mediterranean coast, underlines the international character of Late Antique education and the conspicuous rivalry among schools. The reader will start encountering figures that resurface here and there throughout the book, such as the sophists Prohaeresius

---

[41] Cf. De Vries-van der Velden 2003.

[42] After Chapter One, I chose not to continue discussing the various issues of the school (which are treated from Chapter Three on) because I thought it more useful to present a comprehensive view of rhetoric in the East.

and Himerius, the philosopher Themistius, and Gregory of Nazianzus. With Chapter Three, the international component of the student body of Libanius's school emerges clearly. This chapter delves into the different methods on which he relied in order to recruit his students, that is, strengthening his professional position in Antioch by showing the worth of his oratory and by defeating competitors with all the means available; securing the favor of powerful officials; and creating an effective network of relationships. After he became the municipal sophist of the city, his recruiting efforts concentrated on this network, which consisted of former students and their families, as well as people with whom he had cultural bonds of friendship. Chapter Three begins a series of chapters that follow Libanius's students from the moment they enter the school to when they leave and move on to further studies or various careers.

Chapters Four through Seven allow the reader to enter into closer contact with the letters included in Appendix One. Chapter Four studies students' applications to the school, their initial encounters with the sophist, the diagnostic test he administered to them in order to place them at various levels, and the criteria of evaluation he followed in the reports sent to families. This section probes the issue of innate ability versus upbringing and education as it appears in several ancient authors besides Libanius. It also begins to investigate the question of what a letter writer chose to include (or chose to omit or obscure) in his correspondence. Chapter Five revolves around the curriculum in Libanius's school, but besides describing the various steps that the sophist followed to "sow" and "plant" rhetoric in his pupils, it poses a fundamental question. What were the reasons for the excitement young men who attended a school of rhetoric felt and remembered afterward with longing? Were there features of the curriculum that justified their enthusiasm? The topic of Chapter Six is the length of students' attendance, and especially the abbreviated attendance of most of them. Besides other issues, I investigate with close attention the cost of schooling and students' defections, subjects that the letters barely touch, but that the speeches denounce vehemently. But how crucial was a lengthy education in rhetoric at the hands of a prestigious teacher for a young man who was trying to secure a good career? This is the focus of Chapter Seven, which first considers questions of evaluation of competence and effectiveness (to see if these modern concepts find an application in ancient society), then moves to the choices available to Libanius's students. To measure the relevance of rhetoric in the ancient "resumé," I study here the recommendations that Libanius wrote to provide further assistance to former students. I also inquire about the cultural attainments of governors to verify the validity of the concept of rhetoric as a passport to power, which often occurs in the sources. Besides recapitulating some points, the concluding chapter briefly investigates the presence of silence versus words in the work and life of Libanius. Appendix One contains the dossiers of letters, Appendix Two calculates, as far as this is possible, students' length of attendance, and Appendix Three has a concordance for the letter collection.

Finally, I should say a few words about my translation of the letters. A translation is a balancing act between fidelity and freedom, with translators spending "their lives tottering within this acrobatic space."[43] I have tried to remain fairly close to the Greek text, keeping in mind at the same time that it rarely happens that fidelity in translating individual words fully reproduces the meaning they have in the original.[44] I strictly maintained, however, the distinction between singular and plural first-person pronouns ("I" and "we"). To assume automatically that Libanius used them interchangeably and always pointing to himself is not necessarily correct, in my opinion.[45] The plural often appears to refer not only to Libanius but to his school, with its plurality of teachers.[46] On the whole, I am tempted to quote the words of Frank Cole Babbitt in the preface of his translation of Plutarch: "It is useless to apologize for the translation or to attempt to defend it; it is what it is, but at any rate it has not been done in haste."[47]

---

[43] See Most 2003, 382.

[44] See Benjamin 1992.

[45] Both Norman (1992) and Bradbury (2004a) chose to use these pronouns interchangeably.

[46] The most common example is *par'ēmin* ("by us, in our school," better than "with me"). At times the plural might be humorous. It was, in any case, a conscious choice of the author; cf. Gallay 2003, 1:xliv.

[47] *Plutarch's Moralia*, Loeb Classical Library, vol. 1 (London, 1927), vii.

CHAPTER ONE

Libanius and Rhetoric in Antioch

LIBANIUS: A LIFE, A MAN

An attempt to reconstruct the life and character of any author is fraught with difficulty. The story of Libanius's life has been written many times, first by Libanius himself; yet he remains elusive. Nineteenth-century scholar G. R. Sievers achieved some valuable results, but he accepted with few questions everything Libanius wrote in his speeches and in the letters.[1] A recent work successfully corrected some biographical details, but its exclusive reliance on "facts" hardly allows one to capture the various sides of Libanius.[2] It is necessary to weigh Libanius's statements and opinions against contrasting remarks made at different times and to take into account the tumultuous period when he lived, his mental attitude, which was not always consistent and stable, and the various mediums in which he wrote. Libanius's profession, moreover, contributes to the suspicions of the modern scholar, as if rhetoric would give a definite imprint to his words and a deceiving bent to his mind.

Forming an unfavorable or inaccurate opinion of Libanius is easy. His Greek is often intricate (particularly so in the speeches), much of his work is still not translated, and the single oration familiar to most scholars is his controversial *Autobiography*.[3] It has long been recognized that the first part of the narrative of his life (1–155) was composed in 374 as a complete work that Libanius shared with a select group of friends, but the rest was a private, rambling diary that was added arbitrarily after his death. This somewhat incoherent second part of the *Autobiography,* with its repetitions and dark pessimism, has detracted considerably from Libanius's image. The energetic, indefatigable, communicative teacher devoted to both rhetoric and his students fades away, and we are left with a vision of a disturbed old man and an "embittered egocentric" whiner.[4]

---

[1] Sievers 1868, still very useful.
[2] Wintjes 2005 is currently the most accurate biography of Libanius; it contains a thorough bibliography on pp. 245–76.
[3] See Norman 1965 and 1992; Wolf 1967; Martin and Petit 1979. On the rhetorical motivations of Libanius writing his autobiography, see Schouler 1993.
[4] Heath 2004, 186, reporting the general impression derived from modern accounts of Libanius.

The historian Eunapius, who left a tendentious portrait of Libanius in his *Lives*, declared that he had never met him but knew some of his writings.[5] He probably had access to the *Autobiography* and seems to refer to it when he talks about Libanius's resolve to be a man of the world and not to be buried in a small town.[6] Eunapius's account is an ensemble of sensible observations and plain untruths that betrays on the whole both the writer's taste for a more ornamental oratory than Libanius offered and his determination to be loyal to his teacher Prohaeresius.[7] Eunapius admired Libanius's success with students, his independence, and his refusal of honors, and he rightly underlined his extroverted personality[8] and sense of humor. His criticism of Libanius's allegedly uninspired and weak style derived from a personal dislike for a relatively unadorned oratory where reality took much space, but his remarks on Libanius's ability to give a facelift to old words fallen into desuetude ("as handmaids smooth away signs of old age from their nouveau-riche mistress") are unfair.[9] The result was to make Libanius appear a cold, lifeless, and pedantic writer.

This estimation of his work continued to accompany him, extending to his letters as well. In 1776, Gibbon reported with some satisfaction Bentley's opinion that in the letters, "you feel by the emptiness and deadness of them, that you converse with some dreaming pedant, with his elbow on his desk."[10] Gibbon noted Libanius's fortune and his proud behavior with Julian, who appreciated a sophist who maintained the Greek purity "in a degenerate age"; yet this historian regarded Libanius as a "recluse student whose mind, regardless of his contemporaries, was incessantly fixed on the Trojan War." This drastic, influential judgment erased at a stroke Libanius's activities in the community of Antioch, his political presence, and the actuality of his prose.

I will refrain from recalling in order the minute details of Libanius's life because much has been written on the subject, but I will linger on certain episodes in the course of this book.[11] Born in Antioch in 314,

---

[5] Eunapius VS 16.1.1–2.10, 495–96. See Penella 1990, 100–105.

[6] Cf. *Or.* 1.34, in which Libanius is proud of ridding himself of his "fear of places." Eunapius may have known other orations and some of the letters.

[7] About this sophist and his style, and Eunapius's relationship with him, cf. below, Chapter Two.

[8] In doing so, however, Eunapius underlined Libanius's supposed duplicity; on the comparison with the octopus, cf. below, Chapter Two.

[9] Eunapius VS 16.2.5–6, 496. See the just remonstrations of Schouler (1984, 263–64). Eunapius's remark that Libanius was completely ignorant of rhetorical rules is also difficult to understand.

[10] See Gibbon 1946, 1:704–5. On the causes underlying Gibbon's criticism (particularly with reference to Julian), see Bowersock 2000a, 7–27.

[11] On Libanius's life, see L. Petit 1866. Cf. esp. the very useful introductions in Martin and Petit 1979 and in Norman 1992 and 2000; see also Schouler 2002, and the accurate account of Wintjes 2005. On the years he spent in Athens and the times preceding his appointment in Antioch, cf. Chapters Two and Three below.

Libanius studied rhetoric in Athens between 336 and 340, taught at intervals in Constantinople and Nicomedia, returned to Antioch for the first time in 353, and finally settled in his native city, where he became the official sophist and where he remained from 354 to 393, the approximate date of his death.[12] At the outset, I think it is more useful to give a comprehensive idea of Libanius's character, focusing on elements of his personality that are less well known but must have influenced his relationships with his students and his perception of them. His voluminous writings ("countless," *apeira*, according to the tenth-century lexicon known as *Suda* [*Suidas*]) leave the reader with vivid images of him, but what was Libanius really like? It is difficult to know for certain, of course. These are suggestions.

After his father's death, Libanius was brought up by his mother.[13] Since rhetoric was a men's affair, his mother rarely intrudes in his writings, but her presence can be perceived behind the scenes. Sweet and indulgent, she was nevertheless someone he needed to satisfy. We know comparatively little of Libanius's views on women, but the relationship with his mother offered him the ultimate model.[14] She had decided not to remarry and avoided getting a guardian for her children, wishing to be the only important presence (*ta panta*) in their life until her death.[15] Libanius always returned home after the exertion of declamations and felt an obligation to display his success to her.[16] In *Oration* 35.7 there is a revealing portrait of the mother of a young orator who lost his pride by failing to speak in the Council.[17] Reproaching those of his ex-students who remained silent, Libanius depicted the mother of one of them lamenting her fate at dinner, when she had expected a tale of glory. Libanius's student Hyperechius, who was unable to find a suitable post in the administration after leaving school, was in a similar predicament for failing to fulfill his real duties.[18] Hunting was his main activity, and a hare was the only thing he could bring back to his mother.

Libanius never had a regular family of his own. He resolved very early not to get married because rhetoric was going to be his "bride."[19] A woman of low origin, a servant, became his companion for life and gave him a son, Cimon (sometimes called Arabius), whom he desperately tried to make immune from curial status so that he could avoid financial bur-

---

[12] Wintjes (2005, 235–37) rightly rejects attempts to extend his life to 404.
[13] On Libanius's enlarged family, see Wintjes 2005, 43–62.
[14] See Schouler (1985), who painted the relationship of Libanius with his mother in too-idyllic terms.
[15] *Or.* 1.4. At her death, Libanius reiterates that she was "everything" for him, *Or.* 1.117.
[16] *Or.* 1.117.
[17] On this oration, see Schouler 2004.
[18] See *Ep.* 1443.5 (B45). On the attention to be paid to mothers' needs, see *Ep.* 251 (B66).
[19] *Or.* 1.54. The death of a cousin who was betrothed to him confirmed his resolve.

dens. Cimon's hopes to obtain an official position did not materialize, and he died young. Their relationship, about which Libanius revealed little, to some degree affected his views of his students and was the origin of the envy he felt for their fathers. Libanius presented Cimon to the world as a good orator.[20] He gave the most personal close-up of his son in a letter concerning the athletes for the Olympia in 388 to the iatrosophist Magnus: "I, too, have a youngster who is good at running and speaking and deserves both the victor's crown and the scholar's gown."[21] Yet Cimon's position was always ambiguous. He was the "son born of a good mother," a woman "worthy of many a servant," as Libanius said, praising her only after her death.[22] A late letter written to a student's father in 391 when Cimon was still alive is revelatory (**130**). Complimenting the governor Factinianus on the outstanding qualities of his son, Libanius added, "I now accuse the gods who deprived me of children: I would have them, had I not offended Cyprus," where "children" stood for the legitimate offspring he never had.[23] Aphrodite was angry with him, and, as he wrote in *Oration 5*, "the passion of Aphrodite only existed in order to have children."[24] Cimon died in the same year, and Libanius's first words of grief in letter 1026 confirm his ambivalence: "It is right for me to lament him because he was my son, since indeed he was my son, and the mother he had did not impede that."

Gibbon's comment that Libanius had "a favorable opinion of his superior merit" and displayed it ostentatiously is only true with some qualifications.[25] At the age of thirteen, Libanius experienced a quasi-religious conversion to rhetoric (*erōs tōn logōn*)[26] and remained faithful to his studies for the rest of his life. He says repeatedly that he worked compulsively, did not spare himself any fatigue, and did not indulge in sleep and amusements.[27] Libanius was a man of contradictions, convinced of the

---

[20] It is difficult to say whether this was true.

[21] *Ep.* 843 (N147). On Magnus, see below, Chapter Two.

[22] *Epp.* 959.2 and 1063.5, and *Or.* 1.278. Libanius never mentioned this woman in writing when she was still alive.

[23] As Wolf (1738, ad loc.), I take "Cyprus" as meaning the island of Cypris (Aphrodite), that is, an allusion to his irregular love relationship. I reject the interpretations of other scholars: Sievers (1868, 197 and n. 7) saw an allusion to the intrigues that deprived Cimon of an official position in Cyprus; Festugière (1959, 137 n. 1) disagreed with Sievers, but took "children" as meaning "students."

[24] *Or.* 5.28. On marriage serving only for the procreation of children, see also *Or.* 11.128. Cf., in *Misopogon* 359c, the admiration of Julian for the Celts, "who knew Aphrodite, goddess of marriage, only for the purpose of marrying and having children."

[25] Gibbon 1946, 1:704.

[26] *Or.* 1.5 and 8. Cf. below.

[27] See, e.g., *Or.* 1.53 and 109.

worth of his work, but having occasional doubts about his ability.[28] He usually did not manifest an inner conviction of the superior qualities of his mind but felt (and manifested often) pride in his dedication and contempt for those he considered negligent. In *Oration* 64, a tour de force composed in 361 where he vied with the second-century sophist Aristides to defend the legitimacy of the spectacles of pantomime dancers, he felt the need to justify his personal abstention from such spectacles. The whole passage betrays the acute anxiety of a workaholic, as Libanius cited his raving greed for work (*peri tous ponous aplēstia*) as an excuse. Rhetoric called him away from the pleasures of the table and the baths so that relatives and friends thought he was a bit "touched" (*parapaiein*). People whose love was "to put together words" could all but toil, because it was impossible "to fatten the body and tend the soul" at the same time, and thus he did not hide his scorn for his opponent Acacius, "the marvelous sophist" who lavishly entertained some advocates with wine and food.[29] Students had the same obligation to indulge only in the pleasures of the mind. When some students left the school in the mass exodus from Antioch in the aftermath of the Riot of the Statues in 387, the fact that they returned "fat and with plenty of flesh" was a sure sign for their teacher that they had been idle.[30] Those lazy young men, he reiterated in another speech, did not have any excuse; they spent all their time eating, drinking, sleeping, and avoiding the toil of rhetoric (*Or.* 23.20). Excessive weight was the logical consequence of slacking off and avoiding serious commitment. Subjects other than rhetoric did not require the same labor and did not consume the body. The son of Libanius's ex-student Silvanus, who had originally joined the same school, defected to the Latin teacher and "sported around his abundant flesh" (*Or.* 38.6). A proper dedication to rhetoric was supposed to wear out the body, so that Libanius in a letter of 355/56 found it natural that both he and his student Albanius had fallen ill that year, when rhetorical toil had been intense (*Ep.* 462). Sickly pallor was appreciated in a hardworking pedagogue who dedicated time to writing besides taking care of his ward, but monks had to fake a pale complexion, since they "ate like elephants" and drank freely, if not excessively.[31]

---

[28] From the very beginning, Libanius shows himself as a perfectionist; cf. *Or.* 1.26: "However sufficient my ability might appear to other people, it did not seem so to me." Compare his convinced declaration that the things he did were trifles in *Ep.* 754 (N90).

[29] See *Or.* 64.99 and 106, and *Ep.* 351 (B37), in which he admitted that all his duties prevented him from having regular meals. On his disdain for Acacius 6, see *Ep.* 529 (B28).

[30] *Or.* 34.12. A panic exodus (for fear of retaliation) followed the riots, in which Imperial portraits and statues were demolished. See Wintjes 2005, 213–17.

[31] See pale Dositheus in **163**, and plump monks in *Or.* 30.8.

In 390, Libanius wrote *Oration* 42 to support the candidacy of his secretary Thalassius to the Senate of Constantinople.[32] At the beginning of the speech (3), he gave in a few phrases the outlines of his own life inspired by an all-absorbing love (*erōs*) for rhetoric. At the end (43), he curiously mentioned a portrait of himself that Proclus, an official who was one of the objects of invective in this speech, was guilty of setting up in the City Hall together with portraits of insignificant people who took precedence over Libanius.[33] Though the sophist agreed that "color and canvas" did give distinction, he thought words were more effective. A large part of the speech naturally consisted of a portrait of the virtuous Thalassius, who distinguished himself for his love of eloquence and control of eating, drinking, and sexual desires. He was unselfish, did not care for money, went to great lengths to support his friends and those who worked for him, and did not indulge in spectacles, chariot races, or games. Thalassius refrained from marriage, considered Libanius his own son, and was revered by students and parents. The reader feels that the images of Libanius and Thalassius blend.

Work and learning were a source of pleasure and comfort at any point in time. Libanius compared the excitement some people felt in receiving invitations to the hippodrome or the theater with the acute pleasure children experienced in learning their ABC's (*Or.* 33.8). Likewise, he had only one piece of advice for his distressed friend Seleucus, exiled to an uncivilized location after Julian's death: he should cling to Plato, Demosthenes, and the other writers, and start writing a history of the Persian War.[34] Work brought great solace. A passion for intellectual pursuits compensated for a lack of wealth, control, and power. "I do not have power," he wrote to the influential Modestus in 361, "but I do not mind at all. To me, as to the nightingale, singing is enough."[35] Rhetoric, of course, brought a different type of power, which Libanius was far from disdaining, as he wrote to his student Albanius (7). The pleasure Libanius derived from his work and his burning passion for eloquence must have been to some degree infectious. The excitement communicated by an instructor enamored of his subject is no small gift for a student. In moments of dejection and/or illness, Libanius had to give up declamations, but teaching was his foremost duty, even if he had to do it from his bed at home or from a couch in school.[36] At one point he apparently was "ac-

---

[32] There is a translation of this speech in Norman 2000, 148–67. Thalassius was trying to avoid the burdens of curial status; cf. Petit 1957.

[33] On Proclus, see below. Portraits of Libanius's forebears were also hung in the City Hall, *Or.* 2.10.

[34] Seleucus 1. See *Ep.* 1508 (N142).

[35] Modestus 2; *Ep.* 617 (B73).

[36] Cf. *Or.* 1.142; 34.2 and 17.

cused" of applying himself excessively on behalf of his students by giving them exclusive attention and neglecting everything else (**65**). He took it hard each time a student left him for another teacher, even though he struggled to hold his countenance and "to become like iron" (*Or.* 36.13), but as he grew older, students' defections became more painful to bear. Practicing and teaching rhetoric were two different aspects of the same passion and of a view of the world confined within strict boundaries of *paideia*. This lends amusing overtones to a passage in the moving and sincere funeral oration for Julian. If Julian had prevailed, not only would the Persians have changed their language and dress and cut their hair, but sophists would have turned Persian children into orators, and fair oratorical contests would have measured their ability.[37]

Libanius was deadly serious about his and his students' commitment to rhetoric, yet at times we glimpse a sense of humor that softens his stance. In letter **153** he recalled the pleasurable dinners he had with a group of friends, rhetors and philosophers, who mixed poetry and discussions with merriment.[38] He there described himself as the sophist who drank and said what pleased Dionysus, laughed, and made the others laugh.[39] He claimed to be amicable and relaxed with his assistants, and he contrasted his behavior to the tyrannical or selfish attitudes of his predecessors. He worked with the other teachers in his school on an equal basis, took an interest in their lives, and knew them intimately. They were allowed to laugh and joke with him, and he was the one who sometimes initiated the fun.[40] He confessed that he enjoyed the nickname people gave him, "Libanius the charmer" (*epicharis*), and was genuinely horrified on discovering later in life that some considered him annoying and stern (*barys*).[41] This was unfair, he thought, because he never "clouded over joy" by preventing people from laughing, and when the occasion demanded it, he participated in the general merriment. One may perhaps identify his personal reaction to the holiday mood of the New Year in the description (*ekphrasis*) of the feast he wrote. In depicting the general feasting and laughing, he said in fact that "even the person who knew how to master his desire to laugh, could not but laugh."[42]

---

[37] *Or.* 18.282. Libanius (as a fair teacher) added that results from the new orators would be uneven, but no one would be disparaged or excluded.

[38] Cf. below.

[39] In *Ep.* 316.3, he says that he became a "slave" of wine when he was ill, exactly like his friend Acacius 7.

[40] *Or.* 36.10–12, dated to 386.

[41] See *Or.* 2.19–20. On teachers' nicknames, see Heath 2004, 40–41.

[42] Foerster 1903–27, 8:472–77 (quote from paragraph 6). On the satire and merriment of the Kalends, see Gleason 1986. Cf. below, Chapter Six.

When Libanius declared in *Oration* 2.20 that in the classroom his students experienced a witty teacher who knew how to mix fun and serious work,[43] one wonders how realistic his perception of himself as an educator was, since his extreme dedication to work must have made him sharply intolerant of slackness. And yet, the playful side of his personality sometimes surfaces, as when he described the glorious prowess (*aristeia*) of his student Diogenes at the expense of the sophist Acacius.[44] Libanius was actively involved in this episode of deception of this sophist, who was fooled into believing that Diogenes ("the best actor for the farce") wanted to defect and become his student. "We did not capture Babylon, but seized a store of laughter," a chuckling Libanius wrote to his student Celsus. The use of humor as a pedagogical tool also appears in some of the works destined to his students. Unquenchable laughter echoes aloud in *Declamation 27, The Morose Man and His Son*.[45] The outrageous portrayal of the grouchy man, the embodiment of an unbearable father, who was determined to disown the son who "made a laughingstock" of him, was bound to please students. They must have shared the youth's spontaneous smile when the man, on his way from his farm, tumbled into a muddy pothole in the marketplace. Like the man's son, they had an education in rhetoric and could both defend themselves with the "vomit of words" that the morose man abhorred and take advantage of the laughter of which he was incapable.[46]

Although some of his criticisms were unfair, Eunapius nevertheless remarked that the writings of Libanius "were full of charm and comic wit" (*kōmikē bōmolochia*).[47] Libanius's wit pervades his work and comes unexpectedly, in a flash, leaving a trail of subtly funny and caustic remarks. I will provide a few examples with the warning that his humor is much more effective couched in his pure Greek and against the background of neutral surrounding prose. A vivid image sometimes materializes all of a sudden, and students are the object of Libanius's irony. In one instance, he sends a slave to invite them to one of his declamations. The young men arrive at their leisure, and their teacher's annoyance is palpable when he sees them proceeding to the lecture hall with delicate, unhurried steps as "they march with the gait of brides or, with more truth perhaps, like tight-rope walkers."[48] In *Oration* 43, where he is speaking of students' tendency to switch

---

[43] On jocularity between teachers and students in the classroom, see Heath 2004, 186–87.

[44] See *Ep.* 722 (N85). On Acacius, cf. below.

[45] Cf. also the uncontrollable laughter of the passersby in *Declamation* 28.13, *The Disappointed Parasite*.

[46] See esp. 27.6–11.

[47] Eunapius *VS* 16.2.2, 496.

[48] *Or.* 3.11. Martin (1988, ad loc.) remarks on the novelty of the bride image.

teachers with senseless regularity, Libanius's irritation conjures up an image of irresponsible children at play. The students who move incessantly from one school to another change places like "children playing tag."[49] Again, when most of the students fled from Antioch after the Riot of the Statues, the sneering laughter of Libanius accompanied them. They closed their books, mounted their horses, and ran away "trembling, with teeth chattering, and turning to look behind them as if they were chased, though no one chased them nor was eager to get them" (Or. 23.20).

At times, the effect of a sardonic remark derives from the dry, laconic way in which it is uttered. In a letter written in 355, Libanius presented Acacius, his rival in Antioch, as unable to produce a competing oration; he commented laconically, "My rival promised to speak if his father died, but he is alive, still."[50] Or, in *Oration* 11, Libanius contrasted the situation of inland Antioch with that of coastal cities (37). The reader is offered a charming, bustling spectacle of merchant ships plying their trade, but all of a sudden joy turns into sorrow: the ships sink in front of the very eyes of the proud onlookers, confirming that Antioch's position is preferable. The sudden, cartoon-like vignette is almost amusing in its tragic vividness.

Libanius's prose is usually not built on rhetorical flights but speaks through arresting, concrete images. The teacher Gaudentius,[51] who suffered a stroke in class, is sadly immortalized with his right hand in motion in the act of teaching and in the vain attempt to talk to his pupils (Or. 38.15). In the hymn to Artemis, a frightening, inventive depiction of unruly, wild animals originates from the circus games. The goddess appears as the protector of the human race by keeping wild beasts from invading the cities.[52] Terror strikes everyone when a single beast escapes, and people look for a refuge, lock doors, and scream for help. What would happen, Libanius asks, if the wild animals launched a concerted attack under the guidance of lions?[53] A less wild animal, a horse unable to run, which his cousin Spectatus had given to his nephew, resurfaces in a letter.[54] Libanius concluded dryly that the North Wind, Boreas, who had horses as swift as the wind, was indeed an ancestor of this one, but only in the sense that this horse was able to move when pushed by a strong wind. A striking picture

---

[49] Or. 43.9. It is difficult to render the Greek expression "the game of the corners." The details of this ancient game are unknown, but it might be compared to the game "four-square" (played in the United States but with a ball) or, more appropriately, to the Italian "quattro cantoni," a kind of tag game. Norman (2000, 117) translated "playing at rounders," an old-fashioned British game of baseball.

[50] Ep. 405.9 (N6).

[51] On Gaudentius, see below.

[52] Or. 5.13–15, a prose hymn. Schouler (1984, 437) calls the passage an *ekphrasis*.

[53] Cf. the striding lion mosaic in Kondoleon 2000a, 130, fig. 1.

[54] Ep. 352 (B7).

sometimes is built around the emperor Julian. Advancing in secret along the Danube in 361 after his troops' proclamation, he suddenly appeared at the frontier and caught his enemies by surprise, "exactly like an underwater diver who is hidden under the surface of the sea and escapes the notice of people on the shore as long as he likes" (*Or.* 12.63). After Julian's death, Libanius experienced an acute, physical sense of loss that he expressed by comparing himself to a man who was thirsty and was finally able to lift to his lips a cup of chilled, clear water, which was snatched away from him after only one sip (*Or.* 18.284). The power of Homeric similes was well known to Libanius, who had the natural ability to visualize a situation distinctly, a quality that must have increased the immediacy of his teaching.

Libanius's unrelenting passion for all aspects of his profession and his conviction that saving rhetoric from disregard was his true calling gave his message an urgency that must have been quite effective with his audience. Yet, there were elements of his personality that undoubtedly did make him quite difficult, as his detractors claimed. If I do not spend a proportionate amount of time on this subject here and elsewhere in this book, it is not because I am engaged in a personal crusade to rescue this writer from unfair criticism (a temptation indeed for every scholar who converses with a figure of the past), but rather because my interest is focused on Libanius the teacher and his school. The negative aspects of Libanius have attracted much attention,[55] largely because of the nature of his writings. Most ancient writers did not disclose themselves with the same intensity. We surmise their intentions and crave details, but often end up in a biographical vacuum. Libanius let "tears rain down" upon his writings.[56] His neurosis, paranoia, and tormenting health problems are in full view, to be analyzed from the modern perspective.[57] He recorded with precision details of his mental health, such as insomnia, depression, indulgence in suicidal thoughts, fear for his sanity, feelings of persecution, and complete breakdown, all of which became graver with advancing age. These symptoms often accompanied significant physical ailments (vertigo, migraine, gout, kidney problems), some of which had troubled him from his early years. In his youth, he was sometimes able to use these ills to his advantage to excuse himself from unwanted duty, but later he succumbed utterly to them.[58] In both the *Autobiography* and the letters, Libanius indulged in

---

[55] On Libanius's mental and physical health, cf. Pack 1933. Martin and Petit 1979, 18–21; Molloy 1996, 28–39.

[56] *Ep.* 1064 (N189).

[57] On the well-known episode of the chameleon associated with his migraine and inability to speak, see Bonner 1932; Maltomini 2004.

[58] When he did not want to return to Constantinople, Libanius convinced the governor with the help of his doctors that Antioch's climate was more beneficial to his migraines, *Or.* 1.94.

minute description of his symptoms, lingering sometimes on the possible consequences of accidents that did not occur. A vivid example of this morbid tendency is his description of a riding accident he was able to avoid, the graphic, but counterfactual, details of which culminate with his brains splattered on the cobbles (*Or.* 1.216).

Such insistent recording of physical and mental states was a symptom by itself, but a conscious desire to vie with Aristides provided some rational validation.[59] From his early years, Libanius was a great admirer of the second-century orator, a major exponent of Hellenism and a model of Attic style, who had students when his health allowed him and pronounced *encomia* of two of them.[60] Aristides noted the details of his medical history in his *Sacred Tales*.[61] Both the oration in praise of Antioch (11) and the monody on Nicomedia (61) show clear debts to this illustrious predecessor, and Libanius openly disclosed his literary emulation by dedicating *Oration* 64 to Aristides.[62] The scrutiny of the writings of Aristides seems to have been intense in the 360s, when Libanius was making a name for himself in Antioch and was reading his works, but this writer remained a prominent influence later on.[63] A letter that Libanius sent in 365 to Theodorus, the father of two of his students, testifies to his fascination with Aristides by presenting a tantalizing picture of friends who sent each other portraits of this sophist.[64] On receiving from another friend a first portrait, which showed an Aristides with abundant hair and looking far from sickly, Libanius was perplexed, but the image Theodorus sent him confirmed at least the general features. Libanius looked forward to getting from Theodorus yet another portrait, his third, which showed the whole figure. Was Libanius building a gallery of pictures of a favorite writer? Aristides' portraits certainly played a role in his life, since he disclosed that he read the sophist's works sitting by his portrait, talking to him, concluding that he must have produced those works because it was only "proper that such a handsome figure should be the mother of such discourses."

But besides the neurotic Libanius almost perpetually in crisis, there is an uglier side of his personality, no less real, fed by an unstable state of

---

[59] Martin and Petit (1979, 18–19), who also point to Libanius's desire to show how courageous and enduring he was. On his relationship with Aristides, see Pack 1948. On Aristides' valetudinarianism, see Boulanger 1923, passim; and Luchner 2004, 260–307. On his biography, Behr 1994. Cf. also below, Chapter Five.

[60] See *Or.* 30 and 31 for Apellas and Eteoneus; cf. Behr 1968, 106 n. 39, and 1994, 1163–64; Pernot 1993, 65–66. On the inscriptions concerning the families of these students, see Puech 2002, 486. On Libanius and Aristides, see Swain 2004, 362–73.

[61] See Behr 1968; Swain 1996, 260–74.

[62] On Libanius competing with Aristides in this oration, see Molloy 1996, 86–89.

[63] Cf., e.g., *Ep.* 965, from the year 390.

[64] *Ep.* 1534 (N143). Theodorus 11/iii. It was not unusual to send a letter with one's own portrait; see Aeneas of Gaza *Ep.* 12, and Procopius of Gaza *Epp.* 53, 61, and 94.

mind that became unmanageable in his old age. Though in his youth he was able to maintain independence and a measure of consistency, in his late years some duplicity took hold of him. Constantly preoccupied with making friends, having a following, and having his work appreciated, he was ambivalent or plainly hostile to some people, but showed two different faces in the letters he sent them and in venomous orations delivered to an exclusive group of close supporters. From an early time he appears well aware of the possibility of using speeches to take revenge on certain opponents, and he often indulged this pleasure in his old age. Political invective had well-defined literary traditions,[65] and the diversity of the genre, which we will often see at play, partly accounts for the lack of consistency in letters and speeches. Yet Libanius's behavior is sometimes disconcerting. Consider, for example, writings he addressed to the official Proclus. Some initial enthusiasm for this pagan, cultivated governor subsided with the realization that he was not going to follow the advice of the old sophist. But whereas in the *Autobiography* and in the discourses directed against him, one can follow the escalation of Libanius's invective, in the letters he continued to address Proclus as a dear friend and a benefactor of Antioch.[66] Another official, Rufinus, who was praetorian prefect in the last two years of Libanius's life, was a dark and ruthless personage, a Christian bigot who would have hardly attracted his favor in previous times; but the ill and bitter sophist, who was almost eighty years old, regarded him as a last resource.[67] Most important, Rufinus admired his work. Libanius planned to write a panegyric on him and asked for information about his family and (naturally) on the schools he had attended.[68] He portrayed him in the midst of Antioch's acclaim, showered with rose petals, which he brushed off with an elegant gesture.

Antioch: A Temple of the Muses

Antioch-on-the-Orontes was a sparkling city, as much a protagonist in the works of Libanius as his school.[69] *Oration* 11, the *Antiochikos*, a panegyric of the city that he pronounced on the occasion of the city's Olympic Games in 356, was his belated gift to his homeland, replete with

---

[65] See, e.g., Long 1996, 65–105.
[66] Proclus 6. See *Or.* 1.212 and 221–24; 10; 26; 27; 28; and 42, written in 390. See Martin 1988, 205–11; Wintjes 2005, 205–8. On the tempestuous relationship of Libanius with Proclus, see Swain (2004, 385–90), who says that Libanius "had too strong a grip on reality to adopt Aelius Aristides' solution" (p. 390), that is, dreaming of a perfect situation.
[67] Rufinus 18. Cf. Wintjes 2005, 226–27.
[68] See *Ep.* 1106 (N193), and *Ep.* 1111.
[69] On Antioch, see Foerster 1897; Lassus 1977; and Kondoleon 2000a.

images of beauty.⁷⁰ In later writings dating to the 380s, some negative aspects of Antioch resurface,⁷¹ yet it is impossible at any time to dissociate Libanius from the city where he chose to live and practice. Libanius was a city person who liked to be in the midst of life, and who conceived of the country only as a place where one could assuage stress and disappointment.⁷² The *Antiochikos* glosses over social inequality, ignores the city's Christian churches and the fact that most citizens were Christian, and presents an idealized scenario of perfect and accomplished (pagan) city life. But it was delivered before the Antiocheans and the visitors for the Games, preventing Libanius from altering reality too greatly, as archaeology, especially the city's stunning mosaics, confirms.⁷³ This oration addressed the elite of Antioch, the inhabitants of other cities of Syria who were at the *Olympia*, and the other educated people who read it after its delivery. In 356, Libanius was an accomplished orator who had produced a lot, but he had become Antioch's official sophist only the year before. A panegyric of the city inevitably also addressed the parents of students and prospective students and reassured them of the suitability of Antioch as a "university" town, "a temple of the Muses."⁷⁴

Most of the young men attending Libanius's school resided in Antioch for two or more years without going home for summer vacations.⁷⁵ Though Libanius's insistence on the physical beauties of the city corresponded to the requirements of panegyric, he also meant to show that

---

⁷⁰ The terms "beautiful" and "beauty" appear more than forty times. On the date of the oration, cf. Norman 2000, 3–4. This oration can be considered part of Libanius's *dokimasia* (that is, proof of ability) on his final return to Antioch; cf. below, Chapter Three. On the Olympic Games in Antioch, see Liebeschuetz 1972, 136–44.

⁷¹ In *Or.* 2.26, Libanius says that he is accused of always harping on the city's present misery. In 384, *Or.* 50.31, famine is accompanied by "hordes of flies, snakes, and locusts." In 387, *Or.* 19.6, he considers the city unfortunate because of earthquakes, the Persians' invasions, and riots; yet in *Or.* 19.51, he celebrates Antioch for its appearance and mild climate.

⁷² In 361, after the deaths of friends and relatives, he said he would like to take up farming, *Ep.* 263 (N72). See also *Ep.* 1001 (N175). Cf. letter 55 about Dionysius and the dangerous pleasures of the country. In *Ep.* 1466.2, he deplored that young Iamblichus 2 retreated to the country, but he admitted that at least he was "out of the hurly burly" (B22).

⁷³ See the description of the commons, provided with "wife, children, and a household full of furniture," necessary items for an orderly life (*Antiochikos* 150), and the view of the happy and well-fed poor (253 and 259), with which one should compare the picture of the miserable poor in John Chrysostom; see Kelly 1995, 40. See also the overly optimistic presentation of the generous Council and its relationship with the governors (133–49). The general picture, however, is accurate enough, "granted the purple patches," Norman 2000, 6–7; cf. Kondoleon 2000a; and Cabouret, Gatier, and Saliou 2004. On the mosaics, see Levi 1947; Kondoleon 2000b; and Janine Balty 2004.

⁷⁴ See *Or.* 11.188. Libanius calls schools "temples of the Muses."

⁷⁵ But see the dossier of the student Titianus, who went back and forth from Cilicia.

living in Antioch was enjoyable and productive in every season. Who would not be elated on arriving there? What delight would he find missing? "Don't we have a mild climate, delightful baths, a wonderful market . . . a spring glistening with flowers, a summer that is bright with the colors of the fruit trees and that with its perfumes makes the city into a meadow?"[76] In Antioch, every season had breezes and moderate winds, and Zephyr behaved "democratically" by giving its favors to all.[77] Parents did not need to worry that the environment might be harmful to the health of their loved ones. This is what Libanius reiterated a few years later in a letter that concerned a woman who resisted sending her sons back to school on the pretext of Antioch's (bad) climate: "Tell the mother of the two boys that it is summer here, too, and a moderate wind blows" (**196**).

Water contributed to the appeal and wealth of Antioch, so it is not surprising that it occupies a large space in the *Antiochikos*. The river Orontes, the lake, numerous streams, splendid fountains, and the healing spring waters of the sanctuary of Apollo made Antioch a spectacular city and filled its citizens with pride. The long colonnades also appear to Libanius as "rivers in flood, and the alleys are like streams leading off of them" (201). Antioch was not on the coast, but the Orontes allowed profitable communication with the Mediterranean port of Seleucia Pieria. The distance from the harbor permitted Libanius (and his students) to be sheltered from "the nautical vulgarity" and the coarse cries of a seaport town (38).

Springs, streams, and baths were nowhere as numerous as in the western suburb, Daphne.[78] The Romans were fond of this place, with its abundance of villas, gardens, fountains, and temples. Reading Libanius's description of it, the reader is supposed to leap up and feel like flying, as did the ancient visitor. Its springs were Daphne's chief glory, "palaces of the Nymphs," and Libanius proclaimed that he was convinced that the judgment of Paris had taken place right there (11.241). He immortalized the scene with the three goddesses in his *Progymnasmata* and might have seen the glorious mosaic in the Atrium House, where it was in full view to diners reclined on couches.[79] Libanius's students could enjoy all that Antioch offered, at least occasionally, with no harm. In a letter, he recommended that a father not listen to criticism that his children were studying

---

[76] *Or.* 11.266; Norman (2000, 62) wrongly translates the Greek *osmē* as "color."

[77] *Or.* 11.225. On breezes, 11.31 and 222–226. There is a punctual observation at 226: the breeze makes the clothes of the sleepers lift around their bodies.

[78] On Daphne, *Or.* 11.94–99 and 233–43.

[79] *Diēgēmata* 27 (Foerster 1903–27, 8:50); Kondoleon 2000a, 172, Fig. 58. On the similarity of this mosaic with frescoes from Pompeii because of common models, see Levi 1947, 16–21; Baratte 1978, 90–92; and Janine Balty 2004, 262–63.

in Daphne; the heat was more tolerable there: "They have our permission so that the trees, the waters, and the breezes may make their task more palatable" (**68**).

Antioch "the beautiful and great" was, together with Rome, Alexandria, and Constantinople, one of the four major cities of the Roman world, and its fame spread everywhere.[80] The population included Greeks, Jews, Christians, Romans, and Syrians, with a rough distinction between a Greek-speaking city and an Aramaic-speaking countryside. Inscriptions are not of great help in determining the various languages spoken in northern Syria, but contemporary Greek literary texts provide some indication of actual language usage.[81] Only once does Libanius allude directly to Syriac speakers, artisans who repaired wooden bowls and cried out for customers in the market, but it is very likely that he also spoke Aramaic in his contacts with the local population.[82] Antioch had a great number of visitors who came from all over the world. People moved there for business reasons, to improve their economic position, and to use their learning. Libanius's assistants were not natives, but had moved to Antioch to find more lucrative teaching posts in the (vain) hope of sending part of their revenues back home (*Or.* 31.10).[83] Antioch was generous like Athens, welcoming foreigners and treating them fairly.[84] It offered the advantages of modern "melting pots," such as the possibility of encountering many different cultures, meeting a community of expatriates from one's own, and feeling at home, though in a foreign land. Visiting foreign countries to get acquainted with other people's customs enlarged one's views, thought Libanius, and could benefit a student's education. Thus he wrote with some caution to a father who had criticized his son's decision to reach Antioch only after extensive traveling: "Perhaps seeing many cities has been to his advantage, as it was to Odysseus's" (**206**). By sending their sons to Libanius's school, parents, particularly those who lived in remote regions such as Paphlagonia or Cappadocia, gave them a cosmopolitan experience.

Antioch was renowned for chariot races and theatrical spectacles besides those offered at the Olympic Games. "Dancers, mimes, horses, and drivers" aroused strong passions, and the city governors, in Libanius's view, dedicated much energy to trying to get invited to these spectacles,

---

[80] *Or.* 31.7 and 1.2. On Antioch's population, see Maas 2000.
[81] The inscriptions are almost exclusively Greek, with only a few Syriac inscriptions after the fourth century; see Taylor 2002.
[82] *Or.* 42.31. Cf. below, the people in the workshops who submitted him to a *dokimasia* when he returned to Antioch.
[83] *Or.* 31.10. On Antioch welcoming teachers, cf. *Or.* 11.188.
[84] *Or.* 11.167–68. Cf. the Funeral Oration of Pericles in Thucydides 2.39.

spending whole days attending extravagant shows and whole nights discussing the tactics of the various drivers (*Or.* 45.20–21). Libanius's students, pagans and Christians alike, felt strongly the appeal of the city's entertainments, among them John Chrysostom, who became very fond of the theater in his years in Antioch, but later repudiated those pleasures.[85] In his late orations in particular, Libanius often ranted against his students' lack of commitment to *paideia*.[86] He considered these spectacles detrimental to the study of rhetoric,[87] and his condemnation of races and the theater also extended to those of his ex-students who, after leaving school, showed more enthusiasm for horses than for books. The young men who had to bear liturgies connected with the chariot races had to buy their horses, but after selling them back at the end still retained their full involvement (*Or.* 35.13–14). In the *Antiochikos*, Libanius does not spend excessive words on the theater, the hippodrome, or the baths (another form of entertainment).[88] The audience of this oration had just viewed the Games, and his personal dislike for such spectacles surely limited the attention he dedicated to them, but his determination to show that Antioch was a suitable venue for the education of young men also increased his disinterest.

Presenting the image of an untiring city immersed in productive activities was to Libanius's advantage. In Antioch, sleep was not "the lord of mankind," he said, paraphrasing Homer; rather, people were free of its tyranny.[89] This observation, which served to introduce the much-admired street illumination, extended both to the workshops where people plied their trades and to students' duties. For the sake of efficiency, Libanius was not fond of excessive sleep, exactly like Julian, who, in his opinion, was able to acquire glorious eloquence by spending sleepless nights cultivating it.[90] The emperor "sang much before the birds, creating discourses or taking up the creations of others" (*Or.* 12.94). Some of Libanius's students behaved likewise to his satisfaction. He related to a friend that the latter's young cousins were excellent students but caused the neighbors great annoyance with their loud recitations.[91] Confronting teenagers' customary fondness for sleep, Libanius needed to reassure parents that in Antioch he was standing guard. Yet, on this subject he risked sounding overzealous. His student Gaius had to quit rhetoric because of intolerable

---

[85] See Kelly 1995, 15; and Liebeschuetz 1990, 181–82.
[86] Cf. below. On entertainments and students' distractions in Late Antique Berytus (modern Beirut) in Phoenicia, see Jones Hall 2004, 68–69.
[87] Cf. *Or.* 41.9, trans. Festugière (1959, 228–29).
[88] See *Or.* 11.134–35 and 218–20.
[89] *Or.* 11.266–67; *Iliad* 14.233.
[90] On Julian's moderation of sleep, see Ammianus 25.4.4–5.
[91] *Ep.* 25.7 (N36).

headaches and returned home inconsolable but with some knowledge. "You will say," wrote Libanius to his relatives somewhat inappropriately, "that this boy . . . did not lose time sleeping!" (**87**).

Antioch's major attraction (naturally) consisted of the opportunity to hear and learn the best rhetoric, since Hermes, the god of oratory, had planted its seeds in the city.[92] Antioch held the torch of oratory for Asia and rivaled Athens, which was preeminent in Europe.[93] Quoting Homer's praise for the rich eloquence of Odysseus, Libanius boasted that in Antioch, orators' tongues were "like snowflakes on a winter's day."[94] Because of their mastery of oratory, the members of the Council were able to maintain their independence from governors,[95] and people flocked to the courts of law to learn, as if they were veritable "temples of the Muses." The advocates in the courts were endowed with the best tongues and ears: they improvised fluent discourses and censored other speakers, submitting them to merciless examinations. Because of Antioch's ability to attract the ablest teachers, "swarms of students, like bees," gathered there. Libanius often conceived of oratory as a liquid good that flowed from fountains open to all. Both natives and foreigners could drink at the "spring" of excellence and partake of its waters; even more exciting, in Antioch, an act of volition was not necessary to acquire *paideia*: those who lived and studied there were bound to receive it because the earth emitted a "vapor inducing learning."[96]

A glowing optimism pervades Libanius's oration in praise of his city, so that oratory appears as the only possible key to success. There are as yet no perceivable doubts about the value of Greek rhetorical education or about the existence of other roads to prosperity.[97] At the end of their schooling, some students left Antioch, embarked on promising careers, and went back to their cities to repay them through what they had learned. Their success was the best advertisement for the school, and new enthusiasts headed for Antioch. Others, however, chose to stay on account of their affection for the city; but those who neglected their parents and homeland because of Antioch's charms were to be pardoned, in Libanius's opinion. A few years later, he seems to have changed his mind. An ex-student, Leontius, kept clinging to the city and refused advantageous

---

[92] Cf. the treatment of oratory in *Or.* 11.139, 141, and 181–92. In the late oration 35.9, dated to 388, Antioch still shines for oratory, which is its wall of defense.

[93] On the rivalry between the two cities, see below.

[94] *Ep.* 503.3, year 356 (B53); *Iliad* 3.222.

[95] Libanius highly praises the Council in *Oration* 11, esp. 133–52. Cf. the indifference of John Malalas to Antioch's civic institutions: Liebeschuetz 2004.

[96] See *Or.* 34.10 and 27; 11.192.

[97] Contrast, e.g., *Or.* 62, which dates to 382.

working conditions elsewhere.[98] This young man, a lover of the Muses who had to be ready for the courts and for earning money, did not know his true interests. Insist, wrote the teacher to an official, and "force him to come to his senses" (*Ep.* 1523.4).

THE SCHOOL OF LIBANIUS

Libanius's school will occupy us for the rest of this book, but here I provide a preliminary overview of its location, the student body, the ages for admission, and especially the teachers other than Libanius who were part of the faculty. As we go through the evidence here and elsewhere, we will have to start evaluating the weight of Libanius's presence versus that of other teachers who worked there. This is the first time that a whole institution of learning emerges from antiquity, together with the names and identities of several teachers and details about their respective work.[99] Was Antioch's municipal school the product of a successful collaborative effort? To what extent was Libanius an overpowering element?

One looks in vain for the remains of Libanius's school in Antioch. Its location varied according to his growing success, but it never occupied premises specifically designed for educational purposes. It was the norm in antiquity that teachers at various levels were at the mercy of circumstances and of their own popularity.[100] In Antioch, Libanius taught at home the fifteen students he had brought from Constantinople, then moved to more visible private quarters on the fringe of the city square, and settled in the city hall on becoming Antioch's official sophist. The *chorus* of Libanius included only male students, because girls did not have access to this stage of schooling, even though some of them might have received a sophisticated education from family members or private instructors.[101] A rhetorical education was the prerogative of young men of good family who wanted to have access to positions that would ultimately also benefit their cities. This is what Libanius underlined in *Oration* 31,

---

[98] Leontius xvi: *Ep.* 1523, written in 365.

[99] Quintilian apparently used assistants, but he is the only personality that emerges from the *Institutio oratoria*.

[100] Cf. Cribiore 2001, 21–34; Libanius *Or.* 1.101–2 and 104. Cf. below, Chapter Two.

[101] On *chorus*, cf. Petit 1956a, 21. The same terminology appears sporadically in Himerius (e.g., *Or.* 54.1) and Themistius (e.g., *Or.* 23.294). Libanius (and Himerius as well, passim) often calls the group of students *agelē* ("herd") and *poimnion* ("flock"). On girls' education, see Cribiore 2001, 56 and 74–101. The wife of Seleucus 1, Alexandra, whose letters might have interested Libanius and to whom he wrote and sent books, had a superior education, but she was the daughter and sister of grammarians, *Epp.* 734 (B155) and 771; cf. Schouler 1985, 130–31.

For the Teachers, when he told the inhabitants of Antioch that even if they had no sons of adequate age or were fathers only of daughters, the education of the citizens was supposed to be their business (6). The young men who studied in Antioch generally belonged to the upper class, with the exception of the sons of a few unimportant decurions and teachers.[102] Almost all were of good birth, according to the general assumption in antiquity that people of low birth did not feel attracted to higher studies; but *eugeneia* ("high birth") was not always associated with financial prosperity.[103] Thus some students belonged to families with proud pasts but uncertain prospects, and a few had encountered difficult or even tragic circumstances before arriving in Antioch. As a rule, they were privileged young men from sheltered backgrounds and were accompanied by pedagogues who kept watch over their morals and academic progress *in loco parentis.* Some of these students were accustomed to living away from home, but for many, Antioch was the furthest away from home they had ever been.

We have only approximate information about the ages of these young men, and consequently the appropriate age at which to begin the study of rhetoric. We are rarely told how old they were when they joined the school, and what information we can obtain, usually thanks to outside sources, is bound to be confusing. Thus Euphemius, Amphilochius's son, appears to be at the school when he was eleven (**16**), and Marcianus started to attend at an older age than usual (**138**). In 370, a law of Valentinian stipulated twenty years as an upper age limit for rhetoric and twenty-five for the study of law, but exceptions were not unheard of.[104] The traditional starting age of fourteen or fifteen can probably be maintained on average, while keeping in mind that some flexibility is needed.[105] The scholastic cursus of Libanius, for example, is usually considered quite eccentric, but was it really so? He was under the tutelage of a grammarian before starting rhetoric at about thirteen years of age; at the age of fourteen, he probably attended lectures of a grammarian and a rhetor at the same time; he then remained in the class of a grammarian for five years until he was twenty; and at twenty-two, he went to study rhetoric in Athens.[106] The average student undoubtedly followed a more orderly course

[102] Decurions (*curiales*) were members of a municipal council. Among them there were notable differences in social and financial status.

[103] On the high birth of intellectuals, see Fowden 1982, 49–51. On the status of the students of Libanius, cf. below, Chapter Four.

[104] *Cod. Theod.* 14.9.1, cf. Petit 1956a, 139.

[105] See Walden 1912, 293 n. 1; Cribiore 2001, 56.

[106] See Booth (1983), who plausibly argued that Libanius experienced a conversion to rhetoric at thirteen, against the traditional date of fifteen of, e.g., Petit 1956a, 139.

of studies,[107] but Libanius's school career should be taken as an indication that others may have made similar choices, since there were no strict rules governing schooling.

It was the custom of ancient families to send sons of different ages away to school together. The dossiers of letters of Libanius's students present many such cases: the presence of two or more brothers studying together warded off homesickness and guaranteed families a measure of control.[108] This habit transcended time and space. Thus at the end of the second century, Theon, "high priest of the Nile," sent his three sons to study in Alexandria, even though they were at different levels (from the elementary to the rhetorical stage), so that they contributed mutually to their educational and housing needs.[109] At the turn of the sixteenth century, Bruno and Basilius, the children of Johann Amerbach, studied together away from home. After studying Latin for three years in a boarding school not too far from home when they were respectively thirteen and nine years old, in 1500 they attempted unsuccessfully to pursue their education at the declining University of Basel. They soon transferred to the University of Paris, which was the most prestigious in northern Europe and the alma mater of their father, and they remained there for five years, without ever going back home. At that time the younger student, Basilius, was only fourteen (the minimum age of entrance at the university) and had to study some grammar.[110]

The importance Libanius attached to the study of the classics was one of the reasons why he occasionally may have worked in tandem with some grammarians in Antioch. His correspondence shows that he maintained good relations with a number of them.[111] Good foundations were fundamental; otherwise, one ran the risk of imitating the "wretched" moderns (Or. 1.23). It cannot be ruled out that some students attended the classes of a grammarian outside of Libanius's school and of a rhetor within the school at the same time, as Libanius himself had done. But we should not go so far as to include grammarians as integral part of the

---

[107] With the grammarian first and then with the rhetor; cf. Cribiore 2001, 53–59.

[108] See Strategius and Albanius; Apolinarius and Gemellus; the sons of Caesarius; Diophantes and his brother; the sons of Hesychius; the sons of Hierius; the sons of Eumathius; the sons of Eusebius x; the sons of Eupator; the sons of Hestiaeus; the sons of Priscianus; the sons of Palladius; the sons of Pompeianus; the sons of Sabinus; the sons of Theodorus; and Titianus and the other boys in his family.

[109] See P.Oxy. XVIII.2190; Cribiore 2001, 57–59 and 121–23. In the same letter, the sons of Apollonios are also studying together.

[110] Halporn 2000, 149; Rashdall 1987, 3:352.

[111] Didymus 1, who had been active in the 320s, was Libanius's own teacher and was the father of his student Rhetorius, letters **171** and **172** (Kaster 1988, 269–70). See also in 358 the grammarian Tiberinus (Kaster 1988, 267–68), and Alexander in the year 364 (Kaster 1988, 239).

faculty. After the work of Paul Petit, it became common belief that in the school of Libanius, students could study *grammatikē* (grammar and the poets) with grammarians, and rhetoric with rhetors.[112] It should be emphasized, however, that Libanius's school was exclusively a school of rhetoric, where he taught with the help of other rhetors. Not only would such a school model combining various levels be highly unusual,[113] but an investigation of the sources shows that there is no proof that any of the grammarians teaching in Antioch were working specifically in Libanius's school. It is necessary to examine the evidence with some attention.

Five teachers appear in Petit's list of grammarians supposedly teaching with Libanius: Julius, Eudaemon, Harpocration, Cleobulus, and Calliopius.[114] A slight misinterpretation of *Ep.* 454, written in the year 355/ 56, is largely responsible for the assumption concerning the first three. In writing to his uncle, who had asked how things were with him, Libanius responded that the situation (i.e., number of students, enrollment, his competitors, and the like) was the same as before. He used a generic expression, *ta de peri tous neous* ("the things concerning the students"), which does not refer necessarily only to his own establishment but to the general situation. He turned in fact to his relationship with other teachers in Antioch, Julius and Eudaemon, who were his rivals.[115] The grammarian Julius is portrayed not as an associate, but as a competitor who resented his success and "wasted away in sorrow."[116] Likewise, Libanius presents Eudaemon as a rival of his who was scheming "because things were difficult for him" (*Ep.* 454.4). It is highly unlikely, moreover, that Eudaemon

---

[112] Petit (1956a, 85–86) sought to prove this, and Kaster (1988, 303 and 401; *PLRE* I, passim) subscribed to this view as well. I followed this view in Cribiore 2001, 37–38, but a thorough examination of the letters convinced me that it is untenable. Such a school would be equivalent to an American junior high combined with a high school. Petit may have been influenced by the fact that in France, too, grades six through twelve are often considered a high school as a whole.

[113] Grammarians, however, sometimes took up the teaching of elementary letters; see Booth 1979a and 1979b; and Cribiore 2001, 36–40. In the fifth century, the grammarian Horapollon seems to have taught in Alexandria in the same educational complex that housed sophists and philosophers; see Zacharias Scholasticus, Kugener 1903. The various disciplines, however, were not under a single master and were separated; the whole can be regarded as an anticipation of a medieval university.

[114] Julius 1, Eudaemon 2, Harpocration (*PLRE* I, p. 408), Cleobulus 1, and Calliopius 3/v.

[115] In *Ep.* 454.4 (N14), Kaster (1988, 303 and 401), following Petit, took the words *ta peri tous neous* to mean "the affairs touching his school" and concluded, albeit with some hesitation, that all three teachers worked in Libanius's establishment.

[116] Julius, therefore, was not a supporter of Libanius, as Norman (1992, 1:396, n. to *Ep.* 454) rightly showed. Cf. on the collaboration of rhetors and grammarians in Constantinople, *Or.* 1.44, and below, Chapter Three.

was a grammarian, and the same is true for Harpocration.[117] Eudaemon, who made peace with Libanius in later years, was a rhetor and friend of Harpocration, a sophist who was also a poet and who later moved to Constantinople, much to Libanius's chagrin.[118]

Nor does anything compel us to consider the last two teachers on the list as grammarians who were Libanius's associates. The fact that Libanius depicted Cleobulus as a "Phoenix" (that is, an initial teacher) for Libanius's student Bassianus and said that he helped him grow his "wings" only suggests that he was possibly a grammarian, but not specifically in Libanius's school (31).[119] Since Cleobulus had taught Libanius himself, it is only natural that their relations were so cordial that the latter often interceded in his interest.[120] The evidence about the other teacher, Calliopius, is harder to disentangle.[121] Was he really a grammarian or an elementary teacher, since he taught Libanius's son? A few facts about him are known. He had studied rhetoric with Zenobius and thus "drank from the same bowl in the garden of the Muses," as Libanius had done (*Ep.* 18.2). He worked in Libanius's school "lightening his burden with the students" (*Ep.* 625.4). Libanius praised his oratorical ability when he became an advocate and was in charge of the emperor's correspondence as *magister epistularum* at a later time. Together with Libanius, he ranted against those students who went to Rome to learn Latin. Scholars have noted the contradiction between his later high status and his previous career as "lowly" *didaskalos* tutoring an elementary student. The only evidence that supposedly shows Calliopius as a low teacher in Libanius's school is that of the teachings he imparted to Libanius's son Cimon together with his own father. Several factors, however, need to be taken into account. Calliopius might have taught Cimon at his own house, and the fact that he did so together with his father seems to support the assump-

---

[117] *PLRE* (I, p. 289) rightly considers Eudaemon a rhetor; Kaster (1988, 400–403 and 410–11) thinks that this is likely.

[118] There is no contradiction in the fact that Harpocration was a poet but did not teach poetry. In *Ep.* 364.5–6, he is said to be "clever at instilling in the young the works of the ancients" (*ta tōn palaiōn*), but this expression does not necessarily refer to the poets; see, e.g., *Ep.* 561.7 and 1064.1. In *Ep.* 368 (Cabouret 2000, no. 15), Libanius says that Harpocration is a sophist. When he tells Themistius, "He is leaving us," the turn of phrase does not necessarily mean "our school," but might mean "Antioch" or "our friendship."

[119] Wolf (1952, 73) does not regard him as an associate of Libanius. Was Cleobulus surely a grammarian? The evidence is not strictly compelling. Norman (2000, 67) considers him a rhetor.

[120] *Epp.* 68.1 and 361.2 show that he had been the teacher of young Libanius. Cf. Kaster 1988, 256–58.

[121] Calliopius 3/v, who taught Cimon with his father. See a discussion of all of the evidence in Kaster (1988, 250–52), who nevertheless considered him a grammarian. The letters in question are *Epp.* 18, 625 (B124), 678 (where Cimon is called *paidion*), and 951 (N167).

tion that this was not a regular teaching done in the City Hall, when the other students were present. Cimon is usually considered seven years old in *Ep.* 678 because Libanius calls him *paidion,* but was he really so young? Diminutives are often used as terms of endearment, as the papyri show, and Cimon was not necessarily a "small boy," but in 361 could have been ten or eleven year old.[122] I suggest that Calliopius was a rhetor (as his education shows) and was one of Libanius's assistants. Together with his father (who was perhaps a teacher of younger students), he did Libanius a favor by tutoring Cimon (the verb used in *Ep.* 625.6 is *plattein,* "to form") so that the latter could catch up and become part of the regular classes.[123] Altogether, the evidence that is usually considered in support of the fact that grammarians were part of Libanius's *chorus* is so shaky as to become nonexistent. The fact that Libanius failed to mention these grammarians, who were supposedly his collaborators, in *Oration* 31, *To the Antiocheans for the Teachers,* seems to confirm these findings.

According to this oration, in which Libanius lamented the pitiful economic condition of his assistants, in 361 four other rhetors worked at the school.[124] The corpus of letters surely reveals the identity of three of them at that time, Gaudentius, Uranius, and Herodianus, and we can now add Calliopius as a fourth rhetor. A few more rhetors assisted Libanius in later years.[125] It is of interest to investigate the types of people with whom Libanius chose to associate. From Gaudentius and Uranius he could not expect many surprises. They had been assistant teachers of Zenobius (Libanius's predecessor), were experienced, could provide valuable information on prospective students, and were accustomed to subordinate positions. Gaudentius, a dedicated *didaskalos,* was already "old" in 356 but continued to teach until he was past eighty.[126] An inscription on his family tomb commemorates him for being an advocate (maybe before teaching), but it does not mention his work as teacher, a sign that advocacy was considered a higher achievement.[127] Uranius was a teacher at the school

---

[122] It is usually assumed that he was born after Libanius settled in Antioch, but it is possible that Libanius's relationship with Cimon's mother started in Constantinople. The fact that Libanius was engaged to his uncle's daughter should not have been a difficulty. In the papyri, the adjective *micros* ("little," "young") is not necessarily related to age; cf. Cribiore 2001; 95.

[123] Note in *Ep.* 678.3 that Cimon needs to be supported for rhetoric (*eis logous*).

[124] He did not disclose their names. Translation and interpretation of this oration is in Norman 2000, 66–83.

[125] In identifying Libanius's assistants, Wolf (1952, 67–75) is generally more reliable than Petit (1956a, 87–90).

[126] Gaudentius 2. See 204 and *Epp.* 749, 543. Libanius accepted his son as a student with no tuition; cf. *Or.* 38 and below, Chapter Six.

[127] Wolf (1952, 67–69) thus wrongly denied that the teacher and the advocate were the same person. See the whole discussion in Puech 2002, 261–62, commenting on inscription 118.

(not a sort of pedagogue whom Libanius lodged in his house).[128] Presumably he was not very young, as he had a family and shared with Libanius "the care of the herd of students, my way of life, joys, sorrows, everything" (*Ep.* 357.2).

In 355/56, Libanius wrote to his uncle that the third teacher, Herodianus, had approached him: he wanted Libanius to become his "master" (*kyrios*) and wished to live on the same terms as Uranius.[129] Herodianus, a Phoenician, was part of the faculty in 361 and earned a short leave of absence to inspect his small possessions in Phoenicia, which he needed because "his earnings from his professions were even smaller" (*Ep.* 640). Two years later, Herodianus, who appears to be the only assistant who offered the least bit of resistance to his master, complained of inadequate attention but received meager consolation: Libanius told him that when a master has many horses, each one does not get sufficient love (*Ep.* 1415).

At a later date, in the 380s, two of Libanius's ex-students, Calliopius and Eusebius, taught with him.[130] Libanius presented the first as "quite content with the second rank, even though he could aim at the first place" (*Or.* 62.35) and described his feelings of loss when this assistant died in 392. Calliopius gave the students knowledge of the ancient writers, was a very capable rhetor, and had an excellent character; his death badly damaged the school.[131] Libanius mourned him as his own "son, not by blood but reared by my labors" (*Ep.* 1051 [N184]). This is the way he also referred to his other assistant in those years, Eusebius, "my child, connected by eloquence" (*Ep.* 960.2 [N170]). Eusebius, however, was of a higher rank than Libanius's other assistants, being the only one whom he called "sophist."[132] Even though he still "pastured the flock" under

---

[128] He does not appear in *PLRE* I. Cf. Wolf 1952, 67. Petit (1956a, 28 and 145–46) thinks that he and Herodianus were "pensionnaires" of Libanius and supposes that Libanius put them up in his own house together with some students, but his hypothesis cannot be supported. In *Ep.* 357.2, the word *diaita* means "way of life," not "table." Uranius had a family and could not live with Libanius; *Or.* 31.11, moreover, discloses that the four assistants either rented some rooms or bought a house. Petit envisioned Uranius as the person who took care of the students whom Libanius lodged, but according to *Ep.* 357, Uranius took care of all the students (*agelē*).

[129] Herodianus 2. There is no evidence that he was an ex-student of Libanius, contra Petit (1956a, 28), who did not follow in this case the same stringent criteria devised to identify the other students. See the right interpretation of *Ep.* 454 in Norman 1992, no. 14. The expression *kyrios*, moreover, is never used to indicate a teacher-student relationship.

[130] Calliopius 4/iv and Eusebius 24/xxii. We do not know anything about Theotecnus (64), who may have been an assistant of some sort.

[131] See *Epp.* 1051, 1063, and 1064 (N184, N188, and N189).

[132] *Or.* 54.52. See also *Or.* 1.258 and *Epp.* 904–8 concerning the Council's attempt to deprive him of immunity (N154–159). On the whole affair, see Pack 1935, 121–23; Liebeschuetz 1972, 267–69; and Norman 1992, 454–59.

Libanius's supervision (*Ep*. 904), his duties went beyond the reading and explication of the ancient texts: he "made orators" (*Ep*. 907.3 [N154]). Libanius did not resent that in 388, Eusebius composed acclaimed panegyrics on Theodosius and Arcadius; quite the opposite: he felt that his own prestige was increased (*Or*. 1.258). Eusebius had become an ally in the war against Athens, so that "those who came out of the Athenian schools became admirers of him and myself, of me for what I gave, of him for what he received."

In *Oration* 31, Libanius depicted his assistants as servants of Apollo, "no less precious to him than swans," and yet they were underpaid and undervalued, things for which he held the citizens of Antioch responsible. But in spite of Libanius's proclamation of their competence and request for the same financial treatment that his predecessor, Zenobius, had enjoyed,[133] they did not have the authority of full *didaskaloi*, but occupied subordinate positions, had to render account to him in everything, and followed his directions even in assigning readings to students, as we will see.[134] Libanius always chose as assistants individuals who could not or did not want to challenge his overpowering personality. Only in his late years, forced by his frailty, did he share some power with one of them, Eusebius, a "son." We see already that Libanius was his school.

OTHER SOPHISTS IN ANTIOCH

What precedes highlights some of the difficulties that we will also encounter in the following chapter in identifying teachers of rhetoric. Strict terminology helps only to a limited extent because of the ambiguity of the terms "sophist" and "rhetor."[135] Most of Libanius's assistants were rhetors, not sophists, but taught rhetoric. The term "sophist," meaning "professor of rhetoric," is present in the literary texts in the first century B.C.E. but appears much later in inscriptions. A rhetor could teach the rudiments of eloquence, could give applauded performances, or could be active only in the law courts. I will not include in my account all rhetors, therefore, but I will cover those who appear to have taught. Though Libanius's was the only municipal school, others sophists taught in Antioch and had schools that were sponsored privately. A young Libanius looked with envy upon those who were established enough to use temples (such as the Museum and the temple of Tyche) for their lessons.[136] Libanius's writings disclose

---

[133] See *Or*. 11.20–21; Zenobius farmed a land that belonged to the city.
[134] Cf. below, Chapter Five.
[135] See Bowersock 1969, 12–14; Brunt 1994; and Puech 2002, 10–15.
[136] *Or*. 1.101–4; *Ep*. 88 (N45); Schemmel 1908.

some information about his predecessors and shed some light on the various stages of his feud with the sophist Acacius, who aspired to the same municipal chair. But after Libanius emerged victorious and Acacius left for Palestine, information about other practitioners of rhetoric in the city is scarce, and these teachers recede into an anonymous darkness.

In the second half of the third century, the presbyter Malchion seems to have been the chief teacher of rhetoric in Antioch. The convoluted Greek of Eusebius ("He was at the head of the occupation of the Hellenic schools in Antioch") is far from clear, but Jerome affirms that Malchion "taught rhetoric with great distinction."[137] Aedesius was a sophist in the city before Libanius was born, but almost nothing is known about him.[138] He was the predecessor of Ulpianus, who may be identified with the teacher whom Libanius followed with some nonchalance without recognizing at first his real worth.[139] In contrasting his own benevolent attitude toward his assistants, an older Libanius depicted Ulpianus as a manipulative despot who treated the other teachers like schoolboys: they had to jump up when he arrived, kept their heads bowed, were in fear of a thrashing, and had to pay him part of their fees. His death left a vacuum, and the rest of the sophists seemed "mere shadows of teachers" to a discontented Libanius in search of a real mentor. And shadows they remain to us, except for Zenobius (Ulpianus's successor) and Olympianus. Libanius, who had attended Zenobius's classes before going to Athens, considered his natural capabilities (*physis*) inferior to his predecessor's. He was not as tyrannical, yet he, too, was a self-centered master, ignored his assistants altogether, and did not even know their names (*Or.* 36.10–11).[140] It is still possible, however, that the rivalry that later arose between them, when Libanius was impatient to take his place, colored his estimation of his teacher. Olympianus is probably also to be numbered among the inept sophists left in Antioch after Ulpianus's demise. Though he mentions Olympianus in a letter, Libanius entirely ignores his achievements as he sings the praises of Saturninus, the best of his classmates, around whom the other students assembled in awe when he declaimed in class (*Ep.* 1489).[141]

---

[137] No mention in *PLRE* I; Barnes 1973, 145. Cf. Millar 1971, 16. Eusebius *Hist. eccl.* 7.29.2; Jerome *De viris illustribus* 71.

[138] See *Or.* 4.9, in which Libanius says that Aedesius 1 was in good mental health when he died; and cf. Martin 1988, 287–88.

[139] Ulpianus 1 (*Or.* 1.8), not Aedesius 1 (*PLRE* I, p. 14), taught at Emesa before coming to Antioch; see below, Chapter Two.

[140] Zenobius (*PLRE* I, p. 991). Libanius never ceased considering Zenobius a rival against whom he had to measure up. On their relationship, see below, Chapter Three.

[141] Olympianus 1; Saturninus 5/ii.

When Libanius arrived in Antioch, Zenobius was close to retiring, and the Phoenician Acacius was the most promising candidate for the post.[142] The *Autobiography* and the letters record the phases of their antagonistic relationship: periodic defeats of Acacius, who withdrew to other provinces; Libanius's gestures of rapprochement; a vain covenant between them not to abduct the other's students; and a final, ugly episode involving plagiarism and bribery that brought the governor's condemnation and Acacius's disgrace.[143] And yet, the way Libanius first introduces his rival in the *Autobiography*[144] warns the reader that the narrative may be colored by a later perspective. Acacius is described as "the Phoenician admired for his profession, the son and grandson of teachers, respected no less on this account than for his *logoi*" (90). Such a personage, one feels, could not remain a permanent enemy. Punctually in fact, a less-threatening Acacius begins to undergo a slow mutation, and becomes first an ally of circumstance (110), and then a colleague worthy of some respect.

A letter testifies that things were starting to change already in 358/59, before Acacius's final departure in 360 (**165**). Responding to a father who was returning his son to his care and had criticized his rival, a stiff-lipped Libanius retorted, "It is equally absurd to praise those who are mediocre and not to admire those who are good. By not considering Acacius one of the retinue of Hermes, you cause me, and especially the god, pain." Capturing Libanius's real opinion of his opponent's ability is difficult. The letters that he addressed to him after Acacius moved to Caesarea contain Libanius's suspicious protestations of regret for the latter's absence and admiration for his rhetoric.[145] Yet nowhere in the correspondence or in the narrative of his life did Libanius clearly discredit the power of his rival's eloquence. The image of him that emerges from Libanius's writings is that of a tranquil gentleman endowed with Levantine nonchalance toward work, who could not conceive from where the high productivity of his opponent came, who kept on promising orations without delivering them, and made frantic, cramming efforts only at the end—in

---

[142] Acacius 6, but the entry in *PLRE* I contains some imprecision. He was a native of Phoenicia, and taught there and in Caesarea (in Palestine) besides Antioch. On Acacius (not Eubulus) being Libanius's rival, see Wolf 1952, 93–94; Martin and Petit 1979, 228–29. Swain (2004, 377 n. 75), wrongly in my opinion, continues to identify the rival with Eubulus.

[143] See *Or.* 1.90–91, 109–15, and 120; *Epp.* 390, 391, 405 (N3, N4, and N6), 439, 454 (N14), 529 (B8), 555, and 722 (N85). On the correct sequence of Acacius's movements, see Martin and Petit 1979, 236–37.

[144] Cf. also *Ep.* 405 (N6).

[145] See, e.g., *Epp.* 274, 754 (N90), and 815 (N101).

sum, a negligent (but perhaps gifted) rhetor, an easy target for the indefatigable Libanius.[146]

The fact that Eunapius thought highly of Acacius does not shed much light on the issue of his actual merits. His commendations of his "sophistic force, inspiration, and sonorous diction" seem to put him on the same plane as Eunapius's models of perfect rhetoric.[147] Eunapius's reflexive dislike for what he regarded as the dry, unruffled oratory of Libanius and his disbelief in the latter's (unmerited) success is transparent. He maintained that Libanius dedicated his essay *On Genius* (*Peri euphyias*) to Acacius, who had defeated him because of his natural qualities.[148] It is unnecessary to suppose that Eunapius took a statement of Libanius out of context.[149] Libanius conceded defeat other times, always showing how a student had learned from him to the point of producing impeccable work.[150] It is likely, moreover, that an essay on natural endowments contained a treatment of hard work (*ponos*), the foil of *physis*, that is, an area in which Libanius found Acacius deficient.

After Acacius's disappearance, there is scant information about sophists teaching in the city.[151] In a letter that dates to 363 (*Ep.* 1361), Libanius mentions Marius, who was then governor of Phoenicia, and calls him a sophist.[152] The fact that in the same letter, Libanius by contrast calls "rhetor" a certain advocate, and that other letters attest the trust he had in Marius's ability to evaluate rhetoric, indicates that the latter had had a teaching position of some sort, even though it is not completely certain that he taught in Antioch. The same letter (1361) also mentions as possible sophists in Antioch a Theodorus and a Julianus.[153] The name of another rhetor who taught (*paideuonti*), Philumenus, whose rhetoric Libanius valued, resurfaces from a letter (*Ep.* 1355) in which he appears to have married the daughter of an eminent man.[154]

---

[146] Cf. *Or.* 1.109 and 110; *Ep.* 405.7–9. See also letter **18**, in which he alludes to Acacius by chastising "those who work not at making discourses but at slandering those who do."

[147] Eunapius *VS* 17, 497. Cf. below. On various reasons for Eunapius's praise of Acacius, see Penella 1990, 107–8.

[148] Cf. also Libanius *Ep.* 405.

[149] Penella 1990, 108.

[150] See *Ep. Lib.-Bas.* 4, complimenting Basil (cf. Chapter Three, note 87), and **159** and **160** praising Parthenopaeus.

[151] I do not include Ulpianus 2, whom *PLRE* (I, p. 973) wrongly treats as a student of Libanius and a possible sophist on the basis of *Epp.* 648 and 1353. The word *hetairos* in *Ep.* 1353.1.1 means "friend" or "schoolmate," not "student." For an occurrence of this word with both meanings in the same letter, cf. **124**.

[152] Marius 1; cf. Bradbury 2004a, 175–78.

[153] Theodorus 10; Julianus xxi.

[154] He does not appear in *PLRE* I. The expression "by us" probably meant "in Antioch."

A former student of Libanius, Celsus, may have taught rhetoric in Antioch for a short period before switching to an official career.[155] He returned to Antioch from Constantinople in 361 after studying with the philosopher Themistius, and in a letter of the following year, Libanius praised Celsus's versatile intellect and his gentle disposition (he did not bite!), regretting that he was abandoning the academic career (783). In those years, the sophist Strategius had a *chorus* in the city, but his position is difficult to define. He spent his summers in his native Euphratensis, and taught for at least a year in Phoenicia. Libanius recommended him to the governor of Phoenicia in 364, when Strategius (appropriately called "the bee") was harassed by a certain man (dubbed "the crocodile"), who thus "deprived the students of their teacher, penalizing him both in the schools there and in the school here" (*Ep.* 1145).[156] Equally uncertain is the teaching role of the rhetor Malchus, for whom Libanius wrote a series of recommendations in 356. He appears as teaching (*trephein*) the young son (*paidion*) of the governor Modestus in 361, and it is possible that he gave him some rudiments of rhetoric.[157]

In spite of problems created by desertions and indiscipline, Libanius's school maintained its standing in Antioch in the 380s. Others sophists were teaching as well, but no names emerge from Libanius's writings because of their geographical proximity and relative lack of threat to him.[158] In those years, the dangers to Libanius's school came from other disciplines, not from practitioners of the same art.[159] Some bickering still clouded his relationships with other members of the teaching profession, but he proclaimed, albeit in vain, that they all had to be united to face common enemies.

---

[155] Celsus 3/i; cf. below, Chapters Two and Three.

[156] Strategius 1/iii (*Epp.* 1145, 1146, and 1527, and 100). The word *chorois* in this context probably refers to "schools" and not to circles of educated people. Petit (1956a, 89–90) struggled to interpret an admittedly difficult dossier of letters, but his conclusion (that Strategius taught in Libanius's school) cannot be accepted. In those years, Libanius called his assistants "rhetors," and his tone in letters referring to Strategius is not paternal. In 100 Hieron was not in Antioch anymore (and probably studied with Libanius only for one year), but followed the classes of Strategius, maybe in Phoenicia. In this case, 100 should be rather dated to 364. The letters contained in Ms. V are in a state of confusion.

[157] *PLRE* (I, p. 539) regards Malchus as a tutor, but Libanius often uses the verb *trephein* for teaching (and teaching rhetoric). The word *paidion* does not necessarily refer to a very young child; see above.

[158] I do not think that Antiochus 9 was a sophist. Foerster identified him as such in the introduction to *Or.* 39 (1903–27, 3:264), but the students mentioned at *Or.* 39.16–17 were not his students.

[159] In *Or.* 43, Libanius hoped to bring all the sophists to a covenant to limit desertions. In *Or.* 36, he hinted that the culprit in the chameleon episode (see note 57 above) might have been another teacher, but he did not reveal his name.

CHAPTER TWO

Schools and Sophists in the Roman East

THE RHETORICAL education imparted by Libanius and other teachers in Antioch was the last stage of an educational pattern that appears, for all intents and purposes, to have been obligatory for males from the upper classes.[1] But did rhetoric uniformly pervade the cultural fabric of the Roman East, or was it confined to a few isolated islands of *paideia*? An investigation concerning other schools of rhetoric in the Roman East can help us evaluate the significance of Antioch vis-à-vis other educational centers so that we may begin to understand the nature of the competition that Libanius faced. It also sheds some light on Libanius's relations with sophists who practiced outside his immediate sphere. These contacts, maintained mostly through correspondence, reveal past encounters, sometimes dating back to the rhetors' shared school days in Athens. It is therefore possible to reconstruct the complex web of academic interactions upon which Libanius's recruitment relied heavily and which was part of the larger network of *philia* ("friendship") with former students, and their families and acquaintances.[2] An important caveat, however, is that more sophists than those we can recover were active in those years, since Libanius's correspondence does not put us in touch with sophists he did not like or did not know well.

Information concerning sophists teaching in various locations is extremely uneven. When Libanius is the major source, we gain some details but are often unable to verify the accuracy of the information. His correspondence, however, is so extensive and spans so many decades that one can hope for some perspective. Lack of impartiality also characterizes the reports of Eunapius concerning sophists in Athens. Eunapius's exuberance and partisanship make for vivid and colorful accounts whose veracity needs to (but often cannot) be weighed against other available sources. Yet Libanius and Eunapius provide a wealth of details that make a picture we know only in outline appear deceptively complete.

Regrettably, inscriptions provide little help in verifying or supplementing information from the literary sources. Whereas they almost punc-

[1] On the ambiguity of the terms "sophist" and "rhetor" and the difficulty in identifying teachers of rhetoric, see above, Chapter One.
[2] On this, see below, Chapter Three.

tually reflect the world evoked by the *Lives of the Sophists* of the second-century sophist Philostratus, personages who appear in Eunapius and Libanius are only occasionally present in the epigraphic documentation.[3] This phenomenon is obviously not due to a decline in the presence of sophists. When an inscription commemorates a sophist or a rhetor who did some teaching, it is mostly because of some other benefactions,[4] or because he had a high position in the administration or was a court intellectual who celebrated the glory of the powerful. After the third century, a sophist was no longer the acclaimed celebrity to whom a proud city might erect a statue, and the cases of Prohaeresius, Libanius, and a few others are exceptional.[5] Generally a sophist's rhetorical performances were still appreciated, but he was regarded as a professional in charge of a school, and his name disappeared from monuments.[6] It is telling that no inscription celebrates Himerius in spite of his fame, but it is more surprising that the name of Themistius is not incised anywhere.

Themistius's works, in any case, and particularly those that offer some information about his life and career, are fundamental sources for this inquiry, and the same is true for the correspondence of the Cappadocian fathers, who were in contact with sophists operating in that area. The cases of sophists who are known from the sources considered above contrast sharply with those for which the main or unique source is the lexicon known as *Suda,* which provides skeletal entries on various personages, giving little more than names, patronymics, and (more rarely) titles of works. The inevitable consequence is a lack of uniformity in my treatment of individual sophists. The meager information about some is counterbalanced by the extensive accounts concerning Prohaeresius and Himerius in Athens and Themistius in Constantinople.

THE SETTING

The accommodations of Libanius's school changed repeatedly until he became the official sophist of Antioch. From that time on, he designated the premises he used in the city hall with the term "school" (*didaskaleion*) and apparently never taught again (not even when he was sick) in his own house, which he had employed for the purpose when he had only a few

---

[3] See Puech 2002, 7–8.

[4] See, e.g., the case of the rhetor Iamblichus 2 (student of Libanius), who gave money to build fortifications of the walls of Athens in the 390s and was honored by two inscriptions. Cameron 1967a; Puech 2002, 313–14.

[5] On Prohaeresius, see below. No statues dedicated to Libanius are extant, but he says in *Or.* 2.14 that "many great cities" erected statues for him.

[6] Consider by contrast the inscriptions for Aristides; Puech 2002, 138–45.

students.[7] Antioch's city hall possessed "a covered lecture room (*theatron*) and four colonnades that surrounded a courtyard that had been turned into a garden" with trees of various kinds (*Or.* 22.31). Libanius used the "theater" for his and his students' declamations and for regular classes. The ending of his *Hymn for Artemis* takes place in this hall, where he was expecting the students to arrive (*Or.* 5.45–52). It was a monumental room with an imposing entrance and, on the opposite side, there were two seats, one of which was his chair (*thronos*). Lecture halls for the teaching of law (*auditoria*) existed in fourth-century Berytus, according to the author of the *Expositio totius mundi et gentium*, and in Late Antique Alexandria, a series of fifteen limestone *auditoria* have recently come to light next to similar constructions that were previously discovered.[8] They show seats for the teacher or lecturer and rows of seats for the students and strongly suggest a building complex for higher education, mainly grammar, rhetoric, and philosophy.

The information about the teaching premises of the sophists we will encounter in this chapter is admittedly scanty, but (with the help of some imagination) it will serve nonetheless to locate the activities of individuals, concerning which we are largely in the dark.[9] Archaeological finds sometimes converge with the literary sources to provide some background. This is the case for the teaching of rhetoric at Athens in the fourth century. Eunapius tells us that the relations between the townspeople and the sophists with their followings were so tense that the latter refrained from declaiming in the city and used "private lecture-rooms" (*idiōtika theatra*) away from the city center. He himself had seen the house of the sophist Julianus, which passed to his successor Prohaeresius. In spite of its simplicity, it looked like a holy temple of education where students could "breathe the fragrance of Hermes and the Muses." It was adorned with statues of former pupils, and it possessed a small marble lecture-room, which was suitable for classes and declamations.[10]

---

[7] Cf. above, Chapter One: he taught fifteen students at the very beginning, then twice that.

[8] *Expositio totius mundi et gentium* 25, which probably dates to the middle of the fourth century (Rougé 1966, 9–26 and in particular 19, where he dates the work to 359). The *Theodosian Code* has rulings concerning *auditoria* in Constantinople: 13.3.6 in the fourth century; and 6.21.1, 14.9.3, and 15.1.53 in the fifth century. On *auditoria* in Berytus, see Jones Hall 2004, 66–67. On *auditoria* for higher education in Alexandria, see Cribiore 2001, 34, a preliminary discussion on the basis of what was previously known. On the new teaching halls, see Cribiore forthcoming c and d.

[9] No teaching quarters, for example, have resurfaced in Constantinople, but the baths of Zeusippus, with their abundant statuary, openly alluded to the values of *paideia*; see Bassett 2004, 51–58.

[10] Eunapius *VS* 9.1, 4–6, 483.

Sophists must have frequently used their own quarters for teaching, particularly when they could afford spacious accommodations. In the second century, Philostratus relates that the wealthy sophist Proclus had a library (*thēkē bibliōn*) in one of his houses in Athens and used it to teach.[11] Two centuries later, the Athenian sophist Himerius testifies to a similar arrangement. His short *Oration* 64 is centered on a small lecture-room, a "temple to Hermes and the Muses, a beautiful, sacred place," where he had learned to declaim and to which he returned after delivering orations abroad in many splendid theaters. Visitors preferred to see the houses of Demosthenes, Socrates, or Pindar, said Himerius, rather than the magnificent abodes of the wealthy, and likewise his students were not supposed to spurn the exiguous *theatron* where they toiled at rhetoric.[12] A divine presence (Apollo and the Muses) could be perceived there, just as in the small workshop of the great sculptor Phidias, which was inhabited by Zeus.

Archaeologists have identified a group of fourth-century houses built on the slopes of the Areopagus in Athens as possibly belonging to teachers and used for teaching.[13] These four houses were distinguished by their exceptional size in relation to an average Athenian home and were rich in sculptures.[14] In all of them, the focal point is a large room preceded by a peristyle court and ending usually in an apse with niches for statuary. Although the apse is not present in the largest of these houses, its wide hall with niches suitable for sculptures seems to have had the same function as the apsidal rooms.[15] It is likely that these halls were *theatra* used for teaching and lecturing. A similar large room opening onto a wide apse is visible in the remains of a spacious and more sumptuous house on the south side of the Acropolis. The house in question has been identified as that of Plutarch, the head of the Neoplatonic school at Athens, and passed to his successors Syrianus and Proclus.[16] The similarity with the houses on the Areopagus strengthens the hypothesis that the latter also belonged to teachers: in all of these buildings, private, domestic quarters appear together with a large hall suitable for teaching and lecturing.

---

[11] Philostratus *VS* 2.21, 604; he had four houses, two of which were in Athens.

[12] This is the same "theater" to which the sophist happily returns in *Or.* 54.1.

[13] See Frantz 1988, esp. pp. 37–48.

[14] Statues of Herakles and Hermes, the god of rhetoric, seem particularly suitable to an educational environment.

[15] Athanassiadi (1999, 343–47) made the plausible suggestion that this house (C) was then bequeathed to the philosopher Damascius in the fifth century to serve as residence and teaching quarters for him and other philosophers.

[16] A passage in the *Vita Procli* 29 (Saffrey and Segonds 2001), written by Marinus, Proclus's successor, identifies its location.

Another grand house with shield portraits and busts of philosophers, dating from the Late Antique period, has been discovered at Aphrodisias in Caria.[17] Its imposing size and opulence would be appropriate for the mansion of a local grandee, but the house also features an apsidal hall that is too large for a library and is decorated with a series of niches with busts of past and contemporary thinkers, most of which are set in a tondo frame. The house has been identified as a prestigious philosophical school or, in any case, a school of higher learning. The marble portraits present a series of figures from the classical past (Pindar, Alexander, Alcibiades, Socrates, Aristotle, Pythagoras, Apollonius of Tyana); the posthumous representations of an old philosopher and the contemporary portrait of an adolescent boy; and the masterful bust of a man plausibly identified as a sophist. The pairs Aristotle and Alexander and Socrates and Alcibiades represent teacher and pupil, and the same idea is conveyed by the portrait of the boy in his early teens, who could be the sophist's student rather than the philosopher's.[18] The image of the sophist was meant to represent a contemporary individual, whose identification as a teacher of rhetoric rests on his dress, the short, trimmed beard, and the longish hair typical of an intellectual—on the whole, a man of the world and a public figure. The portrait of Pindar, which has been considered "highly unusual" (insofar as he was a poet)[19] would also fit well into the context of rhetorical education. We will see how important the lyric poet was for sophists like Himerius or for Gregory of Nazianzus, and it is not by chance that Pindar is represented in a different series of marble tondi also coming from late Roman Aphrodisias but now lost.[20]

This brief survey of archaeological finds probably related to education would not be complete without at least a mention of mosaic images. Fifteen Late Antique mosaic panels, which probably come from Syria and are dated to the late fourth to early fifth centuries, have recently been published.[21] These mosaics represent the life story of a youth. One panel depicts his *paideia*, which is personified as a woman who seems to pull the words out of the mouth of a seated figure. This figure, a man called Alexandros, sits on a high chair and may have been a teacher of rhetoric. He is lecturing to a group of students who appear to be seated at a higher

---

[17] See Smith 1990. The Roman house was renovated several times, and the shield portraits were probably added in the fourth and fifth centuries.

[18] It is possible that the boy's portrait stood for a whole category rather than representing a particularly gifted or prematurely deceased pupil.

[19] Smith 1990, 153.

[20] On Pindar, see below. These six portraits were destroyed in 1922, and only descriptions and some illustrations survive. They represented Pindar, Menander, two goddesses, and two young men.

[21] Marinescu, Cox, and Wachter 2005.

level, maybe on the stone seats of a *theatron*. Several houses in the Roman East display floor mosaics with images of poets, rhetors, and philosophers, which were somewhat unusual in Late Antiquity. Thus from Apamea in Syria, where rhetoric and philosophy were taught, a house beneath a Christian church with a floor plan similar to the houses described above was decorated with three mosaics representing scenes from the *Odyssey* and Socrates surrounded by Sages.[22] Socrates and the Seven Sages are arranged around the Muse Calliope in a mosaic from Heliopolis in Phoenicia, and an inscription in the same house says that "the builder of the house was worthy of the wisdom of Eudoxius, the philosopher-disciple of Plato."[23] A very suggestive but fragmentary mosaic was recently discovered in Seleucia in Pamphylia.[24] This yet-unpublished mosaic shows Homer, the *Iliad* and the *Odyssey* inscribed in the center, surrounded by a remarkable array of panel busts of philosophers, orators, historians, and poets: one could thus walk on the whole *enkyklios paideia*.

THE SCHOOL OF ATHENS

Athens loomed large and distant in the eyes of Libanius, Gregory of Nazianzus, and all those who went there to study rhetoric, or at least to gain "the reputation of having learned it."[25] The place was seductive for many reasons: its physical setting, the memories of its classical past, taxing but engrossing studies, friends, and youth itself. Libanius's love of the city sometimes resurfaces, yet his attitude is ambiguous and mostly negative. Before looking at the various figures who taught at Athens in an attempt to define the city's significance in rhetorical studies,[26] it is useful to record briefly some of Libanius's experiences.

The *Autobiography*, which reconsidered the period Libanius spent in Athens almost thirty-five years before, has a generally bleak outlook on

---

[22] Balty 1972. Cf. Smith 1990, 151–52.

[23] Another mosaic on the birth of Alexander includes Aristotle among other figures. See Chéhab 1958–59, 31–50 and plates 15–20 and 22–25. A philosopher by the name Eudoxius is not known, but two sophists by that name are known from Cappadocia, see below.

[24] Cf., in Smith 1990, 151–53, the survey of mosaics from the late Roman Eastern and Western worlds, including a description of the mosaic at Seleucia.

[25] Letter 200, in which Libanius was attempting to lure Titianus away from Attica in 362. On students in Athens, see Bernardi 1990 and Watts 2006, 41–47.

[26] I mention for the sake of completeness four sophists who taught in various regions of the Greek world. At the turn of the fourth century, Metrophanes 1 taught in Phrygia and Metrophanes 2 practiced in Boeotia (*Suda* 1009 and 1010). They both wrote several rhetorical works. In the time of the emperor Constantine, Palladius 1 was a sophist in Macedonia (Methone) and wrote several speeches and declamations. Pyrrhus 3 was a sophist in Crete in the fourth century; cf. the inscriptions in Puech 2002, 431–33.

his studies there. The tone of disappointed hope and frustration that pervades his arrival in the city inspires the rest of the account. A discontented Libanius learned to survive the rough handling of students, to hide a lack of enthusiasm for the teachers, and to bear what were in his eyes mediocre public declamations (*Or.* 1.16–17). It is likely, however, that on the whole his experience was less disastrous. This grim tale changes, in fact, into a joyful and playful account in a letter written in 365, where Libanius recalled his "great, past happiness."[27] Though this is one of many examples of a different treatment of an issue according to genre that one encounters in his work, the letter's protagonist (a High Priest of Athens who reports on the city's loyalty to the memory of Julian) must have helped to give this work a positive color. In spite of Libanius's general unwillingness to give Athens any credit, it is there that his rhetoric assumed the shape that allowed him to write, perform, and teach with great success, and there that he formed strong friendships that would sustain him for the rest of his life.[28] These tenacious relationships, centered on a common Athenian experience, resurface in his correspondence and were regarded as strong bonds based on *paideia* by other people as well (**198**).

Athens always remained for Libanius the model against which he measured his ability as a teacher and his capacity to satisfy and retain his students. He considered the city's reputation as maker of orators utterly usurped. In the blissful five years that he spent in Nicomedia, he tasted the sweetest triumph when his students were content with the teaching he provided and did not (as they had done in the past) try to run to Athens "in order to get inferior stuff."[29] Libanius compared the checking of the flow of students to Athens with the diversion of a stream, and likened the outraged Athenian sophists to old-fashioned farmers unable to accept a change for the better. Eunapius's unfavorable opinion of Libanius must contain an echo of that polemic and of Athens's "denunciation" of Bithynia as undermining its interests. To Libanius's bitter disappointment, the trend reversed itself when he had to move back to the uncultured environment and inclement weather of Constantinople: students deserted his classes and sailed to Greece or to Phoenicia.[30]

Libanius's chance to return to Athens in triumph, claiming the place for himself on equal terms, came a few years later when he was formally invited.[31] The governor Strategius Musonianus[32] protested the rigid hiring

---

[27] *Ep.* 1458 (B159). The date is tentative.
[28] In Antioch he had studied rhetoric for little time and erratically.
[29] Years 344–49, *Or.* 1.53.
[30] *Or.* 1.76. On the law school of Berytus in Phoenicia, cf. below.
[31] In 352/53, before his return to Antioch.
[32] *PLRE* I, pp. 611–12.

practices of the Athenian faculty, saying that Athens received students from everywhere but was unwilling to admit sophists from abroad. Yet, after spending many words to describe to his readers his elation, Libanius refused the invitation. Fear of the violence and competition of the Athenian academic environment was the reason he gave; since he anticipated with typical self-assurance that his ability would have exposed the incompetence of the others, there is no wonder that he forecast war. But the desire to be closer to his family and city, and to be the unquestionable leader of a less-intimidating scholarly community, must have played some role. Athens always remained for him the environment where nothing impaired teaching and learning, and thus an object of envy. When he wrote to the sophist Gerontius of Apamea in 363, "I consider you more blessed than the sophists in Athens," his remark was based upon salary and teaching "in peace."[33] Students resided untroubled in Athens for many years, and education was their only obligation (Libanius thought), whereas his own students had challenges and responsibilities they could not (or did not want to) avoid and often opted for a shorter attendance. With their more or less sophisticated training in rhetoric, young men looked for jobs as advocates or in the administration rather than becoming rhetors or sophists,[34] and such temptations were particularly real in Antioch, which was often the seat of the Imperial court. In Libanius's opinion, in fact, this affliction (*kakon*) affected fortunate Athens much less (*Or.* 62.15).

The school of Athens was legendary. Young Libanius in Antioch had heard with longing of the rhetorical feats of sophists like Tlepolemus and Callinicus, who taught there at the turn of the fourth century.[35] Eunapius related extensive information about Julianus of Cappadocia,[36] who belonged to the generation before that of Prohaeresius, but recorded only the names of some of Julianus's contemporaries, which are supplemented by the entries of the *Suda*. Julianus "dominated" (*tyrannein*) Athens from a cultural standpoint.[37] There were other sophists who shared Julianus's fame and who "touched beauty somewhat," but they were inferior to him. In the early period at Athens, Eunapius declared, the most famous

---

[33] Letter 88, on Gerontius; cf. below.

[34] Cf. below, Chapter Six.

[35] *Or.* 1.11. Tlepolemus (*PLRE* I, p. 920) and Callinicus from Petra (pp. 173–74). (Callinicus 2, mentioned by the *Suda*, seems too late.)

[36] Julianus 5: Eunapius VS 9.1–2, 482–85. Puech (2002, 316–18, no. 143) cautiously mentions the identification with the Julianus of an Egyptian inscription. I will not dedicate much attention to the sophists mentioned by Eunapius because Penella (1990) has treated the subject exhaustively.

[37] Cracco Ruggini (1971, 424) remarked that for the first time, terms such as *tyrannos* and *tyrannein* lost every political nuance and referred only to cultural preeminence.

professors were the Egyptian Paulus of Lycopolis and Andromachus, who started his career in Nicomedia under Diocletian. The latter had as a pupil Siricius from Palestine, who taught in Athens in the early fourth century and wrote on *progymnasmata* and declamations.[38]

A family of philosophers (and sophists perhaps) from Apamea, all called Sopater, deserves attention. Little is certain about the role as sophist of Sopater 1 (a well-renowned philosopher-pupil of Iamblichus) who was executed under Constantine.[39] Eunapius's description of him as a very able speaker might be the origin of the report in the *Suda* (845) that he also was a sophist.[40] But there is another entry in the *Suda* (unmentioned in modern scholarship) for a Sopater, whom I will call Sopater 3 to distinguish him from Sopater 2, the philosopher from Apamea, son of the previous one and uncle of Libanius's student Iamblichus.[41] Sopater 3 (*Suda* 848) was supposedly a sophist from Apamea or Alexandria, and was apparently the author of epitomes and of a collection of "stories" (*historiai*). The identification of this personage with the Sopater who appears in the writings of the ninth-century patriarch Photius is secure. Photius dedicated much space to him, describing his twelve books in detail, but the beginning of his entry is very similar to the *Suda*, whose source he may have been.[42] It is uncertain, in any case, if Sopater 3 existed, if he had any relation to the other homonyms, or (perhaps more likely) if he should be identified with Sopater 1.

Among the contemporaries of Julianus, Eunapius left unmentioned the sophist Genethlius, who had a notable scholarly career in Athens but died at a very young age.[43] According to the *Suda*, in Athens he was the rival of the Callinicus mentioned above. They were both natives of Petra and provide an example of a competition born in early times. Epagathus and the Spartan Apsines also gained a considerable reputation. The latter belonged to a learned family; his father Onesimus was a sophist and a historian, and his grandfather Apsines taught rhetoric in Athens in the third century.[44] Eunapius devoted some of his most memorable pages to a dramatic dispute between Apsines' and Julianus's pupils, during the course of which students were thrown into chains, Prohaeresius shone in a vehe-

---

[38] Eunapius VS 4.3.1, 457; Andromachus 2; Siricius, not mentioned by Eunapius, *PLRE* I, p. 845, and *Suda* s.v.

[39] Eunapius VS 6.2–3, 462–64; *RE* 3A.1 (1927): 1006–7; Cameron 1967a, 146–48; and Penella 1990, 49–53, 56–57.

[40] Cf. Penella 1990, 50 n. 25.

[41] Sopater 2, also called a philosopher by Libanius *Or.* 18.187.

[42] Photius (810–93 C.E.) *Bibl.* Cod. 161; Henry 1960, vol. 2: "His work is a collection of many various stories and writings."

[43] *PLRE* I, p. 390.

[44] Apsines 2, Onesimus 2, and Apsines 1.

ment speech, Julianus wept from emotion, and the Roman proconsul applauded like a schoolboy.[45] Eunapius described Themistocles, who was the head of the *chorus* of Apsines and bore the responsibility for the incident, as a bold and insolent young man. At a later time, when Libanius met Themistocles in Constantinople, he was a member of a stimulating and jolly group of intellectuals.[46]

Five of the pupils of Julianus of Cappadocia taught at Athens, a fact that confirms the validity of Strategius Musonianus's complaint that foreigners outside of that circle were excluded from teaching there. The Tuscianus mentioned by Eunapius might be the eloquent official, the "craftsman of discourses" (*Ep.* 345), who appears in Libanius's letters, but the identification is not compelling.[47] Libanius does not mention Hephaestion, who shared with Prohaeresius a close friendship and a cloak they took turns wearing.[48] Before reaching Athens, both of these rhetors had studied in Antioch with one Ulpianus, probably to be identified as the great sophist whose classes Libanius initially followed, for the sake of form only, and without real passion.[49] Eunapius did not leave a full biographical sketch of Hephaestion, who retired from the competition for Julianus's chair, left Athens, and died.[50] One suspects that one reason for the silence might be that the model friendship with Prohaeresius had become strained.

When Libanius reached Athens, he found as teachers the three other students of Julianus who were competing to succeed him. He was forced to follow the classes of Diophantus but also attended the lectures of those "other two," that is, Epiphanius, who was his original choice, and Prohaeresius.[51] Students were automatically divided according to provenance, so that Libanius had expected to be the student of the Syrian Epi-

---

[45] Eunapius VS 9.2.1–20, 483–85.

[46] Seeck (1906, s.v.) accepted the identification of the Eunapian Themistocles with the scholar by that name in Libanius's *Ep.* 436 (B29), **149**, and **153**; see below.

[47] *Ep.* 345 (N27). Eunapius esteemed Tuscianus (*VS* 10.4.2, 488), but did not provide a separate portrait of him because he had spoken of him in his *History*. Penella (1990, 138 and n. 49) finds other reasons for Eunapius's neglect of Tuscianus and fully accepts the identification with the official mentioned by Libanius. Wintjes (2005, 128 n. 72) distinguishes between two different persons, as in *PLRE* I.

[48] Eunapius VS 10.3.5, 487. Both teachers and students of rhetoric in Athens wore the red *tribōn*, which was dark grey for the philosophers; see a *scholion* to Gregory of Nazianzus *Patrologia Graeca* (*PG*) 36, 906A; Bernardi 1990, 88. On poverty in higher education, cf. below, Chapter Six.

[49] Cf. Chapter One.

[50] Eunapius VS 10.3.12, 487. Penella (1990, 80) surmises that the main reason for Eunapius's cursory treatment of Hephaestion was his premature death.

[51] *Or.* 1.16. At 1.85, Libanius mentioned the rough treatment of Diophantus at the hands of some thugs.

phanius. Eunapius considered Epiphanius vastly superior to Diophantus, of whom he had the lowest opinion. One surmises that the precision and "excessive accuracy" that the Eunapian prefect of Illyricum, Anatolius, found ridiculous in Epiphanius during his visit to Athens suited Libanius more than the spectacular rhetoric of Prohaeresius.[52] Like many people, Anatolius thought that Prohaeresius was the only rhetor worthy of admiration. He laughed at the students who enthusiastically applauded the other sophists and pitied their fathers, who had chosen them as teachers.

The competition for the professorial chair at Athens drew a great number of candidates and aroused the interest of the whole Roman world, with different nations favoring their own athletes of the word. Sopolis and Parnasius were the only candidates who were brought from the outside, but they were inferior competitors in Eunapius's view.[53] Despite "knocking diligently at the Muse's door," Sopolis could manage to capture only a tiny amount of her divine breath, yet this was sufficient to draw adoring audiences. Apparently the Muse's door remained shut to Parnasius, who was of a lesser caliber and had limited following.

The Divine Prohaeresius

Eunapius gives an idealized account of his teacher.[54] Prohaeresius, who with his unusually tall stature, striking physical beauty, ample gestures, and sonorous rhetoric bewitched the young men in his following, among whom were Gregory of Nazianzus and Basil of Caesarea.[55] It was difficult to resist him. His orations were masterpieces of showmanship. With his head high, he surveyed the theater, let out a flood of vehement, overwhelming eloquence as he treated several themes, and "leapt in the air like one inspired."[56] At the end of his speech, adoring people licked his breast and kissed his hands and feet as if he were the statue of a god,

---

[52] Eunapius VS 11.1–12.4, 493–94, on Epiphanius and Diophantus, and 10.6.14, 491, on the opinion of Anatolius 3, *PLRE* I, pp. 59–60. On the distinction between the Eunapian Anatolius and the Anatolius who was prefect in 357–60, see Penella 1990, 90–91, and Bradbury 2000.

[53] Eunapius VS 10.3.9–10, 487; 13; and 15, 494.

[54] Eunapius VS 101.1–108.4, 485–93.

[55] Biographers often describe their subject's tall stature and handsome appearance, as Marinus does for Proclus (*Vita Procli* 3, ed. Saffrey and Segonds), Damascius for Isidore (*Isid.* Epit. Photius 16 and 49, ed. Zintzen), and Eunapius for Priscus or Maximus of Ephesus (VS 8.1.2, 481, and 7.1.1–3, 473); but Prohaeresius's presentation seems exceptional, VS 107.1–2, 492.

[56] Cf., in Eunapius VS 23.502, the performance of Chrysanthius with hair sticking up and eyes that showed that his soul was dancing.

Hermes himself.⁵⁷ But for Libanius, Prohaeresius was only one "of the others." Why the silence?

Prohaeresius must have shone in the classes of Ulpianus and surely left outstanding memories in Antioch, but Libanius almost ignored him. It is possible that in Athens he felt excluded from the closed circle of Prohaeresius's devotees, since he was not fated to be one of his pupils, but Eunapius hinted that Libanius might have chosen not to be part of the group for fear of being obscured by so much talent.⁵⁸ The physical presence and the passionate style of the celebrated orator may have perplexed Libanius. His own style was quite different, and Eunapius's description of it as "weak, lifeless, and uninspired" tells much about Prohaeresius's fire.⁵⁹ Was Libanius the swan and Prohaeresius the goose, or vice versa? In a letter to Themistius, in which Libanius acknowledged the similarity of their writings, he exhorted the philosopher to avoid the vulgar ostentation (*to phortikon*) of other popular rhetors.⁶⁰ The polemic was addressed against those who followed the fashionable Asianic style, Himerius among them. In the fifth century B.C.E., the sophist Gorgias had vied with poetry by appropriating features such as poetic vocabulary and rhythms. This fashion, which can be traced through Asianic orators of the Hellenistic age, continued in the Roman period.⁶¹ Besides ostentatious delivery, these orators' use of rhythms was under criticism. Writers of the Second Sophistic often accused them of "singing," yet recorded how they bewitched their audiences by that.⁶² What we know indirectly of Prohaeresius's style makes it likely that he was an Asianic orator, though we cannot judge for ourselves because none of his writings survive. Libanius preferred not to engage openly against rhetors who followed other fashions. "The flock of geese" should be left in ignorance of others and of themselves, he declared, and be fooled into thinking that they were the truly melodious birds.

The *Suda* records that the great favor Julian showed Libanius was also motivated by his desire to annoy the Athenian sophist.⁶³ The letter Julian

---

⁵⁷ See the narration of Prohaeresius coming back from exile and the account of the speech he gave, Eunapius VS 10.3.14–5.9, 488–90.

⁵⁸ Eunapius VS 16.1.2, 495.

⁵⁹ Eunapius VS 16.2.1, 496.

⁶⁰ *Ep.* 1477 of the year 365 (N141); cf. below.

⁶¹ See Norden 1915, 367–79. A clear distinction of the Asianic and Attic styles can be found in Innes and Winterbottom 1988, 16–19.

⁶² See, e.g., Dio *Or.* 32.68; Lucian *Demon.* 12, *Rhetorum praeceptor* 19; Philostratus VS 1.8, 492; 2.10, 589; and 2.28, 620. Cf. more references in Norden 1915, 375–79. Aristedes composed the most ferocious invective against the Asianic style in *Or.* 50 Keil.

⁶³ *Suda* Λ 486.

wrote Prohaeresius in 361 or 362 is pervaded by irony and is complimentary only on the surface.[64] The beginning ("Why should I not address the noble Prohaeresius?") may hint that relations with the sophist were not completely smooth. Prohaeresius's eloquence was a mighty river in flood, while Julian was inundated by important affairs. Spartan brevity became the emperor, but long, powerful discourses (*makroi logoi*) fit Prohaeresius, a new Protagoras.[65]

Since Prohaeresius was a Christian and lost his official chair under Julian, one may wonder whether this was a decisive source of friction with Libanius.[66] It probably was not. Libanius's real allegiance was to rhetoric, and disagreement in that field was bound to be a matter of graver import. Heeding his own advice to Themistius, Libanius maintained cordial but distant relations with Prohaeresius. He mentions him once in a letter to a governor in which he is trying to secure assistance for a relative of the sophist.[67] Prohaeresius was "the man who benefited the whole world with his rhetoric," and two statues in Rome and at Athens commemorated his eminence.[68] A favor solicited on his behalf resulted in an increase of honor for Libanius. From a distance, Prohaeresius did not look so threatening.

Himerius the Singing Sophist

In 355/56, Libanius wrote a similar letter of support for another sophist, the Bithynian Himerius, who was then teaching at Athens.[69] Himerius had some property in Armenia that was menaced by certain enemies of the Muses. By helping a well-known sophist, the governor Gorgonius was going to give an impressive lesson of *paideia* to his son Aquila, a student of Libanius. Libanius did not mind being generous because Himerius did not pose an immediate threat to him. The two sophists had met in Nicomedia when Libanius was teaching and Himerius was giving a speech, and then perhaps they saw each other again in 362, if Himerius indeed

---

[64] I disagree with Penella (1990, 98) that this letter (31 Bidez) is only full of praises.

[65] Cf. Plato *Prt.*, e.g., 329b.

[66] For the question of Prohaeresius leaving his post, see Penella 1990, 92–94. Eunapius does not mention the exemption that Julian apparently gave him (Jerome *Chron.*, pp. 242–43 Helm). Goulet (2000) doubts that Prohaeresius was a Christian and maintains that Julian's edict required that teachers bring proofs of Hellenism.

[67] *Ep.* 275 (N73), of uncertain date (361?).

[68] Eunapius 10.7.4–5, 492, records only the bronze statue in Rome, erected to "the king of eloquence."

[69] *Ep.* 469; Norman 1992, no. 15. The governor of Armenia was Gorgonius 4. On the chronology of Himerius, see Barnes (1987), who established reliable dates. See also Penella 1990, 98–100.

went to Antioch with Julian. A letter of 362 lets us recover something of Libanius's opinion of this sophist, besides what can be inferred from a comparison of their rhetorical styles. It strongly suggests some antipathy, if the allusion to a rhetor in disgrace refers to Himerius at the time of his visit to Bithynia (*Ep.* 742). The governor of Bithynia, Libanius wrote to his student Celsus, did not disdain poverty, valued authentic rhetoric, and rejected its opposite; that is why he had mocked the "splendidly dressed fellow from Athens," forced him to speak, and let his inadequacy come in the open. The description evokes memories of the petulant and elegant teacher of the short road in Lucian's *Rhetorum praeceptor* (*The Teacher of Rhetoric*).[70] This may look like "good-natured banter rather than barbed insult,"[71] but it was a private joke between a teacher and his student that Himerius would have strongly resented and that disclosed the low regard Libanius had of the latter's eloquence.

Himerius, who was a few years younger than Libanius, was not one of the competitors for Julianus's chair. He taught in Constantinople from 343 to 352, and then at Athens in two subsequent periods. During the period 352–61, he had as pupils Gregory of Nazianzus, Basil of Caesarea, and (supposedly, for a short while) the future emperor Julian,[72] and he taught again from 366 to the 380s after "he hurried" back to Athens at the death of Prohaeresius.[73] Since Eunapius looked at the world through the lens of his loyalty to his teacher, his account of Prohaeresius's rival is not completely innocent, yet he did not fail to show approval for Himerius's style. He defined it as "easily flowing and harmonious" (*eukolos, synērmosmenos*), qualities that we also have a hard time denying Himerius, even though we may have reservations about his eloquence overall. Photius, who preserved long excerpts from twenty-four of his speeches plus shorter ones of others, considered Himerius's style to be endowed with a pleasant clarity, but he recognized that the general readers (*hoi polloi*) might have trouble grasping the meaning of this elevated genre.[74] By contrast, in his surprisingly cursory evaluation of Libanius, Photius declared that he appreciated his school works, but that the rest was

---

[70] In this dialogue, two different teachers lead a student up to rhetoric by a long and a short path; see below, Chapter Six.

[71] Barnes 1987, 212.

[72] Socrates *Hist. eccl.* 4.26.6 (reported thus by Sozomenus, *Hist. eccl.* 6.17.1). Van Dam (2002, 165) accepts it.

[73] Eunapius *VS* 14.1, 494. Barnes (1987, 207–9) sets the date of birth of Himerius at ca. 320.

[74] Cf. Photius Cod. 165. He disapproved of Himerius only for being a pagan and thus "imitating the dogs that secretly bark against us."

marred by obscurity (Cod. 90). Yet, he considered him the Attic rhetor par excellence.[75]

When we read Himerius, we appreciate his lucidity and think we are easily grasping the meaning of the text, but then we doubt whether this can be all. Himerius regarded himself as a singing cicada and as a swan, a melodious bird whose voice would overcome the roaring sea.[76] He envisaged his poetic oratory as something refreshing, novel, even revolutionary. "Since I saw the theaters of Attic eloquence parched, I tried to cure the drought with my discourses, as with shattering rain," he says in the prologue of his *Oration* 68. But as the oration proceeds, the rain becomes an inextinguishable fire, and the poet-orator incites his students to light up the *logoi*. The sophist is a Phidias who molds youth,[77] and yet, says Himerius, Phidias won admiration because of the novelty of his art. God, the great sophist in Heaven, operates in a multiplicity of ways, and a sophist must, too. Discourses cannot be uniform and static but need to be variegated like that "beautiful Homeric meadow," the shield of Achilles.

Every occasion was good for Himerius to proclaim the uniqueness of his art. A large part Himerius's *Oration* 38, which was dedicated to the proconsul of Achaia, Cervonius, concerns the novelty and seriousness of the sophist's message. Himerius seems to defend himself from accusations that his art is light and inconsistent. The poet-orator now is not Pindar or Hesiod but Socrates,[78] who did not teach the type of eloquence that was useful in assemblies but instilled the fruit of wisdom in the tender minds of his students. The comparison seems a bit inappropriate for a sophist accused of singing; it was better suited to Themistius, who appropriated the persona of Socrates to distinguish himself as a philosopher from other sophists.[79] During the years when he taught in Constantinople, Himerius was certainly aware of the important presence of Themistius, who had drawn some criticism to himself. Himerius's oration, in any case, alludes to real discord among the pupils of the various sophists teaching

---

[75] It is possible that Photius did not have access to all the works of Libanius, or that his brief treatment of him was due to the fact that he was well known as the model of Attic oratory and there was no need to expand; see Orth 1928, 70–71.

[76] Himerius *Or.* 40.1 and 59.1. Let us remember the words of Bouché-Leclerq 1909: one sings especially "ce qui ne vaut pas la peine d'être dit." All the citations from Himerius are taken from the text established by Colonna 1951. See also Dübner 1849, and recently Völker 2003, with a translation and commentary on Himerius's speeches and fragments and an excursus on his prose rhythm on pp. 73–78. Robert Penella has just completed an English translation of the orations: *Man and the Word: The Orations of Himerius*, forthcoming.

[77] He is again like Phidias in Himerius *Or.* 64. The lecture room where he teaches is small, like Phidias's workshop.

[78] Cf. also Himerius *Or.* 35.

[79] See, e.g., Themistius *Or.* 20.238, 21.246, 23.285–86, 26.317–18, and 31.352.

in Athens. When some of the students of Gorgias, Prodicus, or Hippias dared to follow Socrates, Himerius says, he was attacked in every way. People also derided his physical appearance and made fun of his face; but Socrates had asked the god to give beauty not to his body but to his soul. Is it excessive to read in these words a veiled polemic against the extraordinarily handsome and dangerously attractive Prohaeresius?

Myth pervades each of Himerius's works, evoking a land beyond time and space. Even though many speeches were composed for specific occasions, myth (or a combination of myths) is an integral part of each one. Reality needs to be extricated from the legendary web to recover some information on Himerius's career, on officials he addressed, and on the ups and downs of his school.[80] In the moving lamentation composed for the death of his young son Rufinus, "a son of the *logoi*" (8), myth is less pervasive, yet some images seem to compromise the integrity of the orator's pain. Thus, for example, Herakles and the fame he acquired through his labors and his journeys are brought in, "but you," says Himerius to his son, "remained in our midst and yet went beyond the pillars of Herakles with your wondrous deeds"—an image that is a bit stilted.

The Muses are a constant presence in Himerius's oratory. In Libanius, the Muses are mentioned with a smile or are part of a set of clichéd expressions obligatorily uttered. Schools are shrines, gardens, or meadows of the Muses, where their sacred rites are celebrated, and students are colts running in these pleasant pastures. People who acquire an education belong to the choirs of the Muses, who can sweeten their fatigues, and those who left their fields might anger them. The Muses can appear in set images together with Apollo or, more often, with Hermes, the god of rhetoric. They protect intellectual activities, as, for instance, the incessant discussions between Libanius and a learned friend: other types of conversation on food, money, or politics are not under their patronage.[81] Himerius, however, attempts to bring the real Muses on the stage. As Apollo tunes his lyre, the Muses dance but are unaware that ruthless Nymphs disguised as goddesses are part of their choir and bring a wild tone to the dance.[82] When it is time to reopen the school, the Muses allow the poet-rhetor the opportunity to declaim in their workshop, just as they gave permission to Hesiod, who rejected the shepherd's pipe and convened with them with

---

[80] For hints on Himerius's career and the governors he addresses, see Barnes 1987. On his school and students, cf. below.

[81] See, e.g., *Epp.* 18.3, 85.1, 154.1, **177**, 263.1, and **190**; *Or.* 11.188, 2.46, and 20.51. The Nymphs stand for the baths built by an official in *Ep.* 1259.8 (B51), and the Muses are considered with an irreverent eye in *Ep.* 1466.3–4 (B22). On talks not supervised by the Muses, see *Ep.* 255 (B151).

[82] Himerius *Or.* 66; the myth is borrowed from Aesop.

his lyre.⁸³ Himerius is a shepherd who always awakens the Muses' dances with his lyre. The Muses dance on Helikon and fill everything with their song, and around them nightingales, swallows, and swans dance.⁸⁴ Unfortunately, in spite of Himerius's earnest efforts, these dances of the Muses are still and their choirs are silent for us.⁸⁵

More Sophists in Athens

We know only the name of a contemporary of Himerius who may have taught rhetoric in Athens, Quintianus, who is mentioned in the title of *Oration 67*, the only part that survives. Himerius seems to have addressed this speech to his undisciplined students, but the possibility that Quintianus was only the ringleader of a misbehaving group of pupils cannot be ruled out. Another oration of Himerius (*Or.* 39) is addressed to Musonius, who learned rhetoric in Alexandria and taught for a while successfully in Athens before entering in the Imperial civil service. Himerius called him a sophist who was able "to mix deeds and actions with eloquence," but his short tenure did not earn him a biographical sketch by Eunapius.⁸⁶

Eunapius does not mention the rhetorician Sopater, of whom several works survive.⁸⁷ This could be an indication that he did not know him, that Sopater belonged to a later generation, or that he did not teach extensively and was instead a rhetor with scholarly interests. That Eunapius ignored him is not surprising, since the biographer dedicated a scant paragraph to Himerius, with whom Sopater apparently had some connection.⁸⁸ Sopater was educated at Athens, and the "son" to whom he addressed his most important surviving work, *Division of Questions* (*Diairesis zētēmatōn*), might have been his pupil.⁸⁹ This work is the best proof of Sopater's interest in education, since it is a textbook in which

---

⁸³ Himerius *Or.* 69.1.

⁸⁴ Himerius *Or.* 22; see also *Or.* 48.3.

⁸⁵ Kennedy (1983, 147), sympathetically reevaluating Himerius's work, attributed the generally low estimation of his writings to the fact that he postdated the lyric poets by so many centuries that his imagery inevitably seems trite.

⁸⁶ Musonius 2; cf. Eunapius *VS* 10.7.13, 493; Ammianus 27.9.6; and Himerius *Or.* 39.8; Puech 2002, 357, on his epitaph reported by Eunapius (*Historia* fr. 43 Blockley). Cf. Penella 1990, 138–39.

⁸⁷ Sopater 2 (*PLRE* II, with a tentative date to the fifth century; *RE* 3A.1 [1927], 1002–6). Innes and Winterbottom (1988) place him tentatively in the late fourth century.

⁸⁸ Much is unsure about this connection; see Innes and Winterbottom 1988, 1.

⁸⁹ Russell (1983, 7 n. 23) prefers to see in Carponianus the actual son of Sopater on the grounds that calling a student "son" was a Christian usage of which there was "no Greek parallel from rhetoric," but the example of Libanius and others show that this is not true; cf. below, Chapter Five.

the teacher-narrator proposes eighty-one themes arranged according to *stasis*. Like Libanius, Sopater did not follow Hermogenes to a great extent, reduced the number of headings, and in general proceeded his own way, an indication that he might have relied on his teaching experience.[90]

After Himerius, Athens's school of rhetoric seems to have continued on a more modest scale. Synesius, who visited the city, probably in 399,[91] left an unflattering and possibly biased portrait of the state of the philosophical and rhetorical studies. Athens's prestige as the capital of learning had lasted to his day. He felt the obligation to visit because people who returned from the city put on airs of superiority and behaved "like demigods amidst mules."[92] But after his journey, Synesius declared that only the historical sights and its honey made Athens venerable. Since the latter was Athens's real glory, the teachers of eloquence did not count on their reputation to attract students, but relied on the jars of honey from the Hymettus.[93] Very little is known of individual sophists at that time. Apronianus and Plutarchus, sophists who lived at the turn of the century, both had a statue built for the praetorian prefect Herculius and are known from the epigraphic documentation.[94] The two inscriptions honor Herculius for the justice he administered, but it is likely that he also deserved the sophists' gratitude for something he had done on behalf of *paideia*. Apronianus is styled as "the powerful sophist of Athens," and the sophist Plutarchus, who defines Herculius as "the steward of the laws," calls himself "steward of discourses" (*mythōn tamiēs*). The city of Athens, moreover, honored Plutarchus, "king of eloquence," with another statue. The possibility that this sophist could be identified with the Plutarchus considered above, the founder of the Neoplatonic school in Athens, cannot be completely ruled out, but it seems unlikely. Two more names are known from (but not only from) Libanius's late correspondence: Aphthonius and Eutropius.[95] The question of whether the former, the author of *Progymnasmata*, was Libanius's student cannot be settled conclusively, but in

---

[90] Cf. below, Chapter 5. On Sopater's relationship with Hermogenes, see Innes and Winterbottom 1988, 2.

[91] For other possible dates and bibliography, see Garzya and Roques 2000, letter 56, n. 3, p. 162

[92] See Synesius *Ep.* 56.

[93] Synesius *Ep.* 136. On this famous letter and on the philosopher Damascius's reaction to it, see Cameron and Long 1993, 56–57.

[94] See Robert 1948, 41–42, 73, and 94–102. On Apronianus, *PLRE* II.1; Puech 2002, 123–24, no. 29. On Plutarchus, Puech 2002, 390–95 (esp. no. 207); he may have been the author of the three inscriptions. Herculius was praetorian prefect in 408–10.

[95] Aphthonius (*PLRE* I, pp. 81–82); Eutropius 4/vii. Puech (2002, 239–40, nos. 107–8) thinks it is possible that two inscriptions referred to the latter sophist.

Epistle 1065, the reference to Aphthonius "showing the seed," that is, the source of his learning, seems to allude to his training with Libanius.[96] The latter told Aphthonius that he was particularly pleased that he was working hard and enjoyed the efforts that went into teaching. Since he was glad of the ties of affection between Aphthonius and Eutropius, it seems possible that the latter was also in Athens. Eutropius was in love with the city and with the teachers he had had in his youth in Athens, but even though he had the same rank (*schēma*) as Libanius and would have been able to declaim and teach, he did not care to. It is to Eutropius that Libanius wrote his last, desperate letter (*Ep.* 1112) in 393. By that point, though, the loss of part of its power made Athens seem distant and small.

Sophists in Constantinople

The resentment Libanius always felt toward the cultural environment of Constantinople is also clear from the fact that he had relatively rare epistolary contacts with teachers working there.[97] An inquiry discloses few names. Bitter feelings against the city constantly resurface in the *Autobiography* except at the beginning of Libanius's career in 340, when the city seemed replete with "many scholars who distinguished themselves for their culture and had convened there from everywhere" (30). The first difficulties made Libanius change his mind. When the grammarian Nicocles offered to hand over to him forty pupils—an indication of the customary collaboration between grammarians and sophists—and tried to entice him by disclosing the large compensation of Bemarchius, the official sophist of the city, he was motivated by a desire to damage an unnamed sophist from Cyzicus who taught in the capital (31).[98] Another sophist from Cappadocia, again unnamed, was appointed when Libanius did not accept his offer (35). Libanius described with incensed words all the machinations of the three sophists.[99]

---

[96] *PLRE* I, s.v., covers the question, including whether Aphthonius was also a student of an unknown rhetor Phasganius. Petit (1956a) did not include him among Libanius's students. Kennedy (2000, 67) considered him a pupil of Libanius, which seems most reasonable.

[97] On the school of Constantinople, see Schemmel 1908.

[98] Nicocles: *PLRE* I, p. 630, and Kaster 1988, no. 106, who recognized that Nicocles was a grammarian. Bemarchius: *PLRE* I, p. 160. There is only one reference to a sophist who was supposed to be appointed in Cyzicus in the year 356, Hierax (*Ep.* 527), but the inhabitants changed their mind.

[99] His troubles during his first sojourn in the city last until *Or.* 1.47. *Ep.* 206 alludes to the governor Limenius's desire to kill him to do a favor to an unnamed sophist, who was Bemarchius. For sophist warfare, cf. below, Chapter Three.

Good relations with Nicocles, however, continued for many years. Libanius often praised the grammarian on account of his students,[100] but disapproved of Nicocles' teaching technique, lectures without using books, in the manner of Socrates (*Ep.* 1487). Affection for Julian was something the two teachers shared. Nicocles taught the poets to the future emperor and was well regarded by him, but was more resilient in accepting his death than Libanius, since a letter shows that the grammarian advised the sophist to come to terms with the loss and confine himself to work (that is, to "the peace of meadows and flowers," as Libanius indignantly put it).[101] In 347–49 in Constantinople, Julian followed not only the classes of Nicocles but also those of the sophist Hecebolius. Libanius declared the latter's utter incompetence, and despised him for binding Julian to himself with oaths, a precaution against defections that does not seem too unreasonable.[102] By the time Libanius left Constantinople for Nicomedia in 344, his utter dislike of professionals in the capital also extended to the public at his own declamations, which he now depicted as superficial and uninterested in culture (*Or.* 1.75–76). Besides Nicocles, none of these teachers left any trace in Libanius's correspondence,[103] but he judged them harshly as a group. In the year 355, he ironically portrayed them as possessing all that sophists were entitled to have: "Large houses, plenty of students, big bellies, and skill in servility."[104] He considered the last quality essential to success—and clearly, at that time, he thought he was exempt from it. In the 390s, a Cappadocian student of Libanius, Zenon, acquired international renown as a sophist in Athens, Rome, and Constantinople, so that "battles, fights for words, and trophies" accompanied him.[105] Naturally, Libanius did not regard him as a rival because his orations also brought glory to the "fountain" of his eloquence.

Themistius

Themistius was the only teacher of higher education in Constantinople with whom Libanius corresponded regularly for a period. After the cus-

---

[100] See *Epp.* 1119 (N122) and 1487. Theodorus iv was a student of Nicocles before joining Libanius's school.

[101] Cf. *Ep.* 1265 (N134). See the introduction of *Ep.* 1368 (B76).

[102] Hecebolius: *PLRE* I, p. 409; Libanius *Or.* 18.12 and 14, where the name of the sophist in question does not directly appear. It is possible that the Hecebolius to whom Julian addressed the literary letter 194 Bidez was the sophist.

[103] In 360 he praised the rhetor Zenas, whose brother helped him against Bemarchius, but he probably did not teach, *Ep.* 206.

[104] *Ep.* 399 (B86).

[105] Zenon 7/iv, *Ep.* 1061; cf. also *Ep.* 1052.

tomary tour of various cities of the East (of which we are badly informed), in 348/49 Themistius settled in Constantinople, obtained the chair of philosophy, and never again moved from the capital for any length of time. Not everything is clear about his relationship with Libanius, in spite of the fact that the latter sent him forty letters and mentioned him in others.[106] Scholars have wondered whether their relationship was brusquely interrupted, since their correspondence ceased in 365 (like all other correspondence of Libanius) and did not resume in 388; but speculations about a definite rift are not productive.[107] It is useful, however, to scrutinize once again a troubled relationship.

Much divided Libanius and Themistius.[108] Their fields of study (philosophy versus oratory) were formally different but nevertheless had much in common, since Themistius was trained in rhetoric and was an acclaimed orator.[109] The polymorphic Themistius, who practiced a combination of philosophy and politics and was much involved with power, was (and remains) a controversial figure.[110] The description that Eunapius gave of Libanius's personality, that he could beat the octopus in assimilating himself to all sorts of men, seems more apt for Themistius, whom Eunapius ignored in his works, in spite of his contemporary fame.[111] In many of his letters, Libanius appealed to Themistius's power of persuasion and to the important friendships he nurtured that could help his recommendees. Themistius was not as weak as other rhetors, who were "ghosts" and "shadows"; he was strong and did not have to

---

[106] The correspondence of Themistius is lost, except perhaps for remnants of a letter written in the margin of one manuscript of *Ep.* 241 of Libanius (N42); cf. Vanderspoel 1995, 110–11. Wintjes (2005, 135–49), the scholar who last examined Libanius's and Themistius's relationship from a factual viewpoint, concluded that there is very little that is certain in spite of the abundance of Libanius's correspondence.

[107] Cf. Dagron 1968, 38 and n. 14. There is only one allusion to Themistius in *Ep.* 18 of the year 388.

[108] Dagron (1968, 36–42 and passim) explores the various sides of their relationship and their differences. See also Bouchery 1936, passim.

[109] For the combination of rhetoric and philosophy, cf. Evagoras 1 and Aquila 1, who were both probably at Athens in the late third to early fourth century. A student of Libanius, Jamblichus 2, had an excellent reputation in both fields. On Neoplatonist philosophers very interested in rhetoric, see Heather 1998, 127. In the second century, Aristides had a position between rhetoric and philosophy; cf. Moreschini 1994. On the rivalry between rhetoric and philosophy in Late Antique Alexandria, see Cribiore forthcoming d.

[110] For a sympathetic account of his political philosophy, see Vanderspoel 1995; for a more realistic account of him as "a skilful propagandist" and an expert in manipulation, see Heather 1998. On his rhetoric of praise, see Penella 2000b. Late Antique philosophy was a generally isolated discipline unless it associated with rhetoric; cf. Fowden 1982, 51–59.

[111] Eunapius *VS* 16.1, 495. Themistius was avoided in Neoplatonic circles. For other reasons for the exclusion, see Penella 1990, 137.

rely only on students "nauseated" by learning (*Ep.* 301). Libanius often mentions Themistius's influence with ambiguous, flattering words. Themistius cultivated governors and reproached Libanius for not adopting a similar attitude.[112] His friends were friends to the gods, and his enemies were enemies to the gods themselves (*Ep.* 405). The palace was open to him, but Themistius had to remember to send his speeches not only to those in power, but also to those who (like Libanius) "had ears."[113] The advent and fast disappearance of Julian undoubtedly brought more disagreement. The pagan philosopher was not on bad terms with the emperor, probably addressed to him in 357 a treatise called the *Risâlat*,[114] and must have benefited from the new impulse toward Hellenism. At the same time, neither did he share the same enthusiasm as Libanius for the ruler, nor did he lament the death of a friend, as Libanius did.[115] The sophist in Antioch remained a man tenaciously anchored to the past, "who ran to the countryside and talked to the rocks" in distress (*Ep.* 1455). Themistius avoided the rhetor in his grief and optimistically looked to the future as an advisor to Christian emperors.[116]

With so much to unite but also to divide them, it is not surprising that the correspondence reveals or hints at some disaffection. Its causes were multifarious, but professional rivalries (an area in which Libanius was very sensitive) likely played a great role. It is from this viewpoint that I will consider Libanius's and Themistius's relationship. They had met in Constantinople in the early 350s and were part of a group of friends that included the learned doctor Olympius and the philosopher Themistocles.[117] Letters evoke those merry gatherings of intellectuals where listening was "more pleasurable than eating" (**149**; see also **153**). In that period, Libanius met Themistius's son, whom he declared (*Ep.* 575), he himself "nourished with the exhortations of Isocrates." One wonders if Libanius gave the boy the advice of honoring and imitating his father, which often occurs in the *Ad Demonicum*.[118] Immediately after, in 355,

---

[112] *Ep.* 476: Norman 1992, no. 16.

[113] *Ep.* 1186 (N128); *Ep.* 368.4, Cabouret 2000, no. 15.

[114] This treatise is only preserved in two Arab copies, was likely to be addressed to Julian, and might have been the panegyric to the emperor mentioned by Libanius in *Epp.* 818 and 1430 (N102 and N116). See Vanderspoel 1995, 126–34 and 244–49.

[115] Vandespoel 1995, 115–34; Dagron 1968, 230–35. Julian, in any case, read and used Themistius; see Bouffartigue 1992, 296–300.

[116] *Ep.* 1430 (N116). Wintjes (2005, 145) maintains that the advent of the emperor Valens marked a definite change, and the relationship of Themistius and Libanius became similar to that of a patron and client. This seems excessive.

[117] Olympius 4/i. On the identification of Themistocles with the pupil of Apsines, see above.

[118] See, e.g., *Ad Demonicum* 9, 14, and 16. On the popularity of this work with students of all ages, see Cribiore 2001, 106 and 203–4. Most of the allusions to Isocrates in Themistius, moreover, come from this oration: Heather 1998, 130.

Libanius did not shrink from defending to his friend his own decision to teach in Antioch, which provided him with plenty of students, whereas in Constantinople teaching was unproductive, he thought.[119] His attempts to woo Themistius for Antioch did not meet with success, since the philosopher visited the city in 356/57 but did not stay long. Libanius declared that Themistius had brought wisdom to Antioch and had brought his friend to tears, reminding him of the past (*Ep.* 518). Themistius chose Constantinople and the limelight. Libanius refused to become a senator in that city (*Ep.* 62), and the two friends met only in letters afterward.

In Constantinople, Themistius found plenty of success as a teacher, in spite of Libanius's predictions, and perhaps to his dismay. A letter sent in 362/63 refers to a disagreement that seems to be have a professional basis.[120] Themistius had previously given his friend a lesson about his own character, as if Libanius did not know him already from the twelve years of their acquaintance. Libanius, who had complimented him on the power of his oratory many times,[121] admitted that Themistius was also a philosopher and that he had plenty of happy students in Constantinople who could learn the truth together with eloquence, since Plato himself taught "noble things with beautiful language." Libanius declared that he was not silent about the superior skills of Themistius and assured him that his own students heard his praises.[122]

In writing to him, Libanius often commended Themistius as a rhetor. He recognized that he was the best at criticizing Libanius's own mistakes and in extolling his merits (*Ep.* 551). In his ability, he was more similar to his father, Demosthenes, than Telemachus was to Odysseus (*Ep.* 368). His political power came from his reputation and the discourses he composed (*Ep.* 1495).[123] In 365, Libanius still basked in Themistius's approval and declared that their orations "had the same form, came from the same parents, were brothers, and actually twins."[124] The closeness to Themistius and the spontaneous recognition that he had good rhetorical skills, however, was bound to produce some rivalry. Themistius, after all, was a philosopher, albeit a political philosopher, and could treat rhetoric with

---

[119] *Ep.* 434 (N12).

[120] *Ep.* 793 (B85).

[121] See, e.g., *Ep.* 241 (N42), where he declined to rate Themistius as a philosopher but applauded his rhetorical skills.

[122] *Ep.* 793 (B85). Toward the end, a better translation, in my opinion, is "whoever came to me to learn rhetoric," instead of "whoever came to speak with me." Libanius is alluding to his students.

[123] Vanderspoel (1995, 107 n. 171) claims that Libanius might have exaggerated Themistius's power.

[124] *Ep.* 1477 (N141); cf. above. Compare a similar statement in *Ep.* 376.5.

some nonchalance—even distance himself from it.[125] Libanius admired philosophy from afar.[126] Rhetoric was a way of life for him.

Themistius taught and worked in Constantinople, a city of powerful people, which Libanius compared to the god Apollo,[127] and he had divine influence, too. He was Athena for the student Dianius (**49**), and, like Zeus, could not be opposed (*Epp.* 62 [N51] and 368). The poor Dianius went to ask the philosopher's help with Themistius's discourses, "not in his backpack or in books, but stored in his memory and soul." Libanius was impotent on this occasion, but with Themistius's assistance, Dianius "would be able to avoid even the Styx." Themistius's help was repeatedly invoked on behalf of the grammarian Cleobulus (*Epp.* 68 and 91), and of the Egyptian poet and rhetor Harpocration, who practiced in Antioch, but transferred to the capital at Themistius's urging. The beginning of *Ep.* 368 shows a flattering Libanius who is only half smiling. Not only did Themistius have the power of persuasion, but he also possessed the force of a tyrant and violently broke Libanius's and Antioch's ties with Harpocration.[128] Themistius bragged about his popularity and said that students ran to his school from everywhere (*Or.* 23.204). Why did he call rhetors to Constantinople? For Libanius there was only one answer: he needed students.

An ex-student of Libanius who was a rhetor, Celsus, abandoned Antioch for the capital, where he became a senator and also followed Themistius's classes. Libanius did what he could to detain him, but to no avail,[129] and Celsus landed in the philosopher's pond. "You have your student Celsus," Libanius wrote to Themistius (*Ep.* 1477 [N141]). "Let Celsus have his good fortune, and let mine go as it likes," he concluded bitterly (*Ep.* 86 [N44]). Students looked forward to studies in the capital, and Libanius was exasperated. The matter-of-fact observation he made to Themistius in *Ep.* 376, "One cannot say that our students are not also yours," concealed some acrimony. He resented being left behind, becoming part of the past, letting other people reap the fruits of what he had sown, and allowing them "to be honored because of my work."[130] He might criticize Themistius's philosophical practice or be a little jealous

---

[125] See Vanderspoel 1995, 1–23; Penella 2000a, 4–5.
[126] See his admiration for the philosophical knowledge of Julian, *Or.* 13.13 and 15.27–28, or the exaggerated claim that his assistant Thalassius was a philosopher, *Or.* 42.9 and 40.22.
[127] *Ep.* 62.8: Libanius prefers Antioch, compared to the mortal Idas.
[128] Harpocration: *PLRE* I, p. 408. Cf. *Ep.* 364 (Norman 1992, no. 29), where the ties of Harpocration with a fellow teacher, Eudaemon 2, are severed.
[129] Celsus 3/i studied with Libanius in Nicomedia. See *Epp.* 86 and 1477 (N44 and N141).
[130] Cf. **200** to Celsus, about Titianus leaving for Athens.

of his influence, but what he could not handle was his own bruised ego as a teacher and the success of another in his stead. When his student Julianus left Antioch to follow the classes of Themistius, Libanius remarked that Julianus's pleasure at what he would find in the capital was greater than the sorrow for what he left behind. The harbor of Themistius was more competitive, that of Libanius could "offer only small gains." Themistius could discuss philosophy, astronomy, and poetry.[131] When Libanius marveled at this student's eagerness to go to Constantinople, Julianus replied, "Do not be surprised, Themistius is responsible for this change. He attracts and charms by offering great things" (**118**). Throughout his life, Libanius was at his most bitter when he had to admit his inadequacy in retaining his students and started to doubt that his school and Antioch could cater to all of their cultural needs. Rhetoric, however, was not enough for many who looked for new skills, such as shorthand, Latin, and Roman law. Philosophy was another card that Libanius could not play.

OTHER TEACHERS OF RHETORIC

Less is known of specific teachers of rhetoric in the fourth-century Eastern Empire. The survey here, covering first the Anatolian plateau and proceeding along the Mediterranean coast to Arabia and Egypt, does not produce strong personalities that allow focused attention, but it does document exhaustingly Libanius's contacts with other professionals and the existence of schools eventually competing with Antioch for students. Libanius usually had a friendly rapport with the sophists who resurface from his correspondence. He had met several of them in Athens during his years of training, and others were in contact with his students. The following account documents the occasional difficulties sophists encountered, such as problems with immunity from curial duties, the discomfort they experienced in their location and consequent mobility in the search of better teaching positions, and sometimes utter dissatisfaction with their profession and its lack of influence. It also shows exhaustingly these teachers' temperaments and rivalries with each other.[132] These animosities derived from competition and jealousy between cities or within the same community.[133] The conviction that "it was necessary to take up bows and arrows, the proper weapons of sophists," as Libanius said in *Ep.* 956, was apparently widespread.

---

[131] Julianus 15, letter **117**. In comparing Julianus to a merchant, Libanius seems to suggest that he could come back to him, or in any case might soon leave Themistius, too.
[132] Cf. Chapter Three; and Bowersock 1969, 89–100.
[133] Cf. Cracco Ruggini 1971, 423–24.

Lydia and Caria

In the middle of the fourth century in Sardis, the capital of Lydia, the Neoplatonist philosopher Chrysanthius taught philosophy to Eunapius. After spending more than four years in Athens, Eunapius went back to his native Sardis, where he taught rhetoric until the end of his life. In his *Lives,* Eunapius discussed last the sophist Nymphidianus, who was a native of Smyrna. Like his brother, the philosopher Maximus, he enjoyed the favor of Julian and held a prestigious office.[134] He had not been educated at Athens, yet Eunapius granted that he was an excellent sophist.

Scant information survives about the teaching of rhetoric in Aphrodisias in Caria, which the archaeological finds (discussed above) identify as a center of higher learning. The only name that emerges from the fourth-century epigraphic documentation is that of Eupeithius, for whom the city had set up a stone image. Very little is known about him besides the fact that he had a name ideal for a sophist ("He who persuades well"), which was carried only by another sophist in the fifth century, who may have been his descendant. Since he was characterized only by the term *sophos* (that is, "wise" or "learned"), much is also unsure about his actual profession.[135] Inscriptions testify that rhetoric was cultivated in Aphrodisias in the second and third centuries.[136] Likewise, this city appears to be an active intellectual center in the fifth century, because the sophist Eustephius was a native of this place, and Proclus was styled "sophist of the city" by Zacharias the rhetor.[137] Since some continuity is to be expected, it is very likely that this city, which had a tradition of philosophical teaching for several centuries, was also able to offer rhetorical instruction in the fourth century.

Lycia, Pamphylia, and Cilicia

Sophists in the provinces of Lycia, Pamphylia, and Cilicia were tied to Libanius by common years of study in Athens or by the fact that they were related to his students. Severus taught rhetoric in Lycia from 359 to 365. He was the same age as Libanius and had received his training in Athens with him. There he had also studied philosophy with his fellow

---

[134] Maximus 21. Eunapius *VS* 18.1–3, 497. He was appointed *Magister epistularum Graecarum,* that is, he was in charge of the Imperial correspondence.

[135] See Roueché (1989, 57–58, no. 33), who dates the inscription to the mid- to late fourth century, and Puech (2002, 238–39), who dates it to the third. Both scholars include him as a sophist, but with some doubts. On Eupeithius, sophist or philosopher in the fifth century, see *PLRE* II, s.v.

[136] See Robert 1989, 395–98; Puech 2002, 165–74.

[137] Eustephius: *PLRE* II, pp. 436–37, and Proclus 5; Kugener 1903, 39. On the intellectual life of Aphrodisias in the fifth century, see Roueché 1989, 85–93.

citizen Maximus.[138] Several letters of Libanius concern Severus's difficulty in receiving the immunity from curial duties to which he was entitled, because, as Libanius wrote Themistius, "it is not only rich people who make cities illustrious, but also those who toil at education."[139]

The only sophist known from Pamphylia is Argeius, of whose ability Libanius had the highest opinion. His country of origin is unknown,[140] but it is conceivable that he had studied with Libanius, who strongly identified with his successes in *Ep.* 1008. Libanius praised the beauty of his rhetoric and admired his facility and speed in composing speeches that were "sweeter than honey," expressing his hope that he would receive some specimens.[141]

Libanius's correspondence discloses three names of teachers of rhetoric in Cilicia: Quirinus, the father of his student Honoratus; Demetrius, the uncle of two of his students; and Acacius, the father of Titianus.[142] Quirinus was older than Libanius, who highly esteemed his eloquence and considered him his teacher. Before embarking on a successful career as a governor, he had occupied a sophist's chair. It is not completely clear where he taught, but Cilicia is a good guess, since he had properties there.[143] The sophist Demetrius was based in Tarsus, whose inhabitants were "lovers of learning" (*philologoi*).[144] He wrote several speeches and called himself a student of Libanius because he was in constant touch with his oratory (Libanius *Ep.* 606). There was a continuous exchange of speeches and compliments for rhetorical ability between them, and the annoyance of Demetrius when the son of his widowed sister ran away to study with Libanius only indicates that there must have been another capable sophist in Tarsus who could have instructed his nephew. Acacius was an orator of the first caliber who had studied in Athens, and who also was a poet.[145] He sent his son technical advice on rhetoric by letter (Libanius *Ep.* 127) and was his son's and his cousin's instructor in rhetoric when they were home. He did not take up any other teaching

---

[138] Severus 9/v; Maximus 10.

[139] *Ep.* 664: Cabouret 2000, no. 46.

[140] Argeius taught some of Libanius's students; see **129, 130,** and **206**. *PLRE* I wrongly affirms that he was from Berytus, likely from the mention of this city in letter **129**. Libanius was actually concerned that the student in question might be sent to learn Roman law.

[141] See *Ep.* 862.4: he hoped that the vicar Domnio 2, who never tired of listening to orations, could bring him some of Argeius's works "by persuasion or by force."

[142] Demetrius 2/i was the uncle of an unnamed student (**48** and *Ep.* 23 [B144]) and of Calycius; most of the letters to Acacius 7/iii are translated by Festugière (1959, 164–79). Cf. Appendix One, the dossiers of Honoratus, Titianus, Calycius, and Philoxenus.

[143] Quirinus: *PLRE* I, pp. 760–61. See letter **104**; *Ep.* 366 (B35).

[144] *Ep.* 1353 (B149).

[145] Cf. below, Chapter Five.

duty, however, supposedly because he feared the commitment that a real appointment (*thronos*) required.[146]

Cappadocia

At the beginning of the fourth century, Asterius taught rhetoric in Cappadocia, but he abandoned the profession when he became a Christian scholar, and the *Suda* also reports that one Eustochius, a sophist, wrote a life of the emperor Constantius.[147] We will see that some of Libanius's students came from Cappadocia, and it is conceivable that they had a smattering of rhetoric there before going to Antioch.[148] An inscription from Tyana, which should probably be dated to the fourth century, immortalizes one Sarapion, "by far the best of teachers, who educated the eloquent citizens of Tyana for the Muses."[149]

Both Gregory of Nazianzus and Basil studied rhetoric at Caesarea, which Gregory celebrated as "the metropolis of the *logoi*."[150] A letter that Gregory apparently addressed in 359 to the father of a student testifies that, on returning from Athens, he taught eloquence in Nazianzus, probably for a short time.[151] He did not approve of a career as a sophist, and he reproached Basil's younger brother, Gregory of Nyssa, for aspiring to become one, putting down the Christian books and intoxicating himself with writings that were "bitter and could not be drunk."[152] In the middle of the century, Strategius, who corresponded with Gregory of Nyssa, practiced as a sophist in the city of Caesarea, and Basil wrote two letters to another sophist, Leontius, a real "nightingale," who was located some distance from the city.[153] Basil and Gregory of Nazianzus were in touch

---

[146] *Ep.* 735.7 (B127). Libanius also valued highly the skills of the young rhetor Evagoras 1 (*Ep.* 137), who may have never taught. In Libanius's view, Evagoras was excessively complimentary in comparing him to Demosthenes, because "often the same chest holds rags and a most beautiful garment" (*Ep.* 809). Pace PLRE I, Hierocles 3 was not a sophist. He was considered a teacher on the basis of *Ep.* 517, where the verb *didaskein* is used in the sense of "to inform."

[147] Asterius 2; Eustochius 2.

[148] See below, Chapter Three.

[149] See Merkelbach and Stauber 1998–2002, 3:44. I think Sarapion was a teacher of rhetoric rather than a grammarian. On two students of Libanius coming from Tyana, see *Ep.* 1014.

[150] Gregory of Nazianzus *Or.* 43.13; Gallay 1943, 31–32. On sophists from Cappadocia with whom Basil was in contact, see Cadiou 1966.

[151] *Ep.* 3 Gallay. See also his *Ep.* 179.

[152] *Ep.* 11.4 Gallay. On Gregory's bad opinion of rhetoric, see his *Epp.* 176, 178, 191, and 233.

[153] Strategius 3 and Leontius 10. Basil *Epp.* 20, 21. Basil regarded Leontius as a splendid rhetor who could not remain in silence.

with Amphilochius, who was Gregory's uncle, Libanius's fellow student in Athens, and the father of two of his students, including the future bishop of Iconium.[154] Amphilochius was an advocate, but apparently also taught rhetoric, since Libanius praised him as an educator (*paideutēs*, *Ep.* 670). A letter of Gregory indicates that he was not too pleased when his son became bishop (*Ep.* 63). Libanius went to school with a gifted rhetor (a cicada) and poet from Cappadocia, Philippus, whom he considered "a winged nursling of the Muses and an imitator of Homer."[155] A letter of Libanius (**139**) is the only testimony of the presence in Cappadocia in the 360s of the sophist Palladius, whom Libanius recommended as a suitable teacher for Marcus (the son of the governor Acacius), who nurtured premature ambition for office.[156]

Later, in the 380s, Gregory of Nazianzus mentioned, or addressed letters to, other sophists: Eudoxius father and son, Stagirius, and Eustochius.[157] Gregory had the highest opinion of the older Eudoxius, as he wrote to Themistius (*Ep.* 38), but mostly dealt with his son, who taught rhetoric to the children of his nephew Nicobulus and especially to the latter's son by the same name. The younger Eudoxius was probably located in a town smaller than Caesarea, because Nicobulus later moved to the school of Stagirius in Caesarea in search of more advanced instruction.[158] As a small-town teacher, Eudoxius commanded perhaps less reverence than his colleagues in the city. In his letter of introduction of the new students (**174**), Gregory made sure to tell him bluntly to behave appropriately because he himself could "judge rhetoric, evaluate commitment, and advance the status of good teachers through praises." Eudoxius, in any case, had other qualities of character, was Christian, and knew "how to feel shame, unlike other rhetors" (Gregory *Ep.* 178). The sophist Stagirius was pagan and may have studied rhetoric in Athens like his rival Eustochius, who bitterly complained that Gregory's grandnephew was not entrusted to him. The wisdom of age or experience counted little when a sophist felt his honor was in question. After vainly trying to exculpate himself by putting the blame on the young man's father, Gregory appealed

---

[154] See letter **16**, Amphilochius 2 father of Amphilochius 4.

[155] *Ep.* 1427; cf. below, Chapter Five. See also *Ep.* 1223. Philippus 3/ii entrusted his children to Libanius for a very short time; cf. below, Chapter Three. He may have never taught.

[156] Palladius 8/xi; Acacius 8/i. On Marcus, see below, Chapter Three.

[157] Eudoxius 1 and 2; Stagirius, *PLRE* I, p. 851; and Eustochius 5 (well known to the emperor Julian; cf. Julian's letter 41 Bidez). *PLRE* I, p. 12, considers the recipient of letter 235 of Gregory of Nazianzus, a sophist named Adamantius 2, who, however, had only some interest in rhetoric.

[158] Since the rival of Stagirius, Eustochius 5, was located in Caesarea, it is very likely that Stagirius himself was in the same city; otherwise Gregory would have had an easy way to excuse himself.

to the character of the two sophists and to the necessity of setting a good example. His words may have fallen on deaf ears.

Galatia

In Galatia, another region that contributed heavily to Libanius's recruitment, Hellespontius taught rhetoric. Libanius wrote to him in 355/56, commenting on the fact that he had not yet seen the sophist's son, who was visiting Antioch (*Ep.* 461).[159] Libanius expressed regret that Hellespontius could not be present at one of his orations, since he was a favorable judge. Hellespontius in his old age became a student of the well-known Chrysanthius of Sardis, presumably learning philosophy.[160] In his last journey, he went to Apamea in Bithynia, where one of his students was apparently a Procopius, who became a sophist.[161] Libanius also had cordial relations with Androcles, who taught rhetoric in Ancyra in 364 and who sent him his former student Eusebius xx, from the prestigious family of Agesilaus (77). Even though he did not have a first-hand knowledge of Androcles' eloquence, Libanius inferred from his writing that he possessed wondrous skills—and of course hurried to compliment him.

At a later time, Ablabius taught rhetoric in Ancyra.[162] In this case, a surface cordiality hid some professional resentment. *Ep.* 921, which Libanius sent to Ablabius in 390, alluded to fond memories of a previous visit. Libanius did evoke with longing "the narrow path close to the house" where Ablabius composed his discourses (better than the Forum at Rome!), but he regretted that he did not receive any students from him. A letter written a year later shows that the solicitation brought some results (*Ep.* 1015). Letoius vi joined the school, and a pleased Libanius encouraged Ablabius to send the other students he had promised . . . unless, of course, he "found fault with the school." It appears that at this time, Ablabius was still a pagan, as he was when he received letter 233 from Gregory of Nazianzus, who reminded him that "playing among young men" was supposed to be a temporary occupation, but that the acquisition of virtue was the final goal. Ablabius later became a priest and a bishop.

Another school of rhetoric in Galatia in those years was located at Tavium, where Paeonius 2/ii, Libanius's student in 359, taught, together

---

[159] Petit includes this young man among the students of Libanius, but the matter is far from certain. This youth would have been more solicitous if Libanius were his designated teacher, and not simply "a friend of his father."

[160] On Chrysanthius, see Penella 1990, 5–6 and passim. Rhetoric was highly valued also in a philosopher.

[161] Procopius 10. Eunapius *VS* 23.4.11–12, 6.2–7, 504–5.

[162] Ablabius 2/i.

with the rhetor Phalerius. *Ep.* 1080 is of great interest because it shows a school's beginnings. Paeonius went to Tavium first, but such was his reputation as a student of Libanius that Phalerius, who was teaching elsewhere, moved there. Libanius suggested that Paeonius was "a harbor" for the other, who would acquire fame and wealth. But then, softening his stance, he presented Phalerius as a lover of learning and a "student-teacher," who cared not only to teach what he knew, as he had done before, but also to learn new things from his colleague.[163]

Bithynia, Paphlagonia, and Armenia

The emperor Diocletian had appointed a teacher of Latin rhetoric in Nicomedia, L. Caecilius Firmianus, who dedicated himself to scholarly work because he did not have enough pupils.[164] In the same period, as Eunapius informs us, Andromachus taught Greek rhetoric in the city, but then moved to Athens.[165] After Libanius left Constantinople to teach in Nicomedia, another war ensued with an anonymous sophist of strong temperament, a neurotic, dangerous fellow who had alienated the local senate.[166] Libanius found an ally in an older local teacher of rhetoric, Alcimus, "a son of a god," who was arrested with him when Libanius was falsely accused of murder, remained his friend for many years, and was regarded as a skillful educator.[167]

Bithynia had some traditions of rhetoric. The sophist Himerius, who was a native of Prusias, followed in the footsteps of his father Ameinias, a rhetor perhaps in the same region.[168] An inscription found at Prusa ad Olympum and tentatively dated to the third–fourth century C.E. on the basis of the script is a further testimony that rhetoric was cultivated in Bithynia. This stele honored a teacher, Cornutus, "who tended the Muses and adorned the *logoi*." Cornutus's student, Firmus, dedicated the decorated marble stele with a metrical inscription as a repayment for what his teacher had done.[169]

No information exists about teachers of rhetoric in Paphlagonia. Four students of Libanius came from there, and might have had initial instruction at home before leaving for Antioch, since this was common prac-

---

[163] Jones (1973, 999) asserts incorrectly that Phalerius was Libanius's student and intended to teach grammar.
[164] *PLRE* I, p. 338. There is no other information about teachers of Latin in Bithynia.
[165] Andromachus 2, Eunapius *VS* 4.3.2–3, 457.
[166] *Or.* 1.49–50 and 62–72.
[167] *PLRE* I, pp. 38–39; *Or.* 1.68. On Basil taking the place of Alcimus for a while, see below, Chapter Three. On this sophist as a good educator, *Ep.* 397; Cabouret 2000, no. 2.
[168] Cf. *Suda*, s.v. Himerius.
[169] See Merkelbach and Stauber 1998–2002, 4:149.

tice.¹⁷⁰ It is also possible that no regular teaching of rhetoric took place there. Paphlagonia was the birthplace of Themistius, who pursued his higher education in a small city of Pontus, Neocaesarea, with a teacher who taught him "ability in rhetoric and what is suitable on festive occasions."¹⁷¹ The identity of this teacher is unknown, but it is unlikely that he was the father of Basil the Great, who was a grammarian.¹⁷²

In Armenia, Libanius possessed a steadfast ally, Leontius, a fellow student from Antioch, who occupied several offices.¹⁷³ He had studied with Zenobius and Gaudentius and acquired the latter's gratitude through an honor he bestowed on his son (*Ep.* 749). Leontius had been the first teacher of rhetoric of some Armenian students of Libanius, such as Maximus, the sons of Philagrius, and probably also Anatolius.¹⁷⁴ Parents who selected teachers other than Libanius embarrassed Leontius, who then refrained from writing to the sophist. But Leontius's loyalty was not an issue: Libanius reassured him that he did not hold him responsible for the fact that his "nestlings" went somewhere else (**161**).

Syria and Phoenicia

The competition of Antioch did not suffocate the teaching of rhetoric in the rest of Syria. In the first part of the fourth century, Ulpianus taught at Emesa before becoming the teacher of Prohaeresius, and perhaps of Libanius, too, in Antioch. His scholarly activity was considerable if he can be identified with the Ulpianus who was author of numerous rhetorical works.¹⁷⁵ In the middle of the century, a father and a son, both by the name Apollinarius, taught in Laodicea.¹⁷⁶ The father, a native of Alexandria, was a grammarian and had previously taught in Berytus. The son taught rhetoric and imitated Pindar, Euripides, and Menander; later he became bishop of Laodicea. The city of Apamea had a tradition of philosophical studies. The Neoplatonist philosopher and theurgist Iamblichus, called "the divine" by his disciples and admirers, taught there. Eunapius

---

¹⁷⁰ See Petit 1956a, 114. One of the students was Alexander 4/ii.

¹⁷¹ Themistius *Or.* 27.332d–333b. The emphasis was on epideictic oratory.

¹⁷² Vanderspoel (1995, 34–38) identifies the teacher with Basil's father. See, however, the description of the latter's skills in Gregory of Nazianzus *Or.* 43.12; cf. Van Dam 2003a, 18–22.

¹⁷³ Leontius 9/iv.

¹⁷⁴ Maximus xvii and Anatolius v. He also taught a young rhetor, Cleopater, who visited Antioch in 358 or 361, pleasing Libanius greatly in all respects (*Ep.* 279).

¹⁷⁵ Ulpianus 1, who might be identical with Ulpianus 4 (*PLRE* I, p. 974), sophist at Emesa in the fourth or fifth century. Cf. Penella 1990, 84 and n. 12.

¹⁷⁶ Socrates (*Hist. eccl.* 2.46.2), who says that they lived at the time of the sophist Epiphanius 1. Barnes 1973, 140.

found his style lacking in clarity and charm, a criticism that was probably a matter of personal taste.[177] It is only natural that Iamblichus was schooled in rhetoric. He composed a treatise on rhetorical subjects, in which he mentioned Homer and Demosthenes; a fragment of the treatise is preserved by Syrianus. He also was the teacher of some members of that family of philosophers, sophists, or both who were all called Sopater.[178] Iamblichus belonged to the generation before Libanius, who called Apamea "the beloved of Iamblichus and the mother of Sopater" (*Ep.* 1389.3) and said that he was the "head of the *chorus*" of the school and "resembled the gods" (*Or.* 52.21). In 363, Libanius thought that the sophist Gerontius had a blessed appointment in the same city with plenty of students and forecasted a lucrative career for him with a splendid house, a rich wife, servants, and plenty of land (**88**). Gerontius received from the city a high salary, and one of his speeches earned a special commendation from his citizens. He was dissatisfied, however, and the letter's beginning may hint at some competition and bickering among colleagues so that (jokingly or not) Gerontius asked Libanius to give him a teaching position in Antioch. A few years later, Libanius complimented him for the numerous pupils (bees) he had, probably still in Apamea, for whom he was "a meadow teeming with flowers" (*Ep.* 1396). Gerontius's relations with Libanius had ups and downs, but in 388 the two appeared reconciled (*Ep.* 863).[179] In the same year, the citizens of Chalcis ad Belum chose a sophist by the name of Domninus as teacher in their city,[180] but the governor Eustathius, who had a good rhetorical education, did not ratify the appointment for unknown reasons. Libanius added this "unjust and shameful" fact to his other grievances against this governor in *Or.* 54.48. Chalcis grew in size and importance from the fourth century on and was a significant center of Hellenism.[181] It was the birthplace of the philosopher Iamblichus, who may have taught there at the beginning, and was a center of Neoplatonist polytheism. The fact that no other sophists from there are known is certainly an accident of the sources.

An investigation of schools of rhetoric in Phoenicia discloses few names.[182] Libanius did not communicate with sophists practicing there,

---

[177] Eunapius *VS* 5.1.2–4, 458, and 5.3.6, 460. Penella 1990, 47–48. Cf. the different views of Damascius (*Isid.* Epit. Photius 34, Zintzen), who criticized Iamblichus's magniloquence, and of the author of the Ps.-Julianic letters (who considered him a pupil of Hermes, god of eloquence, 181.449D and 184.420A Bidez-Cumont).

[178] *Peri kriseōs aristou logou,* Syrianus, *In Hermogenem commentaria* 1, p. 9 Rabe; Bidez 1919, 34–35. On Sopater, see above.

[179] Cf. the dossier of Gerontius vi, the son of the sophist Gerontius 3/iii.

[180] Domninus 5.

[181] See Bowersock 2000b, 261, and 2002. Ammianus (24.1.9) reports that Julian greatly increased its population.

[182] On Phoenicia in the fourth century, see Jones Hall 2004, 105–7.

presumably because this was the country of Acacius (his competitor for the "throne" of Antioch), which was loyal to him. We have seen that the sophist Strategius, who taught for a year in Phoenicia, was in touch with Libanius, who respected him.[183] A family of sophists appears active in Sidon in the early fourth century, with Gymnasius and his son Theon.[184] A papyrus found in Hermopolis in Egypt, which contains two *epicedia* for professors at Berytus, refers to a school of Greek rhetoric.[185] The better-preserved poem eulogizes a renowned sophist, a star of the lecture room, who was beloved by his students and died before going to teach in Constantinople. It is likely that these *epicedia* were pronounced at Berytus and then brought to Egypt. A student of Libanius, Parthenopaeus, was a rhetor in Tyre in the 390s, but there is no indication that he taught. From Tyre he sent orations to Libanius, who rejoiced, feeling that his student (Achilles) was superior to himself (Achilles' father Peleus).[186]

Berytus possessed a celebrated school for the teaching of Roman law. It is useful to mention some of the teachers who had frequent contacts with Libanius, even though the study of law followed or partly replaced that of rhetoric.[187] Domnio, whom Libanius sometimes called Domninus, was the professor to whom he referred those of his students who wished to learn Roman law in the period 356–64.[188] Libanius was on very friendly terms with him and felt free to ask for special consideration for his students—in particular for the older ones, who, in his opinion, needed an accelerated course of study. In the same period, Scylacius taught law at Berytus.[189] We are not informed whether he received students from Antioch, even though Libanius thought highly of his skills and accepted with pleasure Scylacius's recommendation of a young pupil, the son of Julianus (**119**). Much later, in 388, Libanius recommended his student Parnasius to Sebastianus, who was probably a teacher of law in that city.[190] Silanus, who taught law somewhere (probably in Constantinople), should be mentioned, too. Libanius corresponded with him in the years 355–57.[191] *Ep.* 433 testifies to Libanius's attempt to make Antioch educationally self-sufficient. He seemingly invited Silanus to teach there, saying that many admired him, "and young men need a teacher of law."

---

[183] See above, Chapter One.
[184] Gymnasius 1 and Theon 1.
[185] D. L. Page, *Select Papyri*, vol. 3 (Cambridge, Mass., 1970), no. 138.
[186] Letters **159** and **160**. Another student of Libanius, Magnus 12/iii, was a rhetor (but not a teacher) in this region in the 360s; cf. below, Chapter Seven.
[187] See below, Chapter Seven.
[188] Domnio 1. Cf. **28**, **101**, **156**, and **175**.
[189] Scylacius 2/ii, *Ep.* 1431 (N114).
[190] Sebastianus 3/iii, cf. *Ep.* 912. There is no further information about this teacher.
[191] Silanus 1; Libanius wrote to him several times, *Ep.* 433 (B162).

Palestine

There are many indications that the study of rhetoric thrived in Palestine, but ascertaining the state of Greek education, and higher education in particular, in this province is a project in itself.[192] The head of the Jewish community in Galilee was the Jewish Patriarch, and some letters between him and Libanius survive.[193] Libanius complained to the councilors of Antioch that their ungenerous financial treatment of teachers and disrespect for education caused some to flee to Caesarea, a "lesser city," which compensated sophists lavishly (*Or.* 31.42). Before going to Alexandria and then to Athens, Gregory of Nazianzus spent some time studying rhetoric with Thespesius at Caesarea, where, a century before, Origen founded a famous Christian school. In an epitaph (4), Gregory celebrated Thespesius's ability in improvisation and rhetoric, which was worthy of the high standard of Athens. The possibility that Thespesius also gave Gregory some knowledge of grammar and the poets cannot be ruled out.[194] Some uncertainty also exists about the precise identity of another teacher, Eudaemon, who was the recipient or subject of ten letters of Libanius.[195] Since Libanius repeatedly called him a rhetor, he must have had some expertise in rhetoric besides being a grammarian and the author of various grammatical and poetical works, as the *Suda* (E. 3407) relates. This "friend of the Muses" (*Ep.* 108), whose geographical mobility and ability to step out from his profession is notable, was a teacher of rhetoric at Elusa in the Negev for a short period, and taught in Antioch for an even shorter time, before leaving for Constantinople. In those years, Helpidius had a chair of rhetoric in Palestine.[196] He had studied in Athens and had acquired glory with his discourses (*Ep.* 546), but after teaching for a few years, by 361 he was apparently burned out. Helpidius left his *chorus*, practiced rhetoric ("sang") for some time in Antioch (*Ep.* 299), then opted for a career as an advocate in Constantinople. As Libanius wrote to Themistius, Helpidius, who had a chair and wore the appropriate teaching garb, was dismayed at the lack of power of teachers and

---

[192] It deserves more attention than I can dedicate to it now. Scholars of Jewish history have studied this issue very superficially; see Hezser 2001, 90–109. On various aspects of culture in Late Antique Galilee, see Levine 1992.

[193] Letters addressed to the Jewish Patriarch are, e.g., *Epp.* 914, 917, 1084, and 1105. He is sometimes considered the addressee of 206 (supposedly about his son), but I do not accept this identification.

[194] Thespesius 2, who was not (or not only) a grammarian (*pace PLRE* I, which is based on the lemma to the epitaph), as Gallay (1943, 32–33) recognized. Cf. the reservations of Kaster (1988, no. 268).

[195] Eudaemon 3/i, rhetor, advocate, poet, and possibly grammarian. Cf. the detailed discussion of Kaster 1988, 279–82, no. 55. *Ep.* 108 (B69). Cf. below, Chapter Five.

[196] Helpidius 3, who taught from 357 to 361.

abandoned the life of a cicada (*Ep.* 301). Gaza was probably a successful center for the study of rhetoric in the fourth century, but no names of sophists have survived. In *Or.* 55, however, Libanius rants against a powerful sophist who "owned" this city and tried to attract a former student who had reverted to Antioch.[197]

In the last part of the century, a student of Libanius, Priscio, became a successful sophist in Palestine, probably at Caesarea.[198] He was an advocate initially, but then delivered discourses and wrote a panegyric of the emperor in 392. From the time he studied rhetoric, Priscio must have shown a contentious attitude. When he was still in Antioch, he had praised the sophist Panegyrius, who taught in Palestine, but once he arrived there, he declared war on Panegyrius (*Ep.* 956).[199] By not confining himself to instructing students, Priscio disregarded his old teacher's lessons. Two years later, in 392, the story repeated itself. It is possible that Priscio had nurtured in Antioch an enmity toward the student Hilarius, who later became the governor of Palestine. In spite of exhortations and vain promises, the two were again up in arms.[200] Libanius, who thought that success would divert Priscio's attention to something more constructive, acknowledged the collapse of his long-standing dream of an educational family where students were brothers and the same stern father had the duty to dispense unwelcome reprimands.[201]

Arabia and Egypt

When a sophist acquired an important post in the civil service, he "honored all the race of the sophists," who could prove that their strength did not consist merely of words.[202] Two sophists are attested as becoming governors of Arabia in 362/63 and 392 after teaching in undisclosed locations. The first, Belaeus, had learned to apply "persuasion and coercion" as a teacher, and this enabled him to remedy injustices.[203] The soph-

---

[197] Cf. below, Chapter Three. Gaza's intellectual life flourished in the fifth and sixth centuries with figures like Aeneas of Gaza, Zacharias Scholasticus, and Procopius of Gaza. On Late Antique scholarly contacts between Gaza and Alexandria, see Watts 2004, 15–16.

[198] *PLRE* I, p. 729. He might be identified with the sophist who left Antioch for Caesarea, *Or.* 31.42.

[199] On the temperament of sophists, cf. below. See also *Ep.* 453 to Heracleianus 2/i, a pugnacious rhetor who did not mind "shooting" in his speeches to defend Libanius from criticism.

[200] See *Ep.* 1053 (N185). Hilarius 8.

[201] It should be added that in the 390s, the grammarian Diphilus taught in Palestine and "brought the old poets to the minds of his students," *Ep.* 969. See *PLRE* I, p. 261; Kaster 1988, no. 49. Diphilus's father was the grammarian Danaus: Kaster 1988, no. 43.

[202] Libanius, *Ep.* 747.

[203] See *Ep.* 819 (N103). *PLRE* I, p. 160.

ist Bonus, who became governor in 392, seems to have been a student of Libanius, since the latter told him bluntly that he had not been a good student but had become such an outstanding teacher that many of his pupils "adorned the land."[204] The only sophist attested as having a school in Arabia in the 390s is Abureius.[205] In reading his letter (a labor of love, *erōtikon*), Libanius blushed because he could not recognize in himself the qualities eulogized: the strength of an Ajax, a second youth, hair (blond) borrowed from the *Odyssey*?[206] One could imagine an irrepressible laughter, but Libanius kindly lauded the sophist's flowing words and wished that the Muses would keep him as a teacher of young men in love with rhetoric.

In Egypt, rhetoric apparently started to decline in the Roman period.[207] When, in a long digression, the fourth-century historian Ammianus expanded on the glories of Alexandria, he cited medicine and philosophy as its current claims to fame but did not mention literary and rhetorical studies.[208] The fourth-century writer of the *Expositio totius mundi et gentium* went only a little further. In magnifying the beauty and merits of Egypt, and of Alexandria especially, he mentioned rather vaguely literary scholars (*sapientiam litterarum scientes*) besides doctors and philosophers.[209] The papyrological evidence does not change the picture, but it is possible that our view of rhetorical education in the capital would be different if more papyri from Alexandria had survived and if we did not have to rely only on the few texts produced in Alexandria but transported elsewhere.[210] From Libanius, one derives mixed information. In a late oration, he claimed to have "terrified many sophists in Egypt," but one cannot evaluate realistically this statement, since only a few names resurface from his work.[211] A couple of letters regard Castricius, a sophist who

---

[204] Out of fear of being inadequate, Bonus refrained from writing to his old teacher, *Ep.* 1035. Petit does not include Bonus among the students.

[205] *PLRE* I, p. 5, rejects Foerster's emendation of this sophist's name. It is highly likely that Abureius's school was located in Arabia because he wrote a panegyric on Bonus when the latter served there.

[206] *Ep.* 1016, *Od.* 13.399 and 431. Cf. his embarrassment in receiving the poetic panegyric that Gaius i, uncle of his student, wrote in praise of him, *Ep.* 825; cf. below, Chapter Five.

[207] About the decline in Alexandria, see Bowersock 1969, 20–21. Schubert (1995) argues against this view, but not completely successfully.

[208] Ammianus 22.15–22; at 22.16.16, he mentions philological studies in the Hellenistic period, with Aristarchus.

[209] See *Expositio totius mundi et gentium* 34–37 (esp. 34.25–30 [Rougé 1966]). Interestingly, the author describes teachers who did not pretend to know everything and taught only things in which they were experts.

[210] On the loss of papyri because of the high water table in the Delta, see Smith 1974, 37.

[211] *Or.* 2.14; cf. below, Chapter Three.

went to Egypt in 364 seeking success. Libanius presented him as "a skillful sophist and a good man, impaired by the foot illness."[212] The prefect of Egypt was Maximus, who had previously been governor of Galatia, so the moment was favorable to rhetoric, because he supported it, liked to listen to declamations, and honored good sophists.[213] Maximus had embellished Ancyra with buildings, fountains, and springs, had augmented the number of sophists, and had instituted contests among them. Libanius advised Castricius that he should "use his tongue for ears that knew how to judge" (*Ep.* 1117).

Much later, in 388, another sophist moved to Egypt to teach. Gessius, a native of Egypt, had been a student of Libanius in Constantinople or Nicomedia, and after leaving school had shown no interest in marriage, so that his old teacher regretted that he would not be able to teach his children.[214] After a good career, dreams of grandeur brought him to disaster, and he met a violent death.[215] The *Suda* records the activity of a sophist, Alexander, who worked in the fourth century and had been the pupil of Julianus, perhaps the professor at Athens.[216] He might have been a native of Alexandria if his identification as the brother of the sophist Eusebius is secure. Eunapius, who reports that the latter was Egyptian and studied in Athens with Prohaeresius, did not have a good opinion of his talent, and that confirmed his conviction that, while the Egyptians adored poetry, "Hermes, who requires serious study, has departed from them."[217]

Magnus, one of the five iatrosophists mentioned by Eunapius, presided over a school of medicine in Alexandria.[218] A pupil of Zenon of Cyprus, he lived at the end of the third and beginning of the fourth century, established a well-renowned school of medicine, and trained as a doctor and as a sophist.[219] Eunapius wrote that not all of his pupils were equally good in both fields; he regarded Magnus with a touch of con-

---

[212] Castricius 2/ii, *Ep.* 1177.

[213] Maximus 19/vi, *Ep.* 1230 (B112). Libanius often appealed to him.

[214] Gessius 1/i, see 90. Cf. *PLRE* I, pp. 394–95.

[215] On the poems of Palladas concerning Gessius, see Cameron 1964, 279–92. The fact that Gessius did not want to get married should not be taken as a sign that he was a Christian with a propensity for monastic life. He might have been quite young at the time, and Libanius's remarks are not unusual.

[216] *Suda* A1128, Alexander 8; Iulianus 5.

[217] Eunapius *VS* 10.7.10–13, 493. Cf. Chapter Five. Eusebius 12 abandoned an oratorical contest in Rome, and Musonius 2, who taught rhetoric in Athens for a while, prevailed. Another Egyptian teaching in Athens was Paulus of Lycopolis; see above.

[218] Eunapius *VS* 19–22.2.4, 497–99, on the five iatrosophists. Magnus 7/iv. On these iatrosophists, see Penella 1990, 109–17, and Cracco Ruggini 2003. I am covering only the Magnus who was Libanius's correspondent.

[219] *Pace* Penella, for chronological reasons it is still advisable to distinguish this doctor, Zenon 2, from the doctor with whom Libanius corresponded (*Ep.* 171), Zenon 4.

80 • Chapter Two

tempt because he was less good as a physician than as a rhetor. Nevertheless, Magnus had a large following, and students flocked to his lessons. One of those young men was a relative of his and a student of Libanius, Chrysogonus, who ran to Egypt at Magnus's call but discovered how untrustworthy he was. Chrysogonus fell sick from disappointment, left Egypt, and tried to take advantage of the rhetoric he had learned in Antioch but had half-forgotten (**45**).

Sophists in Unknown Locations

For the sake of completeness, a few other sophists who worked in undisclosed locations should be mentioned. Libanius wrote in 356 to Theodorus 7/ii, who had some connection with Egypt, since the letter mentions the river Nile.[220] Theodorus had worked hard at rhetoric in Athens but showed much (false?) modesty. He recommended some students to Libanius, but it is unclear whether they were his own pupils. In the year 358, Libanius mentioned another sophist, Dionysius, who carried a letter to his friend Ecdicius in Cilicia. Unfortunately, this letter expands much more on Ecdicius's passion for beautiful envelopes than on its carrier, who might have taught in Cilicia.[221] In 390, Paulus, a successful teacher, appeared to be concerned for his métier (*Ep.* 961).[222] Libanius reassured him, saying that "those who had a taste of him" would always remain his and would not be persuaded to make worse choices. Paulus was apparently confronting the common problem of defections.[223]

Some Conclusions

There is no strict correlation between the abundance of data from some sources and a commensurate strength of rhetorical studies in a given area. Rhetoric in Cappadocia, for example, was not necessarily stronger than in Galatia, even though more sophists are known in the former province because of the correspondence of the Cappadocian fathers. The data above is neither complete nor binding. Yet, it is possible to observe certain trends in the formation of definite educational areas.

In the fourth century, Athens remained the leading educational center and the ultimate harbor for those who aspired to (and could afford) a

[220] Theodorus 7/ii, *Ep.* 487.
[221] *Ep.* 347, Dionysius 5; Ecdicius ii, Petit 1994, 86–87.
[222] Paulus iii in Seeck 1906; not accounted for in *PLRE* I.
[223] To these, one should add the sophist Lucianus, to whom Julian supposedly addressed a short, complimentary letter (197 Bidez), but much is unsure about him.

highly competitive education. It had a loftier reputation than Antioch or Constantinople, even though it appears (albeit from the one-sided evidence) that its outstanding fame was rather based on past traditions and the direct contact with revered antiquities that it offered. The impression of Libanius in 362 of the inadequacy of some of the Athenian teachers who "because of old age would need to sleep peacefully with their bellies full," however, may not have been completely biased (200), and it converged with Synesius's opinion of the whole faculty half a century later. In a letter, the sophist Aeneas of Gaza rejoiced that Athenian students completed their education in Gaza and not in their own city.[224] Yet, in the fifth and sixth centuries, Athens continued to be considered the university town against which one had to measure a rhetorical school's success.

Constantinople also was a major center of higher education in the fourth century, and one of the stepping-stones to reach Athens. Its educational capacities may have been greater than what we are able to glimpse through the sources. More information concerning sophists teaching in the capital would surface if the letters of Themistius had survived and if Libanius's attitude had been less hostile. Libanius always wished a preeminent role for Antioch, replacing Athens as an educational magnet and limiting the lure of Constantinople as a center of power, but his attempts were often frustrated. We will see that he also spent considerable energy to bring the teaching of Latin and Roman law to his city in order to make it a self-sufficient educational community, but again, his efforts were thwarted.[225]

These three capitals of learning exerted a considerable pull on both teachers and students. It is not surprising that some protested the trend that rewarded some centers at the expense of others that may have been obscure but were nonetheless very good. Thus Themistius, who had a less-impeccable schooling than Libanius, justified his initial training in "barbaric" Pontus and defended those good sophists who taught in small, decentralized locations that did not usually appeal to students.[226] But students were not the only ones to avoid small provincial centers. The geographical mobility of teachers was not a new phenomenon, but it became more pronounced in Late Antiquity.[227] Sophists moved with great freedom and left lesser educational centers in search of better economic treatment, larger student bodies, and more prestige. More rarely, some less ambitious teachers aimed to go back and teach in their homelands. Higher education in other provinces was more or less flourishing, but the authority of the

---

[224] *Ep.* 18; Massa Positano 1962, 48–49 and 105–10.
[225] Cf. below, Chapter Seven.
[226] See *Or.* 27; cf. below, Chapter Six.
[227] See Kaster 1988, 126–28, esp. 127 and n. 150.

three major centers remained intact, notwithstanding the existence of good but lesser schools of rhetoric nearby. Palestine offers a good example of this phenomenon, with sophists moving elsewhere in spite of the healthy state of local rhetoric. All the same, the thick network of schools of rhetoric in the Roman East appears incredibly vital to the modern observer. Though other disciplines, such as Roman law and Latin, were threatening it, rhetoric was determined to survive.

Libanius tried to use all of his connections in order to attract students from small centers. Through the help (or connivance) of sophists who had been former students, his own fellow students in Athens, and "companions" (*hetairoi*) of various origin,[228] he made sure that Antioch could be at least the second station in the course to Athens. In certain provinces, such as Armenia, Bithynia, or Galatia, the network of sophists was to his advantage, while the evidence shows that he was out of touch with teachers practicing in Cappadocia or Phoenicia. It is possible to see the outline of a phenomenon that is more clearly illuminated when one examines the dossiers of Libanius's students. The study of rhetoric did not generally take place in a single school. Most students gradually moved from their hometown school to one in a larger town, and often ended up in a third school in one of the top educational centers.[229] This was not the traditional division between elementary, grammatical, and rhetorical schools, but a progression through more refined stages of the knowledge of rhetoric. For the sons of privilege, the boundaries between town, city, and metropolis did not exist. Because of this, and because many students chose to have only a veneer of rhetoric,[230] Libanius's hopes of very long attendance for each of his pupils were often disappointed.

---

[228] See below, Chapter Three.
[229] On mobility of students, see Watts 2004. Cf. also Kaster 1988, 21–23.
[230] See below, Chapter Six.

CHAPTER THREE

The Network

IN THE SPRING of 363, Libanius, who was then a well-renowned sophist in Antioch, wrote to Alexander, whom the emperor Julian, upon his recent departure for Persia, had appointed as governor of Syria (*Ep.* 838).¹ Libanius thanked the governor for trying to increase the number of his students, but suggested a different strategy. "Leave the numerous assemblies of people alone," he told him, "and do not criticize the other sophists or accuse the parents. Look instead for those young men whom you lately enrolled as advocates, call them, and point them out when they speak."² Alexander was a hot-headed polytheist, prone to excess, and he was regarded by Julian as a fit punishment for the citizens of Antioch, who had offended their emperor.³ Since Libanius did not approve of the governor's harsh conduct on other occasions, it is natural to see the methods that Alexander is said in this letter to have favored as unusual, and in contrast to the sophist's own prudent policy.⁴ The reality could not be more different.

The school of Libanius was presented in the previous chapters as an existing entity with certain characteristics, an institution that rivaled other educational centers in Athens and in the Roman East. But now we take a step back. The current chapter addresses how this school became such a prominent center for the study of rhetoric that Libanius could conceive the hope of dethroning Athens.

The temptation to keep their sheltered sons next to home must have been great for those notables who lived in provinces where the teaching of rhetoric was well established. There were many centers that boasted good teachers and could seriously challenge Antioch. Some causes for the eminence of Antioch as an educational magnet already emerge from what I said above. The school's roots were prestigious. Libanius's predecessors

---

¹ Alexander 5 *consularis Syriae* (a rank attached to the governor) was dismissed by Jovian later in 363; Ammianus 23.2.3.

² This letter was translated, e.g., by Wolf (1952, 84–85), who rendered *kyklos* as "round-about," and by Bradbury (2004a, no. 94), who translated the word as "school." I render the word as "assemblies" because I think Libanius is alluding to cultivating contacts with many people.

³ See Julian *Misopogon*, and Libanius *Or.* 16, on the emperor's anger. Cf. Labriola 1974; Alonso-Núñez 1979; and Benedetti 1981.

⁴ Alexander, in any case, showed personal favor to Libanius. Petit (1956a, 107) saw in the statements of this letter a reflection of the moderate, liberal attitude of the sophist.

(Ulpianus in particular) had such an excellent reputation that they were able to attract youths from other provinces. Antioch itself, which was often the seat of the Imperial court and was the administrative center of Syria and a vital metropolis that valued culture, could be a good launching pad for those who aspired to positions in the administration. Yet it is essential to keep in mind that in antiquity, the traditions of a school had limited value when they did not support a personality of equivalent stature. A school *was* a certain teacher and ceased to be or fell into decline when he disappeared. Schools of rhetoric in Antioch continued to exist after Libanius, but without the same renown.

Libanius's ability to attract students depended on his prestige as a sophist, which he cultivated all his life. Officials who complied with his recruiting efforts and historical circumstances that valued rhetorical education also advanced his fortune. The first part of this chapter will focus on these matters. But the strategies the governor Alexander was relying on to increase the number of Libanius's students—waging war on rival sophists, exercising pressure on parents, and cultivating contacts—were standard methods of recruitment, on which Libanius, like everyone else, relied. The size of his *chorus* was always a passionate concern of his, since, as he declared, in any school the number of the pupils mirrored the teacher's merits.[5] Whereas all the factors noted above undoubtedly contributed to the popularity of Libanius (and of other teachers in antiquity), my concern here is to identify the salient reasons for his success in attracting students. In this inquiry, we must keep in mind that recruitment efforts did not amount to a monumental set of strategies valid in any time. A good recruiter, such as Libanius, had to vary his moves and adapt to circumstances.

Proof of Ability: The *Dokimasia*

In 363, Libanius was well established, having occupied the official chair of rhetoric at Antioch since 354, when he was forty years old. From the time he became a private teacher in Constantinople in 340 until the end of his life, his energy was channeled in two directions: proving his rhetorical power (*dynamis*) in public speeches, and acquiring and nurturing a following of students. But during his years of study, and generally before securing his official chair, his foremost concerns were to increase and prove his knowledge and to brace himself against competition. In spite of his general disillusionment with the state of rhetoric in Athens, he would

[5] *Or.* 31.30, where Libanius refutes the notion that the number of students is an indication of a teacher's income.

have remained there for four more years had circumstances not brought him back east. Libanius thought that further studies were necessary because he feared that his professors might want to test his knowledge by an "infinite examination" (*myria basanō*).[6]

A practicing rhetor needed to prove his ability throughout the course of his career. Here, I focus on a crucial test that awaited students on their return home, the *dokimasia*, in which they had to exhibit their learning and ability. This test, which marked a youth's admission into society and was of foremost importance for an aspiring sophist, has so far escaped scholarly attention in spite of its great significance in assessing the societal value of the acquisition of *paideia* (literary culture, and here rhetoric especially). Interest in a youth's education was not limited to his family; rather, sending a young man to study rhetoric, Latin, or Roman law concerned to some degree all of the educated people (the *pepaideumenoi*) of the community. In a revealing passage in *Or.* 49, the city's notables accompany the young men ready to embark for Rome or Phoenicia: "They congratulate them, wish them well, and send them off" (27–28). The *principales* were proud to send one of their own to a distant place of learning to represent their city.[7] But, upon returning, a youth had to earn his city's approval and render an account of what he had received. In the words of Odysseus, "It was shameful to stay for so long and come back empty" (*Iliad* 2.298). A student had to prove he had assimilated instruction by standing brilliantly on his own in learned encounters with his fellow citizens, by giving dazzling rhetorical displays—in sum, by submitting to a full examination, which Libanius calls a *dokimasia* (*Or.* 55.32).

Returning to his country after many years in Athens, Gregory of Nazianzus knew that the performance (which he called disparagingly a "dance") was a mandatory rite of passage and submitted to it even though he considered it futile. He felt he had to satisfy the "sick" expectations of his fellow citizens, who regarded it as a debt owed to them.[8] The same predicament awaited Libanius's students at the end of their training. The *dokimasia* by the city was a test for trainer and trainee, a stamp of proven value, permission to take a chosen way in life, and a guarantee of future students for a young sophist. At his return, the student Anaxentius was expected to deliver a panegyric in praise of his city, which Libanius presents as the mandatory performance for everybody (*Or.* 55.34). But in spite of their teacher's encouragement, students viewed the *dokimasia* with

---

[6] *Or.* 1.26. One can only guess to what types of "proof" he was alluding, maybe extemporaneous speeches on difficult themes.

[7] Libanius did not share in the enthusiasm, but rather felt that the departures depleted the city council.

[8] *Carm.* 2.1.11.265–76.

trepidation, and even attempted to postpone their return because of it. The student Julianus was one such "coward" who did not trust his excellent capacities. The year before, he had returned home in haste because his mother had been murdered. Back in school, he required considerable prodding to return to his city in Pisidia to celebrate the triumph his teacher had predicted (121). His fellow citizens rejoiced in the talent he had acquired, and after his performance in the theater, they honored him "like a god." Libanius felt justly compensated. One feels that the announcement of a triumphant *dokimasia* brought him more relief—and certainly more excitement—when the success of a student was greater than expected. After several years of study, for example, in 360 Libanius's beloved Hyperechius went back to Ancyra, a city that relished rhetoric and welcomed public performances.[9] He conquered the city "with his fluent tongue and charm" and was regarded by the citizens as an ideal son for his composure and gentlemanly demeanor (108). In a letter laced with an intoxicating joy (109), Libanius told the young man's father that he thanked the people of "sacred" Ancyra, the "benefactors" who deserved "crowns and prayers." At the same time, he quickly assured his recipient that his son had indeed passed the test of approval on his own merit.

The *dokimasia* had awaited Libanius after his four years of study in Athens, but he was able to postpone it by making several detours. Instead of returning immediately to Antioch, he accompanied Crispinus, a fellow student from Pontus, who had to go back home for his *dokimasia*. "Being a cautious young man who had never tasted such ordeals, [Crispinus] was justly alarmed because he was going to show the skill in declamation learned in Athens to people who were clever and dedicated to culture" (*Or.* 1.27). Despite their hesitation, the two young men triumphed together in every town they passed through. The resounding success he and Crispinus obtained, as they were hailed as "benefactors of Athens," apparently served to dissolve or attenuate Libanius's doubts of his own worth (*Or.* 1.29).

Witnessing Crispinus's *dokimasia* must have made the predicament appear less daunting, but Libanius's presentation to his native city finally occurred thirteen years after he left Athens, when the emperor Constantius granted him four months' leave from Constantinople to return to Antioch in 353. It is worthwhile to dedicate some attention to this passage because the test Libanius went through consecrated his rights to be a sophist in the city and to have a following of students. In the

---

[9] On Hyperechius, a student cherished by Libanius in spite of his apparent mediocrity, cf. Pack 1935, 36–37. On Ancyra, see Foss 1977, 29–87, and Mitchell 1993, 2:84–91. Letters 1 and 11 show that about ten years before, around 350, Libanius had enjoyed a visit of several months in this city.

Autobiography, the narration of Libanius's *dokimasia* (*Or.* 1.86–89) has the visionary and illusory texture of a literary dream. Put down in writing twenty years later, the performance acquired a learned veneer but retained the manic quality of a youth's fantasy. The young Libanius contemplating with relish Antioch's temples and colonnades is reminiscent of the young Lucian in the narrative of his career, sowing rhetoric from his chariot.[10] Libanius says that the test to which his city submitted him started in the workshops (*ergastēria*) with "questioning on every side"—a tantalizing reference in terms of locating exactly the audience of this examination.[11] He refers to a stratum of society, the artisan population, that is usually not associated with literary culture but that, as we will see below, might have had some claims in evaluating competence. Although this is one of many testimonies concerning Libanius's open attitude toward the working classes and attesting his desire for social intercourse with them,[12] it indicates that a young man's performance had to find approval at many levels of society and was not the exclusive concern of the supposedly educated (*pepaideumenoi*). At the second stage of the *dokimasia*—a public declamation in which Libanius had to prove "who he was"—most of the people who packed the hall (to the point of sleeping there the night before) had definite claims to culture. The narrative of the lecture itself is feverish and paradoxical and owes something to miracle tales. Libanius's words empowered the elderly, the slow, the sick, and the gouty to jump up in acclamation. The boisterous performance was punctuated by the cries of an audience relishing the triumph of one of their own.

The whole passage, which surely was intended to appeal to an Antiochene audience with its display of piety and patriotism,[13] meant more than that. As he twice underlines, at the beginning and conclusion of the passage (86 and 89), Libanius's triumphant acceptance by his city disproved his detractors in Constantinople who claimed that "fellow citizens are bound to envy each other's success." Envy and enmity were necessary ingredients of a *dokimasia*. Even though they do not appear as openly here as at other points in Libanius's life, when he has to overcome the explicit opposition of enemies, he strongly hints at currents of resistance that accompanied his performance. He was intimidated by the eminence of Antioch, "because it is most difficult to win over one so great." At the beginning of the lecture, Libanius looked confidently at the audience, a

---

[10] Lucian *Somn.* 15.

[11] Cf. Themistius's appreciation for the old orators, who spoke with the general population in the workshops, *Or.* 28.342a.

[12] See, e.g., *Or.* 36.4, and *Or.* 58.4–5 and 22.

[13] Norman 1965, 171.

new Achilles rejoicing in anticipation at the weapons he was going to use. At the end, he was a new Agamemnon, having captured Troy.[14]

The capture of Antioch meant that her returned son now had definite claims to occupy the chair of official sophist when this was vacated by the elderly Zenobius. For the rest of his life, Libanius gave numerous acclaimed oratorical displays, but none had the same significance as the one in which his fellow citizens put the stamp of approval on his ability as rhetor. After his first return to Antioch, and particularly when he came back to the city to reside there indefinitely, an impressive number of orations legitimized his claims.[15] As soon as he settled down to teach, students flocked to him, and the class of fifteen he had brought from Constantinople grew to fifty "in a few days."[16] Accounts of this period in the letters and the *Autobiography* testify to his breathless activity and to people's scrutiny of his teaching.[17] Having found Libanius "a good craftsman of discourses," educated people examined (*dokimazein*) his ability to produce orators as good as himself.[18]

Scrutiny of Libanius's pedagogic talent would continue all his life, as his success as a teacher was periodically in dispute. It will be one of the concerns of this book to try to ascertain whether the detractors of his teaching skills were idle "flies," who, as he said, bit him for no reason, or whether their criticism had some basis.[19] The question now at hand is whether recognition of Libanius as a skillful orator and his ability to attract and keep students were so strictly interdependent that the one automatically implied the other. This was certainly the case at the beginning of his career, but it seems that later, other factors heavily influenced the process of recruitment.

OFFICIAL SUPPORT

Although in the letter mentioned at the beginning of this chapter, Libanius tried to change the governor's actions, he had to acknowledge that Alexander was doing everything in his power "to take students away from

---

[14] Libanius used again the metaphor of capturing Troy for a young rhetor, Evagoras 2, wishing that he could win, *Ep.* 1440.2.

[15] *Or.* 11, written in 356 in praise of Antioch, could be considered an extension of his *dokimasia*. See *Or.* 11.1, on his feverish activity.

[16] *Ep.* 450.6 (N6).

[17] Cf. *Or.* 1.90–105. *Ep.* 391 (N4) and 450. See Petit (1956a, 98–100), who paraphrased *Ep.* 450. Cf. also Wolf 1952, 28–29.

[18] *Ep.* 450.5–6.

[19] Cf. **8** and **12**. Petit (1956a, 99 n. 25) simply found "curious" the fact that Libanius's adversaries criticized him from this point of view.

those who teach elsewhere and to bring here students scattered throughout Syria" (*Ep.* 838.5). The *Autobiography* and the letters show that from the beginning of his career, Libanius dealt with officials who either promoted his interests or upheld rival sophists at his expense, but the question is whether the help he periodically received from the top was critical to his success.[20] Governors might try to damage a sophist's following by not attending his declamations, thus undermining people's confidence in his ability.[21] But they might also side more clearly with his opponents and be part of what Libanius perceived as a "conspiracy" (*synomosia*), inflicting permanent damage to his reputation and jeopardizing his very survival. Resisting, therefore, was a sign of "much lunacy" (*pollēs apoplexias*), and abandoning one's post and moving elsewhere was a counsel of desperation that had sometimes to be adopted.[22]

Yet, the inclination of a member of the administration might change, causing him suddenly to withdraw support from a competitor. The wavering favor of the governor Philagrius[23] is a significant example of the subtle shifts of opinion and the variable currents that determined recruitment. Philagrius originally helped the supporter of a rival of Libanius simply because "the two had gone to school together in Athens, did each other favors, and were going to continue to do so thereafter."[24] The ties that bound two fellow students were powerful. Gregory of Nazianzus choked with emotion upon receiving a letter from the same Philagrius, who had studied in Athens with him as well. The name itself in the letter's first line suddenly called to his mind a world of past joys: "The cities, the work, the common table, the 'lovely comradeship,' as Homer says, the play times, the serious pursuits, the sweats of rhetoric, the common teachers, and the height of hopes."[25] Yet, school ties might be weakened or severed by a new way of life or stronger cultural attractions. Not only was the cultivated mind of Philagrius offended by the violent, mad behavior of the rival of Libanius, but he became hopelessly enamored of a speech delivered at that time by Libanius. "When he rose to leave, he was a lover (*erastēs*), and right away by means of letters mustered and brought to my own school his relatives who were studying with others and the sons of his friends" (*Or.* 1.72). A burning love for Libanius's rhetoric (and probably some sense of justice) translated in this case into immediate and practi-

---

[20] On the power and functions of governors at the times of Libanius, see Cabouret 2002 and 2004. See also Rouéché 1998.
[21] See, e.g., *Or.* 1.42.
[22] See, e.g., *Or.* 1.45–47: according to Libanius, the governor Limenius hoped to kill him and tried every means to indict him on an accusation of magic.
[23] Philagrius 5, *PLRE* I, p. 694.
[24] *Or.* 1.66; see also *Or.* 1.72.
[25] Gregory of Nazianzus *Ep.* 30.2. Cf. also *Epp.* 31–36, sent to the same friend.

cal measures for recruitment. In evaluating this episode, we should not forget that this is Libanius's own account of the events and that he has the tendency to see opposition and favor in highly personal terms. Yet the episode seems to be unique. He does not disclose other cases of governors openly turning themselves into recruiters, and he appears to have received indirect, effective assistance from the top. When he was in Constantinople, for example, all successive governors held him in much honor until Strategius, "steered by the Muses," revived a decree of the Senate, so that he received honorific and financial help from the emperor in the form of revenues from land.[26]

After he was permanently installed in Antioch as official sophist, the accession of Julian must have resulted in an increase of students. Libanius discloses the new vitality of rhetoric, for which the emperor was responsible. As Julian journeyed to Syria, governors approached him with gifts of rhetoric (their own speeches) instead of "the boars, birds, and bucks that used to be offered," and cultivated men endowed with rhetorical skills were put at the head of cities. The emperor made himself available to teachers throughout his journey, and, following his example, governors made teachers their intimates.[27] But after Julian's death, those same teachers "were turned away from [governors'] doors like murderers," and students shunned the *logoi*, which seemed to offer weak means of support.[28] It is difficult to know whether Libanius reaped conspicuous (albeit temporary) fruits from Julian's well-known edict of 17 June 362 that barred Christians from teaching grammar, rhetoric, and philosophy.[29] Even though the edict's impact was not felt immediately, it is possible that some new students came to the school as a result of it. Ammianus thought that one had to bury that harsh measure in eternal silence, and silence is what Libanius offers.[30] Silence versus speech is for him always a charged gesture, and in this case might indicate a measure of disapproval.[31]

An account of the letters concerned with education and of the numbers, year by year, of new versus returning students does not show clearly that

---

[26] *Or.* 1.80. It is unclear from the passage whether Libanius also received emoluments from the city, as Norman (1965, 169) maintains. Kaster (1983, 40–41) is against this view.

[27] *Or.* 18.158–59 and 161.

[28] *Or.* 18.288.

[29] See *Cod. Theod.* 13.3.5, and Julian *Ep.* 61 Bidez. The literature on the edict is abundant. See, e.g., Bowersock 1978, 83–85; Banchich 1993; Hunt 1998, 66–67; and Bringmann 2004, 123–28. Athanassiadi (1981) is isolated in justifying Julian's policy; cf. Bowersock 1983. On the motivations of the edict and Gregory of Nazianzus's response, see Elm 2001. Goulet (2000) maintains that the edict was not explicitly directed against Christian teachers.

[30] Ammianus 22.10.6; cf. 25.4.20.

[31] Libanius did not approve of Julian entirely and did not share his view concerning the Council in Antioch and his new style of Hellenic religion. Was he also afraid to lose his Christian students if he openly approved of the edict? See Wiemer 1995a, 108–10.

Julian's rule and demise had any impact on enrollment.[32] The high enrollment to which the letters of 362/63 bear witness refers to students from abroad, who might have been attracted by Libanius's amicable relations with the emperor. The relatively low figures in the previous year probably reflect local recruitment and a higher percentage of Antiochene students, who naturally are almost absent from the letters. The fortunes of the school appear unimpaired well after Julian's death, however; in 365, the letters' sequence is interrupted, but the school seems still to be thriving after the gap. Libanius enjoyed occasional good relations with some officials under Valens's rule, as a letter to the powerful and cultivated Saturninius Salutius testifies.[33] Here Libanius made a connection between this governor's policy and school recruitment. By continuing to place men with a rhetorical education in the governors' seats, Salutius implicitly helped Libanius's cause. The teacher gratefully acknowledged that he "improved the standing of rhetoric in the eyes of those who occupy official posts and thus filled our schools with students, inspiring a passion for rhetoric in those who hoped for equal honors." Salutius's support was a direct, albeit isolated, continuation of Julian's in times much changed. Afterward, the bitter allegations Libanius leveled against most officials, and the acrimony that characterized most of his contacts with power,[34] make it unlikely that endorsement from the top, which was helpful at the beginning and occasionally later, continued to be the determinant of the school's success.

SOPHISTS' WARFARE

In *Oration* 2.14, written in the early 380s, Libanius acknowledged that he had beaten many opponents: "I defeated such and such sophist, reduced so and so to silence, I brought down another and overthrew another one, I made another run away, and I terrified the many sophists in Egypt and those three in Athens." Acute animosity among sophists is not a novelty of Late Antiquity, but it seems to be a mark of a profession ruled by vanity and outward appearance.[35] The hostile relations with

---

[32] Petit (1956a, 77–80) struggles to interpret the existing data, which he finds surprising. Wintjes (2005, 151–62, 175–76) rightly maintains that Libanius was still influential under Jovian but lost students in the period 371–78.

[33] See *Ep.* 1224 of the year 364, Cabouret 2000, no. 72 (B168). For Saturninus Secundus Salutius, see *PLRE* I, pp. 814–17; Vanderspoel 1995, 139–41 and 156. See also *Ep.* 1233 (B169), written to a poet who was assessor of Salutius and favored rhetoric.

[34] Cf. Norman 1983, 168–69.

[35] For the period of the Second Sophistic, see Bowersock 1969, 89–100, esp. 89, where he remarks on the exquisite character of such educated polemic. Much violence resurfaces from Libanius's *Or.* 1.

other sophists, which sometimes amounted to war (*polemos*),³⁶ contribute to the heated tone of the beginning of Libanius's *Autobiography*. In every city where he engaged in public competitions and attempted to attract students, he had to wrestle with the resentment or open antagonism of other teachers fighting for their own survival. The outlandish feuds he describes are familiar to the reader of Eunapius or Himerius and have already attracted some scholarly attention.³⁷ Here I focus on the forces motivating them and on the question of whether Libanius himself had any part in them. Surely we cannot rest assured that, as one scholar has said, "Only the smallest sophists acted in that barbarous spirit."³⁸ Libanius's *Autobiography* invariably presents him as the victim of other sophists' persecution, but of course, this narrative is not as transparent as it purports to be.

The scenario of the opposition Libanius initially found in Constantinople repeated itself with few changes wherever he moved. The two professors installed in the city were dismayed at his sudden success as rhetor and recruiter. They were at different points in their careers, but were equally alarmed. One "had never bloomed into tenure (*archē*)," and so had never reached "power" (*to dynasthai*), whereas the other "had finished blooming," and had therefore lost power.³⁹ Grief was their first reaction, and insults and abuse followed, escalating to open violence and a charge of magic once a third sophist became involved.⁴⁰ The "ostentation and vanity inseparable from the profession" of sophist⁴¹ were certainly at the heart of these feuds, but genuine concern for their livelihood also motivated the initiators of such disturbances. The crowds of students were fickle and followed the call of fashion, and a teacher could spare no effort to retain his following.

Grief (*penthos* or *lypē*) was invariably the first reaction of a sophist who saw his career in jeopardy, and this was accompanied by fear (*phobos*) and envy (*phthonos*).⁴² Envy, a powerful force in academia at all times, could make a sophist "choke" at the number and variety of a rival's declamations, as happened to Acacius, Libanius's opponent (*Or.* 1.109). Fear forged temporary alliances, which were not based on true

---

³⁶ Cf. *Or.* 1.91.
³⁷ See, e.g., Eunapius *VS* 9.1.6–9.2.21, 483–85; Himerius *Or.* 4.9 and 19. On the feuds accompanying the appointments of ancient professors, see Walden 1912, 130–61.
³⁸ So Walden 1912, 159.
³⁹ *Or.* 1.38. Norman (1992, vol. 1, ad loc.) slightly mistranslates as "one had never enjoyed any success." *Archē* refers to a full professorship, "tenure," as *Or.* 55.10 and 23 show.
⁴⁰ The continuous accusations of magic that are a consequence of success are almost tedious in their occurrence but need to be taken very seriously.
⁴¹ These are the fundamental causes according to Norman (1983, 167).
⁴² See, e.g., *Or.* 1.44.

friendship. As Libanius observed, a sophist who "barked by himself" got nowhere (*Or.* 1.44). He needed a "gang" (*symmoria*) of his own and found it in other sophists and grammarians who feared an intruder. Gambling and drinking parties with those in power also promoted one's career. Certain aspects of social life, such as "go[ing] drinking with men of influence, and wast[ing] most of the day and night around the table" (*Or.* 1.75), cemented strong, albeit false, friendships, so that one who shrank from this behavior might be considered "an enemy" by those who counted.

Like the fickle associations shaped by fear, professional feuds might not be long-lasting. They were based not on principle, but on utility. The enmity between Libanius and Acacius of Caesarea, which evolved into a somewhat cordial relationship once the latter left Antioch, is an example.[43] Real friendships based on mutual respect had more chance to continue unchanged and, as I show below, friendly relations were the main sources for recruitment. Yet the principle of *mors tua vita mea* might lead a candidate anxious for a professorship to undermine his mentor. In the *Autobiography*, the confused account of Libanius's relations with old Zenobius reveals not only Libanius's desire to present him in a bad light, but also his awareness that he had behaved improperly toward his teacher.[44] As soon as Zenobius uttered some half-promises that he might be willing some day to relinquish his position, Libanius started to scheme to take his place. His machinations were so premature that they caused Zenobius's understandable resentment (*Or.* 1.100). A year later, in 355, the old teacher conveniently died, and his post became available. This was the sequence of events, but the narrative is unduly dramatic. Zenobius, guilty of not disappearing at Libanius's bidding, is presented as a participant in the riots of 354, which, by distorted chronology, are made to last until an illness caused his demise.[45] Libanius thus granted himself a fitting opportunity to display his generous treatment of his *didaskalos*, proving that "a kindly spirit" entered Antioch with him (*Or.* 1.96). He showed himself weeping at the sight of Zenobius in prison; composing a panegyric that caused the emperor to forgive the teacher; visiting his sickbed every day (in spite of Zenobius's displeasure, we are told);[46] and finally pronouncing a funeral oration for him. The reader inevitably perceives the illness of Zenobius, "which separated him from his students" (*Or.* 1.104), as a just retribution for his rejection of his former student.

---

[43] Acacius 6.

[44] Norman (1992, 1:161 n. b) shows the distorted chronology of events. Libanius was not always grateful to his old teacher, as Schemmel ([1907] 1983, 4) maintains.

[45] See esp. *Or.* 1.104, with the juxtaposition of Acacius, the decurion Eubulus, and Zenobius.

[46] Libanius says that at times he was turned away (*Or.* 1.105).

We may convince ourselves that Libanius was incapable of the most violent behavior toward other sophists, yet he was certainly guilty of scheming for his position like everyone else. *Oration 55*, which to date has attracted almost no attention, illuminates the animosity of sophists in their quest for pupils as well as the aspirations of students to succeed their teachers.[47] Its date is uncertain, but it appears to be the work of an energetic Libanius, not yet undermined by old age. Libanius himself remarked that he limited the length of this speech, which resembles an unusually developed rhetorical letter addressed to a student. As the speech progressively reveals, this pupil, Anaxentius,[48] abandoned the classes of a sophist in Gaza to attend those of Libanius in Antioch. Unlike Antioch, Gaza appears to have had only one sophist who had full power (*dynamis*) and "owned the city" (*Or.* 55.6). In an attempt to recover his pupil, his old teacher proceeded to harass the lad's father, making at the same time irresistible promises to Anaxentius that he would become his teaching assistant on his return and would one day take his place. The threats that the sophist of Gaza leveled against both Anaxentius and his father (not only words but also deeds) are unclear, but were of such a serious nature that both father and son could have ended up in prison or killed.[49] Even allowing for some exaggeration, a sophist did not spare his weapons to recover a runaway. This speech's argument rests partly on an *encomium* of fathers praised for their capacity to suffer for their sons in the name of education, but its principal interest lies in the realistic details about the strategies teachers employed to keep their following.

Libanius anticipated that on his return, Anaxentius would have to make a formal oath binding himself to his former teacher forever,[50] and then would be allowed to "tend the flock" with the latter (*Or.* 55.7–8). The assistant professor would meet the sophist everywhere—at school, in the baths, in the shops, and at dinner parties at the sophist's home[51]—but each encounter would be pervaded by common mistrust. A few mythological comparisons, such as Midas versus Demosthenes, Croesus versus Lysias, learned Athens versus rich Egyptian Thebes, suggest that Anaxentius might be seduced by the promise of earning some money. Libanius even contemplated the possibility that the young man might die before the professor, having wasted his life in a vain search for tenure (*archē, Or.*

---

[47] This oration is partially translated by Festugière (1959, 434–41), who barely comments on it.

[48] Anaxentius does not appear in the epistolary.

[49] Festugière (1959, 434 n. 2) might be right in arguing for the threat of a liturgy (that is, some kind of civil service), but the wording is very confused.

[50] On Libanius's mistrust of oaths, see below.

[51] Cf. the gatherings of Libanius and his friends, **149** and **153**.

55.10).[52] But even if he could obtain a full professorship upon the death of his mentor, he would live regretting that "treasure" of real rhetoric that Libanius alone could offer him. A fraudulent and incompetent teacher was a laughable donkey[53] covered by a lion skin, and his foolish student was a second Phaethon who received a deadly gift and was unable to fly.[54] With patience and hard work and with his father's applause,[55] however, Anaxentius would obtain his chair (*thronos*) through a decree of the city's Council, as Libanius himself had done.

In this oration, Libanius betrays a suspiciously close familiarity with the irritation and fear of the betrayed professor as well as with his capability for vengeance. One is able to put into perspective the concerns of some parents that repeatedly surface in the letters and to assess the validity of the sophist's reassuring statements that he would never harm a returning student.[56] In all of his works, Libanius reveals an intimate and painful knowledge of the problem of students' defections. None of the remedies he tried, neither war nor a peaceful covenant with other sophists, had lasting results.[57] But even though his relations with other professionals occasionally were tense, these personal animosities were a far cry from the open hostilities that marked the beginning of his career, when the recruitment of students depended heavily on warfare.

Rivalry among teachers in their quest for students, in any case, was a constant of education in antiquity. The letters of the anonymous professor in tenth-century Constantinople again testify of tense relations. Whereas this professor's correspondence with one teacher has a collegial tone and mostly revolves around academic themes, the letters to two other teachers reveal a background of acute hostility with complaints about improperly seizing students and threats to turn to higher civil and religious authorities in order to redress iniquities.[58]

Size of the School and Geographical Recruitment of Students

The size of Libanius's school and the geographical areas from which his students came are important factors in considering his recruitment. Liban-

---

[52] The situation is not unrealistic. Many of Libanius's students died very young.

[53] On changing a horse for a donkey, see *Or.* 62.61; cf. the proverb by the sophist Zenobius (2.33) and the grammarian Diogenes (1.96). By leaving their studies and dedicating themselves to practical affairs too soon, students became donkeys.

[54] Libanius used the classic myth of Phaethon, who became a completely positive figure in Late Antiquity; see MacCoull 2004.

[55] Cf. the applauding father in Lucian *Somn.* 16.

[56] See, e.g., 35.

[57] See below, and *Or.* 43.

[58] See Anon. Lond. *Epp.* 19, 23, 67, 36, 51, and 68; Markopoulos 2000.

ius was constantly preoccupied with the size of his *chorus* and never ceased measuring his fortunes as a teacher by it. His remarks on his oscillating students' numbers are precious insofar they are unique in antiquity. When Libanius first arrived in Constantinople, the grammarian Nicocles offered him a post of professor (*archein*) right there and promised forty students (*Or.* 1.31).[59] Even though this project did not materialize, with his transfer to Nicomedia, Libanius's popularity was such that he made the whole city his lecture room (*Or.* 1.53–55). His return to Constantinople in 349, however, brought disappointment: Libanius was left to confront the inclement weather (all that snow) and the disappearance of his students, who did not survive the capital's high style and lack of taste.[60] Finally, in Antioch, his initial following of fifteen pupils climbed to fifty in a few days, so that he "could not get through them all before sunset" and was forced to skip lunch, a detail reported with some pride to a friend.[61]

During the rest of his career, Libanius remained a rather popular teacher, yet concerns about the number of his students always plagued him to such an extent that others were well aware of them. In 357, at the height of his popularity, an official, Jovinus,[62] could play on his anxiety and hope to patch things up with him merely by sending him a new pupil (*Ep.* 554). Libanius's "flock," moreover, might decline temporarily because of external events, such as a plague and famine in 385,[63] or be sharply diminished—down to twelve and then to seven—when there was a mass exodus of the population from Antioch after the Riot of the Statues in 387 (*Or.* 34.14). At that time, old and disillusioned, Libanius bitterly complained about the behavior of his bad students (a legion, versus a handful of decent ones, in the opinion or argument of the moment, *Or.* 3.27–33). In spite of their rowdy conduct, he confessed that he could not let them go and thus reduce his numbers because his opponents would rejoice, seeing his professorship (*archē*) compromised. He preferred to continue like a general in command of an infamous army, taking precautions that his soldiers would not fall into the hands of the enemy.

---

[59] See above, Chapter Two, and below. Libanius's language in the oration suggests a full teaching position (not an assistantship). Wintjes (2005, 78–81) underlines that Libanius is trying to aggrandize himself because the fast narration seems to refer to a position of official sophist.

[60] *Or.* 1.76. On Libanius's dislike of snow that forced people to stay in bed, see *Or.* 11.32. Cf. Eunapius's dislike of Constantinople and its inhabitants, VS 6.2.7–9, 462–63; Penella 1990, 135.

[61] *Or.* 1.104 and *Ep.* 405.6; cf. above.

[62] Jovinus 1, cf. Petit 1956a, 104.

[63] Cf. *Or.* 1.233: he spent his days joylessly but was glad that his pupils found safety.

Libanius's letters allow one to surely identify 196 of his students, and of these, 134 can be placed in a period of fifteen school years.[64] The numbers for each year, therefore, are not very high, with a maximum of twenty-six students in 359/60. It is essential to underline that the data refer almost exclusively to young men coming from abroad, since there was no need to write to students from families in Antioch and the vicinity. We have seen above that Libanius's students suddenly reached fifty in a few days in 354, when he took Zenobius's place. Even though he mentioned "citizens and strangers" among them, it is reasonable to suppose that his sudden renown brought faster results in Antioch and nearby places. A high cumulative number, close to eighty, for the initial period of the school, when the letters testify to many students from abroad, would sharply decline to about fifteen in his last years, if one, relying only on the data from the letters, maintains the same proportion of students from the city and of those from abroad.[65]

Recruitment, however, must have depended heavily on Antioch at all times. Plenty of factors (such as difficulties of communication and lower costs) favored keeping boys in their home cities when a professor of international renown was available and if there was no need to learn disciplines that were offered somewhere else.[66] In *Oration* 3, written in his late years, Libanius reminisced about the old times, when students (clearly from the city) memorized his speeches as soon as he delivered them and then repeated them for the following three or four days to their fathers at home. In those days, fathers approved when their sons fought for their professor, even though they saw with their very eyes "the evidence of the battles" on their bodies.[67]

Attendance of Antiochene students was particularly high in Libanius's last years, so that there is no need to posit a sharp decline in his popularity, even though the figures from the letters (which concern students from abroad) are low.[68] In Theodosius's times, he continued to enjoy a lasting reputation, and the emperor honored him by sending him letters, allowing

---

[64] From 354 to 365 and from 388 to 393, cf. the table in Petit 1956a, 60–61. Sixty-one of the students cannot be placed exactly, sometimes because they attended his classes in Constantinople or Nicomedia.

[65] Petit does briefly discuss the number of potential students from Antioch (1956a, 66–71), but he seems to forget about these students in the rest of his book, even when he considers the whole school. Schemmel ([1907] 1983, 57) envisages an average of fifty to eighty students.

[66] Students in need of learning Roman law went to Berytus or Rome. Others, such as Titianus, hoped to give the final touches to their rhetoric by going to Athens; cf. below, Chapter Seven.

[67] See *Or.* 23.16–18 and 22.

[68] Petit (1956a, 70), who relies exclusively on the data from the letters, is forced to conclude that attendance was extremely low at that time.

his illegitimate son Cimon to inherit, and dismissing charges of treason and magic.[69] A letter (so far unnoticed) that Libanius wrote in 390 to the sophist Ablabius, moreover, makes significant remarks about geographical distance in relation to attendance.[70] A falling out between the two friends was accompanied by cold relations with other Galatians who had also avoided Libanius's school.[71] "I am not likely to have forgotten my first children," wrote Libanius, "but these children have probably forgotten those who were fathers to them. And perhaps this is not unreasonable: there is a vast territory between us, and my later students come from nearby places" (*Ep.* 921).

That in Libanius's later years his students came largely from nearby places is also confirmed by some of his speeches. His remarks in *Or.* 23 that during the Riot of the Statues students anxiously contacted their families by letter and were told to leave by their worried parents who sent letters in response are understandable if those parents lived not too far from Antioch, so that letters could reach their destinations in a relatively short time. Likewise, in *Oration 4*, written in 391, Libanius, who was reacting to accusations of being feebleminded, retorted that fathers (that is, mostly from the city) could see the situation themselves and could testify that this was not true.[72] Since the letters refer almost exclusively to students from other provinces, they leave in the dark Libanius's maneuvers for recruiting in Antioch and its vicinity. A rare case is represented by a letter (**137**) sent to his friend Marcellinus of Apamea. Although students usually did not encounter their teacher before entering the school, the son of Marcellinus had some preliminary intercourse with Libanius because of his proximity. Asking Marcellinus for a favor on behalf of someone else, Libanius was positive that Marcellinus's son would intercede for him "in order that he may find me gentle in memory of this favor, once he joins my school." This striking, lapidary message could rouse our indignation if we did not keep in mind that no discontinuity existed in antiquity between professional and personal relations.[73]

The locus classicus to verify the origins of Libanius's students is a passage in *Oration 62*, written in 382, when he was still willing and able to

---

[69] Wiemer (1995b) has conclusively put to rest scholars' assumptions (e.g., Norman 1992, 1:278–79; Liebeschuetz 1972, 186–92; Martin 1988, 248–50, note to *Or.* 2.8) that Libanius received the quaestorship with Julian and an honorary prefecture with Theodosius.

[70] *Ep.* 921; on Ablabius 2/i, see above, Chapter Two. *Ep.* 921 is not mentioned by Petit.

[71] A high number of students from Galatia had attended Libanius's school in previous years; see Petit 1956a, 129–32.

[72] *Or.* 4.11. Libanius refers to "those parents who bring their sons to me," but the letters do not show many examples of parents from abroad bringing their sons to school. His remarks about his students coming from far away seem exaggerated.

[73] See Kaster 1988, 69, on a different example taken from Libanius.

try to override criticism concerning the success (or failure) of his pupils. It is worthwhile to revisit this passage since it corresponds more closely than it is usually thought with the data extrapolated from the letters.

> I will say what I can prove, that I have children (for it is right so to call those who have enjoyed attendance with me), some in Thrace and the capital, others in Bithynia, or Hellespontus, Caria, and Ionia, and you could find some in Paphlagonia, if you wished to, and in Cappadocia—not many there, for not many have come to me from there, but still you would find some. In the cities of Galatia, however, you would see many and no less a number in Armenia. Again, the Cilicians outnumber them, and these, too, are far outnumbered by the Syrians. And if you go to the Euphrates and cross the river and go to the cities beyond, you will come across some of my companions, and perhaps not bad ones either. Both Phoenicia and Palestine are under some obligation to me, together with Arabia, Isauria, Pisidia, and Phrygia. (*Or.* 62.27–28)

The provinces mentioned in *Oration* 62 can be identified in the rest of Libanius's work as places of origin of his students both before and after he settled in Antioch. But in addition, this passage makes specific quantitative observations that can be brought into agreement with the information furnished by the letters, provided one takes into account certain general norms of communication with students and their families.[74] I argued above for a high number of students from Antioch and the vicinity, which cannot be quantified exactly. We can reasonably suppose that, before attending his school, most of the students from Syria (or at least their families) had the chance to contact Libanius directly, in a preliminary visit to Antioch. Speaking of another city in Syria, for example, Libanius says that there was "much coming and going" between the two cities (*Or.* 34.20). For this reason, an insignificant number of Syrians as well as a relatively low number of Cilicians figure in the letters.[75] Libanius says that Syrian and Cilician students vastly outnumbered students from Galatia and Armenia, who were quite numerous, judging from the correspondence.[76] His words are consistent with the data from the letters if one acknowledges that he recruited through means other than letters and must have evaluated potential candidates through personal, direct contacts whenever possible. If we keep in mind that the students who reappear in the correspondence are a fraction of the total, Libanius's words in this

---

[74] Petit (1956a, 114) affirms that this text agrees "perfectly" with the data from the letters but then proceeds to say that the data from Cappadocia do not correspond. He also considers less precise correspondences concerning the students from Syria and Cilicia.

[75] Cilicia was not too far from Antioch. Cf. the Cilician student Titianus and his father, who traveled back and forth.

[76] Petit 1956a, 114: 7 Syrians, 14 Cilicians, 16 Galatians, and 20 Armenians.

oration realistically correspond to the contingents from the various areas of recruitment. There is no reason to question his matter-of-fact observation that he did not have a vast following in Cappadocia.

BASIL AS STUDENT AND RECRUITER

As we will see, one of the foremost activities of an alumnus on behalf of his alma mater was procuring new students. Basil the Great exerted himself to some degree in this direction, using his influence with his fellow Cappadocians. But evaluating this aspect of his proselytizing as well as assessing the contingents of pupils from this region make it imperative to confront once again the questions of whether Basil studied with Libanius and whether the extant correspondence between them is authentic.

Basil's education is a matter of controversy. Even though scholars have long shown the inaccuracy of the testimony of Socrates (followed in this by Sozomen) that Basil and Gregory of Nazianzus went to Athens and then perfected their eloquence at Antioch with Libanius, this view still maintains some hold.[77] A ranking of Antioch above the school of Athens certainly would have made Libanius ecstatic, but it is unrealistic. Basil was indeed a student of Libanius, but not in Antioch and not for long. After studying in Caesarea in Cappadocia and on his way to refine his rhetoric in Athens, Basil resided in Constantinople and, as Gregory of Nazianzus says, being naturally gifted, "in a short time" took advantage of the teachings of philosophers and rhetors.[78] In those years (348 or 349), Libanius taught in Nicomedia and Constantinople. A letter of Basil's brother, Gregory of Nyssa, where he refers to Basil as "student" (*mathētēs*) of Libanius, makes the connection.[79] The value of this testimony resides in the fact that Gregory underlines a distinction between the direct teachings that Basil received from Libanius and his own indirect knowledge of the sophist, since he knew Libanius's writings through his brother and by reading his speeches.

With regard to the letters that Basil and Libanius supposedly exchanged, by and large scholars have been divided into two groups. Those who have studied Libanius's works have accepted that two of his letters, which tradition handed down with the rest of the correspondence (*Epp.*

---

[77] Socrates *Hist. eccl.* 4.26; Sozomen *Hist. eccl.* 6.17. There is no evidence that Gregory was ever a student of Libanius. On the inaccuracy of these accounts, see Festugière 1959, 409–10. Meredith (1995, 21) still accepts the testimonies. Other scholars accept that Basil was Libanius's student but do not point to a specific place; Cadiou (1966), for example, argues in favor of that on the basis of their correspondence with sophists they both knew.

[78] Gregory of Nazianzus *Or.* 43.14.

[79] Letter 13, Maraval 1990, 194–200.

501 and 647), were addressed to St. Basil, but they have generally dismissed the authenticity (or declined to address the question) of those letters that are part of Basil's corpus.[80] Scholars of Basil, on the other hand, did not take into consideration or hastily rejected the two letters in the Libanian corpus, but considered authentic a large portion of those letters handed down with Basil's correspondence.[81]

In taking up again, albeit in a short compass, the issue of the authenticity of the letters, let us start from those two that have the greatest chance of being authentic, since they are part of Libanius's corpus. *Ep.* 501 shows that Basil, after leaving Athens in 355, took the place of the sophist Alcimus in Nicomedia for a little while,[82] whereas *Ep.* 647 alludes to an exchange of correspondence between Libanius and Basil and to the latter's interest in the welfare of some of Libanius's students, most likely from Cappadocia.[83] The way is therefore clear to admit the possibility of a further epistolary exchange. In my opinion, the letters that have a greater chance of being authentic are those that allude to Basil's intervention in favor of recruitment of new students from his region.[84] Basil's letter 335 (*Lib.-Bas.* 1), in which he declares his regret in sending students one by one, is a good letter of presentation of a new candidate, with its emphasis on the latter's father. Libanius responded with a letter packed with facts (Basil *Ep.* 336, *Lib.-Bas.* 2). He was grateful for the student, remembered his fondness for Basil's self-control when the latter followed his classes in Nicomedia and Constantinople, and recalled the latter's decision to go to Athens and to take with him Celsus, another student of Libanius in

---

[80] Seeck (1906, 30–34) alone struggled to prove the authenticity of the corpus, which Laube (1913) completely denied. Foerster (*Prolegomena*, 1903–27, 9:197–98) accepted *Epp.* 501 and 647 but doubted that the Basil in question could be Basil the Great. Petit (1956a, 126 and nn. 167–68) concluded that the recipient of these two letters was St. Basil; and Norman (1992, 1:408–9 n. a) followed this view.

[81] See Fedwick (1981b, 5), who accepts in the Libanius-Basil correspondence Basil 335–341, 344, 346, and 358; and Pouchet (1992, 151–75), who accepts Basil 335–40. Cf. also Hauschild 1993, 243 n. 616. Van Dam (2003a, 22 and 24) accepts that Basil was a student of Libanius in Constantinople but does not expand on the subject.

[82] On Alcimus, cf. above, Chapter Two. As Norman (1992, 1:409 n. c) remarks, this information could hardly be the invention of a forger. The objections of Pouchet (1992, 158–59) are not binding: this letter is not unworthy of Libanius; Basil probably stopped in Nicomedia for only a short time; and the letter does not imply that Gregory was also Libanius's student.

[83] Petit (1956a, 126) takes the expression "the students on whose behalf you came to me" as "on whose behalf you wrote to me."

[84] I think that in the Basil correspondence, letters 335, 336, 337, and 338 (*Lib.-Bas.* 1–4) have greatest chance of being authentic, but I have serious doubts about 339 and 340, and I consider the rest forgeries. ("*Lib.-Bas.*" is the standard abbreviation for the short exchange of letters between Basil and Libanius, which is found in Foerster [1903–27] at the end of the second volume of letters.)

Bithynia. Libanius discussed then the situation of another Cappadocian student, Firminus, who left Antioch after only four months to attend a wedding and because he was apparently recalled by his city for some curial obligations.[85] The situation was not uncommon, and Libanius's subtle competition with Athens, when he polemically wondered whether the same imposition would have applied to that city, rings true.[86]

With a further letter (337, *Lib.-Bas.* 3), Basil sent his teacher two more students from Cappadocia for whom he requested special consideration, even though the second was of poor economic condition. According to Libanius's response (338, *Lib.-Bas.* 4), that short, perfectly balanced letter roused his enthusiasm; he showed it to friends and declared joyfully that Basil had surpassed him as a writer of elegant letters. This was not an isolated reaction on the part of Libanius, who took great pride in the accomplishments of his students, as when he declared that his student Parthenopaeus had surpassed himself in an oration he wrote.[87] A century later, Zacharias Scholasticus, who wrote the *Vita Severi* in Alexandria, must have believed in the authenticity of at least this letter, since he said that Severus knew the epistolary exchange of Basil and Libanius and agreed that Basil was the winner as a letter writer.[88] Scholars who denied this letter's authenticity raised another problem. Libanius's words ("I know that you will often write: 'Here, another Cappadocian is coming.' I think that you will send me many since you praise me always and everywhere") appeared to them as contradicting his statements in *Oration 62*.[89] One should take into account, however, that the words refer to a future eventuality and to a wish that might not have had anything to do with reality. Libanius, moreover, looked at the number of students from Cappadocia from the perspective of the much larger contingents from nearby regions. Attempts to augment artificially the number of Cappadocians

---

[85] Celsus 3/i and Firminus 3/ii. The abundance of proper names and historical situations is in itself a mark of authenticity.

[86] Pouchet (1992, 160–62) argues that this letter should be regarded as two separate letters and that one letter, in which Basil presented Firminus, is missing. This is unnecessary because there are some long letters of Libanius that cover several subjects, and Firminus might not have been introduced by Basil (or not necessarily through a letter), who nevertheless took an interest in him, as a Cappadocian.

[87] See **159** and **160**. On Libanius defeated by Acacius, see above, Chapter One. The mention of Alypius 4 and his uncle Hierocles 3 and of the stingy teachers of the past (probably an allusion to Ulpianus, cf. above, *Or.* 36.10, Chapter One) might be evidence in favor of this letter's authenticity.

[88] See Kugener 1903, 13. The Greek text is lost, and only a few Greek words survive in the Syriac translation. On the reliability of Zacharias as a historian, see E. Honigmann, *Patristic Studies* (Vatican, 1953), 197–98; O. Bardenhewer, *Geschichte der altkirchlichen Literatur 5* (Freiburg i. Br., 1932), 112–16.

[89] Laube (1913, 36) denied the letter's authenticity because of this.

known from Libanius's correspondence in order to make the letter and the speech agree are misguided. The twelve students included by Paul Petit as Cappadocians must be scaled back to eight, not a large group and a size that justifies Libanius's remark.[90]

The last point deserves to be clarified in some detail, since this will also shed some light on aspects of recruitment. Four young men—the two sons of Philippus, Marcus, and Letoius vi—need to be removed from the list of students from Cappadocia who regularly attended Libanius's classes. In 364, Libanius sent a letter to the rhetor and poet Philippus complimenting him as "a cicada who must show something ancient or fashion something new."[91] This fellow student of Libanius, who possibly followed Julian to Antioch, had taken advantage of this occasion to give recitals from his poems, at the same time bringing his sons to school. Fearing the reaction after Julian's death, Philippus had quickly withdrawn his sons, causing a cooling of his relationship with Libanius. He protested that the sophist wronged him by not writing to him afterward, without thinking that he had annoyed Libanius and that, "by bringing his sons and quickly taking them back, he had wronged both them and himself" (*Ep.* 1223). The sons of Philippus, who attended the school for such a short time, cannot be counted as regular students.

The other two young men included incorrectly among Cappadocian students were Marcus and Letoius, who had only an indirect connection with that region. On leaving Libanius's school after less than a year, Marcus went to Cappadocia simply because his father Acacius had a post there at the time. Libanius thought he could continue his training in rhetoric in that province under the guidance of Palladius, one of those who practiced "the art of Hermes."[92] Likewise, Letoius vi, acting as a recruiter, brought to Antioch two students from Cappadocia, but he seems to have had a transitory connection with the region. He came to Libanius from Pamphylia and learned some rhetoric there under the tutelage of Argeius.[93]

"Don't I know my students?" Libanius contended in a speech at the end of his life. "Don't I know their fathers and where they come from, their

---

[90] Petit 1956a, 119. His figures are consequently accepted by Van Dam (2002, 61).

[91] *Ep.* 1223 (B104); cf. also *Ep.* 1425 from an earlier period. Philippus 3 (cf. below, Chapter Five) was possibly identical with the rhetor who was friendly with Julian. Wiemer (1995a, 50 n. 181) suggests that he was the poet mentioned in Libanius's *Ep.* 779.2 who followed the emperor to Antioch, where he recited his poems. On his relation with Julian, see Van Dam 2002, 174–75.

[92] See letter **139**, Acacius 8.

[93] See letters **129**, **130**, and **131**, from the same year 391. Seeck (1906, 251) thinks that all of these young men went to Libanius through the agency of his friend Quirinus iv, probably also a Pamphylian.

names and situations, and who has money and who does not?"[94] He surely did, and this knowledge was a fundamental basis for his recruitment.

A CIRCLE OF ALUMNI

Former students and their families and friends were of paramount importance in advertising the value of an education under the tutelage of Libanius. Alumni (*hoi tou phoitan apēllagmenoi*) occasionally got together to remember the old times, and a stiff remark of Libanius allows us a glimpse at these reunions.[95] Reacting with indignation at a nasty prank at the expense of a certain pedagogue, Libanius commented acidly that the guilty students would have been unable to boast about it even in those jolly gatherings, when people recounted the school enterprises of the past. School reunions, probably more exuberant than Libanius allowed, must have taken place among former students living near each other. As a rule, however, contacts between Libanius and alumni and among ex-students themselves were maintained through a well-orchestrated correspondence.[96]

Today, keeping alumni connected to an institution requires no less effort, but in the United States, the task is achieved through a variety of means. Besides regular mail, e-mail solicitations, newsletters, and technologies such as the establishment of an online alumni community provide ways to interact with former students.[97] A college or university may also send its representatives periodically to various parts of the country to visit alumni and fundraise. Libanius's school did not have an institutional identity separate from the rhetor himself. Even though other teachers were involved, it was Libanius who fully embodied his institution. After traveling in his youth, he was mostly stationed in Antioch, delivered his orations there, and complained bitterly when he had to leave the city.[98] Regular fundraising was not one of his concerns, and he generally did not ask alumni to support the school financially. Like representatives of European institutions, he may have suffered to some degree from the "ivory tower syndrome," which recognized teaching and research as sacrosanct but dismissed as unseemly any request for money. But at the same

---

[94] *Or.* 4.14, written after 391.

[95] *Or.* 58.33, a late oration of reproof against some students guilty of tossing a certain pedagogue up and down in a blanket.

[96] On the epistolary network of Libanius, see Bradbury 2004b.

[97] Other means may consist of radio and newspaper ads and some television advertising.

[98] Cf. *Ep.* 802 (N98), written to Julian in 363, when Libanius was almost fifty years old. He initially accompanied the emperor, who was leaving for Persia, but found that short journey almost unbearable.

time, his students, mostly from the upper class, could afford to pay the tuition, and only on occasion did Libanius look for donors who would give some financial aid to a needy pupil.[99]

In spite of many diverse modern resources, direct-mail marketing is still one the most effective strategies modern institutions use to keep alumni connected and to recruit new students. Libanius relied exclusively on this means of communication. Most of the letters he wrote were geared toward maintaining a healthy alumni community through which he could provide employment and connections to young men just out of school, as well as look for potential supporters and new students.[100] Libanius was well aware that the degree to which alumni identify with and feel loyal to their school depends on the extent to which they are nurtured by their alma mater. Consequently, he did not spare efforts to foster the individual members of his community, which spread out over several provinces. He wrote letters constantly throughout the year, but in the summer he had to devote particular attention to that task and felt himself the target of the incessant requests of people who knew that he was free from teaching and took advantage of what they called his "leisure" (*scholē*). Libanius felt enveloped by a thick cloud of things to do—a Homeric cloud, naturally.[101] In composing letters, he mostly avoided formulaic expressions and themes, but crafted each one artfully. Each letter had to represent the cultural values he embodied.

But writing a letter to keep channels of communication open was only the first step. As today, any written solicitation must be read to be successful. Libanius's letters were sometimes ignored, a fact that can be attributed only in part to the erratic state of mail delivery in antiquity.[102] The words he wrote to a student's father, "Are you going to avoid my letter, too, and will you throw it away on finding the name of the sender?" acknowledge an unpleasant reality (**65**). The querulous accusations that he often leveled against his ex-students ("I taught you how to write, but you are silent")[103] show the difficulties he encountered in keeping alive old ties. One suspects that his desire for frequent communications may have been thwarted by the requirements of style his students felt they needed to observe.[104] An alumnus's return letter was no simple endeavor

---

[99] Cf. below, Chapter Six.

[100] On the social role of his correspondence in general, see Cabouret 2001.

[101] See *Ep*. 650 (B152), written in 361 to his dear friend Fortunatianus 1. The image of the rock covered by a continuous cloud refers to *Odyssey* 12.73.

[102] For high officials ignoring his letters, see *Epp*. 558 and 604, and Brown 1992, 46–47 and n. 59. In *Ep*. 185.3 (B42), Libanius dismisses impatiently all possible excuses for ignoring his pleas.

[103] See, e.g., **99**, written to Hyperechius, a former student who sent his son to his school.

[104] See below, Chapter Five.

but had to echo beautifully the sender's message. One never ceased to be a student of Libanius.

The types of people who responded to Libanius's calls are the same that can be identified as givers and supporters of modern institutions. The Procopius, governor of Cilicia, who provided some sort of financial aid to the needy student Dionysius is a fitting representative of the category of wealthy philanthropists who felt an obligation to be generous.[105] Dionysius himself might embody the figure of the debtor, with a sense of obligation toward his school. Libanius actively supported him in all occasions, and gratitude turned Dionysius into an energetic recruiter who repeatedly exerted himself in trying to persuade a reluctant father to give his sons to Libanius. "I marvel," Libanius wrote after the boys finally came, "that, with all your eloquence, you drove out [this father's] fear slowly and did not persuade him to be confident right away."[106]

In all times, the best method for a community of alumni to grow is evangelism. The enthusiast who passionately believes in an institution enlists the most friends. Libanius had many such students, and this was his strength. Aetius, for example, who "never fussed over anything for gain but who would take any pains for a good cause," was an ideal recruiter.[107] He passionately promoted Libanius's school by persuading young men to leave Ancyra, even though he never gave them accompanying letters for his mentor. "Are you trying to spare papyrus and ink?" wrote back a grateful Libanius, somewhat dryly. He needed the enthusiasm of such supporters, particularly in his late, difficult years, even though a natural restraint made him shrink from what he considered exaggerated praise. His student Heracleius had always behaved like a "lover" with him, but in the 390s, his raving commendations of Libanius's peerless eloquence embarrassed the teacher, who (modestly) declared that "this god to whom the bow and the torch belong often forces us to think of the ugly as beautiful."[108] Another energetic supporter was his ex-student Severinus, who "fought battles" against those who slandered Libanius's teaching, repaying him with deeds that "Hermes and the Muses saw."[109] In those dark years, he gratefully acknowledged the goodwill of the governor Factinianus, who sent him his son, considering "his writing a blessed thing." Libanius uttered a cry of triumph with him: "This is like shouting to all

---

[105] See 53, a masterful letter. On Dionysius, see below, Chapter Seven.

[106] See 67, written a few years after Dionysius left school. Eumathius apparently considered Libanius harsh and stiff.

[107] Aetius ii, a recommendation for his good character, *Ep.* 674. See also *Epp.* 733 and 769, where he appears as helping Libanius but refraining from writing to him.

[108] See *Epp.* 1002 (N176) and 993.

[109] See *Ep.* 980; see also 879.

men: 'Fathers, send your dear sons to an old man, who still knows how to work hard, and let neither distance nor the sea keep you away'" (**130**). We have seen, however, that the boundaries of his students' world were shrinking and drawing ever closer to home.

A NETWORK OF FRIENDS

In the fifth century B.C.E., the orator Lysias, after dismissing the possibility that two of his characters might have been related by kinship, proceeded to show that they did not even share the strong ties of a common upbringing, that is, they were not *ek paideias philoi*.[110] In this text, the meaning of *paideia* is not yet confined to the later meaning of "culture and education acquired through schooling."[111] In later centuries, the old bonds created by a common cultural environment remained the strongest, and Libanius relied on them to cement relationships and bridge the distance between himself and his sources for recruitment.

An inquiry on ties of *philia* in Libanius is not bound to reveal a uniform set of feelings and obligations. Friendship, even when confined to a specific area and period, remains an overdetermined concept with shades of meaning, from a spontaneous, unselfish relationship to a social bond with its own code of behavior.[112] We have seen above that Libanius dismissed as manifestations of an inferior *philia* those utilitarian, transitory bonds born out of social intercourse that allowed career advancement. False friends were everywhere, and one had to stay on guard. Many people who drank together "would happily drink each other's blood."[113] Yet we have seen that Libanius also indulged some ephemeral contacts camouflaged as friendships or, worse, addressed and flattered some people as friends in his letters while attacking them as fierce enemies in his discourses.[114] Notwithstanding the diversity of format, there is no denying that he was a man of contradictions. But as a man with great capacity to love as well as to grieve and inveigh, he also enjoyed intimate friendships, which often originated from his studies and were always centered on a common passion for learning. *Philia* could sometimes be for him "a carefully nurtured art of friendship,"[115] but often it was a deeply felt bond.

[110] Lysias 20.11.
[111] See Cribiore 2001, 243–44.
[112] Cf. Konstan 1997, 1–23.
[113] *Ep.* 119.9 (B132).
[114] Cf. above, Introduction and Chapter One.
[115] So Brown 1992, 45. One could say what Libanius said about a dear friend, that he himself "practiced (*meletan*) friendship"; see *Ep.* 33 (N37.3).

It is curious that the *Autobiography* discloses the many frustrations of Libanius's student life in Athens but is silent about the strong relationships he established with other students, which resurface in letters written over the course of his life. There is, however, a single exception. Inborn eloquence and modesty were bound to make a friend of his fellow student Crispinus. Their connection was revealed at the end of their studies, when Libanius followed him in a tour of oratorical display. Friendship, he said, was the main motivation of his decision and made him overcome his hesitation over leaving Athens (*Or.* 1.27–28). As he looked back upon that event, Libanius recognized its pivotal importance in his life (*Or.* 1.34). The course of his career (*schēma*), both as a teacher and as an orator, derived from that single, momentous decision to be the friend and ally of a fellow student. Because of this, Libanius ventured out of what was at the time a comfortable position.

In the narrative of his life, Libanius acknowledges that the period he spent in Nicomedia surpassed every other in happiness. Frequent, triumphant declamations accompanied sure success as a teacher, represented by what he calls "chains" (*hormathoi*) of students, a word that suggests pupils linked to each other by a common discipline and by the various connections that influenced their enrollment (*Or.* 1.51). "The possession of true friends is the greatest beginning of all happiness," Libanius wrote (*Or.* 1.56), comparing the friendships he found in Nicomedia with examples from Euripides and Homer.[116] This passage not only "parade[s] the classical virtue of friendship" in the attempt to respond to criticism caused by his absence from Antioch,[117] but also refers to long-lasting bonds of affection. In the same way, the literary texture of *Oration 8, On Poverty*, which celebrates the value of friendship, effaces neither the warmth of feelings for, nor the assistance from, the true friends Libanius had lost over the years. Rich in friends, he could say with Xenophon that "he could see with many eyes, hear with many ears, and use many hands and whole bodies" through the advice and help he received from his friends (*Or.* 8.7).[118] The rich man who had few friends was both rich and poor, as was the wealthy man deprived of culture (*Or.* 8.12–13). The two motifs are not juxtaposed by chance in this oration. In Libanius, friendship could not be conceived of outside of the *logoi*.

Paul Petit has shown that the term *hetairos* ("companion") might designate a student, a political partisan, or the member of a religious group.[119]

---

[116] Euripides *Or.* 1155–57; Homer *Iliad* 18.79–93.

[117] So Norman 1965, 163.

[118] Cf. Xenophon *Mem.* 2.4.7. Orations on friendship were part of the repertoire of a sophist, cf. Themistius and *Or.* 22.

[119] Petit (1956a, 36–40), who looked at this term as a helpful designation in establishing the list of students.

For Libanius, "companions" were the links in the complex network he used for recruitment: ex-students and their families and friends, his own schoolmates, other teachers of grammar and rhetoric with whom he was on friendly terms, and the educated people who believed that his teaching still imparted a valuable message. Choices in matters of religion did not play a fundamental role in identifying a *hetairos* because they could be circumvented by *paideia*. In defining the quality of the bond between *hetairoi*, Aristotle likened it to that between brothers, based on a commonality of tastes and character and equality of station and age. *Hetairoi* were like brothers who had been brought up together and educated in the same way.[120] But whereas education was the common bond among Libanius's "companions," status and age were not essential.

Friendship, affection, and trust were fundamental in the relations between teachers and students. In addition to the many places where Libanius manifested affection toward his students and called them his children,[121] a single passage starkly notes the fracture of those bonds. In a late oration, Libanius reveals the alarming proportion of students defecting, a phenomenon that supposedly had been quite exceptional in his school days. Those students guilty of disloyalty to their teacher acquired a tarnished reputation and were abandoned by their friends because their behavior signified that "they did not know the meaning of friendship."[122] The sophist Himerius, too, with his customary overflowing rhetoric, inveighed against those students who dared to spend even a single day away from their teacher's *philia* and who found something "sweeter than his tongue."[123] The *philia* between a teacher and a student was similar to the bond Aristotle saw between a father and his child: although a teacher was not responsible for a youth's existence, he was nonetheless the source of his upbringing and education.[124] But the rapport of *philia* between teacher and pupil, which was somewhat unbalanced during the years of study, reached a degree of equality when, at the end of schooling, a student automatically became part of the network used for recruitment.

Prosopographical inquiries have disclosed the rich texture of relations that were at the heart of Libanius's recruitment in each region. But whereas elements such as social origin or religious affiliation had some weight, bonds of friendship cemented by a common cultural upbringing

---

[120] Aristotle, e.g., *Eth. Nic.* 8.5.3, 1157b23–25; 8.12, 1161b35–1162a15. Cf. Konstan 1997, 67–78.
[121] On this, see below, Chapter Five.
[122] *Or.* 43.8. On defections, see below, Chapter Six.
[123] Himerius *Or.* 54.1.
[124] Aristotle *Eth. Nic.* 8.11, 1161a16–19. On unequal friendship, see Konstan 1996, 74–78.

were the equalizer. On his return to Antioch for his *dokimasia*, Libanius remarked on his pleasure in seeing again the "bands" (*ethnoi*) of school friends he had left behind. Some had become governors, others were advocates, and the city derived its strength from the number of its cultivated people. In each of the other provinces from which he enlisted students, Libanius found support in old schoolmates from Antioch and Athens and their friends, in addition to his own former students. It is only by keeping in mind the tenacity of this "old boys"' network that one can explain the apparent anomalies of recruitment region-by-region and the discrepancies in the students' social status and religious preferences. Thus the predominantly Christian student population from a province such as Cappadocia needs to take into account as recruiters Basil and Amphilochius, a fellow student of Libanius in Athens.[125] By supporting one of their own, school fellows appropriated Libanius's success, aggrandized themselves, and hinted that they would be equally great in the same situation. So Libanius remarked to Ecdicius, who constantly persuaded students to "run" to Antioch and dedicated his life to advancing the cause of friends, "You know that, if I look brilliant, you, too, have a good reputation, and if I do not seem too bad a teacher, this would also profit you, in case you choose to teach. People are not unaware of our common studies in Athens" (**198**). Another letter to the same friend, who had just sent him more students, eloquently started, "A friend's children have come to a friend through a friend" (**204**). This was the essence of Libanius's recruitment.

---

[125] Amphilochius 2.

CHAPTER FOUR

Admission and Evaluation

WE ARE NOW entering the school of Libanius together with his students. In doing so, we will delve more into the letter dossiers, and rely less on the orations. This chapter will also serve as a commentary on some of the letters that appear bare and uninteresting at first glance but actually illuminate many aspects of ancient schooling.

Application and admission to Libanius's school seems to have been relatively simple when compared to the cumbersome process of modern college admission, yet much advanced preparation was necessary to establish contact between Libanius and his "companions" (*hetairoi*). In the case of families who were not from the immediate vicinity of Antioch, considerable correspondence, in the form of letters of presentation and application and acknowledgments of acceptance, was involved. Letters also provided the major channel of communication between the school and families, conveying information about a student's progress.

It should be emphasized that the letters Libanius exchanged with relatives, friends, and teachers testify to the existence of genres and subgenres that the ancient epistolary theorists did not mention specifically. When authors such as Ps.-Demetrius and Ps.-Libanius classified letters according to type, they were driven by a desire for symmetry and order, and were concentrating on tone and style, rather than on the occasion of the letters, thus generating rigid categories.[1] But the epistolary medium was flexible and adaptable to the circumstances of real life. Categorizing letters according to their function is not straightforward either, because of the refusal of most correspondence to perform a single communicative role; but in some cases among Libanius's letters (as in letters that responded to letters of application to his school or reported on a student's performance), a particular function does exercise a monopolizing effect. Besides pointing to new social and cultural aspects of ancient education, such letters reveal Libanius's criteria for accepting students and his standards

[1] On the collection of Ps.-Demetrius, see above, Introduction. Ps.-Libanius's collection was dated between the fourth and sixth centuries. See Valentin Weichert, ed., *Demetrii et Libanii qui feruntur ΤΥΠΟΙ ΕΠΙΣΤΟΛΙΚΟΙ et ΕΠΙΣΤΟΛΙΜΑΙΟΙ ΧΑΡΑΚΤΗΡΕΣ* (Leipzig, 1910); Libanius *Epistolary Styles* (Foerster 1903–27, vol. 9); Malherbe 1988. The letters of Cicero, which were genuine correspondence, and those of Pliny, which were revised for publication, show how narrow and limiting the criteria used for classification were.

of evaluation. This chapter will begin to pay close attention to questions regarding Libanius's fairness and competence as an educator that will reverberate throughout the book.

More than in what precedes, the focus is now on Libanius as head of a school and educator. Even though his position as official sophist of Antioch was never in jeopardy, the letters testify to his constant struggle to increase the number of his students and attract the offspring of the best families of the Roman East. Higher education was generally viewed in a negative light in antiquity (and, indeed, until very recently) because of its inequality and elitism: beyond the elementary stages, it reached only boys of the upper classes. Libanius occasionally protested that his revenues were limited because many of his students were poor (*Ep.* 340), and the letters reveal some cases of orphans who needed financial support to pursue their studies,[2] but the majority of his students came from the top social and economic echelons.

Yet, it is instructive to consider as a comparison that today much inequality still exists in the principles for admission to the top American universities. We pride ourselves on the idea that this system of higher education is based on a multitude of private and public institutions that are meritocracies, to which students have access because of their efforts and talents and not because of the advantages of their birth. Yet doubts have emerged about this grand fiction of contemporary education.[3] Top colleges, which have become more diverse through some representation of racial minorities and by drawing from a broader geographic base, nevertheless show that class more than race is the organizing principle of higher education.[4] For students admitted to the most prestigious private institutions and to the most select state universities, class background (that is, parents' income, occupation, and education) is the most fundamental factor. In this respect, similar principles applied to the school of Libanius.

Application

The application to an ancient institution of higher learning was generally made in writing: private letters of relatives and friends paved the way to entrance. Libanius stiffly reminded a father, who sent his sons without a

---

[2] Dionysius, for example.

[3] Cf. e.g., Sacks 2003; Michaels 2004; and Leonhardt 2004. See also Steinberg 2003.

[4] Besides having the ability to pay tuition that continues to increase, upper-class students can afford summer programs, preparation classes for entrance examinations, and sometimes private admission counselors.

letter of introduction because he trusted Libanius's familiarity with the people of his city, that there was a "custom for recommendations" (*nomos prosrēseōs*) that dictated that a student's application be carefully orchestrated (**168**). Exceptions to this convention were rare. Students might arrive at school in the company of relatives or acquaintances who could vouch for their family's worth. A father accompanied a son to Antioch and brought along other children in the hope that they would be inspired by rhetoric (**75**);[5] a widowed mother undertook the long, perilous journey from Armenia in order to "take care of things at the beginning" for her son (**128**). When the relations between a family and Libanius were distant or tense, it was useful to find a suitable "ferryman" (*porthmeus*) to accompany the children and ingratiate them with the teacher. Letter **154** reveals some hostility toward an Armenian father, Olympius, which the good words of a governor and an ex-student escorting his children sought to dispel.[6] The escort was so cherished an alumnus that Libanius fervently declared that the children of an enemy brought by him would automatically become his friends.[7] Letters of introduction sent by ex-students gave Libanius the added pleasures of verifying that they were faithful to him and had not forgotten the principles of good prose-writing he had instilled. When a favorite student such as Hyperechius omitted writing a recommendation for three new recruits he sent (**111**) and for a relative who reached Antioch with three other letters, Libanius felt betrayed and complained vigorously.[8] Naturally, no letters of presentation were given when a young man went to Antioch against his family's wishes: for these students, a driving passion for rhetoric (in addition to a suitable family background) was the best introduction (**48** and **206**).

How many letters were supposed to precede or accompany a student's arrival in order to secure his entrance? Was one letter sufficient when a student belonged to an outstanding family? The documentation is not uniform. It appears that Libanius usually responded with a single letter of acceptance, only much more rarely replying to several letters. Yet the cases of students who were strongly supported by written introductions (as the letters Libanius wrote back to their recommenders indicate) show

---

[5] Cf. Philippus *Ep.* 1223. Achillius probably brought his son and then remained for a while (**1**). Agathius came with his older brother (**4**), but it is likely that letters preceded them.

[6] Petit (1956a, 134) suspects that Olympius was Christian, but this is not strictly necessary. Besides an escort, his sons had letters from him and from the governor Eutherius (cf. *Ep.* 269).

[7] Cf. also **162**, where a man takes his brother together with the sons of Philagrius, who had attended Acacius's school first. In **132**, a new student, Letoius vi, brings two more boys.

[8] Letter **116**, Eusebius xx. Cf. also Aetius (*Epp.* 733 and 769).

114 • Chapter Four

that three or four letters of application must have been the norm.⁹ Our perception is skewed by the fact that Libanius responded only to fathers or to those relatives who were primarily responsible for a youth and usually ignored other correspondents. His acknowledgment of letters from senders other than family members meant that he was most flattered to receive the student in question, or felt close to a recommender, or was indebted to a sophist who sent him students.

Even though requesting letters was to some degree the task of the aspiring student, who, before applying to study with Libanius, visited relatives and acquaintances who might be suitable recommenders (**111** and **116**), the student's family was a powerful presence in the background, and it is likely that fathers not only wrote their own letters, but also solicited them from others. Caesarius of Armenia, for example, must have personally engineered an effective application for his sons, who were "guilty" of having first attended the classes of another rhetor. The Iphicrates who wrote a letter for them disclosed Caesarius's fears that Libanius might be ill-disposed toward the newcomers (**35**).

Fathers were able and practical letter-writers. They urged acceptance (**130**), sent appealing messages evoking memories of their own studies in Athens with Libanius and of happy periods spent in his company (**1**), and tried to mollify him by criticizing other sophists in Antioch to whom they had first entrusted their sons (**165**). In normal circumstances, sophists who had imparted the first knowledge of rhetoric to a student when he was still home became automatic allies of a family. The poet and rhetor Acacius, like the student Gaius and his relatives, lived in Cilicia, and it was with Acacius that Gaius "participated in the sacred rites" of rhetoric for a short time (**86**). Being in Antioch to visit his son Titianus, Acacius manifested his personal affection for Gaius and disclosed how much his parents loved this boy, so that "his mother took him up to the border and parted from him with difficulty" (**85**). Libanius found the detail so appealing (in addition to the recommendations of Acacius and of the boy's father and uncle, naturally) that he protested his full commitment and declared himself to be Gaius's "fourth father" (**86**).

Recommendations from previous teachers were desirable when a boy had lost his father. Since a mother was apparently not an acceptable recommender,¹⁰ it was customary to enlist all other possible writers. Male relatives represented the family. Zenodotus, a grandfather, wrote a letter for his grandson, but Libanius regretted that the student's late father, who

---

⁹ Students introduced by many letters are Eusebius xx, Gaius ii, and Letoius vi, who did not need more recommendations than others since their families were eminent.

¹⁰ There are no instances of letters written by mothers, even though some of them may have possessed a good education.

had attended his school, would not bring him himself, "just as an athlete brings his son to the same trainer" (**133**). Doubtless a student such as Eusebius xx, whom Libanius had held in his arms when he was a baby and who came from a prestigious family of Ancyra, did not need much introduction. Yet his three uncles—Strategius and Albanius (who had studied with Libanius), and Olympius—wrote letters of presentation for him (**75** and **76**), and Androcles, his first teacher of rhetoric, added his own, which generated an obsequious epistolary exchange (**77**).[11] Androcles commended Libanius by saying that he was sending Eusebius to a Phidias who would mold him, a comparison not very original but flattering, which the sophist Himerius applied several times to himself.[12] Libanius in turn lauded the clarity, inventiveness, and style of Androcles' brief but striking letter, which was the product of "a good craftsman of discourses." There was no standardized format, style, or length for letters of presentation, but each correspondent brought his original contribution, and a short but elegant message was appreciated.

It is not surprising that cordiality informed the rapport of Libanius with those teachers who brought him students.[13] In his letter on behalf of Letoius, the Pamphylian sophist Argeius had underlined the superiority of Libanius's teaching. Libanius promptly declined the compliment and insisted on the equivalence of their two springs of learning (**129**). The letter of Argeius was written so masterfully, he declared, that it should have convinced Letoius not to sail anywhere else because he was getting a more than adequate instruction at home. Yet a teacher's recommendation might bring some displeasure. A touch of envy surfaces in the words of another sophist who saw a source of revenue escape to Antioch. The beginning of Libanius's *Ep.* 340 to the teacher Aresius, which also concerns another matter, deserves to be quoted:

> Your nurslings are excellent, and you sent us a gift, though not of gold, which you say my feast has provided in abundance. And yet it is not much: many are the poor. I think that to take from those who are not rich is like stripping a corpse. But let us assume that it is a lot, such as the river gave to the king of the Lydians and, if you wish, more beautiful than gold from Colophon—how can it be like the sons of Hierius, your students? He begot them good at learning rhetoric, but you put some rhetoric into them.

Aresius of Cilicia, probably reluctant to lose three students, had ironically emphasized the munificence of his gift to Libanius. Libanius's annoyance

---

[11] On Androcles, see above, Chapter Two, and below, Chapter Five.

[12] Himerius *Or.* 64 and 68. Libanius called Acacius 7 a Phidias because he composed a marvelous speech on Asclepius, *Ep.* 1342.3 (B148).

[13] Cf. also Scylacius 2/ii, a teacher of law, who recommended a student (**119**).

can be detected from his quick denial of any handsome revenues derived from his teaching, but he soon regained his composure. The three new students, he said, were more precious than gold; and no wonder, since Aresius had taught them rhetoric!

Confidentiality was not an issue in letters of presentation, so that the sophist Argeius read his letter to the student who carried it, although the boy was still apparently unaware of its rhetorical beauty (**129**). When the recommender was a father, secrecy was even more out of the question. In a rush of enthusiasm, Libanius started to tell the son of Parnasius about the cherished memories of school days he shared with his father, but the newly arrived student cut him off, saying that the story was well known to him and everything was written in the letter (**1**). Lack of privacy characterized most ancient correspondence, and a carrier was often charged with supplementing the content of a message, even when it did not concern him directly.[14] The fact that Libanius's replies to letters of introduction never allude to the student who is applying unless he has met him in person may be an indication that letters of application glided somewhat over a student's qualifications and concentrated on other matters. Previous study under a grammarian did not provide a young man with a formal transcript that a family could produce as part of the procedure for admission. Libanius never acknowledged receipt of any recommendation written by a grammarian and attached some importance only to previous training in rhetoric.

A letter of application, which perhaps contained a few generalities about a student, focused on his extended family, social connections, and home city. Judging from his letters of acknowledgment, Libanius considered a family's nobility (*eugeneia*) and culture more important qualifications than material wealth. He strongly desired the offspring of certain families and triumphed when they finally arrived. His enthusiasm then was boundless: he applauded, crowned himself, and twined garlands for the gods.[15] The sons of a certain Hestiaeus were able to study in Antioch, even though Libanius had never made their father's acquaintance and the orphan children were in dire economic straits (**92**). His ties of affection with the family, however, were strong because he had gone to school with the students' uncles and was on intimate terms with their grandfather. His reply to a friend who had recommended two new students significantly

---

[14] Carriers did not relay information mechanically. On carriers of Christian letters living with the community afterward and becoming part of its spiritual life, see Conybeare 2000, 31–40. On lack of privacy in medieval letters also caused by the state of literacy, see Constable 1976, 11.

[15] See **176** and *Ep.* 735 (B127). At other times, he indicates that he had expected a student impatiently, e.g., **133**.

highlights his main criteria for admission. He wrote: "Right away I was pleased with them because of their father and also, when some time passed, because of their natural talents" (**204**). Recognizable family features confirmed that a student was the latest ring of a family chain that included prominent forebears (**36**). "We are trying to make your son quite like his grandfather and uncle and such as will bring credit to his father," he wrote solemnly to a parent (**41**).[16]

Geographical origin also was a reason for acceptance, particularly when Libanius had triumphed in a city and felt the obligation to nurture one of its sons. In a late oration (62.6), he declared that a teacher's failure to produce worthy citizens because of incompetence or bad judgment had to be regarded as conscious deceit of and irreparable injury to that city. A letter of acknowledgment such as the one he sent a father underlines many elements (**4**): *Paideia*, says Libanius, was a necessity for this family, which had to preserve the good reputation for learning that the grandfather had acquired.[17] Among the reasons Libanius gladly accepted the newcomer were the boy's father and uncles, and the city of Ancyra, to which he was grateful. This city is at the center of another letter that replied to the orphan Eusebius's maternal uncle (**76**).[18] In a curious geographical tour of obligations, Libanius acknowledged first his desire to please the province as a whole (Galatia), next zeroed in on Ancyra, which he valued more than other cities, and finally focused on the student's family living there.

STUDENTS ARRIVE

Students came to the school in the fall, or sometimes in the middle of the school year. They probably lodged with acquaintances or rented some rooms in the city.[19] The idea that Libanius put up some of them in his house is not supported by facts,[20] and the supposition that students were guests in some local inns (*pandokeia*) is also unlikely, particularly because of the common Late Antique association of these hostels with low moral-

---

[16] Cf. also **1** and **86**, which point to the culture of family members.

[17] The mention of *sophia* ("wisdom") may allude to the fact that Agathius's grandfather (and not his father, as in B160) was a philosopher; cf. Cribiore 2004. The word, however, which is relatively common in inscriptions (see Puech 2002, 15 and 238–39), may simply point to the excellent learning of a person.

[18] It is possible that Libanius was not very close to him.

[19] Cf. *Ep.* 25 (N36) below, Chapter Five: these students had neighbors. On students lodging with friends in Egypt, see Cribiore 2001, 115–17.

[20] See Petit 1956a, 145–46. The letters that Petit cites do not support his idea, and letter **9** shows only that Strategius was a sort of graduate student assistant.

ity and crime.²¹ Those from far away were always accompanied by pedagogues who supervised them, were glued to them like "shadows," warded off enemies like "dogs," and protected them as securely as "a chamber of Danaë."²² As Libanius and Philostratus show, pedagogues were present at the delivery of special declamations, but it is unclear whether they participated further.²³ The presence of these attendants at the side of the Antiochene students was probably mandatory as well, and Libanius's son Cimon in fact had a slave pedagogue.²⁴ A passage in a late oration actually indicates that families that lived nearby did not entirely relinquish their supervision but maintained some direct control over their offspring, so that students rehearsed speeches with their fathers for several days in a row (*Or.* 3.17). Pedagogues derived their authority from fathers and were "powerless" in case a student was an orphan, as young Libanius was (*Or.* 1.12). But if a young man was motivated, a tutor was less necessary because "love of rhetoric would suffice [a] lad for a pedagogue" (**192**).²⁵

Naturally, there were good and bad pedagogues, and both kinds appear in Libanius's writings. When tutors acquire a name and a distinct identity in his correspondence, they almost invariably appear as a positive presence.²⁶ They are kind, conscientious, learned, and gladly perform a job that is beneath their actual capacities (**177, 2**, and **163**). They act like doctors, healing their wards' physical diseases and the mental distress a family might undergo upon hearing calumnies against Libanius (**18** and **19**). They contribute highly to a student's success, particularly when motivation and self-discipline are lacking (**47**), and they deserve gratitude and adequate compensation. Libanius even goes to the unusual extent of reproaching two of his favorite students (the "Dioscuri" Apolinarius and Gemellus, who are always mentioned together) for "throwing away" their pedagogue and ungratefully leaving him in Antioch after completing their education (**20**).

Unflattering portraits of individual pedagogues are rare in the letters. Where are those meddling pedagogues Libanius encountered in his first

---

²¹ Festugière (1959, 110 n. 1) interprets in this sense *Or.* 25.48, but the passage only means that Libanius wants to have a good reputation with people who come to the city. On *pandokeia* and their bad reputation (at least in literature), see Remie Constable 2003, 11–39.

²² See **192** and **20**, *Or.* 34.29. On the role of pedagogues, see Cribiore 2001, 47–50.

²³ See Libanius *Or.* 34; Philostratus *VS* 2.21, 604: students sit in groups, and pedagogues sit in the middle in order to prevent noise and jeering.

²⁴ *Ep.* 734 (B155). The pedagogue was a gift of Seleucus 1, who sent Libanius other slaves, too.

²⁵ Cf. **103**, where the desire for excellence is like a pedagogue for Honoratus.

²⁶ See, however, the portrait of the violent pedagogue who beat his student like a sailor beating the sea, **183**; and the pedagogue who gave bad advice in **100**.

years in Antioch and considered representative of a whole dark category of individuals whose power derived from "selling students"?[27] Where are those odious tutors to whom he later confessed that a teacher had to defer and whose favor he needed to win by money or special treatment?[28] Libanius composed *Oration* 34 to respond to the slanders of a certain pedagogue, who seems to function as the voice of an offensive category of employees of lower social status; he did not leave any traces in the letters. Two conclusions suggest themselves—and they can be verified for other matters, too. Libanius considered speeches a more suitable (and sheltered) vehicle for his vituperations and did not mind lashing out against people who were less distinguishable for their individual traits; but he might also have avoided communicating with families on this and other unpleasant subjects. The voice of the sophist from distant Antioch had to assuage parents' preoccupations and not alert them about trouble.

It is no surprise that the interpretation pedagogues gave of their authority and responsibilities might be extreme. Comparative evidence suggests that this was a common difficulty when students resided away from home without receiving parental visits. When the sons of Johann Amerbach went to study at the University of Paris in 1501, their father put them under the supervision of a man whose basic functions were to watch over and discipline them, handle their finances, and place them in the care of a teacher. The correspondence of the printer with his children and this attendant reveals a progressive deterioration of the situation and abuses of authority that led to deception, poor academic results, and plenty of frustration.[29] Yet this tutor's letters to Amerbach were reassuring, smooth messages that kept him in the dark. Even though no ancient correspondence between pedagogues and families has survived, these sixteenth-century letters alert us to the possibility of similar occurrences.[30] Parents were left in ignorance, and Libanius's letters were meant to remedy the lack of information only to a small degree.

For his sons' sake, Amerbach also tried to establish a small network of business and personal acquaintances on which they could rely, but this support system was impotent in the face of their tutor's manipulations. Fourth-century parents made similar attempts, and a few examples of friends and relatives keeping an eye on Libanius's students emerge from

---

[27] *Ep.* 405.8.
[28] *Or.* 43.9. See also *Or.* 25.47.
[29] See, e.g., Halporn 2000, 155–57, letter 100. It is hardly believable that, in spite of Amerbach's protests, this attendant succeeded in keeping the two students with an inferior teacher, with whom they wasted time and money and learned little.
[30] The pedagogue Dositheus was probably one of those who kept in close touch, **163**.

the letters.³¹ Most significant is the dossier of the son of Stratonicus of Euphratensis. The lack of a good education, for which this father excused himself, may have augmented his anxiety. A capable pedagogue took care of his son during the single year he attended the school (**177**), but a family friend also made sure to verify that he was learning, tested his knowledge of Homeric verses, and made a complete report to the father. In addition, a fellow citizen of Stratonicus monitored the young man's behavior and social life with such diligence that he deserved some financial compensation (**179**).

In the fourth century, most fathers apparently behaved like Johann Amerbach, who never visited his sons at school during their five years of attendance and attempted to check on their progress from afar. In Libanius's correspondence, the references to students' and parents' personal contacts are quite limited. The examples of close supervision provided by fathers such as Achillius and Acacius, who visited often or repeatedly recalled their sons, are counterbalanced by the much more frequent occurrences of parents who dealt with difficulties through writing, declining Libanius's invitations to come to Antioch.³²

First Meeting: The Diagnostic

Distances and the fact that there was no uncertainty in their decision kept the students who resided far away from visiting the school beforehand. When Libanius met them for the first time, his delight in noticing physical resemblances to other family members is palpable. One feels that his school was crowded not only with students but with their relatives as well, or with their shadows. "I saw you in your sons: so many of your physical traits have come to them," he wrote to a father (**173**). He reported to another that his son was like him in "appearance, deportment, way of walking" (**176**). He scrutinized the physical features of a youth in search of common family traits,³³ but his acute sense of observation and some humor might betray him. A father shared with his son an imposing

---

³¹ See Julianus viii, who urged his nephew Calycius on because the student's father asked him to, **187**. See also **107** and **91**. In *Ep.* 647 (N78), Basil visits students from Cappadocia studying in Antioch.

³² For Achillius, see **1** and **3**; Festugière (1959, 439 n. 1) suspected that he was the omnipresent father who acted as a pedagogue in *Or.* 55.28. Titianus's and Gaius ii's dossiers show that Acacius 7/iii visited Antioch (**86**) and often recalled his son home. Another father willing to visit his son was Macarius (**135**). Libanius repeatedly (but in vain) invited Heortius (**181** and **182**), but rejoiced with Philagrius because of an imminent visit (*Ep.* 176).

³³ See **36**. Cf. **143**, in which he found family resemblances in a student's gestures, movements, and voice.

Syrian nose, but even though, as Libanius wrote to him, "others consider the likeness of children to their fathers a blessing," the father took umbrage at some gauche comments of the sophist and threatened to withdraw the boy (**44**). Libanius's letter, with its pointed and slightly ironic Homeric references followed by a well-meant apology, is a masterpiece of savoir faire.

The variety in age, ability, and preparation of the newcomers rendered necessary the equivalent of a diagnostic, which Libanius administered personally.[34] Letter **119** shows most clearly the sequence of steps involved in meeting a new student. After remarking with pleasure the physical resemblance of the son of Julianus to his father (something Libanius found charming "not only in a human being but in a colt, a calf, a bird, and in all living things"), Libanius proceeded to "[test] his intellectual capacity" (*peira tēs dianoias*), which reassured him that the likeness was complete.[35] We can only guess at the content of this "trial," which may have consisted of giving the pupil some directions to follow, ascertaining his linguistic ability in the oral and written register, and perhaps presenting him with some conundrums of logic. In letter **1**, Libanius used a different terminology to describe the same procedure. He had to "examine" the youth, that is, literally, to "prove by ringing" (*diakōdōnizein*) that the novice was of real value and not a pale, counterfeit copy of the brilliant father Libanius knew from his school days. By "testing his nature," that is, "applying a touchstone" (*prosagein basanon*) to his natural talent (*physis*), he found in him predisposition to the new studies.[36] The phrase Libanius used, saying that the youth's nature was "quick to grasp the principles of rhetoric," had a solemn, poetic ring that doubly pleased this father.[37]

The preliminary evaluation of a newcomer addressed his readiness for rhetoric. Thus, after meeting them, Libanius concluded that the son of Parnasius was "fit" (*epitēdeios*) to take advantage of his teachings (**1**), and that Letoius was "ready to receive rhetoric" (*dynamenos*, **128**).[38] As another educator, Quintilian in first-century Rome, asserted, a teacher entrusted with a new student had to evaluate right away "his ability and his nature" (*ingenium et naturam*). Since Quintilian recognized memory and imitation as the most crucial preliminary talents to possess, he might

---

[34] Cf. Cribiore 2003, 15–16.

[35] The same term, *peira*, occurs in **38**. It does not refer specifically to an initial test but to a general evaluation. For the use of the term in letters of recommendation, see below, Chapter Seven.

[36] On the *topos* of *physis* occurring in rhetoric, see Pernot 1993, 157–58.

[37] In the note ad loc., Foerster thought it could be a citation of a passage from Sophocles or Euripides.

[38] He thus forecasted that the newly arrived Agathius was going to be a stimulating student (**4**).

have examined his novices in these areas. The ability to distinguish students' qualities was the mark of a good teacher of rhetoric as well as of the gymnastic trainer, who had to test a boy in all ways as soon as he first entered a gymnasium. Only then could a teacher adapt his instruction to individual needs.[39]

In Antioch, the diagnostic test did not affect admission but functioned primarily as a placement test. Geographical distances and the regard he had for most families prevented Libanius from rejecting a newly arrived student (however incompetent).[40] It is likely that a student's knowledge of Homer and other poetic texts played a role in the preliminary evaluation of his capacities, since the poets were the protagonists of his future exercises. A young boy's ability to produce from memory passages from the orators duly impressed the sophist, who praised the son of Julianus because of the Demosthenes he had "stored up in his soul" (**119**); and he compared Julianus, who dismissed his son's preparation, to a farmer always greedy for more. Information on intellectual qualities and literary preparation converged so that a student could be assigned to an appropriate "group" (*symmoria*).

Remediation geared to instruct students in subjects not previously available to them or to give them more solid basic skills has a long tradition in modern education. The placement of students into small groups according to ability was Libanius's solution; thus the issue of remediation may have brought less frustration to him than to the modern college educator. The students who converged upon Antioch from many areas of the Roman East were the products of a rather uniform system of education that proceeded along mandatory tracks. Though students' academic levels might be different, their linguistic skills were the only relevant foundation. The ancient lack of requirements concerning mathematics, science, or history finds a suitable comparison in the preparation for admission to the first colonial colleges. Knowledge of classical languages (ability to write Latin prose and verse and to decline and conjugate Greek nouns and verbs) was the only requirement for admission to Harvard in 1636.[41] It took almost two centuries for new requirements to be added.

THE REPORTS

At the mercy of what their sons and pedagogues chose to disclose, parents demanded some verification. Libanius, burdened by school duties and

---

[39] Quintilian 1.3.1 and 2.8.1–3.

[40] No letter alludes to such an occurrence.

[41] Boyer (1987, 27–28), who cites Arthur Levine, *Handbook on Undergraduate Curriculum* (San Francisco, 1978), 540.

scholarly work, usually preferred to confine letter-writing to the summer, but reports to families had a priority over other correspondence.[42] It is possible that the urgency with which reports had to be compiled led to their limited length, since they are usually a short paragraph, unless they form a section of a longer letter. Parents insisted on getting information, and Libanius could not always keep up with their requests. A father finally received a report after the "many" letters he allegedly sent to Antioch (**2**), and another father's complaint of lack of news forced an old and sick Libanius to justify his silence by the "grief and tears" that oppressed him at that moment (**93**).

Fathers were the customary recipients of reports of progress, but other family members (uncles or grandfathers) received them when a student was an orphan or in case of a specific concern. The fatherless student Philoxenus, for instance, was the subject of three reports: one to a relative who had recommended that he should be admitted (**195**), and two more to his maternal uncle (**193** and **198**). No report was sent to his mother, even though she was actively involved in his education. Reports went occasionally to people outside of a boy's immediate family when they had shown a close interest in his education and had worked toward his acceptance.[43]

Parental need to receive information about academic progress can be verified in many times and environments, yet one should refrain from presenting a too-idyllic picture of family relations. Some parents did not take a close interest in their sons, or maintained some detachment, because they trusted the safety net built around them. Libanius's letters testify to the concerns of those parents who solicited close contacts with him but are almost silent about those who did not. The dossier of the student Themistius alerts us not only to the presence of fathers with a stand-offish attitude, but also to the chance of missing such cases. Libanius's close acquaintance with Themistius's father made him overcome his hesitations at "playing the busybody" by intruding in delicate matters.[44] Libanius astutely presented him with the pathetic portrayal of a student in tears and without books, yet of a respectful son who had simply surrendered to the evidence that his close-fisted father had forgotten him. Such behavior was not justified because Themistius's father was a wealthy man and did not need the contributions of friends to be able to send some money, but could well afford to "spend some of his possessions on the most valuable of his possessions." These were stinging words. No wonder this par-

---

[42] Cf. *Ep.* 650.

[43] Ecdicius ii received a thorough report concerning boys whom he sent to Antioch (**204**). Libanius never addressed reports to a boy's previous teacher, since that relationship was cut off.

[44] See *Ep.* 428 of the year 355 (N10).

ent avoided visiting Antioch and opted for less reliable but distant reports by mail (**181** and **182**).

As a rule, however, a host of families concerned with the welfare and academic results of their offspring emerge from Libanius's correspondence. Whatever their motivation—family pride, preoccupation with money and their students' future careers, or desire that their sons obtain the official sanction of *paideia*—these families were thirsty for communication. Centuries before, in Republican Rome, Cicero agonized over the studies of his son Marcus in Athens. With typical pride, he assured Marcus a lavish maintenance consistent with his own standing,[45] but then he demanded equivalent results, which were hard to come by. Marcus was in Athens in the company of a certain Bruttius, who never moved from his side, practiced Latin declamations with him, and was probably a sort of pedagogue.[46] Besides conducting a personal inspection of his son's letters in search of signs of linguistic improvement, Cicero was at the mercy of three channels of communication, exactly like the parents of Libanius's students: vague rumors, the often unreliable information provided by acquaintances who visited Athens, and academic reports sent by teachers.[47]

Cicero's response to his son's academic difficulties provides us with the authentic voice of an ancient parent who confronted a puzzling lack of information. *Mutatis mutandis*, it is of interest to the project at hand because we hear no direct voices of parents through Libanius's correspondence; they are always filtered through the sophist's point of view. Young Marcus studied rhetoric and philosophy in Athens. One of his teachers was Cratippus, who had brought with him from Mytilene some scholars who also taught the young man.[48] After scrutinizing the academic report he received from one of them, Cicero considered a visit to Athens imperative, for his son's sake, or, rather, as he said, for his own (*vel mea potius*). Cicero's friend Atticus, who had forwarded the letter to him, read it as a positive account of Marcus's performance, but the father thought otherwise. Anxiously weighing every word, Cicero concluded that the report was positive only on the surface, but that the teacher's comment that Marcus's performance was good "for the time being" (*quo modo nunc est*) revealed his fundamental lack of trust in the boy.[49]

---

[45] See, e.g., Cic. *Att.* 12.32.

[46] Cic. *Fam.* 16.21.4. Bonner (1977) considers Bruttius a friend.

[47] Inspecting Marcus's letters: *Att.* 14.7 and 15.16; rumors: *Fam.* 16.21.2; and friends' reports: *Fam.* 12.16, where Trebonius congratulates Cicero and reports that Marcus is devoted to his studies, modest, and popular with everybody. He is unable to see, however, that Marcus is also wasting much time.

[48] Leonides, the report's sender, was one of them, *Att.* 14.16 and *Fam.* 16.21.5. He was some sort of assistant teacher and not simply a tutor (as Bonner [1977, 93] calls him).

[49] *Att.* 14.16, "This is not the report of someone who is full of trust, but rather of one who is fearful" (*non est fidentis hoc testimonium, sed potius timentis*).

The report Cicero had received was probably a short communication between whose lines he had to read. In Libanius's correspondence, typical progress reports are brief and stand on their own, unless they are included in longer letters sent to addressees with whom he was particularly close. He often wrote, for example, to the poet and rhetor Acacius, whose literary tastes he shared. Acacius's son Titianus is not the protagonist of these letters, yet the remarks about him provide more details on his school progress than standard reports do. Thus *Ep.* 345 (N27) mentions the customary ingredients of a report, that is, natural endowments and work (*physis* and *ponos*), but also adds that Titianus has the swift enthusiasm of a racing horse, he does not need to be urged (or punished), and his work rouses the admiration of devotees of rhetoric. Likewise, **199** discloses the level this student has reached (rhetorical compositions, *meletai*) and his fast progress in learning, and **192** is a learned and gracious study of his alacrity as well as of the difficulties he will encounter in trying to surpass his father's competence.

Standard reports were self-sufficient communications that provided the necessary but unembellished information on a student's performance. Scholars have wondered how satisfying these messages could have been to families eager to know more.[50] How could a faraway parent rest contented with a few stilted remarks? It was, however, in the nature of reports to summarize a student's standing in school, offering an official verification of the various communications that reached families in other ways. Parents could thus show these reports around as objective proofs of their sons' performance.[51] The correspondence of Johann Amerbach again offers a suitable comparandum. The report he received in 1498 after his children's first year of Latin school reads much like those Libanius sent:

> Know that your children, boys of good breeding, have progressed splendidly in their education in the past year both in the training of their character and their skill in letters, so much that, God willing, they will surely meet your expectation for them.[52]

Another factor to keep in mind in evaluating the effectiveness of written reports is that their carriers served to substantiate their bare lines. Libanius often entrusted his letters to people he knew personally who could elaborate on the particulars of a student's performance. *Ep.* 704 (B179), which he sent to his former student Hyperechius, clarifies an interesting aspect of mail transport: people who delivered letters asked to be lodged

---

[50] Cf. Pack 1935, 36.
[51] *Ta tou neou pragmata,* **91**. See **181**, which shows people's reactions to a boasting father.
[52] Halporn 2000, 138.

and entertained, sometimes at considerable expense to their hosts. It is likely that a letter-bearer also made an effort to deliver some oral information in order to make himself *persona grata*. Libanius alludes a few times to carriers' oral reports. After assuring a father that his sons were not wasting time in the tempting surroundings of Daphne, he declared that he was leaving to the carrier the task of giving him further details (**68**). Carriers felt so invested with their duty that they asked a writer to abridge a letter, since they could report the details, and they complained if he narrated everything.[53] A trusty pedagogue who carried a letter could give a fuller report, so that Libanius omitted any allusion to a student's academic standing in the short communication he wrote: the pedagogue himself, he declared, prevented him from writing at length (**127**).[54] Another written report contains a rapid allusion to the talent and effort of a student, but the father in question could "enjoy good hopes" on the basis of the additional information brought by the letter-carrier (**91**). This letter underlines the true role of written reports, since it shows that the carrier was not satisfied to give only an oral communication but requested a letter as a confirmation (*martyrein*) of the veracity of his words.[55]

Libanius's reports cover fixed areas of performance but do more than dutifully repeat well-worn formulas. No two reports are identical, and all inject at least one personal comment into the evaluation. It must have taken some effort to compress statements artfully into a short compass, and it is wrong to regard these letters as monotonous and uninteresting.[56] We must peruse them slowly, as parents surely did. Consider the laconic **143**, in which the whole family was evaluated. The grandson of Megethius stands out in slow-motion gestures that reverberate back to his father and grandfather, but the family's satisfaction at an external resemblance could extend further to intellectual qualities. Libanius observed that the boy derived the same pleasure from rhetoric as his grandfather once did and was even better than his own father in that respect. It should be noted that the report does not mention actual results. The reports the family of Diophantus received, however, were more explicit. His father was told that he did not have any weakness but was "of the best character and strong in rhetoric" (**61**). At the same time, Libanius felt the need to address another communication to the boy's grandfather (**62**). A letter

---

[53] Cf. *Ep.* 561.2 (B173).

[54] Letter **127** also shows that teachers' and pedagogues' reports were always complementary and subjected to family scrutiny.

[55] The very short message of **170** also needed to be filled up by the carriers, the two students themselves, who had to give their father a final oral report

[56] Reports usually take six or seven lines of the text of Foerster. Petit (1956a, 151) did not think much of them.

sent a year before reveals that the family's anxiety was justified, since apparently a brother was also attending the school, with disastrous results, and Libanius was concerned that this fact might affect the family's perception of Diophantus (**60**). The letter to his grandfather (**62**) called attention to the demeanor of a boy defined eloquently as "a lover of rhetoric but not a lover of bodies."

COMPONENTS OF REPORTS

In a letter mentioned above, Libanius alluded half-jokingly to the uncontentious attitude of a student in spite of his bodily strength (**195**).[57] Good behavior (*tropoi*) was an essential ingredient of success at school and consisted of gentlemanly demeanor (*epieikeia*), lack of insolence (*thrasos*), and a large dose of self-control (*sōphrosynē*) (**62**). Performance at school rested on a well-balanced combination of good character and academic results. Libanius declared that good conduct was essential for those students "who had not yet reached the top of their ability in their studies": boys who did not yet have a good reputation for their eloquence needed to compensate with blameless deportment (*Or.* 58.38). An inner order (*taxis*) regulated school life, and pupils were supposed to stay within the rules of discipline (*Or.* 1.241). The school law (*nomos*) dictated not only respect for and subservience to teachers, but also regard for pedagogues (*Or.* 58.6). It was desirable to be on good terms with schoolmates (**62**), and friendship with the best of them was praised. Parents were less appreciative of their sons' active social life and were concerned when a boy was exceedingly popular (*eudokimein*). Libanius went out of his way to defend Meterius with his father and his old teacher and argued that he was only guilty of having "admired the Syrians and was admired in turn" (**147**, cf. **146**), but in a letter to another addressee, he admitted that the boy "did amuse himself a little," and he tried to win over the recipient by saying that after all, even "the elderly do not disdain horse races" (**148**).

Modesty (*aidōs*) was part of the good student's accouterments. Libanius, who complimented a father because his son knew how to be modest, went to the extent of declaring, "The young man who knows this attracts me and receives more than another" (**74**). The question of the respective weight of ability and good conduct in Libanius's model student will continue to resurface. Are we entitled to suspect that despite protestations to the contrary, he favored the unchallenging but respectful student? Arrogant and difficult pupils made Libanius "curse [his] profession," even

[57] See **195**. Cf. **5**, which praises another strong student, Agathius, who refrained from fighting.

though he might acknowledge these students' academic ability (**5**). The student who was unpretentious and conscious of his deficiencies also possessed a natural sense of shame that governed his actions (*Or.* 58.25 and 33), whereas the one who shunned *paideia* did not have a sense of decency (*Or.* 42.13). Young men who excelled for their good behavior paradoxically lost their youth and became old. They had shed all of the negative characteristics of a youthful deportment, so that people addressed them complimentarily as "old fellows."[58] Libanius consequently urged someone not to judge the conduct of another student by his age, but to "class him among the aged from his conduct."[59]

When a lack of ostentation accompanied intellectual worth, the combination was irresistible, at least for the teacher.[60] The portrait of Julian as a student in Athens that Libanius painted in his *Funeral Oration* (so radically different from that of Gregory of Nazianzus)[61] is strongly redolent not only of his own Athenian experience but also of the expectations he had for his students (*Or.* 18.29–30). Julian's aim was to acquire additional learning, but he ended up "giving instruction rather than receiving it." He was far from a loner and was always surrounded by classmates and other learned fellows. His kindness made him very popular, but he only associated with the best. His remarkable eloquence was attractively accompanied by a modesty that always made him blush (*erythēma*) when he spoke—something slightly awkward in a budding orator. But Julian had every foreseeable quality.

Students' bad behavior reflected unfavorably on the teacher. Libanius felt responsible for the bad conduct of his malicious students (*kakonoi*) and was liable to the accusations of his critics on this score (*Or.* 3.28). The well-behaved student was a good advertisement of a teacher's competence, and as such "could increase the size of the *chorus*" (**83**). For most parents, however, academic progress was of greater import than deportment, unless there were urgent reasons for concern. The reports invariably call attention to two areas: hard work (*ponos*) and inborn talent (*physis*).[62] The intelligent student who worked hard was like a promising plant that was bound to produce fruit (**17**). Students imitated and tried to duplicate not only Libanius's eloquence but also his personal dedication to

---

[58] See **103**: Libanius hurries to tell Honoratus that these remarks were not caused by his white hair.

[59] *Ep.* 571 (N24). The same topic appears in **98** and in *Ep.* 1443 (B45). Wisdom and therefore premature old age are common appurtenances of children who died young in inscriptions, Vérilhac 1982.

[60] But he does not approve of the false modesty of his ex-students, who affect to respect their elders by refraining from speaking in the Council, *Or.* 35.25.

[61] Gregory of Nazianzus *Or.* 5.23, an eyewitness report but prejudiced.

[62] A typical positive report is **91**.

work (**184**). The hard work that produced results was performed with enjoyment. Young men "fell in love" with rhetoric and consequently made every effort to acquire it (**51**), but when an initial motivation was absent, pedagogues were instrumental in instilling it.[63] The grueling labors of rhetoric demanded a dedicated commitment that the negligent student could not hope to avoid, even if (as Libanius ironically underlined) he invoked the gods' help (**84**).

THE POWER OF NATURE

The question of the relation of natural talent on the one hand and training and effort on the other, which was framed centuries before Libanius, continues to be debated today. In the twentieth century, some intellectuals strongly reacted to the conviction inspired by the conquests of science that all human beings are genetically determined. They denied that human thought and behavior were linked exclusively to biology, and posited that human beings are genetically indistinguishable.[64] Today, we have apparently moved beyond the simple dichotomy between heredity and environment, yet claims of the importance of human nature strike people as immoral, since they seem to endorse issues such as racism, sexism, or war. Thus the debate continues between intellectuals who hold that the mind is far from being a blank slate and that biology is a major (if not the major) factor in what we think and do,[65] and others who opt for less clear-cut explanations, believing that human beings are complex system produced by genes and molded by experience.[66]

Ancient society could not take advantage of modern discoveries in the sciences of mind, brain, genes, and evolution, but was naturally less prone to feelings of guilt over endorsing the value of heredity, since it accepted a world of inequality. It confronted the issue of heredity versus environment mostly from the viewpoint of educators such as Isocrates in the fourth century B.C.E., Ps.-Plutarch and Quintilian in the first century C.E., and Libanius. These writers were bound to uphold the relevance of education and to proclaim its ability to improve or transform, but they also had to confront the reality of their students' talents. Even though their discussions are theoretical in some respects and combine different sets of issues, such as philosophy, psychology, and theology,[67]

---

[63] See **2** and **47**.
[64] See, e.g., Gould 1981.
[65] See Pinker 2002.
[66] See Ridley 2003.
[67] See Morgan 1998, 242–43.

their personal experiences as teachers must have had considerable influence on their opinions. Ancient educators were pulled from different directions. On the one hand, in order to empower education, they had to fight the dangerous notion of imperfectability according to which individuals are saddled with their own fatal, inborn flaws. On the other hand, they felt the need to make teachers less dependent on their students' success and less liable to accusations that their own lack of competence and commitment were responsible for failure. Libanius's treatment of the issue of nature versus nurture may appear less systematic than that of the intellectuals who preceded him, since it mostly emerges from his letters, but this discourse finds in him an urgency and vividness that illustrate well the dilemmas educators confronted.

The sophists in fifth-century Athens were the first to frame the question of the relevance of education. Reacting to their predecessors' exclusive trust in an aristocratic concept of heredity, they defended a combination of nature, teaching, and practice as essential to success.[68] Isocrates believed in that educational trinity but acknowledged that teachers did not have the ability to produce natural talent and could only improve innate qualities.[69] Isocrates' conclusion, that the man endowed with excellent natural qualities could be the best of all orators even if he had insignificant training, devalued to a degree the power of teaching and the efficacy of rules that systematized oratory.[70] His position was valid at a time when oratory was still mostly considered a creative process escaping precise classification.

By the first century C.E., rhetoric had developed into a complex art, and it became more difficult to circumvent *paideia*; yet intellectuals never adopted a concept of *tabula rasa* ("blank slate") according to which any individual difference should be attributed not to innate constitution, but to experiences such as upbringing and education.[71] The writer who most appears to believe in education's transformative capacity is Ps.-Plutarch in the essay *The Education of Children*. He upheld the sophists' educational trinity and adopted from Plato the notion that children's minds are impressionable, like wax, and can be molded.[72] Learning and application

---

[68] See H. Diels, *Fragmente der Vorsokratiker*, vol. 2 (Berlin, 1952), 264; and Plato *Protagoras*.

[69] Isocrates considers these issues in *Antidosis* 180–92 and *Against the Sophists* 14–18. Natural talents included an inquisitive mind, a capacity to learn and to remember, the ability to work hard and to project assurance, and the possession of a captivating voice and of a clear diction.

[70] See Isocrates *Against the Sophists* 12.

[71] The expression is commonly attributed to seventeenth-century philosopher John Locke. The concept undermined the aristocratic claim of innate wisdom and merit.

[72] See Plato *Resp.* 377b; he may have taken the concept from the sophists.

could amend a faulty nature so that the child not endowed with natural gifts could nevertheless advance as far as possible (2c). The optimistic claims of the author of this essay seem to derive from his theoretical stance, unsystematic reasoning, literary reminiscences, and consideration of a level of education below rhetoric.

With Quintilian (a rhetor and a sophist), *natura* regained some room: education, persistent study, and extensive practice had to bring out and develop qualities that were inborn. "If natural talent alone were sufficient," he says in a contrary-to-fact clause, "education could be dispensed with."[73] Quintilian made a distinction among the various natural components considered by Isocrates. Education could not remedy a lack of innate mental gifts, but could improve other defective natural talents, such as a weak voice or lack of endurance. Yet Quintilian's stance is still quite optimistic, since he believed that men who were truly dull and unteachable were extremely few. In this way, education possessed ample room to operate and maintained the preeminent position that an educator was bound to assign it.

It is noteworthy that whereas Isocrates spoke of natural talent as inborn without underlining its divine origin, both Ps.-Plutarch and Quintilian posited divine intervention. For the former, it is a god who assigns good natural qualities to a man, and the latter sees in reason's excellence a sign of its divine derivation.[74] Even though both writers insisted on the contribution of fathers to their sons' academic success, they reduced it to external factors. Fathers received children more or less naturally endowed and had to devote the utmost care to fostering the promise that they showed by choosing the right nurses and pedagogues or creating a good language environment.[75] Ps.-Plutarch's brief discussion of "noble birth" (*eugeneia*) did not involve the inheritance of natural qualities from one's forebears, but only referred to the display of pride and assurance of the wellborn (1c).

By Libanius's time, nature had returned fully human. Hermes and the Muses were allies of the student, but they seem personifications of qualities indispensable for learning rather than divine presences in their own right.[76] Fortune (*Tychē*) was an additional external factor that could assure that talent and effort would bring fruit.[77] She served to bring to full

---

[73] Quint. *Inst.* 1, 2.8.8; see also Pr. 26–27; 1.1.1–3; 1.3.1–2; and all of 2.8.

[74] Ps.-Plutarch *De liberis educandis* 2c and Quint. *Inst.* 1.1.1. Morgan (1998, 247–48) notices the paradox that reason, which makes men fully human, needs a divine intervention.

[75] Quint. *Inst.*, e.g., 1.1.1–8; Ps.-Plutarch *De liberis educandis* 4a–5c.

[76] See, however, **177**, where Libanius exhorted an uneducated father to thank the gods. The teacher could not refer to the boy's inborn intellectual gifts.

[77] Cf. **78, 91, 119,** and **176**.

completion a process that originated in the mind and determination of a student. A father was responsible for both the physical and intellectual characteristics of his son, but even when he felt entitled to entertain the highest hopes, he was advised to pray for Fortune's assistance (**176**). We have seen that new students' physical resemblance to relatives made a strong impression on Libanius.[78] During training, he noticed further similarities, such as their willingness to work and learn (*spoudē, prothymia*), their voices, or their powers of memorization (**143**). It was evident to him that a boy inherited the full package of his mental qualities and that he was as "smart" (*anchinous*) as his forebears, especially his father (**119**). Thus a father "planted" (*phyteuein*) in his sons their capacity to learn rhetoric, so that they were ready for their teacher to fill them up with the *logoi* (*Ep.* 340). A good nature was an indispensable prerequisite that enabled a student not only to receive rhetoric, but also to endure its labors (*Or.* 35.13).

Since the reports addressed male members of the family (and fathers especially), they underline the male components of inheritance. Yet Libanius occasionally shows his awareness that both parents contributed to a child's nature. He recognized a mother's participation in a letter to Diophantus's maternal grandfather that stressed that the good, moral traits of the latter were transmitted to the boy through the "blood" of his mother (**63**). Another letter is more explicit in acknowledging parental participation. Libanius wrote to his friend Seleucus, who had a daughter by his accomplished wife Alexandra, saying that he was not surprised at the many natural gifts of his young child.[79] The product of a father (the "sower") and a mother (the "soil") who were both so outstanding was bound to be out of the ordinary. This child was "of a generation of gold."[80]

Libanius's most explicit affirmation of the power and immutability of nature appears in *Oration* 64.[81] In proclaiming his conviction in a sort of

---

[78] He had known many from his school days, so that he could evaluate their intellectual capacities and working habits.

[79] *Ep.* 1473 (N140). In *Ep.* 734.5 (B155), written when the girl was a baby, Libanius complains of receiving no letters from Alexandra and says, "Bid your daughter to write and help her mother." On small children (*nēpioi*) with a great *physis*, see a moving, grandiloquent inscription from Lycaonia written for little Aias, who was "not the great Telamonios, but had the greatest nature in spite of being so little." His death supposedly saddened foreigners and citizens; Merkelbach and Stauber 1998–2002, 3:84.

[80] *Ep.* 1473 (N140). Cf. the Hippocratic treatise *On Generation*, ch. 8, which describes a theory of resemblances that rests on the hypothesis of pangenesis and the existence of sperm in both man and woman: Iain M. Lonie, *The Hippocratic Treatises "On Generation," "On the Nature of the Child," "Diseases IV"* (Berlin, 1981), 137–38.

[81] In this speech, he argued against the corrupting power of pantomimic dances because people's natures were already formed. This view, which he argues here at length, fundamentally corresponds to what resurfaces less systematically in the letters.

genetic determinism, he found allies in the poets (Pindar, Euripides, and Sophocles). He agreed with them that "nothing is more powerful than nature, and nothing has so much power as to change its ways."[82] This amounted to an inevitable acknowledgment of education's limits and incapacity to transform: "In vain you introduce lessons (*mathēseis*) thinking that you will change nature." Such a view, which is not tempered in him, as it is in Quintilian, by a belief that nature is almost universally good, may seem surprising in an educator who so often proclaimed the value of rhetoric. If nature was the sine qua non, what was the role of education?

Good innate qualities were sometimes dormant, and a good education had the capability of rousing them. Before awakening to a passion for study, Libanius himself had been a "sleeping" boy (*katheudōn*), living obliviously in the countryside with his mind occupied with other things (*Or.* 1.4). The individual students who appear in the letters are never described with the appellative "sleeping," which might have been too explicit for parents; but the fact that he emphatically presents some as "wide awake" seems to imply that others were not (**173, 167**). Libanius felt entitled to display his anger at the lethargic students when they were a faceless, generic group. Thus they could function as foils to good, individual students, such as the peerless Faustinus, who "lived among students who were asleep and who believed that rhetoric had no value" (**82**). The same "sleeping," apathetic students lived in his classes and in his orations, but Libanius was often unable to wake them up.[83]

While a good training could not remedy a lack of natural endowments, Libanius sometimes seems to imply that the absence or inferior quality of it might ruin a good nature.[84] Education was crucial in bringing nature's promises to fulfillment but was powerless in the absence of them. The Platonic notion that the minds of children were soft and malleable had limited validity for the pragmatic teacher who occasionally (even in the case of paternal excellence) had to confront a "hard nature" (*sklēra physis*) that resisted instruction.[85] Such students, whom Libanius calls "stones" (*lithoi*), "caused great misery to their teachers" and were unable to derive any profit from education.[86] Some of these "blockheads" were in his classes and displayed their hard nature by standing motionless and

---

[82] *Or.* 64.47, cf. the commentary of Molloy 1996, 216–17.

[83] *Or.* 3.3 and 43.10: "Students sleep, and the teachers do not wake them up" out of fear of losing them.

[84] See *Or.* 18.208–9, where he asserts the importance of training (*meletē*), yet he is mostly concerned with morality.

[85] In *Or.* 38.2, Silvanus, the son of the rhetor Gaudentius 2, has such a nature and requires his teacher's huge efforts.

[86] *Or.* 4.18. The student in question studied law at a later time but never found clients and never went to court.

in complete disinterest when he gave declamations (*Or.* 3.13). For others, such as Calycius, who belonged to a family of unusually dear friends, he fought the suspicion that teaching him rhetoric might be useless. Joining other relatives who urged this young man to work, Libanius paraphrased Aristophanes and wrote to his father: "I believe we are not boiling a stone."[87] Some people, it is true, did not properly evaluate the poor intelligence of their sons (*aphyēs*) and sent them to school because they did not want to appear to be overlooking something, but they wasted their money: these students "had no hopes" (*Or.* 49.23). Libanius's rejection of the unintelligent (or difficult) learner went further than proclaiming him uneducable and depriving him of schooling. His condemnation was unmitigated, so that Diophantus's brother returned to his family with the damning verdict that he "should not have been born" (**60**).[88]

Medical writers such as Galen in the second century upheld the importance of nature as a crucial foundation, but thought that principles and practice had great weight later on. Galen quoted words attributed to Aristides by the comic poet Eupolis: "Nature was the strongest factor, but then I lent nature a ready hand."[89] People should make the greatest efforts to rear a child in the best way so that he could become good, if his nature accepted the teachings. But at the same time, Galen asserted that when nature failed, the blame should not be the educator's. In the reports, Libanius's remarks on the natural talents that his students had inherited were surely meant to tickle family vanity by acknowledging that they had produced outstanding offspring and that his work, albeit crucial to foster the promise, was secondary to theirs. But a significant reason for advocating the preeminence of nature was that such a stand freed the teacher from the responsibility of failure.

Sons of the Gods

Since most reports contain positive assessments of Libanius's students, one is bound to wonder whether parents always entrusted him with paragons of virtue.[90] It is inevitable that a teacher had to do at least some editing in his communications to families. Libanius's exasperated remarks in *Oration 25, On Slavery*, appear to justify some leniency on the part of

---

[87] Letter **187**; Aristophanes *Vesp.* 280; see also *Nub.* 1202; Theognis 568; Plato *Hp. Mai.* 292d, and *Euthydemus* 298a.

[88] See above. The brother disappears from the correspondence.

[89] Eupolis fr. 1.9 Kock; Aristides had to explain the reasons of his excellence. Chapter 7 of Galen, *On the Passions and Errors of the Soul* (trans. P. W. Harkins [Columbus, Ohio, 1963]), covers nature and nurture.

[90] Cf. Petit 1956a, 151.

the professor, who had to render account to a crowd of people who blamed him when he was unable to triumph over a dull nature. Scores of pedagogues, parents, "the mother, the grandmother, and the grandfather" requested that he show that students "were sons of the gods even if they were made of stone" (*Or.* 25.47). Blatant lies, however, had to be avoided. People were not unaware that teachers' fervent declarations might be colored by a desire to please. The glowing reports parents showed around aroused the comments of skeptics who knew that "praising the students even if they are bad is in fact the custom of teachers" (**181**). The parents themselves, who sometimes requested further confirmations, caused Libanius's stiff protestations that he always honored the truth and never told families that students were "sharp when they are dull," or that "those who are wide-awake are sluggish" (**19**). But what about omitting negative remarks and concentrating only on laudable characteristics, a practice commonly advocated for panegyric?[91]

It is likely that Libanius followed these criteria in writing letters to families. Parents could trust favorable comments but had to pay attention to omissions and nuances, and had to pause and agonize over every word, as Cicero had done centuries before.[92] Truly negative remarks are rare in Libanius's reports. When he writes to the father of a student that he "already shows that his voice will become excellent with time," his words partly conceal a negative evaluation but are still colored with optimism (**177**). Not all students were docile learners, but it is telling that Libanius used twice (though never in a report) the expression "persuade and force," which eloquently described his work with certain students.[93] Those words were probably too direct for parents.

But another question that impinges on the formation of the letter collection as a whole concerns the occasional presence of letters that allude to students' difficulties as a thing of the past, even though there are no previous letters that comment on them. Letter **47**, for instance, testifies that "bitter has turned sweet" for the negligent student Daduchius, who underwent a remarkable change, since he presently wished to work on holidays, too. Libanius hoped that the boy's father could undergo a similar transformation, forsaking his bitterness. Since this is the only extant letter concerning Daduchius, one wonders how his father was previously informed. Another student who underwent a change for the better was the

---

[91] Cf. below, Chapter Seven, for Libanius's statement in *Ep.* 19 and his practice in letters of recommendation.

[92] Letters that could give room to anxiety and various interpretations are, e.g., **97**, **143**, **146**, **164**, and **195**.

[93] The expression refers to Julius in **123** and to Letoius ii in *Ep.* 1265 (N134), a letter to the grammarian Nicocles. These were charged words that in general applied to power.

Themistius mentioned above.[94] When Libanius wrote to him approximately at the time when he was named governor of Lycia at age twenty-five, his glowing letter started with an allusion to Themistius's past negligence. "You were unhappy at school, thinking that you were wasting energy in something useless."[95] But, one wonders, where are the negative reports to Themistius's father? Several explanations are possible, all inevitably speculative. We might suppose that the students themselves or their pedagogues delivered the bad news or that unpleasant information was not entrusted to letters but was given directly to letter-carriers or to parents. It would be interesting to know in more detail what ancient letter-writers chose *not* to communicate. But one cannot avoid entertaining the suspicion that whoever put together the letter collection (Libanius or someone after his death) had an interest in presenting Libanius as a successful teacher of "sons of the gods."

---

[94] Themistius 2/iii.

[95] *Ep.* 309, tentatively dated to 361. These words clarify the allusions to the boy's improvements in **181** and **182**.

CHAPTER FIVE

Teaching the *Logoi*

WE HAVE SEEN that Libanius regarded the physical and mental characteristics of his students as inborn. Parents transmitted to their offspring the most subtle bodily and personality traits, including aptitude for rhetoric. Inheritance of parental characteristics was not complete at birth, but continued through the inculcation of working habits, mindset, and cultural values. Teachers were not extraneous to the process. Education consisted (and still largely does, in spite of modern innovations)[1] of an ensemble of mechanisms that transmitted inherited cultural information from one generation to the next. The transmission of culture comprised by "education" was thus analogous (on a cultural level) to the biological transmission of genetic traits: teachers were fathers in their own right.

This chapter begins by considering Libanius's fervent belief in the equivalence of the identity of fathers and teachers, and proceeds with an examination of his role in the education of the emperor Julian. Libanius wrote copiously to guide his students in the reading of the authors, in the compilation of preliminary rhetorical exercises, and in the composition of complete declamations, but the information that one can extrapolate from his orations and letters about the program of studies is admittedly scanty, and it has been therefore mostly neglected. I examine all of this material to see the practical application of the teaching of the art. Since letter-writing was such a significant element in the texture of ancient society, of Libanius's and his students' connections, and of this book as a whole, I also investigate the evidence for teaching epistolary skills at the rhetorical level, a topic that has so far received little attention.

But the fundamental concern underlying the entire chapter (and in a sense, this whole project) is the attempt to find the reasons for the excitement young men felt for education at this level. What exactly were the *logoi*? What did Libanius (and other good sophists as well) communicate to their students that remained with some of them for the rest of their lives? We feel the tenacious passion for this culture in Gregory of Nyssa's resistance to being taken away from it,[2] and Gregory of Nazianzus's nos-

---

[1] See Bourdieu and Passeron 2000.
[2] See the letter of Gregory of Nazianzus to Gregory of Nyssa, *Ep.* 11, and the latter's letter to Libanius, *Ep.* 13 Maraval.

talgic longing for the *logoi* is still alive in his words. The thrill of living in cities such as Antioch or Athens, away from the strict control of their families, in daily contact with their peers, under the care of teachers who supervised their instruction for several years and made them members of new families of the intellect—are all these sufficient reasons to justify adults' yearning for those youthful years of study? Were those young men simply adolescents at play, as John Chrysostom described them,[3] students "who grew old in a long childhood,"[4] who wrote and declaimed their exercises and had plenty of fun with the pyrotechnics of rhetoric? There must have been more to the experience.

FATHER-TEACHER AND TEACHER-FATHER

The image of a father as teacher is not uncommon in antiquity. Whereas direct parental involvement must have been generally more common at low levels of education, there were fathers who were able to teach their sons rhetoric, and occasionally those who actually did so.[5] The possession of a rhetorical education enabled a father to teach at least the rudimentary notions of rhetoric that many students already possessed when they joined the school. Those who had studied under Libanius and later sent him their sons were in a privileged position. Libanius acknowledged the pedagogic work of his former pupil Julianus, who exposed his young son to some Demosthenes before sending him to Antioch. He called him "home teacher" (*eisō didaskalos*) and compared him to a farmer, employing the usual agricultural image of the teacher who sowed and planted information (**119**).[6] Rarer were the cases of fathers who were able to take up and continue their sons' education when circumstances interrupted their schooling in Antioch.[7]

---

[3] *Adversus oppugnatores vitae monasticae* 47.368.8–14. John Chrysostom argued that rhetoric (the "ostentatious display of adolescents at play," *meirakiōn paizontōn ē philotimia*) did not fit philosophers and adult men.

[4] See Bouché-Leclercq 1909, 753.

[5] See Cribiore 2001, 106–8. The sophist Quirinus taught Honoratus (**104**), and Acacius 7/iii taught Titianus (**190, 192,** and **199**). Libanius's father trained Aristophanes of Corynth (*PLRE* I, pp. 106–7) in oratory, see *Or.* 14.7. Fathers who were qualified could test their sons' knowledge in order to check on their teachers' competence, cf. *Or.* 43.16, below, Chapter Seven. Libanius played on the equivalence father/teacher in *Or.* 42.9, when he said that parents wanted their sons to be students of his assistant Thalassius rather than "students" of their own fathers.

[6] Libanius describes his teaching as "meeting with students outside" (*exō,* **124.**1; cf. *Ep.* 351.1, B37). There must have been plenty of those "inside" teachers.

[7] See **27**: Arsenius's father, who had been a fellow student of Libanius, takes over his son's education.

In all times, a student's dependence on and closeness to his teacher might produce mutual feelings of affection, but it is in Late Antiquity that the model teacher-father and student-son was often used to describe pedagogic relations.[8] The sophist Himerius called his concern for his students "love" (*erōs*),[9] and commonly addressed them as his *paides* ("children," "sons"). The philosopher Themistius adopted this way of referring to his pupils, but did not further expand on the concept of paternity.[10] In describing the sophist Apsines' concern for his students (who were implicated in a violent dispute with the pupils of a rival sophist), Eunapius said he was worried for his "children" and used the word *tekna*, a term that usually (but not always) referred to blood relations and was avoided by the purist Libanius.[11] It is the same form of address (together with *hyios*, "son") adopted by Amphilochius of Iconium, a student of Libanius, in his poetic epistle with didactic content for one Seleucus, a student or disciple of some sort.[12]

Affection for his teacher (*erōs*) made a student's work a product of imitation.[13] A student who fell under the spell (*philtron*) of a teacher held him worthy of the same regard he had for his father, "or even more," said Libanius (*Or.* 3.22). Thus a student had two fathers, one who begot him and the other "who persuaded him to love rhetoric."[14] It was this love that made a youth fight fierce battles against pupils of other sophists and ultimately justified in Libanius's eyes this violent practice. In his late,

---

[8] Kaster 1988, 67–69. See, however, in the second century, Philostratus VS 587, on Alexander of Tyre. This usage continued well after the fourth century; see *Ep.* 18 of Aeneas of Gaza (Massa Positano 1962). This is far from being "a Christian usage with a religious flavour" (Russell 1983, 7 n. 23). Naturally, there are exceptions to the use of "son" to indicate a student. Symmachus, for example, regularly referred to a younger correspondent and colleague as *filius.*.

[9] See, e.g, *Or.* 9.30 and 24.20. On his feelings for a student's bad health, cf. *Or.* 45.

[10] See, e.g., Themistius *Or.* 120c1 and 126a2.

[11] Eunapius VS 483, 9.2.7. On a student "son" of Prohaeresius, see VS 486. Cf. Cribiore, "P.Col. inv. 179c2," in *Proceedings of the 24th International Congress of Papyrology*, forthcoming. Dickey (1996, 68–69) pointed out that besides parents, people who acted *in loco parentis*, such as tutors or nurses, also used this term. Libanius calls his students his *paides*, and once called one *hyios* (**109**).

[12] See *Iambi ad Seleucum*, Oberg 1969. This work belongs to a tradition of advice addressed to sons and recalls particularly Basil's *Ad adulescentes*; Wilson 1975; cf. also Rousseau 1994, 49–57. After a generally moralistic opening, lines 33–64 advise Seleucus to study the poets, the historians, the orators, and the philosophers, using his nature (*physis*) to distinguish what is good and bad. The youth is then told to refrain from spectacles of any sort and is guided in choosing books from the Scriptures.

[13] *Or.* 1.23: since he did not follow a single teacher in Athens, Libanius was able to imitate only the classics.

[14] See **136, 194, 202** (Titianus has two fathers), and **86** (Gaius has four). Cf. also **16**: as a true father, Libanius did not need to be thanked for his care.

bitter years, he regretted that his own students shrank from showing him signs of such love, refraining from battles waged on his behalf, and painfully resented that they reacted with indifference (and without "love") at his declamations (*Or.* 3.10). The image of Libanius surrounded by a chorus of faithful students who always remained deeply loyal to him is definitely idealized.[15] Among the unfaithful, John Chrysostom manifested a real hatred for him in his oration *On Babylas,* where he ridiculed his teacher and his religion, and made punctual, bitter remarks on words and phrases extracted from Libanius's *Monody for the Temple of Apollo in Daphne.*[16] Besides the sharp epithets he addressed to Libanius, the deep hostility of the Christian former student comes across in the commentary, where he used abundant mythology and argued with methods he had learned in school. When he quoted Plato, "The Greeks (*Hellēnes*) are children, and an old Greek is nowhere," he brutally demoted the old sophist.[17]

Even during his years of greatest activity, Libanius acknowledged that he had "toiled for many, but . . . suffered because of many" (**23**). Students could be ungrateful to their teachers and sometimes behaved like the proverbial rams, which butted at those who brought them up, rejecting the example of the loving storks, which fed their parents. The late orations show that Libanius's negative perception of the attitudes of some of his students changed for the worse under the influence of his general disenchantment with life. Yet his feelings for at least some of them and the high concept he had of his work as an educator remained unaltered, as the letters from his last years testify.[18] He was elated at their successes, agonized over their defeats, attempted to arrange their marriages, wished they could send him their children,[19] and was distraught at their deaths because "it is painful to be a teacher: he is necessarily the father of many young men, and it is difficult for a father of many not to mourn" (**42**). A random perusal of the dossiers of letters reveals how alive (and much more than a literary convention) the equivalence father-teacher was for Libanius.[20] His own disappointed paternal expectations may partly account for his desire for children of the intellect, even though he was very aware of the more binding connection with

---

[15] But see Petit 1955, 18

[16] *Oration on Babylas* 98–113 (Schatkin 1990); Libanius *Or.* 60, written in 362/63, of which John Chrysostom preserved the only surviving passages.

[17] Plato *Ti.* 22b. John, of course, uses *Hellēnes* in the sense of "pagans."

[18] See, e.g., **159** and **160**.

[19] See **108**, **126**, and **90**.

[20] See, e.g., **9**, **30**, **21**, **103**, **109**, and **162**. See also *Ep.* 1266.5 (B81).

his son Cimon. Though a student was his "son," he acknowledged that Cimon was twice his child: by eloquence and by blood.[21]

SOWING AND PLANTING

Libanius adopted the agricultural metaphors that other writers on education had used before,[22] but whereas in Ps.-Plutarch or Quintilian these were fleeting images, Libanius made them an integral part of the texture of his prose. A teacher was like a farmer who sowed, planted, and cultivated his fields: he was bound to have results in plenty, provided the soil was good. Biological fathers planted seeds in their offspring and created the soil where the farmer-teacher would plant the seeds of rhetoric. An environment favorable to learning helped those seeds grow. In the year 355, while in Constantinople, Libanius, who longed to be in learned Antioch, felt like a frustrated farmer, trying in vain to plow the sea; but his perspective later changed, and in the 380s in Antioch, he regarded himself as a disappointed farmer whose seeds were falling on stones.[23]

The Greek verbs *speirein* ("to sow") and *phyteuein* ("to plant") were both employed with regard to farming, but their meaning also extended to "begetting."[24] As agricultural terms, *speirein* referred to scattering the seed, while *phyteuein* related to planting seedlings or root stock of some sort, usually trees. Whereas the medical writers recognized that women as well as men produced "seed," for Libanius, fathers were the sowers and mothers the soil.[25] In his writings, the terms *speirein* and *phyteuein* denote primarily the actions of fathers and teachers.[26] Libanius so deeply identified himself as a foster parent that in one instance he even appropriated the role of a mother giving birth to a child.[27] We do not have a way of differentiating usages for "sowing" and "planting" knowledge in

[21] Only his students' successes assuaged his grief for Cimon's death, see *Ep.* 960 (N170). The reputation of Priscio made him overcome his sorrow, **124**.

[22] On the occurrence of this metaphor in educational writers, see Morgan 1998, 255–59. See also, e.g., Plato *Resp.* 6.492a; *Phdr.* 276b–277a; Themistius *Or.* 27.338d–339.

[23] In Syria, results could be bountiful, *Ep.* 441 (N13). The image of plowing the sea is reminiscent of Theognis (106–7): "sowing the sea." Seeds falling on stones: *Or.* 2.44 and 68.

[24] A brief inquiry concerning these terms is necessary because Petit (1956a, 2–43), who explored the meanings of several words connected to education, neglected them.

[25] Cf., e.g., the Hippocratic treatise *On Generation* 7.479–81.

[26] In the orations, he sometimes used *phyteuein* metaphorically with reference to negative concepts, such as envy, hatred, or sickness, e.g., *Or.* 12.15, 15.64, and 30.19. Both terms refer occasionally to agriculture.

[27] *Tiktein* (**188**), depicting his emotion at the wedding of a student.

his pupils except in one instance, when Libanius posited a clear distinction. This allows us to revisit the question of whether he in fact regarded the emperor Julian as one of his students.

In Constantinople, Julian was the student of the Christian sophist Hecebolius, who forbade the prince (when he moved to Nicomedia) to follow Libanius's lectures.[28] Since he took pleasure in Libanius's eloquence but did not want to break the oath to his teacher, Julian was able to follow Libanius's classes indirectly, because a courier brought him the sophist's "daily words" (*Or.* 18.12–15). Libanius regretted that he had not "sown" (*speirein*) eloquence in Julian, by which he meant that he had not exposed him to the rudiments of rhetoric (*Or.* 18.12), yet he was in contact with him from those years, as an early letter shows.[29] Julian was in the same position as many other young men who joined his school to perfect their knowledge. Libanius thus claimed that he had "planted the seed of beauty" (*to kalon phyteuein*) in him, and Julian had nurtured it and achieved a splendid epistolary style.

A student's imitation, which resulted in works that echoed those of his teacher, was the most conclusive proof of his attendance. Teachers "begot" their students, who fulfilled their hopes by "begetting" in turn work that reflected their teacher's.[30] If a student's work was better received than his own, a teacher's identification with his "son" sweetened the defeat. Thus when a contest of speeches at a banquet allegedly determined that Libanius was inferior to his student Parthenopaeus, "I, Peleus, was happy of the defeat, and even happier than had I won."[31] What a student's work had in common with his teacher's betrayed his training, so that, for example, scholars have always accepted as a student of Libanius a youth, Olympius, whose speeches "partook of ours."[32] The stylistic similarities in the works of sophists and their students were sometimes so compelling that an audience had trouble attributing them, as letter **125** shows. When Libanius presented to different audiences a speech of his former student Leontius, their reaction (did the student appropriate a speech of his teacher?) brought him such delight that he ended up considering it his. The speech ultimately reached Libanius's students, who kept it, and in a way this consecrated Leontius as teacher, thus fulfilling Liba-

---

[28] On Julian's schooling, see Bouffartigue 1992, 13–42; and Bringmann 2004, 29–42. On the early contacts with Libanius, see Wiemer 1995a, 13–17.

[29] On Julian's use of *progymnasmata*, see Bouffartigue 1992, 523–33. Wiemer (1996) has shown that *Ep.* 13 (B23), dated to 353, was addressed to the future emperor and testifies to their early relationship.

[30] The concept that a rhetor was the "father" of his productions occurs over and over, e.g., *Epp.* **49**, **869**, and **1072**.

[31] See letters **159** and **160**.

[32] See *Ep.* **985**, Olympius xiv; Seeck 1906, 226; and Petit 1956a, 31.

nius's hopes of reproducing a true copy of himself.³³ We still recognize ancient students' imitation of the work of their teachers, as we, for instance, attempt to identify the traces of Libanius in John Chrysostom's early works, which still bear that imprint.³⁴

Libanius says that his fellow citizens insisted that Julian was his student (*mathētēs*) on account of the similarities of their literary productions (*Or.* 15.6). He also acknowledged that the works that they both begot (*tiktein*) were "brothers" and that the beauty of the emperor's letters stood out.³⁵ A letter that he sent to the emperor is highly significant in affirming his and Julian's conviction that Libanius had taught him all his rhetorical skills. Since the emperor's literary productions could rival his, the sophist reported a story meant to amuse him: for a while he had been in fear that the emperor intended to enter a rhetorical contest as his opponent and thus defeat his *didaskalos*.³⁶

It is only natural that, like other gifted students of Libanius, Julian could not escape being assigned a role of teacher. When he went to Athens to acquire more knowledge, Julian was the only student who could "give instruction rather than receiving it" (*Or.* 18.29). Libanius again proclaimed him the best of teachers in *Oration* 15, where Julian's foil was Constantius, presented as a lazy, incompetent teacher who ruined the cities, just as bad sophists could not make good practitioners of rhetoric (67–68). But Julian, the good teacher, had to impose himself upon his subjects (to those willing and unwilling to learn) and had to use the whip as he would have done with lazy students, if he had become a professor in Antioch, and thus a true rival of Libanius (77–78). "The most revered and divine position" that he held was a sufficient excuse for Julian to take a different road.

THE SEEDS OF RHETORIC

Libanius regretted not having exposed Julian to the initial instruction that based rhetoric upon good foundations. He composed a corpus of "preliminary exercises" (*progymnasmata*) and corrected his students' work with-

---

³³ Leontius 14, a good rhetor, apparently never became a teacher. On the wish of most teachers to create other teachers, cf. Amirault 1995.

³⁴ See Fabricius 1962, 118–21; and Hunter 1988. On his early works, see Kelly 1995, 20–23.

³⁵ *Or.* 16.16, and *Ep.* 716.3 (N84).

³⁶ *Ep.* 758 (N95). The pedagogic relationship Julian had with Libanius seems to have been tighter than with the philosopher Priscus 5. He knew the latter's written works and declared in *Ep.* 12.15–17 that he was his "pupil with no title" (*pseudepigraphos mathētēs*).

out relying on his assistants (*Or.* 34.15).³⁷ Is this a good indicator of the fundamental importance he attributed to "sowing" rhetoric, or is it perhaps another sign of his inability to delegate? Theon of Alexandria lamented the fact that in his day, many rhetors avoided these exercises altogether, and both Quintilian and the first-century biographer Suetonius did not approve of the fact that in Rome, grammarians had taken over the preliminaries of rhetoric.³⁸ Libanius probably composed his *progymnasmata* piecemeal, but they were grouped as a collection in later times, and they were arranged to conform to the practice of the later handbooks.³⁹ On the model of later collections, it is tempting to consider Libanius's a manual that went into the hands of his students to prepare them for larger treatises, a "miniature rhetoric," in the words of John of Sardis.⁴⁰ But he probably wrote the individual pieces either as models that his students would recite to internalize their structure or as instruments of verification that they could use to see if their work conformed to the desirable finished products. Both aims were contemplated by Theon of Alexandria.⁴¹ Unlike those in other handbooks, after the short fables and narratives of mythological episodes, Libanius's exercises are full-scale compositions that show not only his literary capacities but also his intention to train his students' critical faculties and independent judgment.

This is not the place to examine Libanius's *Progymnasmata* in depth,⁴² but I would like to focus briefly on his treatment of *encomion* and invective (*psogos*) to try to ascertain the reasons for his decision to be in charge of the "miniature rhetoric." Libanius's *Progymnasmata* include two pieces that he must have used as a pair even though they are widely separated from each other in the manuscripts: the *encomion* and *psogos* of Achilles.⁴³ The *Iliad* was the favorite Homeric poem for readers in antiquity, and Achilles was the hero that Libanius evoked so often in his letters,

---

³⁷ On the teaching of *progymnasmata* in schools of rhetoric, see Pernot 1993, 56–66.

³⁸ Theon 59; Quintilian 2.1; Suetonius *Gram.* 4.4–6; Kaster 1995. Thus Suetonius heard of youths who went directly from the grammarian to the practice in the Forum.

³⁹ The manuscript tradition does not preserve a uniform order; see Schouler 1984, 27. Cf. the collections of *progymnasmata* of Theon of Alexandria in the first century (Patillon and Bolognesi 1997); Ps.-Hermogenes, probably in the third century (in the edition of Hermogenes' works by Rabe); Aphthonius, a student of Libanius, in the fourth century, in the Hermogenic corpus (Rabe); and Nicolaus in the fifth (Teubner ed. by Felten). An English translation of all of these handbooks is in Kennedy 2000.

⁴⁰ Cf. the preface to the *Progymnasmata* of Nicolaus and that of John of Sardis, the earliest of the Byzantine works (probably the ninth century): Rabe 3; Kennedy 2000, 135.

⁴¹ Theon 70–72 (Patillon and Bolognesi 1997, 15 and 17).

⁴² Schouler (1984, 51–138) examines them systematically, but most of the exercises have not been translated. See Cribiore 2001, 220–30, with some examples from Libanius. On *progymnasmata* in general, see Webb 2001.

⁴³ Foerster 1903–27, 8:235–43 (*Laudationes* 3), and 282–90 (*Vituperationes* 1).

orations, and exercises.⁴⁴ Both exercises start with a justification of the legitimacy of a rhetorical treatment of a subject that poetry had apparently exhausted: rhetoric had the power to exploit the theme and to tell the truth. Though it is clear that Libanius did not limit himself to the Homeric text, but drew on the Homeric cycle and on the tradition that is the source of Hyginus's fables, it is impossible to know if he exposed his students to such texts, summarized them for them, or simply presumed their familiarity with them. Both pieces follow a traditional ring structure that starts with Achilles' forebears and ends with the inheritance of glory or madness that he bequeathed his son. In the *encomion,* explaining the reasons why he had become a "lover" (*erastēs*) of Achilles, Libanius follows the traditional elements of his upbringing, such as the nourishment upon the marrow of lions' bones (instead of milk) and the teachings of the centaur Cheiron. The narration of Achilles' participation in the Trojan War brings an indignant denial of the tradition of his hiding in Scyros in feminine garb. Yet Libanius concedes that the hero's yielding to his mother's anxiety would have been enough justification for that. One of the themes that runs through the *encomion* is the healing power of Achilles, who learned medicine from Cheiron, healed Telephus, and brought "healing to the evils" with his concerns for the army wasted by disease. Achilles' behavior is shown as exemplary in every respect: he had no interest in wealth, did not fight for Briseis, and yielded to his destiny in killing Hector.

Achilles' complex character made him an ideal subject for controversy. Libanius exploits various traditions in the exercise of blame, and one cannot but feel the entertaining quality of the tour de force. All the points developed in the *encomion* are thrown into question. Cheiron's body is ridiculed (who would believe a combination of man and horse?) and so is the hero's traditional food in infancy (lion's marrow is fit for a beast, but milk is for humans). Achilles' yielding to his mother's desire that he disguise himself in feminine clothes is regarded as shameful, as is his greed, his attempt to wrench the power from Agamemnon, his craze for women, and his barbarous treatment of Hector. If he killed this hero, moreover, it was not because of his personal valor, but because destiny had so decreed. Was Achilles at least swift of foot? He was, concedes Libanius, but like a useless horse—in sum, he was an animal altogether.

These two exercises allow us to see the mind of Libanius (and of his students, too) at work in firing up the imagination and devising new "positions" as orator-wrestler.⁴⁵ The amusing, fictional aspects of these men-

---

⁴⁴ See Cribiore 2001, 194–97 and 226.
⁴⁵ For education (and rhetorical education in particular) as gymnastics, see Cribiore 2001.

tal games and their organization around set themes should not obscure the creative process they put into play, the critical senses they targeted, and the habit of considering all aspects of a question that they inculcated. The sophist Nicolaus expressed the general dismay that *encomion* was included among the *progymnasmata,* since it was complete in itself and belonged to the panegyrical type of oratory.[46]

Praise and invective were at the core of Libanius's oratorical works, and his students soon learned to take practical advantage of the training. At the end of their studies, the *dokimasia* mostly consisted of the delivery of an *encomion* of the city to which students returned.[47] Titianus delivered an appreciated panegyric in praise of the governor Celsus that filled Libanius with pride, since both the boy and the honoree were his "children." More meaningful were the accomplishments of the student Albanius, who, after only two years of instruction in rhetoric, delivered a panegyric praising the eminent Domitius Modestus that roused the enthusiasm of a rhetor of the caliber of Priscianus.[48] A limited training permitted those who took the short path to rhetoric to perform to satisfaction. In commemorating the death of a student, the sophist Aristides says that Eteoneus died as he was preparing a panegyric, which was probably to be delivered on the occasion of a celebration.[49] Likewise, a rhetorical exercise from Greco-Roman Egypt reproduces an *encomion* of the fig that associates the fruit with a celebration in honor of Hermes and was likely to be pronounced at a festival.[50] In ancient society, there were public performances and contests in which students and aspiring poets could present their work,[51] and governors were all too pleased to accept gifts of the Muses.

No wonder Libanius kept the *progymnasmata* in his own hands. Most students remained in Antioch for a relatively short time, and after the preliminary exercises had limited training in declamation. But an adequate introduction to rhetoric prepared a youth for deliberative and judicial oratory, in addition to oratory for display. The case of the student

---

[46] Nicolaus 47. Panegyric was the only form of classical rhetoric that survived well into the Middle Ages, cf. Constantinides 2003, 41.

[47] Cf. above, Chapter Three. Libanius presents such a panegyric as a mandatory performance in *Or.* 55.34.

[48] Letter 7. See *Ep.* 735.4 (B127). Celsus 3, Domitius Modestus 2, and Priscianus 1. Cf. the panegyric of Tatianus 5 delivered by Priscianus 4, an ex-student (*Ep.* 1021, N178); and the panegyric on the consulship of the same Tatianus by Parthenopaeus, letters **159** and **160**.

[49] Aristides *Or.* 31.10; Pernot 1993, 65.

[50] See *P.Oxy.* XVII.2084; the hand, the roughly decorated title, the prominent mistake in the first title, and the crude drawing (a fig?) identify it as a student's exercise.

[51] Cf. Cribiore 2001, 241–42, for what concerns Egypt.

Severus, against whom Libanius wrote *Oration* 57, is exceptional only because of the extraordinary success he won as a pleader upon leaving Libanius's school.[52] During his second year of attendance, his father stormed into class to take him away, and Libanius's remonstrance (the young man was at the beginning of the art and could not possibly be strong enough to tolerate the sight of the judge and the arrogance of the other advocates!) had no effect. A year later, Severus's victories in court were the talk of Antioch (3–6). This speech amusingly conveys Libanius's ambivalence over the whole affair, in spite of his intention to play the part of the noble mentor. Asking the gods to help Severus, he declared his support for him but also reported the malicious gossip that the youth's resounding success was due to the money he had paid a sorcerer.[53] The reality that Libanius had a hard time accepting was that, with some further training on the job, students with little rhetoric could function rather well in society. The seeds of the "miniature rhetoric" bore plenty of fruit.

RUNNING ON THE SAME TRACK

The curriculum existed as an unchangeable entity outside of a teacher's influence. A teacher's ability to implement and expound it was fundamental, but the curriculum was truly an obligatory course, in every place where rhetoric was taught.[54] In other societies, such as in Roman Egypt (from where abundant Greek educational material resurfaced), learning was governed by order, and knowledge largely followed tradition.[55] The details concerning the curriculum and the ways Libanius implemented it that emerge from his works refer not only to his school but also to other schools of Greek rhetoric disseminated here and there in the Roman Empire. Though Egypt provides the tangible remains of ancient rhetorical education, Syria (through Libanius's school works, orations, and letters) contributes a sort of commentary to those teaching and learning materials.

The easy comparison between Libanius's school and a modern college is inadequate in many respects. A common complaint about the modern American university is that it offers excessive freedom of choice.[56] Stu-

---

[52] No translation of this oration is available. *PLRE* I, p. 834, wrongly remarks that Severus 14 was withdrawn "at Libanius's request for misconduct." Libanius actually pleaded for him to continue his training.

[53] Libanius, therefore, indirectly supports the very old connection between rhetoric and magic.

[54] This is what letters 129 and 77 imply, if one reads beyond the flattering remarks.

[55] Cf. Cribiore 2001. On higher education in early Byzantine Egypt, see Cribiore forthcoming b.

[56] See Schwartz 2004; Rhodes 2001.

dents are confronted with a wide array of courses (many of which provide narrow training) but rarely receive any comprehensive and coherent expression of educational goals and intellectual purposes. Today, the increased diversity and complexity of the curriculum results in a disconnected series of courses that convey mixed messages, and the higher-education system often serves as a job-readiness program with no integration of compartmentalized knowledge.[57] The school of Antioch provided education only in rhetoric (and literature as a whole), but it communicated to all students a shared knowledge of culture. It also furnished a strong model of intellectual authority in the person of Libanius, who never relinquished control and was an intellectually aggressive teacher who nonetheless organized his students' learning and thinking so that they ultimately could empower themselves.[58] Let us now gather the information scattered throughout Libanius's works about the program of study in Antioch, clarifying at the same time some of the issues that reappear in the letters.

Libanius took for granted that the curriculum (*ta pragmata*, "study matters") was the same for everybody (*Or.* 34.15). His resentful response to a pedagogue who criticized the repetitiveness of the program was, "The cause of this is to be found in the curriculum, not in me." With the possible exception of some students who joined the school at a late age,[59] the entire *chorus* "observed the same rules, in the same school, marched on the same path, heard the same voice, and followed the same models."[60] Educational metaphors that often occur in Libanius convey the same message. Education was a liquid good, a spring that flowed for the benefit of those who wished to drink. Those who went to the same school enjoyed the same spring and drank from the same cup of learning.[61] A teacher was a fountain at the disposal of those who were thirsty. It did not pursue potential customers, but it was there if students cared to enjoy its waters.[62]

We have seen above that Libanius did not employ grammarians at his school but was assisted by a number of rhetors whose authority was severely curtailed.[63] Another misconception concerning the curriculum fol-

---

[57] See Gregorian 2004. A comparison with the first colonial colleges will also be out of place. In 1632, the curriculum was fixed and limited at tiny Harvard College, but students studied a different subject every day; cf. Boyer 1987, 60–61. The education offered in Libanius's school has more in common with graduate-school instruction.

[58] On the positive aspects of "progressive traditionalism, which denies that students cannot become active learners with authoritative teachers," see Graff 2003, 261–74.

[59] See below, Chapter Six.

[60] *Or.* 35.21. Cf. Lucian *Rhetorum praeceptor* 9.

[61] See, e.g., letters **72** and **201**, and *Or.* 34.27.

[62] See **162** and **166**. In reality, however, the fountain-teacher looked for drinkers.

[63] See Chapter One.

lowed in Antioch needs to be corrected. The notion that students spent the first two years reading the classics and studying rhetorical theory with his assistants and finally approached Libanius and written exercises in the third year is unsound for several reasons.[64] On this assumption, young men who remained in Antioch for one or two years would see Libanius only from afar. The school based its reputation fundamentally on his accomplishments, and parents would have objected to having their sons only in the charge of lesser teachers. It is certain that Libanius was closely involved in teaching all of his students from the beginning, as he says in a meaningful passage of *Oration* 34.[65] Students, divided into classes of about ten,[66] read texts (*biblia*) under the guidance of an assistant but following Libanius's directions. At the same time, it was Libanius who "corrected and set right" their written exercises of debate and refutation of passages of Homer and Demosthenes (*hamillai*). Pupils therefore had "two teachers instead of one" and "a double advantage."[67]

The term *hamilla*, which only Libanius uses for an exercise of rebuttal of statements of ancient writers, requires some attention.[68] The handbooks of *progymnasmata* include exercises of refutation and confirmation (*anaskeuē* and *kataskeuē*) that taught students to engage in debate. Theon also calls refutation *antirrēsis* and provides an example from Demosthenes' *De corona*.[69] This exercise offered an ideal opportunity for mental gymnastics because it had the potential to grow from a refutation of a simple statement to that of a whole discourse. Theon adds that it is useful for the teacher to compose exercises of this type so that students can recite them and learn to imitate them. Libanius's correspondence shows that in fact, sophists also engaged in this exercise. When he began his teaching in Antioch, he composed a prologue and a *hamilla* against something of Demosthenes.[70] A few years later, he wrote to the sophist Demetrius of Tarsus and included in the letter a *hamilla* against some points of Demosthenes, together with some introductions to speeches (*proagōn*), material

---

[64] Petit 1956a, 65 and 88.

[65] See *Or.* 34.15–16; Norman 2000, 140.

[66] These groupings were called *symmoriai*; cf. 2, the son of Achillius was the best of his group.

[67] *Or.* 34.15–16. I do not agree with Norman's translation, "You gained two for the price of one." The interpretation of Heath (2004, 240) is unnecessarily complicated, in my view. The whole group included at that level read texts with an assistant, and the pupil who wanted to do more demanding things had to wait. He was not qualified to move up, moreover.

[68] Cf. Festugière 1959, 480 n. 3. Heath (2004, 248) advances the suggestion that it could be a paraphrase.

[69] Theon 70. See also Nicolaus 30–34. Cf. Quintilian 5.13, who calls the exercise *refutatio*. It was part of judicial oratory.

[70] See *Ep.* 405 (N6); this piece contained many variations (*morphai*).

that Demetrius had apparently requested.[71] But the gift sent with another letter to the same friend consisted of a dream of sophists composing *hamillai* (*Ep.* 243). In the dream, in his anxious search for Demetrius, Libanius ascended the many steps to a temple and found him there besieged by applauding students as he delivered a *hamilla* in rebuttal of one of Demosthenes' orations against Philip. Wanting Libanius's approval, Demetrius continued his performance in front of him. But when he woke up, Libanius had one regret: "Night wronged me, and I did not retain your words," a rebuke to himself for failing to do what he requested from his students.

"You have taken [your son] from Homer, Demosthenes, and Plato to horses, chariots, and charioteers," wrote Libanius to a father who removed his son from school (because of some misbehavior) in order that he could perform public service (**64**). Epiphanius was at the stage of having two masters, and the decision caused pain both to Theotecnus, who directed his readings, and to Libanius himself. Leaving aside for now the more problematic question of the place of poetry in a rhetorical school, the favor that Demosthenes and Plato enjoyed there was recognized almost universally in antiquity.[72] From the preliminary exercises to the finished orations (*meletai*), a student had to wrestle with Demosthenes and was encouraged to continue reading his speeches when school was over in order to retain his rhetorical facility.[73] It is no wonder that the immobility of the program caused some remonstrations, and that Libanius had to beg his students "not to hate" the orator.[74] These voices of dissent confirm that the program was taxing (especially to the less gifted) and that one had "to suffer a lot for a long time" for the glory of the *logoi*, as Gregory of Nazianzus said in an autobiographical poem.[75]

Libanius's passion for and emulation of Attic oratory elicited comparisons between him and Demosthenes, and he was dubbed "Demosthenes the second" by Byzantine grammarians.[76] He affected to resent such flattering correlations, and in 380 ironically invited his fellow citizens not to make special efforts in order to honor him: in their enthusiastic acclamations that he was a new Demosthenes, they compared "things much differ-

---

[71] *Ep.* 283.5 (N64); Demetrius 2/i.

[72] Cf. Rutherford 1998, 39–43.

[73] The *meletē*, which von Christs, Schmid, and Stählin (1924, 689) appropriately call *Paraderede*, was a speech prepared beforehand and not improvised. Aristides (*Or.* 47.37–39) distinguished it from the *dialexis* and the *lalia*, which were shorter and delivered impromptu.

[74] See *Or.* 35.16. Libanius himself sometimes manifested a bit of impatience with the historical themes of *meletai*; cf. *Ep.* 796.5 (B156), where he wrote that he would never neglect a friend and choose instead to "chatter away about Miltiades or Themistocles."

[75] Gregory of Nazianzus *Carm.* 2.1.1–11.96–98 (Tuilier, Bady, and Bernardi 2004).

[76] Cf. Foerster 1903–27, 1:74 nn. 2 and 3.

ent" (*Or.* 2.24). Yet he had apparently internalized the analogy when, in 387, he accused his pupils of consigning Demosthenes to oblivion because they were unable to respond when they were asked about the subject of one of his (Libanius's!) speeches (*Or.* 3.18). The public must have felt saturated with Attic literature. One may find some awareness of this in remarks Libanius uttered in the defense of the right of his secretary Thalassius to become a senator (*Or.* 42.21–22). After bringing up the details of Demosthenes' personal life and his stance as champion of Greece in order to justify the legitimacy of Thalassius's request, Libanius's impatient remark ("But let us leave aside the Athenian democracy and the Pnyx and the speaker's platform and Solon!") may testify to an acknowledgment that some people felt the need to escape from a past that often looked irrelevant.[77]

The works of the classical authors formed the basis of *paideia*,[78] and Plato was one of the pillars of prose-writing.[79] Theon of Alexandria did not include him among the authors to be read because he rigidly limited himself to rhetors and historians, but Plato was commonly regarded as one of the two greatest prose-writers, with Demosthenes usually occupying the first place. Hermogenes considered Demosthenes the embodiment of perfect style and the most versatile of all authors and paid little attention to Plato, but Aristides' judgment was more nuanced.[80] Libanius's students read Plato with his assistants from the very beginning. A letter presents Calycius absorbed in reading the philosopher upon joining the school (**186**), and in another letter, Libanius recommends Julianus to the philosopher Themistius, saying that the student is able to discuss Plato and philosophy.[81] Libanius encouraged students to dedicate summers to filling themselves with the *logoi* of the ancient writers (**189**). After the second year of attendance, spending the summer with his father in the stifling heat of Cilicia, Titianus read a great deal, so that upon his return, his teacher found that his "soul has become golden" (**197**). The breadth of his reading caused Libanius some surprise, and he vouchsafed that the discourses Titianus produced were now excellent.[82]

---

[77] One could also, however, view this as a standard rhetorical transition.

[78] See *Ep.* 1004.7 (N177).

[79] Libanius did not have a properly philosophical interest in Plato. It is possible that the traditional dichotomy between rhetoric and philosophy played a role; see Norman 1964, 159. On Libanius's attitude toward philosophy, cf. von Christs, Schmid, and Stählin 1924, 996.

[80] See Rutherford 1998, 47–51 and 99–100.

[81] Julianus 15/vii, **117** and **118**. The remark can also be explained by the fact that Themistius was a philosopher.

[82] The addition that some people might not have liked them (because of their ignorance or envy) perhaps indicates some experimentation on the part of this student.

Readings from the ancient authors were combined with selections from the moderns, and from Libanius himself in particular. A letter to Hesychius shows that changes were implemented month by month: students read the classics the first month, integrating them with Libanius's works, and the following month turned to the ancients alone. Afterward, the cycle started again (**93**).[83] It is unfortunately unclear whether they were reading Libanius's elementary rhetorical works or if they engaged from the beginning with complete speeches of his, as they did with Demosthenes', performing some exegesis.[84] Not only did Libanius's work have pedagogical value, but his contemporary reputation was so outstanding that other sophists included him in their reading lists. He says in his *Autobiography* that his works were "in the hands of pupils and teachers alike in every school of rhetoric."[85] In the story of his constant rivalry with Athens, the fact that Eustathius, who became governor of Syria in 388, read his works while studying in the Greek city must have been a private triumph.[86] Eustathius, in any case, read Libanius on his own accord, arousing the anger of the Athenian teacher who caught him doing so. A letter about a student who ran away to Antioch without permission from his family makes one surmise that he was more welcome because of the readings from Libanius he had done with his former teacher, Argeius (**206**). Two other students who were already strong in rhetoric joined Libanius after they had previously "feasted" on his discourses (**168**). Exposing a young man to readings of the sophist whose classes he was going to attend may have also been a matter of collegial etiquette. Thus, in recommending Dianius to the philosopher Themistius, Libanius made sure to tell him that the young man treasured many of his discourses "in his memory and soul" (**49**). Professional rivalries did not prevent Libanius from using Themistius's works in his classes.[87]

---

[83] Festugière (1959, 135) wrongly concludes, in my opinion, that these were summer readings done under the guidance of Libanius. I also do not agree with the interpretation of Heath (2004, 240). Libanius apologizes for not keeping this father abreast of his sons' progress; "myself" (*eme*) in the letter can only refer to his own works (not to a class conducted by him).

[84] The modest remark in letter **69** might refer to these students reading Libanius. "It would not be right for me to tell you in detail about this" may indicate that they appreciated Libanius's prose.

[85] *Or.* 1.155. Eunapius (*VS* 16.2.6, 496) confirms that many of his works were in circulation.

[86] Eustathius 6, *Or.* 44.2–3, a very short speech praising his rhetorical skills, written before 389.

[87] Letter **125** shows that students used the speech that the ex-student Leontius 14 had sent Libanius.

The readings fueled eloquence at all times. We have a welcome glimpse of Libanius himself engrossed in Demosthenes on a summer day, sitting "at the foot of my usual pillar" (*Or.* 1.237). The insistence on preserving the knowledge acquired in school is often present in his work. Students could not afford to remain idle during the summer, and when their education was over, they had to keep in contact with their books. Those who avoided touching books as if they were "snakes" paid the price, lost their gift, and remained silent in the Council (*Or.* 35.13). It rarely happened that someone could keep up otherwise, and Libanius marveled at his cousin Spectatus's masterful display of eloquence, even though he had not touched his books for a long time after entering the Imperial service.[88] Eloquence was not acquired for always but had to be kept alive. The proficient rhetor also needed to practice his "scales." Thus, on returning from a journey to his school, the rhetor Himerius felt the need to exercise like the athlete who won at the Olympic Games and had to continue frequenting the gymnasium (*Or.* 63). When eloquence was left idle or was superseded by other disciplines, such as Roman law or Latin, it slipped away.[89]

After two years in Antioch, the student Titianus was getting "sharpened in the exercises called *meletai*" and was learning fast, the teacher wrote his father (**199**). His work had been excellent from the beginning, and in his second year he was able to produce "outlines for declamations" (*skemmata*, *Ep.* 345.3) that aroused the admiration of knowledgeable critics. The basic difference between declamations and real orations was minimal and mostly rested on the experience and cultivation of a rhetor.[90] In his third year, Titianus was already producing valuable *logoi*. Libanius, who always struggled to advertise his reputation as a teacher, made sure to circulate them among ex-students and rhetors: they were like the first published papers of a modern graduate student.[91] Aware that the boy's father had sent Titianus a letter with some pointed advice on voice-pitch and pauses, Libanius still defended his decision to let others read this student's work as it was, but apologized for his own stylistic imperfections: people in fact criticized him "for being an actor more than a rhetor." This remark brings to mind Eunapius's carping that Libanius was ignorant of rules that even schoolboys knew. Libanius's rhetoric had a degree of independence from current rhetorical theory that some people found disagreeable.

---

[88] See *Ep.* 331 (N35).
[89] Letters **45**, **131**, *Or.* 40.7, and 62.21–23.
[90] For a thorough treatment of Libanius's declamations, see Schouler 1984, 139–221.
[91] See *Ep.* 127.4 (N58). Andronicus 3 and Priscianus 1 read them.

Education was a loud affair: the noise of teaching and learning was overwhelming. Students who declaimed and heard others read aloud in the same environment became accustomed to producing, receiving, and eventually tuning out the rumble of intellection, but a letter shows how exasperatingly loud declamations could be for others. Libanius remarked half-seriously that only one aspect of the performance of two students was unsatisfactory: by rehearsing their declamations at the top of their lungs at night, they prevented the neighbors from sleeping, causing "some to move and others to have a breakdown."[92] Before a declamation could be ready for formal delivery, it had to go through a final revision. This is what the extraordinary finale of the *Hymn to Artemis* discloses (*Or.* 5.43–53). In this prose hymn, Libanius claims that a miraculous intervention of the goddess saved him and his class from death when a marble piece and other stones collapsed from the top of the door of the schoolroom. This tale highlights one aspect of the teaching routine: whereas the other students refrained from coming to school because of a mysterious, premonitory fear, one boy, concerned with his work, brought his declamation to Libanius for a final verification and was able to read 240 lines aloud before the disaster occurred.

When students were ready, they would declaim in front of the entire school. Libanius encouraged this practice as advantageous to everybody: the most advanced students had a chance to exercise criticism (*krisis*); those less able could compare and improve their work; the beginners might develop a sense of emulation (*Or.* 34.27–28). With this performance, which was followed by Libanius's observations and corrections, the school day was over, and those boys who besieged their teachers with their critical remarks about the speaker were invited to leave.[93] Freedom of expression had its time and place in Libanius's school. It is likely that students started to display their work from the end of their second year, but exceptional boys existed, like the fifteen-year-old whose performance opens *Oration 34* (not a beginner in spite of his age). He suspiciously possesses all the qualities of the ideal pupil: he is very young, an orphan, with an excellent mind, from a renowned family, exceptionally modest, prompt in paying the school fees, and able to deliver an impeccable discourse with its introduction. Quintilian's pages help us capture the fun students had at their peers' performances (applause, shouting, jumping up in enthusiasm, all reactions that a teacher had to curb), and a letter of Libanius shows them assembled in admiration around the speaking chair of a schoolmate.[94]

---

[92] *Ep.* 25 (N36). Cf. in fifth-century Constantinople the *Theodosian Code* 14.9.3 on the necessity of separating different classes to prevent students from overcoming each other with their loud voices.

[93] For boys with difficult personalities, cf. 5.3.

[94] Quintilian 2.2.9–13 and Libanius *Ep.* 1489. Suetonius (*De grammaticis et rhetoribus* 10) talks about "open-house" days that sophists organized for their students to display their work; cf. Imber 2001, 210.

When reading Libanius's flowing prose, it is easy to forget that he followed some variant of the complex theory of issues (*stasis*) that Hermogenes codified in the second century.[95] Since Libanius did not write a handbook of rhetoric, we are not informed precisely what particular theoretical views he might have had.[96] At the same time, it is notable that his declamations do not bear many traces of the theory of Hermogenes. This is probably a sign that the latter (the only complete Greek testimony of the issue theory) looms larger in the eyes of modern scholars than in those of his successors, as the different treatment of issues by Sopater seems to confirm.[97] Libanius's students learned that the art of persuasion followed strict principles, which could not be applied mechanically and required a personal analysis of a particular situation, but which were a formidable help in structuring their writing, in creating effective strategies of argument, and in problem-solving. If we still value the ability to communicate effectively orally and in writing, to develop a high level of articulation, to recognize contradictions immediately, and to construct persuasive arguments, Libanius's students did not fare too badly. Their knowledge of subjects other than rhetoric and literature was severely curtailed, but their thinking and ability to dissect problems were sharpened in the process of learning rhetoric. Libanius's statement that "eloquence derives from understanding, and understanding comes from eloquence" was not too extravagant.[98] His students were not only experts (*technitai*) trained to use sophisticated systems of theory and to follow pre-formed templates. The exercises in persuasive argument in which they engaged sparked their creativity to much the same extent that more personal forms of writing would have. The debate on the respective validity of argumentative and creative-writing models continues, but a conflict between them is unnecessary today, as in ancient times.[99]

Love and the *Logoi*

A powerful sophist was a charming Orpheus, a Pied Piper who bewitched students. Himerius often alluded to the myth of Orpheus and depicted the enthralling power of his lyre, and Eunapius called the sophist Chrysantius a harmonious Orpheus, whose *logoi* seduced his students like

---

[95] See Heath 1995.
[96] But it is possible to examine his works on the basis of other theories; see Schouler 1984, 139–221.
[97] See Swain 2004, 360; Innes and Winterbottom 1988, 2.
[98] See *Or.* 12.92. Cf. also *Or.* 49.32: the aims of rhetoric were to "discover the right course of action" and praise that action.
[99] See Graff 2003, 246–60.

beautiful, sweet songs.[100] When Libanius arrived in Antioch, people urged a rival sophist to hurry back if he did not wish to find all the youths following Orpheus, and an empty classroom.[101] Another passage in the *Autobiography* is even more explicit in pointing to passion as the primary motivation of those young men who deserted their old teachers for Libanius (38). Attraction to perfect oratory could not be resisted, and the sophist who drew adoring students to himself could not be accused of "rape," but was only guilty of being "beautiful." After becoming the core component of higher education in the Greek world in the fourth century B.C.E., rhetoric continued to seduce its young audience, even though its material appeal declined, replaced by a more general appeal to cultural values. Libanius was certainly not the first to find an erotic dimension in the force that compelled a youth to devote himself entirely to those taxing studies. By playing ironically on the devotee of rhetoric presented as the "lover" (*erastēs*) and calling the art of rhetoric "his beloved" or "his bride," the Second Sophistic had pointed to a metaphor already in use.[102] The image of youths "in love" with hard work and rhetoric or with Libanius himself (as the one who held the key to it) appears so often in the correspondence that the temptation exists to consider these concepts to be mere clichés for the benefit of parents.[103] Again (as for the concept of intellectual paternity), this temptation must be resisted, at least partially. It is not unusual for pedagogical relations to generate intense emotional and intellectual dynamics,[104] and the passion some of these youths felt for their studies is aptly exemplified by that of Libanius himself or Julian. Libanius's life showed that the seemingly ostentatious words in his *Autobiography* that "my bride was my art" were not empty, and his portrait of Julian spending sleepless nights declaiming his or other people's *logoi* was not a figment of his imagination.[105] We have already identified some of the positive aspects of those studies, but was there more?

Consider the school of the grammarian that students attended before starting rhetoric.[106] The goals achieved there were significant. Finding a

[100] Himerius, e.g., *Or.* 35.34 and 39.5; Eunapius VS 23.3.3, 502.

[101] *Or.* 1.90. See also *Ep.* 838.10 (B94): with some help from the governor Alexander 5, Libanius-Orpheus will get many students.

[102] See, e.g., Lucian *Rhetorum praeceptor* 6 and *Nigr.* Praeface; or Aristides in *Pros tous aitiōmenous oti mē meletōē* 51.421.10 Dindorf. See also Plutarch (*Quaestiones conviviales* 622d), commenting on Euripides, "Love teaches a poet." Cf. the *ardor amoris* in Cicero *De or.* 1.30.

[103] See, e.g., **62, 51, 132, 28**, and *Epp.* 1080.5, 574.4 (B19), 1081.2, and 1060.4. Cf. also, e.g., *Or.* 55.24. The theme of "love" for rhetoric occurs in fourth-century rhetorical prose.

[104] See Simon 1995.

[105] *Or.* 1.54 and 12.94. Cf. also *Or.* 18.18.

[106] See Kaster 1988. See an overview of education at this level in Cribiore 2001, 185–219. See also Morgan 1998, 152–89. On the profession of the grammarian in the West in Late Antiquity, see Schindel 2003.

way through the maze of texts written with no word divisions and almost no lectional signs; learning to read with understanding and expression; "translating" classical Greek texts as if they were written in a foreign idiom; categorizing the language and thus being able to recognize a correct or incorrect form: these were no mean achievements. Yet the grammarian had to build on shaky elementary foundations, worked with texts that did not distinguish between young learners and educated adults, and aimed to deliver precision rather than breadth of vision. The inevitable results of this education were a fragmented and narrow exposure to literature and the development of an analytical capacity that verged on the pedantic and that clogged the mind with minute shreds of information. But the foundations (albeit imperfect) were now in place and could be built upon.[107]

One of the tasks of a sophist, I suggest, was to continue the work of the grammarian by exposing his students to *every* kind of literature (prose as well as poetry) through a radically different method of reading. Prose, which consisted of the works of orators, historians, and some philosophers, received the lion's share of attention, yet poetry was not neglected. The student, who had previously covered relatively brief texts, pausing at grammatical forms and minute points of interest, now had permission to proceed unbridled, "racing along like the horse of Hieron," unencumbered by the grammarian's training wheels.[108] Better mastery of reading techniques and a new emphasis (at least in the first years) on the flow of a text rather than on meticulous glossographical and "historical" observations (*historiai*) finally allowed the student of rhetoric to understand fully the meaning of a literary passage or to start appreciating the development of a theme in the overall work of an author. A look at Libanius's introductions (*hypotheses*) to Demosthenes' orations confirms that he had broad interests when he wanted his pupils to read this author.[109] He omitted the theoretical concerns that were going to prevail later in the course and a point-by-point commentary, used minimal technical language and glosses, gave a general idea of some critical issues, and concentrated on Demosthenes' power. Education at the rhetorical stage gave students a more varied and complete vision of literature, which inevitably entailed some literary appreciation, in addition to consideration of specific rhetorical aspects. For those who savored them, the *logoi* provided not only enjoyable exercises in good company, useful training in oral and written

---

[107] Kaster (1988, 12–13 and n. 4), who points to the burdens of this education that remained with the educated.
[108] See *Ep.* 345 with an allusion to Pindar (N27).
[109] Foerster 1903–27, 8:575–681. See Gibson 1999, and a praise of Libanius's work in Cameron 2004a, 59.

communication, and enhancement of their logical skills, but also the excitement of discovering a world that had only been sampled before.

Scholars have wondered about the pluralism and inclusiveness of the Greek reading lists that appear in several ancient authors, such as Dionysius of Halicarnassus, Quintilian, Dio Chrysostom, and the rhetor Hermogenes.[110] Roman and Greek practice differed considerably because, as Quintilian revealed, little reading was done in Roman schools of rhetoric, as he regretted (2.5.1–17). In compiling an extensive reading list for rhetors, apparently Quintilian could not draw upon personal teaching experience but used Greek sources.[111] Quintilian's catalogue, with its vast list of recommended reading, is usually regarded as the product of idealism, with a view to forming his "good man skilled in speaking," who was destined to rule in the public sphere. There is no doubt that Quintilian adjusted reading practices to serve his paradigmatic purposes, but the question is to what degree he did so. I believe his and other authors' reading lists were more than ideal, theoretical canons and reflected the breadth of reading with which a first-rate orator was supposed to have at least some acquaintance.

The common procedure of trying to infer a writer's readings through his direct quotations from and allusions to other authors is hazardous.[112] Citations depend on personal preferences, on special familiarity with a certain author, on the character of a work in which they are supposed to be included, and on the audience's expectations and level of culture.[113] Scholars who sometimes recognize in passing that citations and allusions tell us what an author read but not *all* that he read still succumb to the temptation to delineate his library and come up with invariably pessimistic considerations on reading ranges.[114] A good example of the inadequacy of citations in disclosing the literary breadth of an ancient author might be Ammianus's revelation that Julian was fond of reading Bacchylides versus the slight interest in poetry and the total ignorance of Bacchylides

---

[110] Dionysius *Peri mimēseōs* 2; Quintilian 10.1; Dio Chrysostom *Or.* 18; Hermogenes *Peri ideōn* 2.10–12; Rutherford 1998, 37–53.

[111] See Tavernini 1953; on the similarities with Hermogenes' list and the supposition that he was Quintilian's main source, see Rutherford 1998, 40–41.

[112] For quotations in Lucian, see Householder 1941; Bouquiaux-Simon 1968; Anderson 1976 and 1978. For Homeric quotations in the Second Sophistic, see Kindstrand 1973. For literary quotations in Plutarch, see Hembold and O'Neil 1959. For allusions and quotations in Julian and for external testimonies of his culture, see Bouffartigue 1992, 51–424.

[113] The observations of Morgan (1998, 94–100) are only partially valid, and her table 19 is not significant, since it compares authors in Quintilian and in Hermogenes (Ps.-Hermogenes?) and Aphthonius who only wrote *progymnasmata*. It appears, therefore, that Hermogenes' quotations of Demosthenes are extremely rare, even though he was his favorite author.

[114] See, e.g., Bouffartigue 1992, 317 and 675–80.

that Julian's quotations reveal.¹¹⁵ Consider also the conclusions drawn about Libanius's limited knowledge of literature.¹¹⁶ Besides the undeniable fact that at this time, readings from some works were on the way to being reduced to Byzantine proportions, are we supposed to believe that he was familiar with such a limited range of authors and works? Is the fact that Libanius did not quote certain works proof that he did not know them? Or is this rather a sign of the fact that he was selective and chose to quote and allude to works that were *very* familiar to his audience, leaving on the side other authors that he had nevertheless read?¹¹⁷ In this case, moreover, it would be paradoxical for Libanius to have had such slight familiarity with literature, since he had received the usual grammatical education before studying rhetoric but then went back to the grammarian for five more years before engaging seriously in rhetoric again. A close reading of some of his works reveals that in fact, his library was richer than might be expected, so that, for example, far from almost ignoring Hellenistic poetry and relying only upon handbooks, he read poets such as Aratus, Callimachus, and Apollonius, who left subtle traces in his work.¹¹⁸ I suggest that fully educated people with scholarly ambitions had a good knowledge of literature, taking into account, of course, what was available at their time. This would explain, for instance, the discrepancy between the more than 100 papyri of Hesiod found in Egypt and the few that clearly belonged to the grammarian's school environment. People learned to appreciate Hesiod in the grammarian's school, but continued to study him at the rhetor's and as educated readers.¹¹⁹

Poetry, which occupies an unusually large proportion of Quintilian's catalogue, is also prominent in other lists. In selecting writers to be imitated, Dionysius started with Homer and other epic poetry and moved to lyric and comedy.¹²⁰ In these lists, poetry occupies the first place and is followed by prose, except in the list of Hermogenes, where it comes last. Yet for Hermogenes, poetry is essential, and Homer rivals Demosthenes as the greatest writer.¹²¹ Hermogenes' placement of poetry in his list, moreover, disconnects it from grammatical studies.¹²² He may not have

---

¹¹⁵ Ammianus 25.4.2: *quem legebat iucunde*. See Bouffartigue (1992, 317–18), who briefly comments on that.

¹¹⁶ Festugière (1959, 216) and Norman (1964) envisioned a limited library, e.g., "Alexandrian poetry is conspicuous for its absence" (Norman 1964, 161).

¹¹⁷ Cf. the remarks of Householder (1941, 70) on Lucian.

¹¹⁸ See Martin 1988, 135, commenting on *Or.* 5.

¹¹⁹ Cribiore 2001, 197–98. People must not have read Hesiod completely on their own.

¹²⁰ The list that Dio compiles to educate the man in political life (less significant for my purpose) also starts with poetry; *Or.* 18.6–8.

¹²¹ Rutherford 1998, 54–63.

¹²² Other writers may have given poetry the first place not only because of its importance, but also because its study was paramount at the school of the grammarian.

attached the same importance to poetry as to prose, but he did regard it highly, specifically for the benefits it brought a rhetor. Prose was the paramount concern of the would-be orator, yet poetry offered canons of style that had to be reckoned with.[123] Consider a passage in Lucian's *Lexiphanes* (22) that underlines the mandatory steps for someone who wanted to be renowned in the *logoi*: "After beginning with the best poets and reading them with teachers, pass to the orators and become familiar with their diction. In due time, go over to Thucydides and Plato, after a careful training in beautiful comedy and majestic tragedy." This account embraces education first under the grammarian and then under the rhetor, where reading supposedly included prose and poetry. Poetry was so important for the student of rhetoric that in the second century as well, Philostratus made the sophist Polemon declare that "while works of prose needed to be brought out by armfuls, the works of poets required wagonloads" (*VS* 539).

Historians of education have emphasized a sharp break between the levels of the grammarian and the rhetor: grammar and poetry on the one hand, and prose on the other. Marrou maintained that from the Hellenistic period on, a youth completed his literary studies with the grammarian, then entered the school of the rhetor, where he concentrated on prose works. This path has been more or less the general consensus since Marrou.[124] The ancient authors themselves, however, hinted at the shifting competence of the teachers at the various levels.[125] Poetry had been the protagonist in the Archaic and Classical periods and was still alive in Roman times, even though in the first and second centuries, prose dominated the literary landscape. The level of poetry in this period was not high, and (for this and other reasons) not much of it survived, yet its role should not be underestimated.[126] Poets often were scholars and men of letters, professionals who traveled to offer their services in commemorating events and people. Some were grammarians, but knowledge of rheto-

---

[123] North (1952) stressed the importance of poetry for the rhetor, focusing on the period from Homer to the second century C.E. She thought, however, that students at the rhetorical level read works of poetry in private, and she did not bring examples of the study of poetry in class.

[124] Marrou 1975, 296. Bonner (1977, 250–87 and 296–307) never mentioned poetry in his treatment of the curriculum with the rhetor; conversely, on p. 250, he asserted that the course of the grammarian did not provide any opportunities for work in prose. See also Clarke 1971, 38: students read orators and historians. Cribiore 2001, 225–30, started to show that the boundaries between levels were far from sharp and there was some poetry at the rhetor's, but Heath (2004, 239) dismissed most of the evidence, too rashly in my opinion. It is necessary to dedicate some attention to this question, which is treated nowhere else.

[125] Quintilian 2.1.

[126] Bowie (1990) focused on Greek poetry in the Antonine age. See also Bowie 1989b.

ric was fundamental to their trade. They often wrote *encomia* and invectives following the rules of the rhetoricians, celebrated weddings with *epithalamia,* and composed epic poems in which the art of panegyric was central. The rhetorical skeleton of these compositions was well in view.

Besides admiring poetry, some rhetors had a first-hand interest in it and composed poems. Aristides wrote both verse and prose hymns. The principal constituents of the latter were those of poetic hymns, and they were often poetic and highly rhythmical. Aristides' statements on the relationship between prose and poetry and his dismissal of the poets' exclusive claim to the composition of hymns are not easy to interpret, yet he (and other sophists as well) did not mean to supplant poetry with prose, but recognized that there were certain boundaries between the genres, and that poetry still maintained an independent role.[127] In the second century, other sophists wrote poetic hymns, hymn-like compositions, and dedicatory epigrams, and they introduced newly composed poetic texts into their prose works.[128] In an age when prose was the literary medium par excellence, poetry was still vital.

But it is in Late Antiquity that poetry enjoyed a remarkable revival, as Alan Cameron has shown.[129] This scholar identified a flourishing school of traveling poets from fourth- and fifth-century Egypt and focused on the resurgence of classicizing poetry all over the Greek and Roman world. Epigraphic dedications were written in elegiacs and hexameters and not in prose, like before,[130] and mythological and didactic poetry were extensively cultivated. We have seen above that one of Libanius's students, Amphilochius, bishop of Iconium, wrote in iambics a didactic letter to a young man, as Libanius himself had written an epistolary prose oration to a student (*Or.* 55). At the end of schooling, a returning youth often pronounced an oration of praise of his city, and Libanius wrote his oration in laudation of Antioch (*Or.* 11). In this he followed a tradition of epideictic oratory that the rhetor Menander had codified, and dedicated a large space to the tutelary deities of the city, revealing the divine favor that Antioch enjoyed from the very beginning. Likewise, in Late Antiquity there was a revival of poetry written in laudation of the mythological origins of cities.[131] The Alexandrian poet Claudian, who went to Italy at the end of the fourth century and composed in the tradition of Roman

---

[127] Aristides *Sarapis* 45 Keil. See Russell 1990b and Bowie 1989a, 213. Aristides' recognition of poetry per se is implicit in his choice to also compose hymns in verse.

[128] See Bowie 1989a.

[129] See Cameron 1965 and 1982, on one of these poets. On poetry in Late Antique culture, see Cameron 2004b.

[130] Cf. Robert 1948.

[131] Such poems were called *patria;* see Cameron 2004b, 330–31.

poets, wrote a number of such *patria*, honoring, for example, the city of Berytus. His debts to rhetoric in his panegyrics and invectives cannot be disputed.[132] Even though Claudian did not follow slavishly (as a previous generation of scholars emphasized) prose rhetorical examples, he was steeped in rhetoric.[133] The rhetorical texture of his poems as well as their structure and themes are a sure indication of the rigorous education in rhetoric he acquired in Alexandria. In many respects, these poems do not differ significantly from patterns of analogous prose composition in Menander and Aphthonius. Like Claudian, not only did poets who cared to engage in the fashionable art of panegyric attend schools of rhetoric, but they could hardly be satisfied with knowledge of poetry attained at the grammarian's.

Knowledge of Greek mythology was mandatory for a student of rhetoric, and for anyone who wanted to be identified as a person of some culture. So many writers in the Roman world dedicated themselves to expounding mythology that it is natural to expect that their works had a wide readership.[134] Students, however, became acquainted with myth at the school of the grammarian directly from poetic texts and must have continued to amplify their knowledge at the rhetor's through reading.[135] Numerous school exercises of mostly mythological *encomia* and *ēthopoiia* in verse have resurfaced from the sands of Egypt.[136] Far from pointing to an eccentric phenomenon and to the exclusive predilection of the Egyptians for poetry,[137] they are symptomatic of the fact that poetry was cultivated in schools of rhetoric anywhere, even though school examples outside of Egypt are hard to come by. It is significant that we are acquainted with some products of schools of rhetoric in Phoenicia because they are preserved in Egyptian papyri. These consist of two *epicedia* eulogizing professors, which were composed in Berytus, and a *logos epibatērios* for the arrival of an eminent personage, written in Tyre.[138] After a prologue in iambics, these exercises continued in hexameters; the *logos epibatērios* was written in a codex that included poetry from Aratus. A

---

[132] See Long 1996, 78–90.

[133] See Struthers 1919; and Fargues 1933, 46–50, 191–231. More recently, see Barr 1981.

[134] See Cameron 2004a, 217–52.

[135] The classical sources cited by mythographers are almost entirely from the poets. Van Rossum-Steenbeek (1998) concluded that mythological material in the subliterary papyri (many of which are associated with schools) was not read in lieu of the texts but was intended to supplement the reading of poetry.

[136] Cribiore 2001, 229–30.

[137] Cf. Eunapius VS 10.7.10–13, 493; above, Chapter Two.

[138] D. L. Page, *Select Papyri*, vol. 3 (Cambridge, Mass., 1970), no. 138. P.Vindob. 29788a; Heitsch 1961, no. 28; A. Zumbo, *Proceedings of the Twenty-Fourth International Congress of Papyrology*, forthcoming. Consider also the *ēthopoiia* in hexameters that the pupil Sulpicius delivered in Rome, Cribiore 2001, 241 and n. 91.

series of fifth-century epigrams in the *Palatine Anthology* is a further indication that cultivating poetry did not stop at the grammarian's.[139] These epigrams are mythological *ēthopoiiai* mostly based on the Trojan cycle, are written in epic (Nonnian) hexameters, and exhibit a remarkable homogeneity that shows that they have to be considered together as a group and that they may have come from the same school.

Libanius enjoyed poetry, and a letter allows us a welcome glimpse of him reciting Homer at the baths, as he waits for a friend.[140] He was not really a poet, however, and had to justify himself to friends, such as Philippus and Fortunatianus, who were rhetors, yet composed verses.[141] "Philippus and I went to school together," he wrote, "but I am on foot while he has wings; he is a nursling of the Muses and emulates Homer."[142] Philippus was a cicada dear to the Muses, and the rhetor Fortunatianus, "in whom a varied swarm of words resided," had the obligation to help him because he was a poet himself.[143] It seems that people trusted Libanius's judgment with regard to poetry and surmised that he composed verses. Gaius, a Cilician poet, composed a poem for the poet and rhetor Eudaemon of Pelusium, and another one in praise of Libanius (the teacher of his nephew), in which he lauded his rhetorical skills so extravagantly that the sophist hesitated to show it around, fearing it would provoke laughter.[144] Libanius approved the gift of a poem to Eudaemon because the latter could respond with another poem, but how could he, a sophist, reciprocate? Gaius apparently had a favor in mind: he sent him another poem and requested a detailed criticism, a sort of commentary, but this provoked a reaction (*Ep.* 1347). "Who wrongly told you that I am a poet? I love poetry, but I do not know how to compose it," Libanius retorted. "Yet I often wished to, but my natural talent did not cooperate." Moreover, he added, he could not bring himself to make a critique of that poem as he would not criticize Homer, Hesiod, and all the other poets as some did: the work of those critics was "lifeless" (*psychros*). Naturally, he felt more qualified to judge rhetoric and commented in detail on an oration on Asclepius his friend Acacius had composed.[145] But Acacius, a leading orator, also was an excellent poet and had equal proficiency in both genres.[146]

---

[139] *Anth. Pal.* 9.451–80; cf. Cameron 1967b.

[140] *Ep.* 430.10 (N11).

[141] Philippus 3/ii and Fortunatianus 1.

[142] See *Ep.* 1427.1. The term "on foot" (*pezos*) refers to prose, and the most notorious reference is to Callimachus *Aetia* 4.1.9.

[143] *Ep.* 1425 (B154).

[144] See *Ep.* 826 (B158). Gaius 1, uncle of the student Gaius ii. For Eudaemon 3, cf. above, Chapter Two.

[145] See *Ep.* 696 (B147). Acacius was Titianus's father.

[146] *Ep.* 127 (N58).

Libanius's conviction that he did not have a talent for poetry apparently arose from some attempts at composing it.[147] He was so fond of a former student that he composed an *epithalamion* for his wedding, in spite of his usual restraint from "singing" such things.[148] When a friend's prayers to Asclepius and his own faith freed him once of his migraines, he again overcame his reticence and declared his intention to visit Asclepius's sanctuary and bring him "a small poem on great things" (*Ep.* 1374.3). He apparently also composed a monody either for Julian or for the temple of Apollo in Daphne, and he wrote a sepulchral epigram for the emperor, which appears in the *Palatine Anthology* in a reduced version under his name and is reported by the historian Zosimus as anonymous.[149] Libanius's poetry was the fruit of exceptional circumstances.

In encountering so often the term *logoi* in fourth-century writers, one might be in doubt about what it included. When Libanius mentions this term, he mostly refers to eloquence in general, but in a few passages he clearly gave it broader significance, in accordance with what other writers did. Although the word *logoi* had many connotations, it was often used almost as a synonym of *paideia,* that is, culture and literary knowledge, and was associated with an education obtained in school.[150] Libanius wrote addressing Julian, "You received in your soul every canon (*idea*) of the *logoi*: compositions rapid or leisurely, letters, dialogues, and the beauty of poetry. In these you produce works of praise, persuasion, compulsion, and charm" (*Or.* 12.92). His thoughts on the inclusiveness of the *logoi* also come across in a letter to the Council of Ancyra.[151] Recommending a poet, Libanius dwelled on the citizens' passion for eloquence. Since they adored every *idea* of the *logoi*, they would not fail to appreciate Dorotheus, who traveled widely, showing his inspiration from the Muses. Libanius also wrote to Themistius that his student Julianus, who was departing from Antioch, was one of those who had mastered all the forms of the *logoi*, so that if the philosopher undertook to study poetry, Julianus would dedicate the most serious attention to it.[152] Themistius offered all kinds of *logoi,* including poetry, and thus attracted and charmed students (**118**).

---

[147] Foerster (1903–27, 11:654–55) reports the evidence for his poetical activity.

[148] See *Ep.* 828; the student was Herculianus son of Hermogenes, *PLRE* I, p. 420.

[149] Cf. Foerster 1903–27, 11:654, 57c, according to what Bernard de Montfaucon read in a manuscript; also p. 666, 89. *Anth. Pal.* 7.747; Zosimus 3.34.6 (a late fifth- or early sixth-century historian from Constantinople).

[150] See Bouffartigue 1992, 603–5.

[151] *Ep.* 1517; Cabouret 2000, no. 78. The poet was Dorotheus 4.

[152] Letter **117**. The *logoi* also include philosophy and astronomy. Poetry is here, as often, called *ta paidika* ("pleasurable, beloved pursuits"). Rhetoric could also be defined thus; see 7.3 and *Ep.* 405.13.

Libanius made poetry an integral part of his classes, as a few passages show. We have seen above that the student Epiphanius devoted himself to Homer under the guidance of one of Libanius's assistants (64) and that the sophist had to rebut the criticism of a pedagogue who objected that in his classes, Homer and Demosthenes were studied ad nauseam (*Or.* 34.15). He noted in a late speech that the value of rhetoric was so low that students were dejected at seeing people with no rhetorical education advance in their careers. They wondered what material advantages they would derive from the labors they had undertaken, fearing that they had covered "many poets, many orators, and all kinds of literature" to no avail (*Or.* 62.12). An excerpt from a late letter gives an insight as to how classes were conducted, and is explicit about the use of poetry in a school of rhetoric. Quintilian had already approved the pedagogical method of assigning each student in turn the task of reading aloud a speech in class, but Libanius went a step further. He conducted a quick audition and selected a student to read and act a play. The practice is not exceptional; Libanius says, "The *usual* texts were in my hands and I was thinking who could be the proper actor for the plays."[153] These customary texts must have contained classical poets, Euripides in particular, since Libanius was "inflamed" by him, as he declared in the year 360 to the poet Eudaemon, who had composed a poem culled from Euripidean material.[154] Libanius does not indicate whether he read this poet's works in class, but in later years he definitely used a similar poem composed by the governor Tatianus, which became a regular school text and underwent three revisions.[155] This epic poem (a combination of Homeric material and original verses) was as popular as the *Iliad* and the *Odyssey* with teachers and students and was used in his school at every level. Libanius said that he also benefited from it and drew inspiration for his own work.

You Think You are Happy and Make Youths Happy

Gregory of Nazianzus wrote to someone embarking on that life of rhetoric that he had renounced, "You think you are happy and make youths happy."[156] One of the enduring fascinations of Gregory's writings is the

---

[153] Quintilian 2.5.6; Libanius *Ep.* 1066.2 (N190). Heath (2004, 239 n. 44) argues that the word "dramas" is "surely metaphorical," but such an elaborately constructed metaphor does not make sense here. Libanius uses the term "drama" metaphorically only once and to the point, alluding to the real "drama" of a student playing a joke on Acacius in *Ep.* 722. The word occurs in his works numerous times, always referring to a play.

[154] See *Ep.* 255.9 (B151).

[155] *Ep.* 990.2–3 (N173), year 390.

[156] *Ep.* 235.4; the addressee had asked him for books that he had put aside.

conflict that still pulsates in his pages between his passion for the *logoi* and Christian expectations. The Gregory who still declared toward the end of his life that he was "Attic" (*Attikos*) and thus consorted with "Attic" people constitutes a paradox that many have attempted to solve.[157] The contradiction between his longing for but partial rejection of the Greek *logoi* and his frequent adoption of myths and citations from literature versus passages where he contrasted to them the truthfulness of the Scripture has been variously interpreted as the incompatibility of two different value systems; a conventional, literary rejection of culture; and a consistent personal conviction of the possibility to integrate the *logoi* with Christianity versus a more intransigent position adopted to convince others.[158]

The ambivalence of Gregory, however, did not extend to every aspect of literary culture. On leaving Athens, he was supposedly offered teaching positions and taught briefly in Cappadocia, but the attraction of a sophistic career did not last long.[159] His nostalgia for the eight years he spent in Athens often recurs in his work, yet he was sharply critical of the "sophistic mania" that reigned there.[160] Like Libanius, he felt estranged from those students who fanatically took the part of one or the other professor: they thought they were intimately involved in those conflicts, but they were like spectators at the games who participated vicariously and failed to notice they were serving the interests of others. The ludic aspects of rhetoric did not escape Gregory. Sophists "played among youths with exercises of fiction" and juggled with Marathon and Salamis, he wrote, but he had stopped "playing and babbling."[161] Their games, contortions, and gesticulations were like those of wrestlers, and "their glory was inglorious."[162] He found amusing and offensive at the same time the arrogance and ostentation of these "external educators" (*exōthen paideutai*), the vulgar aspects of their profession, their search for honors, their dealing with "dreams and shadows," and even their loud voices.[163] Sophists

---

[157] See Gregory of Nazianzus *Ep.* 224, to the governor Africanus 4.

[158] See Ruether 1969, 156–75; Demoen 1993; Van Dam 2002, 195–99.

[159] *Carm.* 2.1.11.254–64 Bernardi, note ad loc. Bernardi supposed that some Christian students offered him a teaching position. See above, Chapter Two.

[160] On his account of the years spent in Athens, see Gregory of Nazianzus *Or.* 43.15–24, and esp. 15 for the word s*ophistomanein*, a *hapax*.

[161] See *Ep.* 178.9, 233.3, and 235.1.

[162] Gregory of Nazianzus *Ep.* 11 was written to Gregory of Nyssa to dissuade him from becoming a sophist. The expression is typically sophistic, but also is vaguely redolent of Aeschylus.

[163] The expression "outside educators" (that is, outside the Church) often occurs in Christian writers to indicate non-Christian teachers. Gregory of Nazianzus *Or.* 43.21; *Ep.* 178. Cameron and Long (1993, 35–36 and n. 90) show numerous examples of this expression applied to learning.

talked incessantly, wrote his friend Basil of Caesarea to the sophist Leontius with mock courtesy: they talked with their students or even to themselves because they were unable to be silent, like nightingales intoxicated by spring.[164] Gregory agreed, yet for him, intimacy with the *logoi* was difficult to resist.[165]

For Gregory, the *logoi* were something "of his own" (*oikeion*), which touched him deeply and were capable of joining friends who had had the same experience, as he wrote to one of his fellow students in Athens.[166] The term *oikeion* with its various meanings ("domestic," "friendly," "personal," and "endearing") captures well Gregory's aching allegiance to culture. Twice he quoted Pindar's "what belongs to us bears heavy" (*to oikeion piezei*) to show how difficult it was to carry and to shed the weight of culture, but he also corrected the poet, for "what belongs to us also gives us pleasure."[167] Rhetoric, cultivated for so many years, had found its way deeply into Gregory's mind. When his brother Caesarius joined Julian's court, and people commented on the seeming paradox of a bishop's son aspiring to power and wealth, it was natural for Gregory to consider the matter an appropriate subject for *meletai*, or to add when writing to Themistius, "great for rhetoric," that he himself was not too bad at it.[168] This cultured way of life, which he confessed he had embraced to a degree, he defended against Julian's appropriation in *Oration* 4. He had earned the power of the *logoi* with "toils by land and sea" and was ready to preserve his rights to them with ferocious indignation. The Greek language, Hellenism, Atticism, and poetry must not be exclusively Julian's property.[169]

Poetry was essential for Gregory to express his vision of the world. His own poetry amounts to more than 17,000 verses in several meters (hexameters, elegiacs, and iambics), his prose is permeated by the poetic words of his predecessors, and he often integrates poetic citations into his text, a technique that rhetors recommended as improving "sweetness."[170] But poetry provided Gregory with much more than a technique. His letters to cultivated pagan and Christian correspondents throughout his life

---

[164] Basil of Caesarea *Ep.* 20.
[165] On the different meaning of the *logoi* for Basil and Gregory, see Van Dam 2003a, 155–84.
[166] See Gregory of Nazianzus *Ep.* 67.1.
[167] Gregory of Nazianzus *Or.* 4.100.3 and *Ep.* 10.12.
[168] Gregory of Nazianzus *Ep.* 7.3. Caesarius 2, a younger brother, was a doctor; *Ep.* 38.2.
[169] Gregory of Nazianzus *Or.* 4.100–109.
[170] On his autobiographical poems, see White 1996; and Tuilier, Bady, and Bernardi 2004. On the significance of Gregory's choice to write in verse, see Cameron 2004b, 333–39. On poetic integrations in Hermogenes, see Rutherford 1998, 58. The integration should remain almost invisible, as it does in Libanius.

testify how easy it was for him to turn to poetry. Homer was not just *your Homer*, as he wrote to a pagan friend, and the myth of Herakles and a minor episode from the *Iliad* were natural comparisons in another letter to a Christian governor who was learned (*logios*).[171] Gregory's poetic knowledge was vast and extended in many directions, including Attic comedy and Callimachus.[172] He must have systematically deepened his familiarity with the poets (and literature in general) during his long years of rhetorical training. The sheer fluency of his poetry, which he composed at great speed, shows that he was constantly reading Homer or the tragedians. The vast readings (prose as well as poetry) heightened both his pleasure and his lingering nostalgia for the *logoi*.

Gregory's writings are the clearest proof of the breadth of the education he received in Athens. His turgid Greek, teeming with allusions, metaphors, and classical references (particularly from Pindar), reminds one of Himerius, traditionally one of Gregory's teachers.[173] Since we have only an indirect knowledge of Prohaeresius, we cannot detect a sure influence from him, even though it is highly likely that his dashing, theatrical rhetoric produced a lasting impression. Gregory says that he followed all the teachers who were practicing in Athens, so his richly poetic style is the product of yet more contacts.[174] His style does not possess the clearness (*saphēneia*) and sweetness (*glykytēs*) of Himerius, and the conflicts inherent in his themes are reflected in his more convoluted prose, which is, however, lucid with sincerity.[175] Himerius the pyrotechnician liked to kindle his torch with Pindaric fire. In the lecture room, he was Pindar, who took up his lyre to sing.[176] Because of his predilection for lyric poetry, Himerius preserved valuable quotations from and allusions to lyric poets, but his own posture as a lyric poet has dubious value since, in spite of all his fire, his words are cold, graceful, and pretentious.[177] His relation to tragic poetry was more distant. In Himerius's *Oration 66*, written on the occasion of a student rebellion, he seems to confront and reject an attempt to make discourses with a tragic beat and a less gentle melody.

---

[171] Gregory of Nazianzus *Epp.* 71 (to Eutropius 2) and 156 (to Asterius 4).

[172] For example, the fourth century B.C.E. poet Anaxilas; cf. Bernardi 1984. On Gregory's deep knowledge of Callimachus, who left numerous traces in all of his works, see Cameron 1995, 334–36.

[173] Norden 1915, 563; Völker 2002, 178.

[174] Gregory of Nazianzus *Or.* 43.22.

[175] For an assessment of Gregory's style, see Kennedy 1983, 215–39.

[176] See Himerius *Or.* 35.9, 60.4, and 62.2.

[177] See H. Gärtner, "Himerios," *Der kleine Pauly*, vol. 2, col. 1149 (Munich, 1975); J. D. Meerwaldt, "Epithalamica I. De Himerio Sapphus imitatore," *Mnemosyne* 7 (1954): 19–38.

Himerius was constantly conversant with the poets. His rhetoric drew diction and imagery from Homer, Hesiod, Pindar, Stesichorus, Ibychus, and the Lesbian poets, who, in his view, provided much-needed liquid nourishment to parched rhetoric.[178] His students were not supposed to always follow rhetorical handbooks or old models such as Demosthenes, but they were encouraged to enrich rhetoric with every kind of voice.[179] A teacher (*mystagōgos*) initiated pupils into mysteries and taught them to fly like eagles that finally left their elders and went "beyond the clouds flying around the mighty sun."[180] Rhetoric was like music. For his students, Himerius was the teacher of the flute or cithara who produced melodies as examples (*paradeigmata*) for them and taught them to "dare" new words (*Or.* 61.3).

Besides style and diction, Himerius's closeness to the poets is also reflected in the themes he treated, such as commemorations of momentous events and personalities, journeys, arrivals, birthdays, and weddings.[181] Many centuries before, Isocrates lamented the superior power (*dynamis*) of poetry versus rhetorical prose: poets "could bewitch their listeners."[182] In addition to using meter and rhythm, they were allowed to treat more themes, to employ many embellishments of language (*kosmoi*) and mythological components, to use exotic and newly coined words, and to embroider their creations with metaphors in order to enhance charm (*charis*). Orators, on the contrary, were at a clear disadvantage. But things had changed considerably: by the fourth century C.E., orators could "bewitch their listeners" as much as poets did, and the *logoi* had acquired the power to bewitch those who knew them, Gregory among many others.

Epistolary Writing: A Form of the *Logoi*

I have investigated elsewhere the little that is known about the teaching of letter-writing in elementary and grammatical schools.[183] People who preferred not to employ scribes needed some epistolary skills. The exchange of correspondence between students at lower levels of education and their families naturally continued for those who left home to study

---

[178] See, e.g., *Or.* 69 (partly translated in Walden 1912, 265–66). On dry rhetoric, cf. *Or.* 68.
[179] See *Or.* 68.11.
[180] *Or.* 54.3. On images of flying connected to learning rhetoric, see Cribiore 2001, 220–21.
[181] Cf. Völker 2002.
[182] Isocrates *Evagoras* 8–11 (*psychagōgein*, 11).
[183] Cribiore 2001, 215–19.

170 • Chapter Five

rhetoric. The historian Ammianus refers to the practical instructions parents compiled for their sons going away to school (16.5.3). In later times, correspondence dealt with financial support and emergencies, such as the need for a student to return home or to leave Antioch during a dangerous riot.[184]

There was, however, another level of epistolary skill that cultivated people needed when they aspired to high office or wished to correspond with a measure of sophistication. Libanius exhorted his student Honoratus, who had just left school, to keep on exercising his skills by writing to his parents and to him: Honoratus needed to be an expert for the time when he would govern a province (**103**). As with rhetorical skills, epistolary ability had to be nourished with books and constant practice.[185] The ancient sources praised the advantages of a good knowledge of the proprieties of letter-writing,[186] but did not expand on how and at what level of education it was inculcated. Modern scholars have advanced the opinion that the teaching of epistolary skills might have been on the fringe of formal rhetorical instruction, but they have adduced no real evidence.[187] Yet there seems to be plenty in both the Western and the Eastern Roman worlds.

The fact that in the fourth century, Julius Victor appended an excursus on letter-writing to a manual of rhetorical theory already points to a connection between rhetorical and epistolary skills.[188] Libanius allows us to make considerable progress in this respect. He regarded letter-writing as an *idea* ("canon") of the *logoi* and proudly believed that he taught Julian to write powerful letters.[189] The compliment he addressed to an ex-student, Aristaenetus, who had studied rhetoric for a year with him and later "made such progress as to reach such competence in epistolary style," reveals that he did not consider letter-writing a skill for the novice; quite the opposite.[190] Letter-writing was an art that was nourished by rhetoric, and Libanius found it hard to comprehend how the sophist Bonus hesitated to correspond, since he had within himself "all the poets, all the

[184] See, e.g., *Ep.* 428 and **89**; *Or.* 55.1 and 23.20.

[185] See **67**; cf. also *Ep.* 842.

[186] See Pliny the Younger *Ep.* 9.9.

[187] Kennedy 1983, 70; Malherbe 1988. Thraede (1970, 180–85) argued that the fact that epistolary topics in fourth-century writers such as Synesius or Ambrose were very similar depended on a common rhetorical education.

[188] Julius Victor *Ars rhetorica* 27, pp. 447–48 Halm. He considers the use of rhetorical devices indispensable for formal epistolary writing.

[189] On Julian's letters, see Bouffartigue 1992, 542–44.

[190] See *Ep.* 1064 (N189). Aristaenetus 2/ii, a relative of Libanius, attended his class for about one year and probably continued elsewhere.

rhetors, and all forms of the *logoi*" (*Ep.* 1035.1). As one recognized the speeches of those who had been trained at the same school, so the letters of those educated together were so similar as to confuse others.¹⁹¹ People, in fact, mistook a letter of a friend who had been trained in Athens together with Libanius for one of his: it had the same beauty and length.¹⁹²

The perfect length of a letter was a matter of discussion for ancient letter-writers. Many times, Libanius concerned himself with the *metron epistolikon* by praising or blaming the length of letters he had received or written.¹⁹³ The length of a letter was a function of its subject, and the rules that governed speeches also applied to letters. Thus Libanius commended the short letter of introduction of Androcles for the same clarity (*saphēneia*), invention (*euresis*), and propriety of diction (*lexis*) that made the discourses of this sophist beautiful (**77**). His correspondents often appear intimidated by Libanius's mastery of the genre, and his reassurances to them clarify his definition of "proficient letter-writing" (*to technikōs epistellein*). People who had the ability to judge the quality of discourses were good critics of letters, too. A good letter showed thoughtful concepts and a language fully Attic, and revealed the character of a person (*Ep.* 1283.2–3). Style depended on the occasion and on the recipient, Libanius told Honoratus (**104**). The crowd was fond of a recherché style, which this student was permitted to use in certain circumstances but not in familiar letters or when corresponding with his teacher. Unnecessary flattery should be avoided in the latter, because it "spoiled the beauty." The similarity of the advice that in Rome Symmachus gave his son is striking: the "darts of rhetoric" (*aculei orationis*) fitted some occasions, but familiar letters had to have a different tone, in between seriousness and jocularity.¹⁹⁴

Libanius's ideas on letter-writing are found throughout his works, but Gregory of Nazianzus composed a didactic letter to explain these principles to his grand-nephew Nicobulus and expatiated on the necessary length, subject, clarity, and elegance of an epistolary message, and on the rhetorical figures that were appropriate to the genre (*Ep.* 51). By way of example, he included a fable: of all the birds, the eagle was the most beautiful because it was not self-conscious of its beauty; a natural and unadorned (*akallōpistos*) style was most desirable in a letter. On another occasion, he acquiesced to Nicobulus's request to have a collection of

---

[191] Cf. Gregory of Nazianzus *Ep.* 52.3: one could distinguish the letters of certain authors as one recognized the children of noble fathers.

[192] See *Ep.* 559 (B31).

[193] See, e.g., *Ep.* 561 (B173). On *modus* in Christian letters, see Conybeare 2000, 23; in Byzantine letters, see Mullett 1981.

[194] Symmachus *Ep.* 7.9.

his letters by quoting Homer and saying that he was sending him "Aphrodite's girdle"—not something erotic, of course, but concerning the *logoi* (*logikos*).[195] Homer, Callimachus,[196] Euristheius, and Herakles still figured in the letters of an old lover of the *logoi*, which were in reality far from unadorned.

There is no doubt that letter-writing was an object of study in schools of rhetoric in both the Western and Eastern worlds.[197] When Symmachus wrote to his son that letters addressed to friends differed considerably from public letters, and that some "insouciance" (*neglegentia*) fitted the former, he added that he was sure that the boy's teacher (*rhetor tuus*) advised him with regard to this (*Ep.* 7). We gather, therefore, that both private and public letters were objects of study in a school of rhetoric, as Libanius confirms. In a letter he addressed to the grandfather of a pupil, also named Libanius,[198] he exhorted him to write his grandchild often, since his letters were vigorous and so well-written that they could serve as models. "I encouraged Libanius to become acquainted with the letters of the old writers and also with these, and to be nourished by the former and by the latter, too," he wrote (**134**). Learning epistolary skills was achieved through the process of imitation that permeated the rest of the *logoi*. As the composition of *progymnasmata* went hand in hand with the reading and digestion of the classics, in the same way a study of the letters of ancient and contemporary writers prepared the ground for epistolary skills. Libanius's allusion to letters of the old writers is intriguing, because so much of the epistolography prior to the fourth century is lost or of questionable authenticity. One surmises that some of the letters handed down under the name of Demosthenes might have been studied by Libanius's students, yet he never alluded to them.[199] Everything else (letters from Isocrates, Herodotus, Thucydides, or Alciphron) is only speculation.

In letters to former students, Libanius often mentioned his pleasure that they were using epistolary skills he had instilled in them. Bassianus was learning to write letters in school and, after leaving, cultivated his ability and elicited his old teacher's approval (**31**). When he wrote a polemic letter to Libanius, the latter could not help admiring its beauty, even if Bassianus had used his "wrestling tricks against [his] trainer" (**33**). The

---

[195] See Gregory of Nazianzus *Ep.* 52. Gregory quoted *Iliad* 14.219, a book that was rarely read and quoted in antiquity; see Cribiore 2001, 197.

[196] See Gregory of Nazianzus *Ep.* 51.3, with an echo from the *Aetia*.

[197] Epistolary writing continued to be taught in schools in Byzantium, see *Anon. Lond.*, letters 104 and 105. The fact that the anonymous professor collected his letters (Markopoulos 2000) probably indicates that they served as models.

[198] See **133** and **134**.

[199] No allusion appears in the introduction to Demosthenes' orations, cf. Gibson 1999, 176.

letter that two brothers sent him upon leaving school was also so accomplished that it made him comment: "Writing a letter with such skill (*technikōs*) is not usual for students who are away but rather for those—if I may say so—who are still meeting with me" (**20**). A letter of another student, Julianus, brought Libanius great joy not only because of its good tidings, but also because "the length of the letter and its charm was showing that I am the father of a good child" (**121**). Considering a letter a gift was an epistolary *topos*,[200] but in this case, an ecstatic Libanius equated the gift to all the money Julianus could send him by selling most of his land. Likewise, a well-written letter from an ex-student, Dionysius, was not only a more valuable gift than the horse that he was gratefully planning to send his teacher, but was "more valuable to me than the horses of Tros and Achilles, and even winged Pegasus" (**54**). Yet, although a letter might be brimming with elegant and impeccable Greek, it was sometimes inadequate return for a great favor, as Libanius reminded the same Dionysius, who meant to send a letter to his "savior" Palladius but should rather compose a long, momentous discourse properly honoring him (**58**).

Writing a letter to a teacher as demanding as Libanius was no small endeavor, and some students dreaded or avoided corresponding altogether. Scylacius "tremble[d] in fear" of looking bad, but since he had covered the most rigorous material in school with good results, he received the stern warning "not to insult" the studies he had done (**180**). Likewise, Hypatius wrote to Libanius apologizing for a letter he thought inadequate, but, the teacher replied, he had good rhetorical and epistolary skills and only needed to not cease practicing (**105**). Another student who had taken Libanius's classes about ten years before spoke highly of him but refrained from corresponding. Libanius, who looked forward to talking about the old times, marveled at the silence, since Basilides was once an elegant letter-writer—unless, he added dryly, that skill had vanished (**30**).[201] But as always, the emperor Julian was the most accomplished pupil. By nurturing the seed Libanius had planted in him, he supposedly became capable of surpassing the fame of his teacher as letter-writer (*Or.* 13.52). This time it was Libanius's turn to declare in a letter to an ex-student that he feared corresponding with Julian because the emperor's letters had a light that was lacking in his own.

---

[200] One sees it already in Demetrius *On Style* 224; cf., e.g., Libanius *Ep.* 1215, where a letter is a gift more precious than gold.

[201] Cf. also **111**, reproaching Hyperechius, who knew the art but did not use it.

CHAPTER SIX

The Long and Short Paths to Rhetoric

THE DIALOGUE *The Teacher of Rhetoric* (*Rhetorum praeceptor*), by the second-century satirist Lucian, is cast in the form of an essay advising a young man who is interested in receiving a rhetorical education. Seduced by the promises of rhetoric (wealth, status, and fame), the student confronts a choice between two different paths: a traditional rhetorical education consisting of many years of strenuous training, and the new, shorter, and easier road to rhetoric, which, according to Lucian, had just been opened. The traditional teacher, who led students up the hill of learning in an ascent that would take many years, made them follow carefully in the footprints of ancient writers such as Demosthenes and Plato.[1] The elegant and effeminate teacher who offered the easy and short path, however, dismissed the need for rigorous training, claiming that a sprinkling of Attic words, the careful selection of easy themes, and the imitation of contemporary models would assure success. Lucian assigned to the charlatan teacher the most outrageous attributes, yet it is likely that he based the figure on some realistic details and that the work has claims to actuality.[2] This dialogue shows how literary reminiscences, imagination, satire, and the real world converge. It is not only an attack against "concert orators,"[3] those sophists Lucian pretends to despise, nor is it merely a variation on the often-recurring theme that younger generations toil less than older ones. It is, in my view, a satirical acknowledgment that two different educational tracks may have already existed in the second century C.E., and that people who followed the shorter route succeeded equally well, if not better, than those who embarked on the traditional course.

This chapter is concerned with the two paths that led to the acquisition of rhetoric, and with what induced students to shorten a long and demanding process. Personal circumstances and the need to start earning, the cost of schooling, a diminished appreciation for traditional rhetoric, or satiation with an education that was somewhat out of touch with reality contributed to the urge to leave the customary path. Parents' insistence

---

[1] Lucian *Rhetorum praeceptor* 9.
[2] See Baldwin 1973; Jones 1986.
[3] See Branham 1989, 3.

that education should bring tangible fruits in a short time can often be verified. In all times (and especially when schooling was not partitioned in mandatory stages), families have tried to interfere with teachers' plans. The anonymous professor who taught in tenth-century Constantinople, for example, protested that some parents wished to accelerate the learning pace of their sons contrary to reason. A bird who had not flown before—he said with rhetorical emphasis—could not fly swiftly at the start, and it was impossible for the Augean stables to be cleaned with one sweep.[4] In Late Antiquity, the wish to acquire an education in rhetoric concentrated in more easily digestible pills went hand in hand with specific cultural aspects. Late Antiquity saw a proliferation of manuals that recycled and summarized knowledge, of commentaries and paraphrases that clarified a text, and of presentations of material in question-and-answer format (*erōtapokriseis*).[5] This period was also distinguished by a gradual development of specialization that peaked in the sixth century.[6] The examples of Libanius, Eunapius, Gregory of Nazianzus, and Basil of Caesarea, among others, have served to foster the view that since Isocrates' time, an education in rhetoric has always involved the sacrifice of an inordinate number of years.[7] But these were "culture heroes," whose choices tell us relatively little about those who needed some rhetoric as training for posts in the administrative bureaus.[8] It has not been sufficiently emphasized, moreover, how both the long and short paths to rhetoric were often fragmented through instruction at the hands of several teachers in different schools. In addition to receiving pupils fresh from the grammarian, Libanius also took others who had learned the rudiments of rhetoric or had progressed to a higher stage with sophists who taught closer to their homes.

In Lucian's dialogue, the main narrator (Lucian himself, for a while) claims that he followed the long path for a number of years without reaping great rewards.[9] Who were the young men who held to the arduous road until the end? When we regard as paradigmatic the schooling of Libanius or Eunapius, we should not lose sight of the fact that they considered an academic career a desirable way of life.[10] Their choice to study rhetoric at Athens involved a long, perilous voyage by land and sea,[11]

---

[4] *Anon. Lond.*, in Markopoulos 2000, *Epp.* 38, 39, and 93.
[5] See Moreschini 1995; Volgers and Zamagni 2004.
[6] Cf. Cameron 1998, 683.
[7] But see the observations of Heath (2004, 321–31), which my study fully confirms.
[8] For a pessimistic view of culture in the fourth century, see MacMullen 1990, 117–29, esp. 125.
[9] Lucian *Rhetorum praeceptor* 8 and 26 (he quit rhetoric).
[10] Gregory of Nazianzus, too, did a little teaching.
[11] See Libanius *Or.* 1.14–15; Gregory of Nazianzus wrote two versions of the storm he encountered in sailing from Alexandria to Athens, *Carm.* 2.1, 1.308–21 and 2.1, 11.121–210. Eunapius fell sick during the voyage, *VS* 10.1.4, 485.

several years spent away from their native countries, and a total immersion in a life cut off from past affections and habits. The experience of Bruno and Basilius Amerbach at the turn of the sixteenth century was similar. After studying for a short time at the University of Basel, which was closer to home, they attended the prestigious University of Paris for five years, communicating with their parents only through letters. Did Libanius try to reconstruct in Antioch an institution comparable to the "university" of Athens, that is, a prestigious educational magnet with the power to retain youths for many years? Was this project remotely successful, or, if not, what were the reasons for its failure? This chapter will investigate all of these matters.

THE LONG ROAD

By buying and studying daily the lectures of Libanius in Nicomedia, the emperor Julian assimilated his style and was in the same (or even better) condition as the sophist's regular students (*hoi synechōs synontes*).[12] The expression "to attend on a continuous basis" (or a variant of it) seldom occurs.[13] The regular attendance that Libanius envisaged consisted of an uninterrupted course of studies lasting for several years, but one is hard pressed to find many students fulfilling this ideal.[14] Some considerations need to be borne in mind in attempting to calculate the length of attendance on the basis of the correspondence.[15] It was in the nature of letters to respond to crisis, to underline exceptional situations, and to ask for help for deserving students compelled through misfortune to interrupt their studies. Libanius, moreover, was probably not in epistolary contact with all parents, communicating primarily with those who had requested information about their sons. Some families may have been intimidated by Libanius's erudition, and thus reluctant to contact him.[16] Many centuries later, others, like Johann Amerbach (a man of culture who had himself attended the University of Paris), may have deemed sufficient the communications they received from their children and their attendants. Yet, even though some negative reports may be missing from the correspondence, the dating of the letters needs further work, and each student's years of

---

[12] Cf. *Or.* 18.15.

[13] See, e.g., 145: Menecrates, who came to Antioch with the intention "to partake of my teaching on a continuous basis," quit because of illness.

[14] On the vague terminology Libanius used to refer to the "whole" of the instruction in rhetoric, cf. below, Chapter Seven.

[15] Cf. Appendix Two. The conclusions I reach there for some students are inevitably speculative.

[16] See, e.g., 177: The first phrase lets us speculate that Stratonicus had a poor education.

attendance cannot be tidily determined,[17] it is nevertheless clear that Libanius regarded so highly his work as a teacher and the well-being of his pupils (both while they attended his school and after) that he probably failed to mention only a few of them in his letters.

It is risky to assume that, when two letters testify that a youth was studying with Libanius in a certain year and then again five years later (with no other letters in between), he necessarily attended for the whole period.[18] Such a scenario could be valid when families lived near Antioch and nearly all communications were in person, but in most cases, no definitive conclusion can be reached. The rigid presupposition that a young man was in school for years without interruption does not take into account numerous factors that might affect his presence. Besides reflecting the modern custom of higher education, this assumption rests on several considerations: Isocrates' statement that, in the fourth century B.C.E., students from all over the Greek world attended a course of three or four years with him; the impression one gets from Quintilian that instruction in rhetoric in first-century C.E. Rome comprised a course of several continuous years; and our knowledge of the long school attendance in Athens of some fourth-century authors.[19] But mentioning students' sometimes sporadic attendance was not helpful to the projects of Isocrates or Quintilian, and the Athens of Libanius's times was an island of learning of exceptional reputation from which a return home was unusual and final.[20]

In their pursuit of rhetoric, young men moved from place to place, starting closer to home and ending eventually in distant Athens. The reputation of certain locations (Antioch among them) was so irresistible that students would often neglect a "nearby spring" of eloquence (**129**). They considered the veneer of a prestigious education indispensable and the lack of distinguished credentials a liability. Libanius benefited and suffered at the same time from this trend. Although his school functioned as a magnet in Anatolia and nearby provinces, he was unable to offset the allure of Athens, where he had studied himself and where some of his students aimed to put the finishing touches on their own schooling.[21] He was not the only one to protest against the trend of studying at an educational center that was rich in traditions, but ultimately equivalent to others. The philosopher Themistius composed a whole oration on this point, defending his training by a good sophist in an obscure town of Pontus.[22]

---

[17] As in Petit 1956a, 46–66.
[18] Petit (1956a) always takes this for granted.
[19] Isoc. *Antid.* 87 and 224; Quint. passim.
[20] On the whole, we base our conclusions concerning a very long attendance in Athens on the schooling of only a few exceptional students.
[21] See Celsus 3 and Titianus.
[22] Them. *Or.* 27, translated in Penella 2000a, 164–74.

178 • Chapter Six

Eloquence, he said, was "winged" and was to be found not only in Attica, even though the *logoi* had appeared there first. A true desire to learn involved more than the urge to visit a foreign place. Both Libanius and Themistius thought that the fame of Athens as an educational center was undeserved, and they regarded students' "need" to go to the source of eloquence as a pose. The wings of eloquence ensured that it was not rooted in any one place, said Themistius.

Determining the length of a complete course with Libanius is a matter of supposition.[23] His statement in the year 388 that Eusebius was the student who attended for the longest time[24] is not accompanied by further information, since the letters that concern this "head of the *chorus*" all date from that year.[25] In spite of his long attendance, Eusebius did not choose a life of teaching, allegedly because of family pressure. A disappointed Libanius remarked that he would have been perfect for the role, since his performance as substitute teacher had been impeccable (**81**). I have already discussed the status of another student, also called Eusebius, who did choose a teaching career.[26] He was a very accomplished rhetor and must have had a lengthy schooling, but no information exists. The attendance of other students who supposedly remained in Antioch for long periods cannot be verified with certainty. Sometimes only two letters separated by many years attest that students were in Antioch, and it is suspicious that Libanius corresponded with relatives of theirs in the interim without mentioning them.

A calculation of length of attendance that rigidly clings to the letters' dates is also of dubious accuracy. Examination of the content of some letters may show that students arrived in the summer (therefore, they attended the following year), went home, and returned the next year, so that the estimates of their attendance need to be reduced.[27] But the opposite may also be true. Students who supposedly attended only for a year (because they are attested in letters for that year only) are likely to have had a longer schooling, since the correspondence that concerns them attests such great diligence and expertise that Libanius nurtured the vain

---

[23] Petit (1956a) made an earnest effort in this direction, but with doubtful results. His statement (64 n. 93) that the complete course lasted five years is only a conjecture.

[24] See **78**, Eusebius 25.

[25] Other students who were *koryphaioi* in different periods were Basilides (**30**) and Julianus xv (**120**). Petit (1956a, 88) supposes that one became "head of the *chorus*" after four to five years.

[26] Eusebius 24; cf. above, Chapter One.

[27] The sons of Philagrius were students of Libanius for two years, not for four. The attendance of Titianus, which for Festugière (1959, 179) amounts to eight years and for Petit (1956a, 63) to five, should also be reduced to three incomplete years.

hope that they were going to embrace an academic career.[28] To sum up, even though the letters do not permit us to achieve precision, and sometimes leave us completely in *aporia*, it is clear that the vast majority of Libanius's students were not in school for anywhere near the number of years that some distinguished contemporary figures were (Libanius included). The attempt of Libanius to supplant Athens and to gather many dedicated students was not very successful. Those who desired a thorough training still went (or wished to go) to Greece, while the majority opted for studying in Antioch for a limited amount of time.

A Shorter Path

The expectations of families and educators often clashed because their goals were different. Parents were aware of Libanius's projects about training but had sometimes planned their children's careers long before. Some rhetoric was necessary, so that one "participated so far as to get a touch of it,"[29] but the long, arduous road was inappropriate in most cases. When parents planned for more financially rewarding careers, they did not communicate their intentions to Libanius.[30] Pandorus, for example, "an eager hunter for rhetoric" who devoted himself to the discipline, was in poor financial condition. After one year of attendance, Libanius recommended him to Celsus for a summer job or some sort of internship (**157**). But at the end of the second year, the youth's father enjoined him to come home: he claimed that he missed him and thought that he possessed the art of rhetoric to a sufficient degree (**158**). Some resentment and insistence followed, and Libanius volunteered to help financially: he sent back to the father the donkeys that were meant to cover the young man's expenses.

That Libanius considered three years of training sufficient for Pandorus does not prove that this was the average attendance. Education in the ancient world was much less standardized than today, and the diagnostic exam for newcomers served to ascertain their readiness. The student Themistius, one of Libanius's best success stories, attended only for two years, but, since he joined the school when he was eighteen years of age, it is likely (though not certain) that he had had some previous instruction in rhetoric.[31] The few sophists who appear in the correspondence through the letters of recommendation they wrote for applicants are probably not

---

[28] See the cases of Faustinus and the son of Marianus.
[29] Cf. *Or.* 33.3: the governor Tisamenus participated little and perforce.
[30] See Julianus above; Severus 14, Chapter Five.
[31] Themistius 2. Apolinarius and Gemellus, who studied with Libanius for one year, might have had some previous training.

the only instructors the students had had before Libanius. Most of the time, we are not informed of the identity of a previous teacher, but some students must have had some training, because they were already strong in rhetoric when they arrived in Antioch.[32] At other times, the scenario is clearer and throws into relief groups of students from a particular location associated with certain sophists. In Armenia, for instance, the sons of Philagrius, Maximus, and perhaps also Anatolius attended the classes of a renowned local teacher, Leontius. Libanius did not mind if boys had received some previous training somewhere else,[33] but he resented it acutely when they followed other sophists in Antioch. Caesarius sent his sons from Armenia to study with a rival teacher, probably Acacius, and when he wanted to transfer them to Libanius's care, he had to excuse himself profusely, engaging the help of a friend and of the provincial governor to gain admission for them.[34] Philopatris, the governor's son, also studied with Acacius first, and both his father's blandishments of Libanius and recommendations from friends are evident from Libanius's letters.[35] Students who left Libanius prematurely might also continue to study with other sophists. Calliopius left Antioch to follow his father, who had become head of the notaries, and Libanius trusted that he was going to keep up with rhetoric with other good teachers.[36] For Marcus, who suddenly "flew away," he suggested the sophist Palladius in Cappadocia, although further training may not have taken place because Marcus was satisfied with the little he knew and was impatient to enter public life.[37]

The preceding tales have already highlighted some of the reasons why students followed the short path to rhetoric. That decision was sometimes made earlier, when children were young.[38] Some families planned a short attendance from the beginning because they needed their sons to start earning by practicing as advocates or entering the administration. But the letters also reveal emergencies of various kinds that led to detours from the long road: ill health,[39] parents' deaths,[40] fathers obtaining posts some-

---

[32] See **168** and **176**, *pros tous logous errōsthai*, "to be strong in rhetoric."

[33] See, e.g., Meterius, who was a student of Alcimus in Nicomedia, **147**.

[34] See **35**, **36**, and **37**.

[35] See letters **99**, **165**, and **166**. We do not know if the sons of Caesarius and Philopatris also studied some rhetoric in Armenia.

[36] Calliopius iii, *Ep.* 362 (N28) and *Ep.* 366 (B35).

[37] See *Ep.* 1174 (B102), and letter **139**.

[38] Besides the son of Marianus, cf. Honoratus, *Ep.* 366 (B35) and dossier. See also *Epp.* 362 and 1399 (B64 and B44): on the young sons of a doctor enrolled in the corps of the imperial couriers (*agents in rebus*), and on young children nominally undertaking a liturgy.

[39] See Gaius (**87**), Menecrates (**145**), and some older students always in the hands of doctors (**205**).

[40] Albanius (**8**), Dionysius (**52**), Faustinus (**82**), Julianus xv (**120**), and Eudocius the son of Caesarius (**40** and *Ep.* 288). See also the observations in *Or.* 55.14.

where else and taking children along,[41] fathers or students themselves compelled to perform financially ruinous public service,[42] and young men entering the army.[43] Age might also shorten a student's path to rhetoric. Libanius's writings sometimes disclose cases of students who joined the school at more advanced ages, even those who were married and had children of their own.[44] In spite of his protestations that the curriculum was the same for everybody, Libanius treated these pupils with special consideration, shortening their course and giving them "concentrated instruction and eagerness, which instills speed in the art" (**101**). It is indicative of his desire to appear fair to everybody that his treatment of these students is mentioned only indirectly, in letters where he suggests an analogous modus operandi to a professor of law.[45]

Families might also have wanted to recall their sons when they suspected indulgence in spectacles and chariot races[46] and questionable moral deportment. The letters, with their veneer of amiable politeness, do not reveal much on this matter. Veiled allusions, perhaps to homosexual behavior, occur in **62** and **98**, while in another letter Libanius discloses his own policy (prompt dismissal) with regard to "what is not decent to mention."[47] The orations, which address a faceless crowd, are less timid and refer to the supposedly unacceptable behavior of a teacher (suspiciously, the Latin teacher) and of students in general.[48] *Oration* 38, an invective written in the year 388, is more direct than usual in pointing to the bold conduct of a student, the son of Silvanus, who had attended Libanius's classes in the past. The only letter that refers to Silvanus (**175**, dating to 359) alludes to his "good character," but the much later oration evokes his learning difficulties and his indecorous conduct: he overlooked the supposedly indecent behavior of his son, who "made many households wretched" by having lovers and procuring lovers for friends (*Or.* 38.8–12). The defection of this young man, who transferred from Liba-

---

[41] Arsenius (**27**) and Polybius (**167**).

[42] Cf., in *Or.* 55, the threats of the sophist of Gaza to Anaxentius's father. See also Asteius (**29**); Epiphanius (**64**), Gerontius vi (**89**), and the son of Argyrius (*Ep.* 113).

[43] The son of Salvius (**174**).

[44] Apringius, Bassus, Hilarinus, Julianus 15, Marcianus, Rufinus (*Ep.* 1352, B157), and the students of letters 204 and 205. See also *Ep.* 1257 to Euphemius i, who was about the same age as Libanius. Both the son-in-law of Caesarius and Calycius were married. The *Autobiography* mentions a Cappadocian student who started rhetoric late (11), and his friend Crispinus, who had his own family (54).

[45] See **101, 26**, and *Ep.* 1131 (B165).

[46] See *Or.* 23.26–27, 41.6–9, 35.13–14 (for ex-students), and letter **190**.

[47] *Ep.* 1330 (N139): expulsion prevented the "contagion" (*nosos*) from spreading.

[48] On teachers (presumably the Latin teacher) smitten by students' graces, see *Or.* 58.29–31, and on students' homosexual penchants, *Or.* 2.57, 62.25, and 64.48.

nius's classes to those of the Latin teacher, puts the objectivity of the report into question.[49]

The short road to rhetoric was well trodden. It was a fairly efficient way to obtain the degree of knowledge that enabled people to acquire the reputation of being educated and the ability to function in the curial administration, advocacy, and provincial government. Students "fell in love with power" and "leapt off" from Libanius's school when they saw an opportunity to partake of it.[50] In spite of his protests, Libanius must have recognized that for the majority, it was an inevitable course. Not only did he refrain from objecting loudly to the short attendance of some students, but he also plumed himself with their successes. The two brothers Strategius and Albanius from Ancyra, for example, attended for one and two years respectively.[51] Strategius left at the beginning of his second year because his father died.[52] His mother and uncle convinced Albanius to quit after two years, and his prosperous career is noteworthy in the light of the fact that a very short training in rhetoric is verifiable in his case.[53] Libanius says unequivocally that Albanius was his "student in the strictest sense of the word," because he did not have other teachers either before or after him (**13**). Yet, with only two years of rhetoric, this young man was Libanius's pride and joy. He was admired by first-rate sophists, delivered an acclaimed panegyric in praise of an important official, preserved his property through legal maneuvers, undertook splendid civil service, spoke in the law courts, and gained the reputation of being a good orator. Libanius respected his choice, assured him that rhetoric was going to be of service no matter what he decided to do, and told him that through the reflection he cast on his teacher, who appeared to be "not only a wrestler but also a good trainer," he had "silenced" the sophist's critics (**8**). When in the 380s he tried to rebut criticism that he had failed to produce outstanding members of society, Libanius included the two brothers in the list (admittedly short) of those who shone as councillors. He mentioned another pair of brothers, Apolinarius and Gemellus, as "directing their community" in Cilicia by virtue of their *paideia*.[54] It is

---

[49] Festugière (1959, 200) takes the whole invective too seriously. We are not sure where this speech was delivered.

[50] See *Ep.* 81 (N47): the student Julianus ix, who followed Libanius from Constantinople, left him despite his potential, and Optatus (below) planned to do the same.

[51] See dossier. Festugière (1959, 153–59) assembled all the letters concerning these two brothers.

[52] *Ep.* 536 says that he left to be as splendid as his father in civil service. It is uncertain whether he had had any previous training in rhetoric. In a short note to his father, *Ep.* 444, Libanius described him as above the majority (*hoi polloi*) in one year only.

[53] Many students attended for a very short time, but it is impossible to know if they had other teachers besides Libanius.

[54] See *Or.* 62.37.

significant that he claimed their success as his in spite of their brief attendance.[55] He told their father that he should be grateful to him because they had "acquired not a little rhetoric, and in such a short time" (**21**).[56] It was an implicit acknowledgment that the short path to rhetoric was an adequate road to worldly success.

THE COST OF EDUCATION

The students mentioned above belonged to well-off families for whom expenses for maintenance and tuition were not important issues in determining length of attendance. Not only did Albanius always pay the school tuition, but he also discharged his debt of gratitude to Libanius in other ways. He entertained him in his house for long periods and sent him monetary gifts years after he had left the school (**11**). Letter 11 revolves around the "ruse" Albanius devised to prevent his teacher from refusing the gift and is an eloquent example of the subtle norms of reciprocity that regulated pedagogic relations. The correspondence shows over and over the multiplicity of meanings of the word *misthos* ("fee," "payment"), which include compensations of various kinds.[57] Besides the specific duties involved in teaching and learning (providing instruction and paying for it), a complex web of gratitude pervaded the process of *paideia* and was part of the larger circle of obligations that formed the texture of ancient society.[58]

Teaching involved not only the obvious pedagogical duties, but also a measure of voluntary goodwill (*eunoia*) that was not strictly dependent upon monetary compensation and would theoretically continue in its absence. A grateful student did not completely discharge his debt to a teacher by paying him a fee, but compensated him in other ways for his generosity. We have seen above that a Bithynian student dedicated a stele with an inscription for his teacher as a "repayment."[59] A teacher considered his pupil's success in life his own true "payment" because it validated and advertised his worth (**11**). Libanius declared that the speaking ability of those who had studied with him, the orations they composed, and their elegant letters were his true compensation (*misthos*) and were better than all the gold and silver they could give him.[60] His words were not only

---

[55] Their father, Anatolius 4, became governor of Phoenicia, and they followed him.
[56] The expression *micros chronos* refers to an attendance of about one year. Cf. in *Ep.* 1081 the *mikra synousia* of Aristaenetus 2.
[57] It was also called *amoibē*; see *Or.* 3.6.
[58] See the distinction between formal and personal reciprocities in Van Wees 1998.
[59] Cf. above, Chapter Two, Firmus "*antēmeipsato.*"
[60] See letters **8**, **63**, **103**, **121**, and **125**.

pedagogic savoir faire. For the modern observer, the gratitude involved in receiving and giving instruction complicates the scenario of compensation for schooling in antiquity. A family's debt of appreciation could be discharged, for example, by helping other young orators who had been the "tent-mates" of their son and studied at the same school.[61] Conversely, a student's disappointed hopes, and the admission (feigned or authentic) of failing to gain the promised knowledge, wiped out any obligations, at least in the eyes of the owing student, who protested that "he had learned nothing, heard nothing" (*Or.* 43.6).

Libanius's sources of revenue as a sophist have been much discussed. He lamented that he was defrauded of money, but was accused of trying to profit unjustly from the system.[62] From various letters and passages in his *Autobiography*—which are admittedly confusing—one can deduce the following.[63] When teaching in Constantinople, Libanius received a regular salary in kind as official sophist (*trophē*), plus some extra emoluments in the form of revenues from Imperial land (*chrēmata*). He was released from that appointment when he was in Antioch, but he remained on the books for a while. After that, the salary was rightly transferred to someone else, but he was also asked to return the money that he had received in the interim period, even though that was not customary. Let us look at the controversial beginning of *Ep.* 572, which dates to 357:

> [1] I did not resent that the imperial salary in kind was given to someone else. I had to become fully disentangled from that, and this happened with the removal of the salary in kind. [2] I regard as a benefactor the person who took it away. With regard to the money, however, which in previous times those who received it did not return, I talked to the governor and I also added that I was bothered by the lack of respect more than by the material loss, but I talked in vain. He did not respond, but it was clear that he found no fault with those who deprived me of it but blamed the one who demanded it back.

In this letter, Libanius does not strike me as particularly greedy,[64] but refers to tradition: other sophists who had been in the same position in the

---

[61] See *Ep.* 1357 (B95).

[62] See Martin and Petit 1979, 226; and Petit 1955, 409. Kaster (1983, 50) argued that Libanius tried to appropriate money unjustly, calling it "an unedifying episode in Libanius's career."

[63] Cf. esp. *Or.* 1.74 and 80; *Epp.* 446, 454 (which allude to the loss of the salary), 480, 572; and *Or.* 31.

[64] But see Kaster (1983, 47), who translates (less naturally in my view): "I spoke to the official concerning the money that they had taken during the time before this and had not given back." Kaster therefore supposes that the sophist did not receive that money, which was diverted to someone else, yet Libanius insisted on getting it, even though he was not entitled to it.

past had not returned the *chrēmata* dispensed according to extraordinary honors. Thus Libanius resented that he had to give the money back. He argued that it was a question of principle rather than an attachment to money per se. The whole episode reveals Libanius's usual attitude of suspicion and resentment when he feared he was being slighted, rather than a desire to profit unjustly. On becoming Antioch's official sophist, he continued to receive the imperial stipend, which was supplemented by fees from his students.[65] Besides pupils' fees, his assistants received meager compensation from the city, and Libanius in 361 appealed to the city Council for augmentation of their salaries.[66]

Parents (or students who received money for this purpose)[67] paid a sophist's fee on the occasion of the celebration of the New Year, that is, in the middle of the school year, which started in the fall.[68] Abuses ensued because students who claimed they had found the instruction disappointing refused to pay and moved to different schools. We do not know how much the tuition was, but it was high. Libanius remarks (with some exaggeration) that families were ready to lose their fortunes to pay for their sons' education, and that the student who became a sophist was able at least to recoup the money he had spent for his studies.[69] But other factors complicate the scenario of school compensations. It is commonly remarked that Libanius did not really exact fees from his students and that his policy was similar to Themistius's,[70] but the practice of both sophists deserves further scrutiny. The letters, moreover, indicate that students brought gifts at the Kalends and on other occasions. The orations include only the official salary and students' fees among a teacher's compensations, yet one wonders whether gifts were gratuities or whether they had any relation to the school fee.

---

[65] In *Or.* 55.23, he expressed his dissatisfaction with the salary. On teachers' economic standing in antiquity, see Kaster 1988, 99–134, and Cribiore 2001, 59–65. The tenth-century letters of the professor in Constantinople also testify to economic hardship and of being paid late or not at all; see Lemerle 1986, 288–90.

[66] *Or.* 31, written in 361, claims that these low salaries were also paid irregularly.

[67] In *Or.* 35.12, Libanius says to those former students who were silent in the Council that they had all the advantages because parents paid their school fees. On students placing the fee in the sophist's hands, see *Or.* 54.17; on their wasting the money for their amusements, *Or.* 3.6.

[68] See *Or.* 9.16–17 and the *ekphrasis* of the Kalends (Foerster 1903–27, 8:472–77), Martin 1988, 202. See Chapter One. Reiske (1791, ad loc.) states that people left the fee on the steps leading to the teacher's chair. *Or.* 54.16–18 contains a reference to a student depositing "the money of the pedagogue" at the feet of the sophist. See also Palladas (*Ant. Pal.* 9.174), who says that a student's nurse brought the fee once a month wrapped up in papyrus and deposited it by the grammarian's chair.

[69] *Or.* 55.21 and 26. Letter 53 implicitly shows that the cost of studies was high.

[70] See, e.g., Martin 1988, 276–77; Norman 2000, 186 n. 7.

In presenting the Council with a realistic view of a teacher's income in 361, Libanius rebutted the common opinion that students' fees constituted a great part of it and admitted for the first time that not everything was well with his profession.[71] The financial ruin of many curial families (compounded with rhetoric's lower prestige) forced him to teach their sons for free. In several late orations, he expanded on his tuition policy with a bitterness that was absent before.[72] In 361, Libanius was offering a tuition exemption for families in financial straits that aroused in them mortification as well as gratitude; by the 380s, however, the poor as well as the well-off supposedly took advantage of Libanius's practice. It seems that a policy that was originally connected solely with low income brought about a general rule of voluntary giving that Libanius thus described: "Those who wish to do so, pay; those who refuse, do not."[73] This practice had infelicitous consequences. Libanius condemned not only the delinquency of students of all economic condition but also their resulting slackness in following his classes.

Libanius's policy on students' fees is vaguely reminiscent of that of the fifth-century B.C.E. sophist Protagoras, to whom he may have referred when he mentioned "those who enriched themselves out of teaching in former times" (*Or.* 31.25). Accused of charging excessively, Protagoras had relied on a kind of honor code: satisfied students paid the fees he exacted, but those who did not want to stated on oath in a temple the value they attributed to what they had learned (*Prt.* 328b–c). In times more precarious for both rhetoric and the personal finances of students, Libanius found it harder than his distant predecessor to rely on a similar code of honor. It was not on sophists but on Socrates himself, however, that the philosopher Themistius modeled his policy.[74] Unlike Libanius, he did not charge his students at all. While he was pleased that he could not be accused of "hunting down any rich young man," Themistius claimed that his prosperous income permitted him not to exact fees, but that the practice per se was not especially noble. His main reason for not boasting of his generosity was that other teachers may have needed such revenues. Was Libanius one of these needy sophists?[75] It does not seem so, yet tradition and his fear of devaluing rhetoric prevented him from waiving tuition altogether.

---

[71] *Or.* 31.25 and 29–32.

[72] *Or.* 36.9; 3.6–9; and 43.6–7 and 13.

[73] In *Or.* 36.9, Libanius adds that his example forced other sophists to imitate this practice.

[74] See Plato *Ap.* 31b–c; Themistius *Or.* 23.249c–d Dindorf, where he is polemical against old and new sophists.

[75] On Libanius's finances, see Petit 1955, 407–11.

A less obvious result of Libanius's ambiguous practice was the stigma attached to all those who did not pay. Thus issues of "justice" (*dikaiosynē*) governed pedagogic relations, so that paying benefited the giver (who acquired a reputation of being honest) as well as the recipient and encouraged better teaching.[76] The student who did not pay because of financial difficulties was under a cloud of suspicion like the rest. Good students paid, said Libanius, and bad ones did not, and the father of Severus, who appealed to his "generosity" (*megalopsychia*) to avoid paying, wrongly trusted that "those who did not pay were on an equal footing with those who did" (*Or.* 57.3).[77] It is no wonder that Libanius accused the governor Eutropius (his target in *Or.* 4) of never paying the tuition to any of his teachers during his school years: besides offending Demeter by taking his son away from the work of the fields, Eutropius's father "offended the Muses by depriving them of their fees."[78] It is only to be expected that the infamous Silvanus of *Oration* 38 never paid anything.[79] When his father, the teacher Gaudentius, mentioned the tuition, Libanius "was vexed" (*Or.* 38.2) and promptly waived it because of collegiality and on account of Gaudentius's income, but one is not surprised at the ensuing dark portrayal of the two insolvents, Silvanus as well as his own son, who studied in turn with Libanius.

The correspondence shows the usual reluctance to mention problematic issues and contains remarks on insolvency only twice, and in a jocular mood. Libanius mentioned to an official his former student Leontius, one of those who failed to pay the tuition, who paid him back, "more than anyone else," by bringing the letter.[80] More ambiguous is his attitude toward a former schoolmate, the father of two students.[81] Are we supposed to believe the sophist's protestations that his chiding remarks about overdue fees were not serious and that his friend should keep the horse he planned to send him? This letter is a good example of the complicated etiquette of giving and receiving in matters of *paideia*.

An education in Roman law, which was quite costly,[82] respected the same social code of gratitude and consideration of students' finances, and Libanius's correspondence also allows us a glance at that. Thus the sophist warned the professor Domnio, who had special regard for needy cases,

---

[76] See *Or.* 9.17. In *Or.* 43.7, the sophist remarked that teachers who did not receive their fees became inefficient because they were not serene enough to concentrate on their books.

[77] Cf. the portrait of the ideal student in *Or.* 34.5. On Severus 14, see *Or.* 57.3.

[78] *Or.* 4.16–17. On the difficulty of identifying this *consularis Siriae*, see Martin 1988, 105–8.

[79] Cf. above.

[80] *Ep.* 1523.2; Leontius xvi.

[81] See letter **71**, Eusebius x.

[82] Professors of law could count only on students' fees, Collinet 1925, 200–204.

that the student Apringius, who wanted to learn the law, might have trouble paying the tuition, but that he was "indeed capable of remembering a favor" (26). Conversely, he pointed to two reasons why the father of a student who could afford it should not object to paying the law school's apparently high fees (96). Poverty forced the teacher to charge a fee that was not excessive if one calculated "the amount of books and the other great things" that he provided. This letter implies, therefore, that the tuition in a law school was higher than in a school of rhetoric, but that it included study materials that Libanius did not provide.[83] Parents of Libanius's students bought "the usual books" for them, and when they neglected to send money, they hampered their children's learning, as if they made their sons "learn archery without a bow."[84] It is only a matter of speculation what else, in addition to the especially heavy books,[85] law professors included in their pupils' package. Besides writing material of various kinds, it is possible that they contributed to students' maintenance to a degree.

Gifts present a further difficulty in forming a coherent picture of compensation. In the second century, Philostratus presents the seemingly unorthodox example of the sophist Alexander of Tyre, who, when offered a gift of fish lying on a silver-and-gold plate, appropriated the precious platter as well (VS 590). Philostratus deals at some length with this incident because it could be interpreted in various ways and probably was not so unusual. In our society, gifts mostly appear as extras, defining relationships that would exist (to some extent) even in their absence; but elsewhere and in antiquity, gifts were a vital part of social life.[86] As a rule, Libanius's fees amounted to money, which he called *chrēmata* or *argyrion* but occasionally showed to be gold coins (*chrysia* and *statērai*).[87] In *Oration* 54 he ranted against the governor Eustathius, who was grateful to him because his son "made lots of progress in a few days," but who did not pay the sophist because he regarded teaching a governor's son to be a sufficient honor. Not only did this student neglect to hand him gold or silver, Libanius said, but Eustathius did not even send him any oil or wine from his properties.[88] These remarks indicate that the tuition could be

---

[83] See, however, *Or.* 62.21, where Libanius implies that youths of the lower classes went to Berytus.

[84] See *Or.* 35.12 and *Ep.* 428 (N10). Libanius used books in his class and disapproved of teachers who did not; on Nicocles, cf. *Ep.* 1487.

[85] On heavy books, see *Ep.* 1203 and *Or.* 4.18.

[86] See Van Wees 1998, 25–29.

[87] See *Or.* 3.6, 31.25, letter 27, and *Or.* 54.17–18. Libanius usually employs the term *statēr* to indicate the golden *solidus*; see Liebeschuetz 1972, 84–85.

[88] Eustathius 6. On Syria's abundant production of olive oil, see Liebeschuetz 1972, 80–81.

covered by items other than money that were not mere gratuities, as the example of the student Pandorus and his donkeys shows (**158**).

One is hard put, however, to distinguish gifts that were mere presents[89] from those that were meant to compensate the sophist for his services. All the wine that the grandfather of a student sent him probably belonged to the latter category (**134**), as perhaps did the two tunics with their silver embroideries that a father gave him (even though Libanius calls them "gifts"): these were expensive items, and their elegance prevented the sophist from wearing them in public (**73**). He sent back another beautiful tunic because it seemed too extravagant; the sender, moreover, could not properly call himself a student of his, and in Libanius's view, the gift was not justified by being a real compensation (*misthos*) (**43**). All the presents he received over the years from another father, Flavianus, seem to be gratuities of some kind.[90] Since presents are usually not random objects of value, Flavianus's gifts also tell us something about Libanius himself. Besides doves that the sophist enjoyed, Flavianus sent him a gazelle, which did not reach him alive and whose fate Libanius lamented because Flavianus had said *mirabilia* about it.[91] The sausages, wine, tunic, and book that he offered the sophist on another occasion served to mollify him (**84**). Flavianus's son, "the little weasel," intended to buy some peace with this compensation (*misthos*): he was not a good student and longed to return home.

Even though Themistius could not be accused of exacting fees, he still had to rebut the charge of being a "mercenary hunter" (*emmisthos thēreutēs*), since his detractors maintained that he bought students: he fed them, gave them money, and distributed among them some of the wheat he received as Imperial salary.[92] The philosopher, however, considered this practice legitimate and refused to discuss the magnitude of his expenses because they aimed at assisting needy students. When Libanius accused a rival sophist in Nicomedia of squandering his patrimony to buy students, he did not mention whether the beneficiaries were in financial need, but

---

[89] Dionysius, a former student, sent Libanius a horse to thank him for his support (**54**), and the horse he wished to receive from Marcus's father (**139**) perhaps was not a gift. On gifts accompanying a Christian letter, but with a different symbolism, see Conybeare 2000, 26–31.

[90] *Ep.* 1332, a witty letter, shows that a Philagrius, who may have not been the Philagrius iii who was father of some students, sent him a bad horse, after Libanius offered him doves.

[91] See *Ep.* 655; the gazelle died either because of the heat or because of the negligence of those who brought it. The letter dates either to 361, when the boy was not in school yet (Flavianus may have planned to send him), or to 365 (Sievers 1868, 139 n. 31), when he was attending.

[92] Imperial salaries were paid in kind. Besides wheat, Themistius received oil, *Or.* 23. 289–92.

it is likely that they required some subventions (*Or.* 1.65).⁹³ He certainly did not find this practice objectionable per se, but he was ready to intervene when a family kept a student in poverty and therefore asked the sophist Demetrius of Tarsus permission to let him "assist" (*symmachein*) his nephew.⁹⁴ Poverty often appears in connection with higher education. Gregory of Nazianzus mentioned poverty among the memories (sweet in retrospect) of his student life, and sore need characterized the school years of Prohaeresius and Hephaestion in Athens.⁹⁵

When parents were unwilling or unable to provide for a student, Libanius tried to organize some financial aid from other sources. The dossier of Dionysius exposes all the "misfortunes" of this orphan and the tenacious help of his teacher. The letter that Libanius wrote to the friend of a former supporter of the youth in the hope that he could help reinstate the interrupted financial aid is a masterpiece of gentle pressure (**53**).⁹⁶ It clarifies that assistance was dependent on real need, on the student's behavior toward the donor, and on his overall personality. Only in case the student's and the donor's financial circumstances changed or the student's attitude did not deserve to be rewarded could the aid be suspended. In a brilliant stroke, Libanius emphasized that a suspension would reflect badly on the former supporter and feigned to believe that the decision had stemmed from a subordinate, without the patron's knowledge, allowing the latter to keep his pride. A letter of the same year, 357, also reports on financial support of poor students. This time one of the sophist's friends in Antioch paid much attention to impoverished students and aided them with prompt generosity.⁹⁷ Two years later, Libanius acknowledged the receipt from the governor Anatolius of 100 *solidi* on behalf of the student Optatus.⁹⁸ Libanius grumbled that Anatolius, who intended to make the student proficient in rhetoric, should have disbursed 1,000 *solidi*, but a letter dating to the summer of the same year shows an amusing "coincidence."⁹⁹ Another student, Julianus, quit the school, encouraged by Anatolius, and Optatus, "falling in love with the power" of his supporter, was doing the same. The governor may have planned from the beginning a limited intervention. It is perhaps not a

---

⁹³ Eunapius (*VS* 10.5.6, 490) discusses more extreme methods of attracting students by providing "expensive banquets and nice-looking servants."

⁹⁴ See *Ep.* 23 (B144). Libanius was referring to more than the tuition.

⁹⁵ See Gregory of Nazianzus *Ep.* 30 to his friend Philagrius, who was equally poor; Eunapius *VS* 10.3.5, 487. When Libanius imagined his life in Athens, he forecasted that he would ask for loans, *Or.* 1.19.

⁹⁶ Letter **56** notes that another student, Julianus xv, was also helping his schoolmate.

⁹⁷ *Ep.* 552; the benefactor was Letoius i.

⁹⁸ *Ep.* 80 (N46), Anatolius 3; Optatus iii.

⁹⁹ *Ep.* 81 (N47). Julianus ix, see above.

coincidence that all the letters that present Libanius's efforts at organizing financial support for his students (including the message to Demetrius) date to the late 350s. The rest of the correspondence does not reveal any more direct interventions. It is possible that Libanius decided to stay out of such matters later on, when the circumstances in which he practiced became more problematic.

DEFECTIONS

The widespread problem of defections (*apostaseis*)—that is, pupils' withdrawal from the classes of one sophist in favor of another—suggests a need for caution in determining students' length of attendance on the basis of the letters.[100] Defections were not confined to the end of the year but occurred throughout it. Some students went from sophist to sophist to end up with their first teacher, and then the cycle restarted. This phenomenon, which apparently reached alarming proportions by the 380s, was not new. Libanius maintains that students' defections attracted universal condemnation and rarely occurred in his schooldays, but they were already frequent at the beginning of his teaching in Antioch, as a letter dated to 355 discloses.[101] At that time, he attributed the cause to the greed of pedagogues who "sold" their wards; he did not dare to find fault with parents seeking a competitive education for their sons or with students' own dissatisfaction. According to a series of late speeches, the problem became acute in the last decade of his life, when he denounced (with some exaggeration) the fact that "every day, pupil after pupil attached themselves to different teachers."[102] He then held parents responsible for the situation because of their lassitude and avarice: they did not interfere with their sons' decisions and encouraged defections in mid-year so that they could cheat teachers out of their fees. In his eyes, newly popular disciplines such as Latin or Roman law also shared the responsibility for the difficulties rhetoric encountered, but rhetoric itself was beyond reproach.

A passage of the *Autobiography*, which has been variously interpreted, refers to Libanius's difficulties in those years and his remedy for this "disturbance" (*tarachē*, 241–42). Since his refusal to declaim did not produce the expected results and some students continued to misbehave, he said

---

[100] This is a problem that Petit overlooked. When some intervening years in a student's attendance are not documented, we cannot automatically assume that he was studying with Libanius.

[101] See *Or.* 43.8 and *Ep.* 405.8 (N6).

[102] See *Or.* 1.241–42; 3.24; 34.20; 36.13; all 43; and 62.25. The installation in 388 of a chair of Latin further encouraged defections; see *Or.* 3.24, and cf. below, Chapter Seven.

that he used some "compulsion (*anagkē*) so that they could not leave, even if they wished to," but declared that he preferred not to mention what it was exactly. This has been enough to arouse the curiosity of scholars.[103] The measure does not seem to refer to the covenant he had openly proposed to the other sophists in Antioch in *Oration* 43. It may have been something less dramatic than the magical practices that have been suggested, yet still something that ran counter to his ideal of a good teacher, so that he preferred not to discuss it. By analogy to what was happening in Athens, it is usually assumed that Libanius always bound his students with an oath, even though he never says he did.[104] He felt a real aversion toward the oath, which in Athens functioned as a sort of contract between a sophist and his students, and in the narrative of his life he repeatedly expressed his dislike for that arbitrary practice by using the same expression (*anagkē*) that he employed with regard to his own later, secretive measures.[105] One suspects that Libanius, the proud teacher, after his loud denunciations of the binding practice of the oath during his schooldays in Athens,[106] felt quite uncomfortable in admitting that in his old age he had to resort to the same methods, particularly if some harsh punishment was then visited upon the transgressor.[107] When teaching in Nicomedia, he sharply blamed the constriction of the oaths that the sophist Hecebolius imposed on Julian and again condemned "all the oaths, constraints (*anagkai*), and bonds" that his rival Acacius used in vain to retain his students.[108] It is not too surprising that he did not feel like discussing a matter that he found controversial.[109] When personal charisma and the unique prestige of a rhetorical education were under attack, he assimilated the weapons of his opponents like that "octopus" Eunapius accused him of being.

Unlike some of the speeches, the letters are sparing with comments on the issue of defections. Mobile students appear twice in connection with the sophist Acacius. In the year 357, Libanius vented his rage at him, since he apparently did not observe some covenant they had stipulated to

---

[103] Martin and Petit (1979, note ad loc.) suggest (but are unable to prove) that he may have resorted to the practice of magic; Norman (2000, 111–13) finds the suggestion attractive.

[104] Norman (2000, 112) takes this practice for granted.

[105] See *Or.* 1.16 and 20: *anagkē* and *prosanagkazein*.

[106] He wrote that people feared that he "might take some fresh line with regard to the oath," *Or.* 1.20.

[107] On punishment in the ancient classroom and on Libanius's ambivalence in this respect, see Cribiore 2001, 65–73.

[108] He deeply disapproved of the "many fearsome oaths" with which Hecebolius had bound Julian in Nicomedia, *Or.* 18.14. He ridiculed Acacius's measures in *Ep.* 450.12.

[109] The awkwardness of the sentence is due to the fact that he did not publish personally the second part of the *Autobiography*.

protect their respective enrollments and took advantage of the discontent of a pupil punished by Libanius (*Ep.* 555). A few years later, after securing a permanent position, Libanius could afford to make fun of defections by playing a trick on his rival with the help of another pupil (*Ep.* 722). Letters to families, however, almost never discuss defections or attempt to recover lost students, and so the correspondence gives us the false impression that "everything was plain sailing," as it had supposedly been for Libanius's predecessors.[110] While letters were by nature vehicles of friendship, Libanius's pride prevented him from pursuing a fleeing student.[111] "I never saw fountains going after those who need to drink," he wrote to a father, saying that he scorned those who wanted to avoid him. But at the same time, this letter reveals the distress that resurfaces in the orations.[112]

Defections were not a problem unique to Antioch.[113] In Athens, students appear to have been equally restless, but their defections were probably confined to other sophists in the city. Himerius's orations hint at students disaffected with the teaching of some sophists and looking for different mentors.[114] The details of his allusive, heavily mythological speeches are sometimes difficult to grasp, but some passages undoubtedly refer to students' dissatisfaction.[115] Whereas Libanius denounced pedagogues and parents as responsible for students' mobility, Himerius focused on pupils' discontent and recklessness. He portrayed the rebellious students who were brought to reason as Nymphs who abandoned the woods to play again in Attica. Now the students' flocks, "which used to leap recklessly," could pasture in peace and return to their folds as if Orpheus or Amphion led them (*Or.* 38.9). Himerius apparently pronounced an extemporaneous speech for a students' revolt, which survives in a mutilated state (*Or.* 16). In the proem, he wishes that his words could be a healing remedy (*pharmakon*), like the draught Helen gave the guests of Menelaus to calm their emotions. In this oration, mythological exam-

---

[110] In *Or.* 43.3, he says that the educational system worked well only for previous sophists.

[111] He wrote to Titianus's father in letter **188** that he was pursuing the boy contrary to his habit, but in this case the boy received instruction from his own father.

[112] See letter **162**; cf. *Or.* 43.6.

[113] Students' mobility also plagued the professor in tenth-century Constantinople. Many letters (and especially 30 and 35 Markopoulos) regard the tense relationship with an individual who convinced some of his students to go to a rival teacher.

[114] Cf. above, Chapter Two. In Himerius *Or.* 35, the students finally come to Socrates' school.

[115] See, e.g., *Or.* 18, where Himerius presents the god Dionysus arriving in India among people who were hostile at the start but then promptly joined the "*chorus*" of the god. His *Or.* 65, which apparently refers to student fights, also contains hints of internal strife: the good *chorus* master needs to eliminate discordant voices. The bad state of preservation of some speeches hampers understanding.

ples follow unremittingly, but they all intend to soothe the anger of what appears to have been a real revolt (*stasis*).

What were the motivations of the students' unrest, one wonders? Why did they feel the urge to continue searching for a better guide to eloquence? Libanius's focus on external agents is not satisfactory and, one suspects, mainly serves to assuage latent anxiety about his own inadequacy.[116] He sheds more light on the matter when he discloses his own disillusionment with his teachers in Athens, even though part of his discontent should be attributed to his exceptional talent and preparation. Himerius's works, however, suggest that students were in need of a change and wished to experiment instead of tirelessly repeating the same forms and content. Far from adopting extreme measures to punish the rebellion, the sophist allowed some innovations, showing his students at the same time that the result might be unharmonious eloquence, or at least eloquence devoid of the pastoral sweetness that he cherished.

Of all the works of Himerius, *Oration 66* shows most clearly that the Late Antique classroom was teeming with discord, which is still detectable, although myth disguises its virulence. Himerius is Apollo surrounded by a chorus of Muses (the good students), among whom are some reckless (*atasthalos*) mountain nymphs (the rebellious students).[117] When they are mingled with the chorus, these nymphs do not distinguish themselves from Muses, but when they attempt to leap and bound in a graceless way, they stand out and anger Apollo. According to the version of Aesop that Himerius is following, the god-sophist does not have recourse to his shafts and refrains from violent punishment,[118] but adapts his lyre to a new, wild song following the nymphs' dance. Mountains, valleys, rivers, and birds (that is, the sophist's audience) are appalled at the offense done to Apollo, and Mount Helikon, disguised as a man, gives voice to everybody's feelings in a full-fledged *ēthopoiia* addressing the rebellious nymphs. In reproaching them for leaving the Muses' workshop, which makes poets out of shepherds, Helikon warns the nymphs that their urge to go to Kithairon, the place for "disgrace, sorrows, and the source of tragedy," will bring them to ruin and madness. Naturally, the nymphs heed the appeal.

Himerius appears aware that students were tired of the old formulas. The proem of another oration (19) expands on the concept of surfeit (*koros*) that ruins the pleasure in what is customary. The sophist's obser-

---

[116] Cf. letter **162**: some people attributed the defections to his inability.

[117] Cf. above, Chapter Two. *Atasthalos* is the appellative that Himerius applies to the "bad" students; see *Or.* 54.1.

[118] The speech, however, recalls the chastising nature of Apollo in the *Iliad* and admits, therefore, that there were different reactions to students' rebellion.

vations that people who live on land would rather be sailors and vice versa, and that men admire the ocean or the pyramids because they are far away, are not original, but the invocation he addresses to his students—"Habit produces surfeit: boys, let us flee from surfeit!"—deserves attention. Perhaps it is not excessive to envisage Himerius's eloquence as a response to his students' protests, or at least to his own realization that rhetoric needed to be reinvigorated. Orators (the poets of the *logoi*), he says in *Oration 68*, were in love with the old models, but it was urgent "to contrive new works of art." Nature was always changing and renewing itself, and a powerful orator had to be like Proteus (fire and water, a lion and a tree) and had to divide his *logoi* into many forms (*idea*, 68.9). The same concept dominates Himerius's *Oration 35*, in which Plato, who had forsaken all other pleasures in life after hearing Socrates, did not model his philosophy solely on him but was able to capture his audience by adopting every form of the *logoi*. Eloquence needed to be like a meadow teeming with every kind of flower, and variety also characterized Homeric poetry or Herodotus's historical prose.

It appears that Himerius gave permission to his students to test their strength and experiment with a novel eloquence. "Yesterday I saw you as you were creating, when you threw away your books and built this improvised theater to the Muses," he told the young men in his following. He considered that theater "stronger than the wall that Demosthenes and the Athenians raised against the Spartans in Pylos" (*Or.* 68.11), words that affirm the superiority of his eloquence with respect to the rhetoric that found its champion in the Athenian orator. Punishment (or compulsion of any type) was not the answer to students' discontent and to those "who dared spend even a single day estranged from my friendship" (*Or.* 54.2). He abhorred those masters who used the whip in lieu of their song to manage their flock: it was his novel song that had to lead them back to the Muses' meadows. This was Himerius's power and the source of the charm that he exercised on many, Gregory of Nazianzus among them. It is unfortunate that in discouraging his students from modeling themselves on the old rhetors and in urging them to search for something new, he also went back to old models and found inspiration in the writings of Archaic poets that were even less relevant to contemporary rhetorical tastes.

But let us now return to the two different paths to rhetoric. In Lucian's dialogue, the traditional teacher, who required a long commitment and huge sums of money, enjoined the student to follow the footprints of a few writers of the past and dug up long-buried speeches, which were no longer relevant but which students were supposed to imitate faithfully. But why revive these speeches in a time of peace, when Philip and Alexander were long gone, Lucian asked?[119] Education built on a set of exempla that were more or less superficially known. In the second century, Lucian was already well aware of the dilemma that confronted rhetoric and education, which was to become more acute later. The long road to rhetoric that Libanius, Himerius, and other sophists promoted in their respective fashions did not have the same appeal as before, even though some persisted in taking it, and a sophisticated rhetorical education was still alive and well in the fifth and sixth centuries and in later Byzantine society.[120] From a cultural and literary point of view, a shorter path was not a change for the better, because with it education was losing the rigor and discipline that had characterized it in the past and were its strength. Yet rhetoric had learned to survive, adapting to social change and to the practical needs of its devotees.

---

[119] *Rhetorum praeceptor* 10.

[120] This is what the works of Aeneas and Procopius of Gaza and of Choricius testify. On the continuity of the system in late Byzantium, see Webb 1994; Browning 1997; Jeffreys 2003; and Constantinides 2003.

CHAPTER SEVEN

After Rhetoric

DIFFERENT EDUCATIONAL PATHS—A LONGER TRADITIONAL EDUCATION in rhetoric and a shorter one that amounted to only a few years—usually led to different choices in life, but whereas some students immediately entered the real world and tried to use their knowledge to enhance their careers, others continued their studies in other fields. My goal in this chapter is to identify the options available to a student of rhetoric when he left school, and ultimately to evaluate the significance of a rhetorical education in securing good positions. Was a complete training in rhetoric at a prestigious school a crucial component of the Late Antique "resumé," or were other factors (such as wealth and high social status) more important? The first step is therefore to investigate what forms of evaluation were available to prove competence both in and after school, and how effectively this information was conveyed.

I will take into consideration the numerous letters of recommendation that Libanius wrote for those young men who needed contacts for their future careers, aspired to jobs in the administration, or wanted to pursue further studies in law or philosophy.[1] Were Libanius's letters efficient instruments of communication, or were they vague "form letters" composed largely of commendatory *loci* and inflated to impress their addressees? Were the details of a student's past performance significant in securing a position, or was attendance in Libanius's school an adequate qualification per se? I will try to ascertain whether letters of recommendation were the only way to evaluate the capacities of a candidate, or whether other (perhaps more effective) means were available. I will then briefly consider the literary and epigraphic evidence on the education of governors to examine whether a thorough rhetorical training was a mandatory requirement for them, or whether an educational veneer was deemed sufficient.

A 1976 study of the importance of competence in appointments to public positions during the Late Antique period concluded that considerations

[1] Petit (1956a, 158) calculated that Libanius wrote recommendations for sixty-four of his students (sometimes several letters each). I have studied the most meaningful of these, about seventy letters; only few of them are included in Appendix One. On the whole, approximately one-third of Libanius's letters are recommendations of some sort.

of competence and training did not on the whole inform appointment procedures, and a candidate was only supposed to show "a general capacity for using any skills."[2] Schooling, therefore, with very few exceptions, would not have been a significant component in supporting a candidate's application, but "was considered a private matter." This study based its conclusions on the almost total absence of tests to ascertain the qualities of an applicant; the use of letters of recommendation that were couched in vague, stereotyped language; and an analogy with the practice, particularly in the West,[3] of appointments made solely on the basis of the candidate's high social status.

It is undeniable that modern concepts of competence do not apply to the ancient world, and that considerations of training and efficiency emerge only sporadically and unsystematically. The official sources barely touch on this subject, but it is to be expected that the testing and practical enforcement of requirements lay with the authority immediately in charge of an appointment; therefore, details of these matters are not discussed in documents whose scope was more universal, and to some degree they escape investigation.[4] We must be skeptical about our ability to extract such information from the sources available. The papyri of Greco-Roman Egypt, for example, which usually provide rich material for verification, are of limited usefulness. There is evidence of some control exercised over applicants to a position, but the papyri in question unfortunately do not fully disclose how comprehensive these "tests" (*basanoi*) were.[5] The reality is, I believe, that certain qualifications were required for some positions, but that testing was largely informal and thus escapes sure detection. Libanius, for example, provides significant but vague information in this respect. He says in an oration that a certain official was nominated as assessor to a military commander, but not because of his experience in the job: there was no need of experience (*empeiria*) in this area, because both the commander and his assessor had to supervise only corporal punishment (*Or.* 33.4). This observation indicates that some qualifications

---

[2] See Pedersen 1976, in particular pp. 45–46. This sound investigation mostly examined Imperial constitutions and official documents.

[3] Jones (1973, 382–83) noticed that the phenomenon was slightly less widespread in the Eastern provinces.

[4] Pedersen 1976, 45.

[5] Pedersen (1976, 37 n. 133) mentioned two papyri, *P.Oxy.* I.40 and *P.Tebt.* II.291. In the first, a doctor seeking immunity for some public service had to give proof of his status by answering a scientific question concerning his practice. In the second papyrus, a priest had to give proof (*apodeixis*) of his knowledge of Hieratic by reading from a book. More significant is another papyrus, *P.Oxy.* I.58, where the appointments of assistants to a treasury official are predicated on passing some undisclosed tests (*basanoi*). Searching through the *Duke Databank of Documentary Papyri* is not helpful, because words such as *apodeixis* or *epitēdeios* occur frequently in other contexts.

were necessary for other positions, particularly so in the military. A letter, moreover, implies that people expected the holders of certain posts (such as the *comes rei privatae,* a prominent financial office) to possess some specific competence for the job:[6] people objected to the recent appointment of one Caesarius on these grounds, and the office-holder himself had doubts about his suitability. Libanius wrote to him saying that Caesarius had proved himself in other positions and was not only a gentleman (*kalos kai agathos*) but was also qualified to handle the matters at hand.[7] While it is definitely unclear how competence for certain offices was tested, this is not dissimilar to what happens nowadays for certain positions: sometimes all that is sought is a *kalos kai agathos* man for the job, and experience is gained during tenure.[8]

The reality is that many factors could come into play in securing a first appointment or advancement. Ability was joined by inheritance of the right to a position, seniority, personal choice of a high-ranking official, influence acquired through recommendations of supporters, or even purchase of office with money. None of these ingredients alone could guarantee a successful outcome. The laws, with their ambiguous and sometimes contradictory rulings, testify that no scheme for promotion had universal application.[9] When an aspirant did not personally know a grandee and did not have access to an influential network, buying an office was a solution.[10] The practice of selling offices was occasionally operative in the centuries before the fourth, but it became more widespread from the end of that century on, as Imperial legislation also proves. Yet reliance on a network of supporters who would propose someone for a position or secure at least an introduction to someone powerful was still a key factor in Libanius's times.[11] In this respect, the vast correspondence of Libanius or Symmachus attests to the efficacy of a system of trading favors.

Assessing Students' Ability

The lack of formal examinations and the seeming absence of precise and objective criteria of evaluation in ancient education only indicate that

---

[6] *Ep.* 1435, addressed to Caesarius 1, who was just nominated.

[7] The historical example he adduces to encourage Caesarius is somewhat amusing: soldiers from Plataea, who were only used to fighting on land, nevertheless did not suffer from sea-sickness when engaging by sea.

[8] Consider, for example, the variety of careers to which a degree in law gives access today in America.

[9] See, on this question, Kelly 2004, 38–40 and 211–13.

[10] See Jones 1973, 391–96; Kelly 2004, 158–65.

[11] On the widespread presence at this time of *suffragium,* that is, influence acquired through powerful support, see Matthews 1989, 270.

modes of evaluation were different than they are today.[12] Assessments of performance and ranking still existed, however, even though they are difficult to verify in detail.[13] Consider, for example, a passage of Lucian's *De mercede conductis* (11). The trembling and sweating of the man who had a salaried post when his master posed some questions to him was surely meant to evoke the behavior of a student who became confused when his teacher asked, "Who was the king of the Achaeans?" Parents received general information about their sons through correspondence. The cursory reports Libanius sent home were based upon his observation of his students. When Libanius started teaching in Antioch, it took him the whole day to "get through all" of his students, and although he later employed assistants, he maintained full control.[14] He was undoubtedly aware of his pupils' ability and ranking. He told a father that his son was the best of his "group" (*symmoria*), and said of another that he was better than most of his classmates.[15] He described another student (who ended up opting for a military career) as better than "the lads his age" and with the potential to surpass older students, too (**174**). Two young men were so outstanding that he made the wish of Agamemnon in Homer, to have "ten like them" (**5** and **30**). Since one of these young men, Basilides, was a *koryphaios* (head of the whole *chorus*), the same might be true of the other, Agathius. In describing the latter's proficiency in rhetoric, Libanius employed the expression *errōsthai* ("to be strong"), which he rarely used and which must have referred to a specific, advanced stage of preparation.[16]

Libanius's students did take a sort of diagnostic test upon entering his school, and this ranked them at the start. Libanius replied to a father who had written urging him to take care of his sons (who had just arrived) that they were so good that he had "entrusted [them] with the task of taking care of others" (**36**). How formal and extensive this *dynamis* was, we cannot tell, and since Libanius had assistant lecturers, it may have amounted to little more than supervision. In tenth-century Constantinople, the letters of the anonymous professor who was the only officially appointed teacher in his school testify to a reality of student-teaching

---

[12] On examinations dominating current university life, see Bourdieu and Passeron 2000, 142–45.

[13] Morgan (1998, 80–82) remarked on the lack of formal examinations, another proof, in her view, of the lack of a definite curriculum. Cf. the vague information, including no allusion to actual results, in a letter a professor sent to Johann Amerbach, Halporn 2000, 188–90.

[14] See *Or.* 1.104 and *Ep.* 405.7.

[15] See **2** and *Ep.* 444.

[16] See letters **61**, **168**, and **176**.

comparable to what occurs in modern universities.[17] Student-teachers (*ekkritoi*, that is, "selected above others") were entrusted with teaching those below their level.[18] Thus the professor retorted to some who had protested the lack of his direct supervision that, since the *ekkritoi* had already mastered that part of the program, teaching beginners was not a challenge for them.[19] In selecting his student-helpers, Libanius used a comparable term (*pro tōn allōn krinein*), but these students may have had less power than their tenth-century counterparts.

The unique position of "head of the *chorus*" (*koryphaios*), however, gave the students who held it considerably more authority over their peers.[20] This was a quasi-formal position that existed in Athens and probably in other schools as well.[21] Outsiders recognized its value, and Libanius was occasionally asked who held that rank at a given time (**80**). On special occasions and in emergencies, these students might have full teaching responsibility.[22] The position was probably intended to encourage gifted students to embark upon academic careers, but not one of the three "heads of the *chorus*" who are mentioned in the letters took that path, a telling sign of rhetoric's diminished prestige.

There are a few glimpses of Libanius evaluating students in the course of his teaching (*synousia*, "getting together"). He corrected the work of pupils of every level, and they brought him tablets filled with their exercises "many times each month."[23] Some were told to come back for comments, and when a speech deserved particular attention, a student had to make an appointment at a suitable time when Libanius was free. But another type of evaluation occurred in the course of formal *epideixeis* that students gave in front of the whole school (*Or.* 5.46). This type of display can be compared with the *disputatio*, a debate between students that went on in front of the masters and the whole audience in the medieval university, followed by an evaluation. Libanius's remarks that when a student's performance was good, the speaker left amid applause, and that the teacher's full commendation amounted to adding nothing to the speech, imply that a sophist corrected unsatisfactory work before the whole student

---

[17] See *Anon. Lond.* Markopoulos 2000, 8–10; Lemerle 1986, 290–92.

[18] They also had to evaluate the stylistic qualities of a rhetorical letter composed by a student, cf. *Anon. Lond.* letters 104 and 105 Markopoulos.

[19] Cf. *Anon. Lond.* letters 81 and 110 Markopoulos.

[20] Eusebius 25, Basilides, and Julianus xv. Faustinus, whom Libanius calls "the best of our students" in **82**, may have held that position.

[21] In *Or.* 1.20, Libanius calls the title *prostatēs* of the *chorus*. In Eunapius VS 9.2.7, 483, the Spartan Themistocles probably had this position among the pupils of Apsines.

[22] Eusebius taught when Libanius was sick, and the students supposedly took full advantage of his classes.

[23] See *Or.* 34.16, *Ep.* 911, and *Or.* 35.22.

body. It was an old custom (*nomos*), and no one had ever challenged a sophist's abstention from a public evaluation of work that met his approval. Declamations before a student audience had been common practice in previous times and societies, and must have formed an effective basis for evaluating competence. Besides Quintilian's allusions to them as part of school routine, in the second century Plutarch described an *apodeixis* ("competition") given in the school of an unknown teacher, Diogenes, "by the young men who were studying literature, geometry, rhetoric, and music."[24] The competitive spirit of those students corresponded to that of their instructors, who went to dinner after the competition and disputed furiously over their cups.

Even though standardized criteria of competence measured precisely through regularly set examinations did not have a place in ancient schools, a teacher knew fairly accurately how one student compared with the others. The terminology through which Libanius conveyed his assessments appears hopelessly vague to us, but those who were familiar with his style were in a better position to judge the reports and letters of recommendation they received.

MEASURING A SOPHIST'S COMPETENCE

We have seen how ferocious the competition for a teaching place could be, but even after securing a position, a sophist was liable to periodic examinations of competence in both areas of his activities: as a rhetor and as a teacher. Libanius disclosed that two years after his permanent installation in Antioch, the audience of people he had invited to a lecture mercilessly underlined every deviation from the norm.[25] The speaker was the target (*toxeuomenos*) of criticism voiced aloud and found a critical examiner (*akribēs euthynos*) everywhere he looked in the theater. With this observation, Libanius intended to flatter the people of Antioch by reference to their perceptive critical faculty (*akribeia*),[26] yet he also rightly emphasized a sophist's vulnerability. In his late years, when his reputation was secure, his complaints were identical.[27] A speaker's prestige depended on the length of the applause he received, so that he was "the slave of anyone who had hands and tongues." He left the lecture room "full of

[24] Quintilian 2.2.9–12; Plut. *Mor.* 736d.
[25] *Or.* 11.189–90. On the date, see Petit 1983; Norman 2000, 3.
[26] Julian's perception of the Antiocheans' education in the *Misopogon* was different.
[27] *Or.* 25.50–51, written after 387. For a partial translation of this speech, see Festugière 1959, 442–43. In a speech on the subject of slavery, Libanius is prone to underline only the negative aspects of a sophist's occupation and only one side of the picture.

pride, as if he were a free man," without fully realizing how subservient he was to each of his hearers, who "could cast a vote on what he said." It is also noteworthy that Libanius stated that the audience comprised "(the merchant),[28] the artisan, the soldier,[29] and the athlete," people usually unconnected with culture.

In the same speech, Libanius also dealt with evaluation of a teacher's work and referred to his need to advertise his worth to all classes of citizens (*Or.* 25.48). A teacher was under a continuous, informal evaluation process. The guardians of the gates and the innkeepers might damage his reputation with visitors to the city. Failure to maintain cordial relations with these and with "even humbler" classes could injure a sophist's "workshop" (*ergastērion*). A teacher also needed to cultivate people who visited Antioch, since they "could make war and dig through his *chorus*," and those who left the city to go abroad might spread damaging rumors if the sophist had not made a positive impression. It speaks for the vagueness of the process of evaluation that most of these people were aware of a teacher's qualifications by hearsay, although some of them might use students as (not necessarily objective) informants. Whereas a speaker's competence was subject to periodic evaluation in open contests, a teacher's competence was harder to measure, as it is today.

In the oration on behalf of his impoverished assistant lecturers, responding to parents' potential criticism of his proposal to supplement their meager salaries, Libanius came close to suggesting a real verification of teaching expertise.[30] The relevant passage is unique insofar as it contains several of the words that in other sources (such as Imperial constitutions and official documents) refer to levels of competence required for public appointments and promotions, terms such as "capable" (*dexios*), "expert" (*epistamenos*), and "incompetent" (*achrēstos, phaulos*).[31] Libanius suggested that remuneration and employment should be contingent on a teacher's competence. If his assistants were competent, that is, "if they were able to benefit the students," they should be rewarded; but if "they were no good at teaching," they should be dismissed. It was necessary for parents who intended to test (*dokimazein*) the rhetors in question over their financial status to conduct a preliminary examination (*basanizein*) of their educational skills. Libanius's argument was sound, and his

---

[28] The manuscripts' *skaios* ("stupid, clumsy") is suspect. Foerster suggested a possible *kapēlos* ("merchant") to accompany the following "artisan."

[29] Libanius usually considered soldiers uneducated people and felt the need to defend his students against their abuses, *Or.* 36.8. He made some exceptions (particularly when he needed them); see, e.g., letter 52, or the letters to the military officer Barbatio (B29–30). On the prejudice against soldiers, cf. *Or.* 47.

[30] *Or.* 31.21, written in 361, a date much debated; see Norman 2000, 67–68.

[31] Cf. below.

pleading may have been successful, but the difficulties of the examination of competence he proposed surely did not escape him.

A distinction between concepts such as competence and effectiveness can hardly be drawn in the ancient sources,[32] and for Libanius, they amounted to much the same thing. Thus the number of pupils not only was an index of the teacher's success, but also pointed to his pedagogic merits (*Or.* 31.30). A teacher's ability was assessed on the basis of his students' success as well. When Libanius in his late years had to confront criticism in this respect, he attempted in vain to sever the connection between his achievements and theirs, while simultaneously specifying what a teacher's responsibilities were (*Or.* 62.6). An educator could fail because of ignorance and inexperience, sluggishness, excessive leniency, and envy (*phthonos*). The last is an unusual notion that might reveal something about Libanius's own experience as a student. A teacher could selfishly keep part of his knowledge for himself and not make it available to his pupils. A young, disappointed Libanius may have encountered such lack of generosity in his instructors in Athens. He seems to be very familiar with this concept, and in the early *Oration 59*, in praising the *paideia* that the emperors Constans and Constantius received from their father, he remarked that Constantinus was necessarily exempt from the "disease" of envy and did not begrudge his "pupils" his knowledge of governing.[33] Libanius declared that the teacher who could be proven guilty of all of the above had to confront not only accusations but actual prosecution and punishment. Yet, even though he felt he could not be indicted for any pedagogic deficiency, his subsequent writings indicate that people continued to measure his competence according to his ability (or lack of it) to produce successful members of society and considered him responsible even when his former students avoided participation in active discussions in the Council.[34] Libanius's answer to this criticism shows that he surrendered to the common opinion that a teacher was to be blamed for the shortcomings of those he had educated, but he defended his ability to identify with two or three success stories. Wasn't it true—he retorted—that a gymnastic trainer could derive his good reputation from only three successful athletes?

---

[32] See Pedersen 1976, 30.

[33] *Or.* 59.34, dated to 344/349; see Malosse 2003, 7–8. Malosse (note ad loc.) tentatively explains Libanius's remarks on the basis of the hostility of Constantinus to his first son Crispus, but I think that they rather emerge from the sophist's ideas about teaching. In later times, Libanius (like Ammianus) showed a poor opinion of Constantius's education. For a favorable (but unlikely, in my opinion) view of the *paideia* of this emperor, see Henck 2001.

[34] See *Or.* 35.20. On the high esteem Libanius had of the role of his former students in the Council, see Schouler 2004.

In any case, the difficulty of adequately measuring an instructor's effectiveness made the issue one with which teachers had to wrestle periodically. It reemerged as Libanius attempted to find a remedy to the problem of students' defections (*Or.* 43.16). He recognized that parents had the obligation and right to test (*exetazein*) their children, and they could do so in person, if they were capable of such an assessment (*krinein*), or else they could employ intermediaries. Most of the fathers of Libanius's students were probably able to conduct an informal examination, but the recourse to outsiders may suggest that an exacting Libanius had in mind a rather technical control that verified a youth's assimilation of the material. Such a meticulous process might result (in his thinking) in a formal charge and a punctilious evaluation of the teacher in question by a board composed of teachers and laymen. A negative assessment might lead to a benevolent admonition or to a pupil's legitimate transfer.

Libanius's suggestions are a measure of his bitterness. These were remedies of desperation that did not have much chance of success, and were perceived as such by the other sophists of Antioch, who resented them.[35] They infringed upon a teacher's independence, a delicate issue in all times. Yet since his speech against defections was addressed to other teachers, Libanius attributed inadequate performance to mere negligence, without touching on more sensitive issues, such as academic qualifications. The "lazy" teacher could become "diligent" (*prothymos*), but there is no hint that the examination might bring to light graver shortcomings. Once more, Libanius revealed the confidence he had in his own didactic competence. If he had any awareness that students' dissatisfaction might be due to his following a repetitive and outdated curriculum, he did not show it.

SOME CHOICES

Libanius urged his students to take "the long road to rhetoric," but (at least in his written work) he indicated that road's length in vague terms. He referred to his ideals for attendance simply by saying that one should not leave before receiving "the whole" (*to pan* or *to holon*), or that one should stay "for the time necessary" (*hoposon axion*): a youth who went back to his country without possessing the whole of rhetoric did not deserve the deference of his cultivated fellow citizens.[36] Only complete training brought preeminence in rhetoric (*dynamis, ischys*), which was

---

[35] See Norman 2000, 112. The tone of *Or.* 36 might show Libanius's isolation.
[36] See *Or.* 55.32–33.

achieved when one was able to transmit eloquence to others.[37] Though Libanius claimed that he was able to produce not only rhetors but sophists, too, his critics retorted that very few of his pupils had taken up teaching. His correspondence confirms that several of his students who had the potential to become teachers disappointed his expectations and pursued other careers.[38] They made a conscious choice, he said, because the present state of rhetoric and the low reputation of the profession were enough to turn them away, but his constant grieving (particularly in his late years) over the supposed troubles sophists endured (low esteem, limited influence, negligible income, little satisfaction with students) may have contributed to students' and parents' lack of enthusiasm for such a career.[39] The profession had gone wrong, he lamented, and pupils avoided it, "like sailors avoid reefs" (Or. 62.32).

Rhetoric had landed on the rocks, and many recognized that it was not the path to worldly success (*eudaimonia*). "Fathers, most foolish of all, avoid these rocks on which you waste your seed. Send your sons instead to rich Rome, where one can reap the fruits that bring success" (Or. 40.5). These were supposedly the words of one of Libanius's detractors, someone who ruined the profession of rhetoric and, by upholding Latin, "further dishonored the Greek language that was already covered with mire." Some families made provisional plans for their sons and thought that whereas a touch of rhetoric was useful, a combination of various skills brought more tangible results. Knowledge of shorthand writing, of the Latin language, and of Roman law appeared to improve the chances of getting coveted posts. It is usually said that Libanius was sharply intolerant of all of these disciplines and that his stance hardened considerably during his late years, when he depicted a general flight from the *logoi*.[40] Libanius's attitude, however, is one of nuances, and its apparent contradictions deserve a closer look. Was the threat of these rival studies so much more urgent toward the end of his life? Did he really undergo a sharp change from early tolerance to uncompromising hostility?[41]

---

[37] See Or. 62.29–30, 36, and Or. 55.33. One supposes that it took an almost equal amount of time for one to become a good rhetor as to become a sophist. Some students, like Parthenopaeus, made that choice.

[38] See, e.g., besides the *koryphaioi*, Albanius, Faustinus, Gerontius, and the son of Marianus. Cf. Wolf 1952, 88–90.

[39] See Or. 62.35, where he acknowledged that his assistant Calliopius's constant bickering discouraged people from taking the long road. On the profession of sophist as a form of slavery to everyone, see Or. 25.46–50.

[40] See Liebeschuetz 1972, 242–55, and Festugière 1959, 411.

[41] See Liebeschuetz 1972, 244; in the 370s, "he himself did not yet suffer from this rivalry," but later Libanius suggests "that the flight from *logoi* was much more general than before"; Bradbury (2004a, 200), commenting on Libanius's invitation to Antioch of a

Shorthand writing (*tōn sēmeiōn hē technē*) threatened rhetoric particularly during the reign of Constantius, who gave preference to men skilled in it and appointed them to the highest positions.[42] These notaries (*hypographeis*) came from humbler classes than students of rhetoric, and Libanius characterized them as "savages" (*barbaroi*) and considered their skills appropriate to slaves. Julian put an end to the practice of his predecessor, and Libanius asserted that, whereas parents had preferred shorthand before or had considered it equal to eloquence and urged their sons to learn it, under this emperor the opposite occurred, so that those who had acquired skill in shorthand turned to the study of rhetoric.[43] Under later emperors, shorthand was still valued, even though it never regained its former predominance; Latin and Roman law, then, represented the strongest threats to eloquence's prestige. The menace of shorthand continued to arouse Libanius's indignation throughout the orations,[44] yet he seems to have considered it a legitimate enhancement for people who were close to him. Thus in early letters, the student Honoratus was admired at court for the "wondrous" combination of rhetoric and shorthand (**103**), and Libanius gave a report to Hierocles' father about the latter's proficiency in rhetoric, adding to it a positive evaluation from his shorthand instructor (**97**). Likewise, he wrote repeated letters in support of a certain Mares, whose commendations included a good reputation as a shorthand writer.[45] And in a late oration written to uphold the nomination of a friend, his beloved secretary Thalassius, Libanius's praise of his skills in this area comes as no surprise.[46]

This differing treatment of a controversial subject (and especially the differentiation according to literary medium) needs to be kept in mind when one attempts to understand Libanius's attitude toward the other two rival disciplines. Latin and Roman law were connected, since some knowledge of Latin was necessary to have access to a school of Roman law, but it is unclear how much Latin students needed in reality. I have

---

teacher of law in 355, calls this "interesting in light of Libanius's later intense hostility to the incursion of legal studies on rhetoric."

[42] See *Or.* 18.158–60, 42.25, and 62.16. Petit 1955, 363–65; Cracco Ruggini 1987, 227–28. Cf. also Kaster 1988, 47–48. See a good survey of the issues connected with shorthand writing in Heath 2004, 259–67. From a second-century papyrus, *P.Oxy.* IV.724, it appears that a period of two years was sufficient to learn to write and read "any text in prose."

[43] See *Or.* 31.28 and 18.160. Cf. also *Ep.* 1224. The great-grandnephews of Gregory of Nazianzus traveled to the city to learn "fast writing" (*tachygraphein*), *Ep.* 157.

[44] In *Or.* 62, which dates to 382, the problem of the success of shorthand writers still troubles students.

[45] See letter **92** and *Epp.* 136 and 244.

[46] See *Or.* 42.25: Thalassius has this accomplishment, but in *Ep.* 929.2, he is described as excellent in morals but "neither great, handsome, nor fast." He probably possessed a minimum of skills.

argued that the evidence of the so-called Latin school exercises found in early Byzantine Egypt shows that minimal competence was required and that students progressing to a school of law needed not much more than a reading knowledge of the language.[47] It is true that Antioch was occasionally the seat of the Imperial court[48] and that the need for Latin may have been more pronounced there than in Egypt, yet most people probably learned it rather superficially. The Roman emperors' knowledge of Latin varied greatly.[49] Libanius wrote that Julian knew Latin perfectly, but added that he could not personally vouch for that, since his own Latin was nonexistent (*Or.* 12.92–94). The emperor's degree of familiarity with Latin, however, is likely to have been "sufficient," as Ammianus said.[50] If one takes into account that Julian had started with this language, that Latin was the first language of his brother Gallus, and that he resided for a long time in the West, the knowledge of most who had learned it as a second language would not have been greater than his. Attitude also mattered. The traditional idea of the Greeks' contempt for Romans and their language has limited validity, yet it should be recognized that, by and large, the Greeks felt linguistically self-sufficient and were not interested in Roman culture and literature.[51] While in Gaul in the year 359, Julian affected some concern for the state of his Greek learning, since the place had made a "barbarian" of him.[52] From Libanius, his relatives, and his friends, one derives the impression that their knowledge of Latin was insufficient or nonexistent.[53] Highly cultivated people like Gregory of Nazianzus declared their ignorance of "the Latin language and things of Italy,"[54] but it is especially the lack of Latin in someone like Themistius that is striking, since he resided in Constantinople, had a close relationship with several emperors, and became urban prefect of this city.[55]

Those who wanted to enter the public administration needed to be able to function in Latin, but it is unclear which level was deemed satis-

[47] Cribiore forthcoming b and e.

[48] Gallus resided there, and so did Julian for a time. Constantius lived in Antioch in his teens and later liked to spend time there; see Libanius *Or.* 11.180. Cf. Malosse 2004.

[49] Constantius knew both languages, and Valens knew only Latin, Themistius *Or.* 6.71cd, 8.105c, 9.126b. Cf. Dagron 1969, 37.

[50] Ammianus 16.5.7. On Julian's Latin, see Bouffartigue 1992, 408–12 and 500–501. On the knowledge of Libanius and other Antiocheans, cf. Liebeschuetz 1972, 247–49

[51] Rochette 1997, 69–83 and 260. In contrast, the Romans felt linguistically humble vis-à-vis Greek; cf. Fögen 2000.

[52] See Julian *Ep.* 8 Bidez.

[53] Cf. Liebeschuetz 1972, 247–48.

[54] Bernardi (1990, 89–90) argues, however, that it is likely that Gregory had a limited knowledge of Latin.

[55] See Gregory of Nazianzus *Ep.* 173, and Gregory of Nyssa *Ep.* 14 to Libanius. Cf. Vanderspoel 1995, 157–58.

factory. Governors could use scribes for both documents and letters and for translations relied on the assistance of those few in their retinue who knew the language.[56] Knowledge of Latin could make a candidate more appealing, and those students who traveled to Rome must have reached a good level in the language, but a veneer of it may have been acceptable. Some teaching of Latin existed in Antioch when Libanius moved there. In this and in later periods, it is not certain at what level this language was taught, but one suspects that speaking of "Latin rhetoric" might be excessive.[57] All that was needed was grammar, practice in reading, and perhaps some ability to translate. Though a good reading knowledge was essential for those who wished to enter a school of law, since legal texts were in Latin in the fourth century, ability to produce fluent rhetorical prose was at most ancillary. The information that is available concerning the teaching of Roman law in Berytus confirms this.[58] The detailed evidence from the *Digest* refers back to the fifth century at least.[59] In the early period, students learned from oral discussions of cases, public and individual *disputationes*, and readings from legal works, which were aided by commentaries, summaries, and works in question-and-answer format.[60] A pedagogical innovation, which was definitely in operation in the fifth century, may have been in preparation before: teachers produced summary translations of Latin legal texts into Greek. These so-called *indices* provided assistance to law students handicapped by their poor knowledge of Latin.[61]

That the teaching of Roman law in Berytus was conducted in Latin is usually considered a given, but in my opinion, it is not certain.[62] This assumption mainly derives from the perception of this city as an island of Roman culture and education. But Berytus was not exclusively a "Roman" city, as is shown by a papyrus discussed above, which contains two *epicedia* for professors of Greek rhetoric.[63] The evidence that is usually invoked to support the fact that teaching in the school of law was

---

[56] On the extensive use of scribes, see Adams 2003, 542.

[57] Libanius ironically calls "rhetor" in *Or.* 40.6 a youth who returned from Rome.

[58] Schulz 1953, 275–76. There were other schools of Roman law in the East, at Constantinople, at Caesarea in Palestine, and at Alexandria, but the school in Berytus was the most prominent until it was destroyed by fire in 551.

[59] Mommsen and Krueger 1985.

[60] Collinet 1925, 220. Scheltema (1970, 9) thinks that these teaching aids existed before the fifth century.

[61] Scheltema 1970, 12–16; McNamee 1998, 273–74.

[62] Schulz (1953, 276) is the only scholar who considered it a priori improbable and unsupported by facts. Yet this idea has strong support; cf. Collinet 1925, 211 and 38–39; Jolowicz 1952, 474; Rochette 1997, 168 and 174; and McNamee 1998.

[63] See above, Chapter Five. See also the older Apollinarius (above, Chapter Two), a Greek grammarian in Berytus.

done in Latin, moreover, can be interpreted in a different way.[64] The testimony of Gregory Thaumaturgus shows only that he needed *some* Latin to attend, and Libanius in *Oration* 2.44 (but elsewhere, too) employs the term *phōnē* in relation to Latin to indicate the language in general, not exclusively spoken language. It is possible, of course, that Latin was the language of instruction for law, but, if so, no evidence exists. Greek was the first language of most of the students at the law school, so that classes might have been conducted (at least partially) in this language.[65]

The letters Libanius sent to his former student Olympius, who was living in Rome in 356/57, prove that he was already well aware that some Latin was necessary in those years when that language was supposedly less threatening to the Greek *logoi,* but Olympius declined the offer "to shepherd the flock" together with him.[66] As a former student, Olympius was part of Libanius's enlarged family. Since Libanius was attempting to incorporate it in the school curriculum, Latin ceased to be (at least for the moment) a hostile presence. It supported his long-standing dream that his school could be a self-sufficient educational center, successfully competing with other institutions. In a letter to a friend, moreover, Libanius could afford to reveal his vulnerability in a way that would be difficult in an argumentative speech directed to a large audience. Olympius did not come to Antioch, but the next year, in 358, another teacher, Celsus, was there, and with him "the Syrians were not deprived of the Italic language."[67] Libanius did not even have a reading knowledge of Latin, but he seems to have admired those who, like Julian or an occasional student, could master both languages.[68]

Latin resurfaces next in Libanius's work mostly in the speeches written in the 380s and after, whose general tone is quite acrimonious.[69] There were then several private teachers of this language in Antioch, and in the year 388, an official chair was instituted. Students devoted themselves to both Greek rhetoric and the Latin language. It is undeniable that in those years, there was a greater pressure to learn Roman law and Latin, yet

---

[64] Gregory Thaumaturgus *Oratio panegyrica in Origenem* 5.57–62; Libanius *Or.* 2.44. This evidence, which had been examined already by Collinet (1925, 38–39) and others, was scrutinized again by Rochette (1997, 170–74).

[65] That lectures in the fifth century were in Greek is common knowledge.

[66] See the dossier of Olympius 4/i, in particular letters **151** and **152**.

[67] Celsus 2/ii; *Ep.* 363.1: the generic expression seems to indicate that Celsus did not teach in Libanius's school. *PLRE* I calls him "Latin rhetor," but it is possible that he was only a language teacher.

[68] Libanius needed to have Latin letters translated, see *Ep.* 1004 and 1036 (N177 and N181). Julianus 15 was the perfect example of a student who honored Greek rhetoric, yet was conversant in Latin, letter **118** and *Ep.* 668 (B79).

[69] See *Or.* 58.21–22, 24, and 29–31; *Or.* 1.255–56; *Or.* 3.24; *Or.* 38.6, ("the laughable African").

Libanius's bitter recriminations in his speeches were not entirely justified by facts. The rival disciplines and the desertion of the Greek *logoi* became the "hobby-horses" that he customarily rode in the choleric speeches of those years.[70] After the failure to appropriate these disciplines by including them in the teaching offered at his school, he was resentfully antagonistic toward them. His angry disillusionment was especially acute when he saw young men embarking for Rome, and he sneered at their high hopes of "office, power, marriage, a life at court, and consorting with the emperor" (*Or.* 43.5). The vast majority, he thought, would come back with nothing.

Libanius's reaction to students traveling to Rome or Berytus was similar to his confrontational attitude toward those who continued their studies in Athens. Their departure for other provinces was the clearest manifestation of his failure to retain them. Contemptuous hostility pervades his account of one of these journeys (*Or.* 40.5–6).[71] The father who sent his sons to Rome "despised" Libanius's teaching, "diminished" his flock, spent lots of money, yet the alleged "ignorance" (*amathia*) of the son who returned[72] delayed for a while the plans of others to sail to Italy. Silence is what this young man brought back from Rome: he had not acquired anything, had forgotten his rhetoric, could neither speak nor pay attention to a speech. Such a "gift of Hermes" was "no better than a slave or a phantom" and (typically) devoted himself only to eating, drinking, sleeping, and enjoying springs and breezes. Yet, when the young man in question became assessor to a governor, young men's trips to Italy resumed: those "harbors, boats, the Adriatic, and the Tiber." Accusations of pederasty and homosexuality seemed, then, effective weapons to an old, acrimonious Libanius composing his last speeches.[73] They are the equivalent of his allegations of magic to explain the rhetorical success of a youth who did not have proper training and serve to justify in his eyes the recourse to other disciplines: Libanius was not responsible for the flight from the *logoi*.[74] Every spring, students went down to the harbor to sail to Berytus or to Italy, and another reason for those journeys was that the protraction of their studies allowed them to postpone service in the Councils for years, or maybe forever, if on their return they could obtain positions that exempted them.[75]

---

[70] See Norman 2000, 89.
[71] No published translation of this speech exists.
[72] Cf. also *Ep.* 951 (N167): youths who come back are "not much different from sheep."
[73] See *Or.* 58.30–31 and 38.6.
[74] See *Or.* 57. Cf. *Ep.* 951, "I am not responsible for the trouble."
[75] See *Or.* 48.22 and 49.26–29. In these orations, the "first" among the decurions (the *principales*) are guilty of favoring the flight from the Council. Libanius's reaction is also due to the desire to defend the independence of the cities from the intrusions of the Roman power; Petit 1955, 347.

Libanius started to lose students to Roman law when he was a young sophist in Constantinople (*Or.* 1.77).[76] The incursion of legal studies on rhetoric no doubt became more pronounced in his late years,[77] but one should be alert to the marked imbalance between the rancorous denunciations in his speeches and the resigned acceptance of his correspondence. Some letters again testify to his attempt to make Antioch a self-sustaining educational magnet by "planting" the study of the law there. When a chair was established, Libanius was directly involved in the search to fill the position, and he wrote first to a teacher of law in Constantinople, Silanus, and then to Domnio; but these projects did not materialize.[78] Likewise, he often recommended his students to the latter, or gracefully assented to their desire to go to Berytus.[79] He resented their attempts to arrange things in secrecy, but was not blind to their quest for more qualifications. A possible objection that most of these letters are relatively early (but later on, necessity made him much more intransigent) needs to take into account a few factors. In his late years, Libanius wrote another recommendation for a student "who desired the law" and continued to praise in his correspondence people knowledgeable in both rhetoric and Roman law.[80] The general imbalance in preservation between his early and late letters, moreover, largely explains why his conciliatory attitude resurfaces a little less in the late correspondence.[81] It is reasonable to expect that Libanius continued to support students who wished to learn Latin and Roman law because he could not help but find their quest justifiable. He wrote letters of recommendation for them and did likewise for those who intended to continue their education in philosophy and medicine.[82]

Other students, who aimed at positions as advocates in the law courts, learned rhetoric for a relatively short time, even when they did not continue to study Roman law. They would gain some skills on the job, after-

---

[76] On professors and students of law in fourth-, fifth-, and sixth-century Berytus, see Jones Hall 2004, 195–220.

[77] Cf. the plight of Diognetus, letters **50** and **51**, when in 388 Tatianus made the study of Roman law a requirement for all advocates; but his law was abrogated later on, see *Ep*. 916.

[78] See *Ep*. 433 (B162) and *Ep*. 209 to Domnio 1. A list of lawyers, law professors, and students in Berytus is in Jones Hall 2004, 280–85.

[79] See letters **26, 28, 96, 101, 156**, and **175**. Even though he had good relations with Domnio, a bit of contempt for his subject can be detected in **26**, when he calls the learning of the law *emporia* ("business, merchandise"); see B166, note 82.

[80] See, in the year 388, *Ep*. 912 to Sebastianus, probably a law teacher; and *Epp*. 974 (year 390) and 1032 (year 393).

[81] The letters from 388–393 C.E. represent only 20 percent of the whole correspondence.

[82] See letters **117** and **118**. Letters **45** and **46** concern Chrysogonus, his only student who tried to learn medicine. On medicine in Late Antiquity, see Jones 1973, 1012–13; and Cracco Ruggini 2003.

ward.[83] As Themistius remarked, eloquence opened the door to some wealth, since a legal profession could be lucrative, especially at higher levels.[84] More students, whose length of attendance varied, aspired to become public advocates in the retinue of some high official with the hope of entering the administration at some point. The best idea—Libanius told Hyperechius—was to persist in the quest for a post with official rank, not aiming at the top straightaway but accepting any offer, however lowly.[85] Libanius also supported young men who sought adlection to the Senate of Constantinople, even though he disapproved of their ambitions. In his opinion, they risked spending much money without achieving real influence and might lose whatever authority they carried at home.[86] For all these young men he wrote recommendations, often several letters for each, and he continued to sustain their applications in later years.

RECOMMENDATIONS OF STUDENTS

Letters of recommendation were integrated into the system, as is shown by an edict of the Code of Theodosius from 370 C.E. that concerned the organization of higher education in Rome and Constantinople: the new students had to be provided with documents from the governors, birth certificates, and letters of recommendation.[87] Helping someone secure a position or simply some favor through *suffragium* was a system normally followed in the fourth century. The addressees of Libanius's letters ranged from high-ranking officeholders to minor provincial notables. One of the governors who received the most letters was the *comes orientis* Modestus, who was in office at Antioch in 358–362 but continued to be an important patron when he moved to Constantinople, as city prefect.[88] Modestus had a huge retinue. Libanius was aware that he received many requests, but his own recognition that one should not "add more cargo to an overburdened ship" did not deter him from asking.[89] One letter in particular, *Ep.* 154 (B70), hints at a governor's priorities in selecting candidates.[90] "I bring you my colts from the Muses' meadows. You see that you have called some of those I gave you but not others. I consider fortunate the former

---

[83] On the various professions open to Libanius's students, see Wolf 1952, 75–92, and the valuable discussion in Petit 1956a, 166–88. On the practical sides of advocacy, see Heath 2004, 309–17; on advocacy practiced in Egypt, cf. Heath 2002b.

[84] See *Or.* 27.339a.

[85] See *Ep.* 1441 (N117).

[86] On the privileges and burdens of senators, see Jones 1973, 523–62.

[87] *Cod. Theod.* 14.9.1.

[88] Modestus 2. On the office of *comes orientis*, see Jones 1973, 592–93.

[89] *Ep.* 617.2 (B73).

[90] Cf. Petit 1956a, 158–59, and note 108 with translation.

because of the honor you gave them and the latter because they long for you." Libanius exhorted Modestus to take special care of those who were not wealthy: speaking and earning money was essential for them, while the rich could afford being silent because their position as aspirants was "no small honor" per se.

Modestus received a steady stream of students who responded to specific promises, which were not always kept, but their teacher was there to "call in the promises" and require honest explanations (*Ep.* 807). The usual interpretation of *Ep.* 154 is that Modestus employed some students and rejected others. The reality appears to have been more nuanced. In Late Antique society, there was a large number of supernumeraries. All of the candidates seem to have been on a sort of standby: some were invited to speak; others remained silent but continued to hope. Silence, the very antithesis of eloquence, is a visible presence in many passages of Libanius.[91] In a letter to another official, Libanius recommended two young and poor advocates (*Ep.* 302). Aware that they might not be given an immediate opportunity to speak, he considered the possibility of listening and enjoying this official's favor advantageous for them, even if they remained silent.

A crowd of hopeful and silent advocates, therefore, hovered around governors. Both of these letters reveal that wealth was an important qualification for a candidate aspiring to a post. Young advocates in need were overlooked, while their rich companions secured appointments. Libanius struggled to remedy the unfairness of the system. A further area in which he disagreed with governors was in the value that should be attached to good birth. Another recommendation of two wellborn but poor advocates, also addressed to Modestus, has Libanius commenting bitterly, "*Eugeneia* is little considered in these days" (293.2). The prominence of a family had many components, such as wealth, power, nobility, and traditions of *paideia*. When economic standing did not correspond to social standing, an application to a job might be fatally compromised. Libanius was particularly sensitive in this respect since he came from an old, distinguished family that had lost its great wealth during the revolt of Eugeneius in 303 C.E. (*Or.* 1.3) He never attempted to recoup those possessions, which were unjustly confiscated, not even when he had an opportunity under Julian (*Or.* 1.125). At the same time, he was convinced that most people, "as far as families go, could not even look me straight in the face."[92]

Before proceeding to an examination of Libanius's letters of recommendation, I would like to refer briefly to the analogous correspondence of a

---

[91] Cf. below, Conclusion.

[92] *Or.* 2.10–11. Some people found him hard to bear because of his perennial glorification of his family.

contemporary illustrious figure, Symmachus, the main supporter of paganism in Rome, with whom Libanius corresponded once, in 391.[93] Symmachus left over 900 letters dating from the middle 360s to 402, and about one quarter of these are recommendations. His correspondence has often been criticized for lack of personal involvement, for rarely reflecting contemporary events, and for its undeniable formalism.[94] Symmachus's letters are artificially wrought, and even their *brevitas* is inflated: much distinguishes them from those of Libanius in style.[95] But a comparison of letters of recommendation written by both authors brings to light further points of divergence. Though the characteristics of Libanius as a writer of recommendations will emerge from what follows, certain features of Symmachus's correspondence throw them into better relief.[96] Symmachus's activity in promoting others (and himself at the same time) appears to have been so systematic and organized that there are a few cases of almost identical letters sent to different people at different times and on behalf of different individuals. Many letters, moreover, do not contain concrete details emphasizing someone's qualifications but are a concoction of stereotyped concepts: they seem to be models in which slightly different data were inserted at different times.[97] In this regard, too, Libanius's more individualized letters distinguish themselves.

The types of employment Libanius's students sought gave opportunities for social and/or economic advancement. Since many people aspired to such appointments, measures were devised to limit their number, while at the same time, other people were detained in compulsory positions and had to undertake mandatory obligations. Libanius had a high opinion of the functions of the members of the city councils,[98] but people who were forced to occupy these positions by compulsory inheritance sometimes had to bear heavy or disproportionate liturgical burdens.[99] Some students of Libanius were in this position, and I start by examining the letters of recommendation on their behalf, since Libanius treated their unfortunate cases with some uniformity.

---

[93] See *Ep.* 1004 (N177). Libanius had met his father in 361 when the latter was in Antioch for an embassy, and had discussed (presumably in Greek) classical literature with him. Symmachus wrote to him in Latin. He knew Greek but may have felt intimidated to write to a foremost Greek sophist; see Bruggisser 1990.

[94] See the defense in Matthews 1974.

[95] On Symmachus's style, see Haverling 1988 (p. 259 on the difference between his and Libanius's letters).

[96] Cf. Roda 1986.

[97] See Roda 1981, 65–66 and 82. Two-thirds of the letters in Book 9 do not have addressees. Naturally, some of the letters, however, required considerable attention from the writer.

[98] On the duties of the *politeuomenoi* (those performing civic duties), see *Or.* 35.3 and 62.38.

[99] On civic services, see Jones 1973, 734–57; Petit 1955, 45–62.

As one would expect, the letters for students in dire circumstances do not bring their academic achievements to the attention of the addressees. Libanius only mentions their schooling in passing, but the fact that they studied with him further entitles them to some assistance.[100] What counts in these letters is the general scenario, the family background, and the presumed injustice suffered. Allusions to possible wealth were naturally out of place, since these young men's claims usually rested on their impoverished condition, but the *eugeneia* and good reputation of a family, and its past services to the community, were central to the petition. A situation might rightly call for urgent redress, as when a father's numerous accomplishments and service in the Senate made the plea of an impoverished orphan more moving.[101] The same situation might be treated differently according to addressee. Libanius, for example, explained in detail the misfortunes of a student to Modestus, who perhaps would not have much time to dedicate to him in person, but described them in a cursory way to another correspondent, who had been Libanius's schoolmate, had children in his school, was an Armenian like the student in question, and would certainly pay a great deal of personal attention to the youth's own pathetic story.[102] Students were sometimes snatched from the midst of their studies by a city council demanding their services. When his father died, one was recalled and "had to go back home exchanging cares for cares, those that befit a student for those fit for a father." The mention of his interrupted attendance was enough to validate Libanius's request for a favor.[103] A student's success in rhetoric paled in dark times. The thorniest case of all was that of Dionysius, who, after surmounting great family difficulties, rejected favorable work offers in order to remain in his fields with "his trees and the birds in them"(55).[104] But country life had its dangers. A grave episode involving the *harpagē* (*raptus*, "rape" or "abduction") of a girl put this young man at risk of losing his head.[105] The urgent letters of Libanius on his behalf naturally do not mention this youth's (veritable) success in eloquence, and show that the teacher could not condone the deed but remembered well "the many years he studied with us."

---

[100] Thus he said that Domninus of Larissa, the father of a besieged young man, "entrusted us with his son so that he could acquire ability in speaking" (*Ep.* 952), and he described in 6 the unfortunate Agroecius as "no different from a son to me."

[101] See *Ep.* 952 and 953: Domninus was a senator in Constantinople.

[102] Agroecius was poor, in bad health, and had five sisters in need of husbands, *Ep.* 293 (B72); see letter 6.

[103] See Eudocius I and the dossier of the sons of Caesarius ii; and see *Ep.* 288. Further letters show that his appeal was successful, *Epp.* 814.1 and 646.

[104] See dossier of Dionysius ii.

[105] On *raptus*, see Evans-Grubbs 1989; Beaucamp 1990–92, 1:107–14; and Karlin-Hayter 1992.

The fact that Dionysius's behavior had been orderly in school ("one might as soon have accused the statues of a sexual misconduct as him," 56) was enough guarantee of a sound moral character.

Let us now turn our attention to those students who asked to be recommended to various teachers because they intended to continue their educations. A few letters concern two young men who were both seized by the *erōs* for philosophy. Julianus wanted to follow the classes of the philosopher Themistius in Constantinople, who considered rhetoric a vehicle to spread his message.[106] It should not come as a surprise, therefore, that the letters for Themistius are an exception among the recommendations addressed to teachers because of their emphasis on academic qualifications. Libanius's evaluation of this student assured him that he was going to be a pupil out of the ordinary. Libanius's detailed remarks were also due to the exceptional qualities of this student. The sophist did not give a full commendation to many. Other letters to powerful officials also emphasize Julianus's cultural achievements, as when Libanius wrote to one of them that such was the charm of his *paideia* that Julianus could capture anyone he wanted and all those who listened to him—doubtless an allusion to the pleasure that the official in question would derive from an eventual interview.[107] The attainments of *paideia,* in any case, usually lost their urgent appeal in recommendations sent years after school: when someone was beyond his first appointment, there was no need to document his school credentials aside from a few generalities.[108] The tenor of letters written for the other student enamored of philosophy, Menecrates, is different. One was addressed to Diophantus, an otherwise unknown philosopher who taught in Egypt: one phrase, "Give this youth a share in the mystery that opens heaven to its partakers," points to the type of philosophy he practiced.[109] Libanius introduced Menecrates as "the finest" (*aristos*) of his students, an adjective that did not refer to academic but to moral qualities and to the nobility of his choice: philosophy over advocacy. For two reasons, Libanius does not praise his success in school: Menecrates' numerous illnesses kept him from receiving all the rhetoric he wanted (**145**), and his school performance did not pertain to Diophantus's field.

Providing information about the academic standing of students who wanted to attend law school was equally irrelevant in Libanius's (and

---

[106] See the dossier of Julianus 15, and cf. above.

[107] *Ep.* 668 (B79) to Clearchus 1.

[108] Recommendations sent to other governors in later years do not discuss Julianus's academic credentials at all. Cf. *Epp.* 1305 to Modestus and 1297 to Datianus.

[109] Letter **144**. He is different from the Diophantus mentioned by Eunapius (*VS* 12, 494); Penella 1990, 94–97 and passim. It is likely that he was a Neoplatonic philosopher.

probably his correspondents') eyes. The numerous letters he sent to Berytus to the professors Domnio and Sebastianus do not contain meaningful comments about rhetorical skills. Some students opted for legal training after trying their skills as literary advocates or went back to school when they were older than usual, but younger students also felt the need to acquire knowledge of Roman law.[110] It may seem surprising that the letters for students seeking higher education are anything but letters of evaluation and amount to little more than asking a personal favor. Among several explanations, one reason for Libanius's silence might be his conviction that the studies of law and rhetoric were mutually exclusive. Legal knowledge did not build on a foundation in rhetoric; by acquiring new notions, a student would automatically wipe out what he previously knew. "The intellect is incapable of acquiring something fresh, retaining at the same time the other," he asserted (*Or.* 62.21–23). Students going to Berytus did not get "an advantage but only an exchange" and would lose all or almost all of their eloquence.[111] The concept of the necessity of continuous work and of memory limitations must be at the base of Libanius's conviction. Another teacher, Quintilian, urged that students learn many subjects and agreed that they had to apply themselves constantly not to lose their knowledge, but he opted for a different solution: the cultivation of many different disciplines together (1.12.6).

In sorting through the many letters recommending good or mediocre students who aimed at coveted posts, one encounters varying combinations of social and economic standing, knowledge of rhetoric, and personality traits. These letters differ considerably in form, length, and degree of eloquence.[112] Some have what Libanius called "laconic brevity"[113] and are brusque and almost imperious; others are vivid sketches replete with details. Libanius the wordsmith (*logōn technitēs*) was powerfully at work in constructing the "image" of those he recommended: some portraits of students are memorable.[114] But we cannot forget that we also see at work in these letters a rhetoric of self-presentation, so that length and style are

---

[110] Libanius did not comment on Apringius's skill as an advocate, with which he was certainly acquainted. Likewise he did not refer to the expertise of Hilarinus (**101**) or Artemon (**28**). Cf. *Ep.* 912 and **156**, which do not contain any comments on ability in rhetoric. Even though in *Ep.* 1131 (B165), Libanius wrote to Domnio that the student in question made discourses, his recommendation revolved around his good, impoverished family.

[111] See also the allusion to students who turned in vain to other subjects in **131**. Cf. Themistius *Or.* 27.339: when the soul was sown and planted, one had to avoid sowing indiscriminately.

[112] Libanius tells an ex-student in **104** that writing standards vary according to addressees.

[113] Cf., e.g., *Ep.* 81 (N47), where he talks about letters of various lengths.

[114] Cf. Roda 1986, 181–82. See, e.g., **5, 49, 175** (B92), **722** (N85), and **82**.

a function of the writer's desire for self-positioning. Through these letters and the responses received, a grandee such as Libanius could establish and test the range of his influence. To come closer to evaluating the veracity and authority of Libanius's letters, it is useful to consider the norms of modern recommendations in the United States. Scholarly attention to these letters (particularly quantitative studies) has been rare.[115] A survey, however, found that a disproportionate number of the internship applicants under consideration were rated at the top of the academic distribution.[116] With few exceptions, faculty members perceive that recommendation letters written on behalf of students and faculty are inflated, a phenomenon that is a legacy of the late 1960s and is also due to the legal constraints under which the letters are written. Compression at the top harms the stronger applicant more than the weaker one. Letters that are invariably positive and replete with superlatives lose credibility and are unhelpful.

Besides Libanius's practice of evaluation in the reports to families, a letter sent to the prominent Anatolius in 358 is the locus classicus to explain his criteria of panegyric (*nomos peri tous epainous*).[117] The serious, programmatic intent of *Ep.* 19 is attested by its original placement at the head of the letter collection, without respecting a chronological order.[118] Responding to Anatolius's criticism that he sang the praises of many people, Libanius retorted that he never praised anyone by attributing nonexistent qualities. "If I did," he said, "I would be lying." He concentrated instead on the positive characteristics of a certain place or person, giving due credit to them while drawing a veil of silence over less-positive qualities. So, for example, he added jokingly, in praising Anatolius, he would laud his industry, foresightedness, or powerful eloquence, but he would not mention the handsome and tall figure that he did not possess. It has been shown that Libanius followed this method of giving praise in his various speeches in honor of royal personages, such as Constantius, Constans, and Julian, and that he applied the same technique in his treatment of the virtues of Antioch in the *Antiochikos*.[119]

The recommendations written on behalf of students are a further confirmation of this practice. It is possible to distinguish on the one hand letters that are not fully commendatory of the candidate's rhetorical abil-

---

[115] See Rosovsky and Hartley 2002 with bibliography; Ryan and Martinson 2000; McCloskey 2002.

[116] Miller and Van Rybroek 1988.

[117] *Ep.* 19 to Anatolius 3 (N40); Bradbury 2000, 178–79. On this and other letters to Anatolius and on Libanius's criteria for praise, see Schouler 1984, 936–39.

[118] Silomon 1909, 29–30; Norman 1992, 35–43.

[119] See Malosse 2000; and Norman 2000, 5.

ity or that praise him for qualities other than scholastic success, and on the other hand letters that are glowing reports of a student's academic qualifications. A few examples will suffice. Bassus was probably not a good student. Libanius extolled only his diligence and conviction that "the sweat that comes from rhetoric was sweeter than wine" (*Ep.* 175), and, even less ambiguously, declared to an addressee: "He acquired something that I hesitate to praise but that perhaps will not seem small to you" (**34**). Likewise, Magnus was not an outstanding student. The four letters that Libanius wrote for this young advocate just out of school[120] are short and a bit peremptory in requesting that the recipients help Magnus earn money; they describe him unenthusiastically as "the son of a good advocate and not too bad himself," and comment that "he hunted for the *logoi* for so long at our school."[121] Two other students' most credible claim to special consideration was their poverty (*Ep.* 1245). While in school, they had spent most of their time in the hands of doctors, so that Libanius candidly declared, "They have not yet acquired sufficient ability in rhetoric in order to perform their best in what they have come for."

Libanius considered a letter "the greatest gift" that he could give a student (**145**).[122] His profound concern that his pupils find suitable employment is evident. But when he felt that he could not wholeheartedly commend their eloquence beyond the fact that they had taken his classes, he concentrated on other qualities. Excellent *tropoi* were fundamental for those students who did not reach great results, and he relied on them when necessary (*Or.* 58.38). A candidate might also be warmly supported on account of his urgent need of a job or his kinship with someone the recipient knew well (**49**). One of the warmest and longest letters, for example, extolled the praises of a young man who had followed the class of another sophist before joining Libanius.[123] Libanius praised him for his illustrious family; all his activities on behalf of the school; his friendly good nature; his lack of interest in wealth and generosity to the needy; but he did not even mention this youth's skills in eloquence. In this case, moreover, the student, Majorinus, who was the son of a senator and prefect by the same name, derived excellent credentials from his father's status.[124] A respondent to a modern American questionnaire on whether let-

---

[120] Magnus 12/iii; Petit thinks he was in school in 355/56, but we can only say that he was a friend of Calliopius who attended the school in the years 355 to 358. Since Libanius said that he attended his classes for a very long time, in the year 364 (the date of the recommendations) he may have just left the school.

[121] See *Epp.* 303, 1270, 1271, and 1272.

[122] He sometimes sent many "gifts" together; cf. the package for Hyperechius, **114**.

[123] See *Ep.* 560 (B87).

[124] See the epitaph of Majorinus Senior, Puech 2002, 341–42. He was not a consul, as in Bradbury 2004a, no. 87, n. 8.

ters of recommendation that inflate achievements are unethical defended her personal (and maybe rare) way of writing letters by saying, "I emphasize strong points . . . make some comments about the person's personal characteristics . . . I am not inflating with untruths, but I am certainly shaping the contents of the letter."[125] Libanius's method of praising his "bad" students was similar, and perhaps more honest, since he omitted any allusion to their ability. A comment of the contemporary Roman rhetor Julius Victor, "Recommendations should be written truthfully, or not at all," shows that Libanius was operating according to ancient standards, at least theoretical ones.[126]

Rhetoric, however, is central to the letters recommending the "good" students (*hoi epainoumenoi mathētai*), those who were models for others (*Or.* 43.15). A young man might be described as sharing a passion for rhetoric identical to Libanius's (*Ep.* 203), another might be styled as "a true friend of Hermes," who gave him a power of eloquence that deserved the teacher's admiration (*Ep.* 269).[127] Of another, who was destined to join the court *officiales*, Libanius said that his ability would allow him to be "great defending people on trial or great in the same position where I am," which was the highest commendation (**140**). Among the virtues of his pupil Aristaenetus was the fact that he knew how to speak, but also how to be silent;[128] that he regarded the power of rhetoric (which he truly loved) much above wealth; and that he composed a panegyric in praise of Libanius that made him blush (*Ep.* 1081). But it is probably Eusebius, for whom Libanius wrote four glowing letters, who deserved the highest recognition: he had become an orator of a high standard.[129]

Ancient letters of recommendation have so far attracted limited attention, but an observation that is commonly made is that they did not convey enough information and relied on vague, generalized terminology. No doubt the letters of a rhetor of the caliber of Libanius are often much more concise than current recommendations, but one should beware of imposing modern criteria. Libanius's letters were far from unable to convey the information needed by the recipients. Set expressions defining competence, such as "worthy, well-deserving" (*axios*), "suitable" (*epitēdeios*), and "effective" (*chrēsimos*), are almost absent in these letters.[130]

---

[125] See Ryan and Martinson 2000, 50.

[126] *Ars rhetorica* 27. Julius Victor continues by saying that proper recommendations are those given to dear friends.

[127] For pagans and Christians alike, friendship with the divine meant power, Brown 1978, 63–64.

[128] Libanius considered as virtues his students' capacity to speak and to be silent; cf. letter 154.

[129] See the dossier of Eusebius 25/xxviii.

[130] These are the terms that most often appear in the ancient sources to define competence; Pedersen 1976, 30. But see *Ep.* 302, where the students in question are quickly

In describing the ability (or inability) of a candidate, Libanius, unlike Symmachus, varied his locutions and individually crafted every epistolary "gift" for each student.[131]

THE INTERVIEW

Another point that deserves attention is that letters of recommendation served to introduce an applicant to someone he might meet in person. The candidate himself usually carried the letter (or letters) written on his behalf. Confidentiality was not an issue, as it is today, when students are advised to waive their right to know the contents of a letter. Carriers were probably familiar with their own letters of reference, and Libanius may have read his recommendations to the students who were still in Antioch, as he said another teacher of rhetoric had done.[132] A letter was only one of the ingredients necessary to secure an appointment. It served (though not invariably) to open a door, but the aspirant who obtained entry had to prove his own credentials.

The practice of seeing a candidate in person and judging him after a direct inspection must have been widespread, but little attention has been paid to it. Both Symmachus and Libanius testify to the existence of an interview that served to test the qualities mentioned in a recommendation.[133] Libanius usually called this type of test *peira*, "trial"; he twice employed the verb *peiran* in the same context and once the term *dokimazein*, "to test."[134] The interview was a common practice when someone sought employment or useful contacts. Libanius mentioned interviews in about fifteen instances, but this practice must have been common. The term *peira* was used sometimes in a slightly ambiguous way: one cannot exclude the possibility that the "trial" of a person consisted of more than a single encounter.[135] Most often the "trial" appears to be in direct connection with the delivery of a letter of recommendation and served to validate

---

described to an official as "deserving your attention because of their eloquence and characters."

[131] These letters, therefore, are not couched in "the uncontroversial banalities" of correspondence, as Kelly (2004, 159) maintains.

[132] Argeius, see 129.

[133] See, e.g., Symmachus *Ep.* 1.41 and 72, where the interview is called *primus aditus*. In 2.16, a recommendee's submission to inspection (*examen*) is reserved for novices.

[134] The noun is often accompanied by the verb *lambanein*, "to make a trial." Letters in which the term *peira* appears are: *Epp.* 62, 71, 203, 301, 309, 425, 574, 810, 1228, 1331, and 1525. See also 110.5, and *Epp.* 1229.4 and 1441.4 (N117) (the verb *peiran*). In *Ep.* 1229.4, I retain the reading *peirason* of Wolf 1738, ad loc.

[135] See *Ep.* 62.4 (N51).

its content.[136] An interview was also supposed to disclose some qualities not mentioned in a letter, so that Libanius, for example, after singing loud praises of someone, wrote to an official: "Now, you will think that I am exaggerating, but when you 'try' him you will learn that I have kept silent about many of his qualities."[137]

The same term used for job interviews (*peira*) also referred to the diagnostic test that served to assess a student's ability before entering the school.[138] The encounters that followed a letter of recommendation had a similar purpose. In a letter that Libanius wrote for Iamblicus, after noting his family's eminence, he invited his correspondent to test his student's "judgment" (*gnōmē*), which would arouse his admiration.[139] A capability to handle pressing matters and general good sense were also in question, but another purpose of this type of interview was to test an aspirant's education.[140] An interview was a clever, learned exchange in which the participants "set up a system of instant communication" through their *paideia*,[141] mutually wrestled with rhetoric, and proved that they belonged to the higher world of the elect. When Libanius recommended an able speaker to the philosopher Themistius, he added, "It is up to you to 'try' him by listening and speaking to him. He is marvelous at shaking those who hear him with the beauty of his words" (*Ep*. 301).

A fundamental difference between the *peira* that functioned as a placement test and that which occurred at the end of schooling was the significance of the latter in securing an appointment. The story of Hyperechius, a student who attended Libanius's classes for many years, is exemplary. In spite of the flood of letters that Libanius sent to influential people, Hyperechius never obtained the position he wanted. Shunning the sophist in disillusionment, in 366 he became commander of some auxiliaries in the revolt of Procopius in spite of his complete inexperience and was prob-

---

[136] *Ep*. 71: "You will see when you interview (*peiran*) him that I do not know how to praise bad people"; and *Ep*. 1525: "Give him an interview and you will be persuaded that he deserves to join your retinue."

[137] *Ep*. 1228. Paianius (a student perhaps) has disappeared from every prosopography and is not mentioned by Petit (1956a) (unless he should be identified with Paeonius i). Libanius wrote four letters for him, 1226–29, in which he called him a *hetairos*, an ambiguous term that very often referred to students.

[138] Cf. above, Chapter Four.

[139] *Ep*. 574 (B19). This is one of nine letters recommending Iamblichus 2, who was probably Libanius's student, judging from 107; but he was not included in Petit 1956a. On his prominent family, see Cameron 1967a, and cf. above, Chapter Two.

[140] See *Ep*. 203.2–3; Hermolaus was an advocate but followed Libanius's classes at the same time, and so increased his own "power."

[141] Brown 1992, 40.

224 • Chapter Seven

ably killed.[142] He disappeared from the documentation, leaving the reader "with the feeling that he was less sinning than sinned against."[143] Scholars have wondered about reasons for his failure to obtain a post "malgré sa gentillesse et ses talents."[144]

A careful reading of all of the letters concerning Hyperechius discloses that he was probably not much out of the ordinary. One perceives a degree of surprise on the part of Libanius in the warm congratulations he sent when Heperechius gave a speech for display in his native city, after leaving Antioch (**109**). Hyperechius's chief merits consisted of a pleasant personality, moral goodness, affability, but also the capacity to keep silent and to listen respectfully. One searches in vain for enthusiastic commendatory *loci* in the letters that date to 361, after he left the school. Despite the fact that comments on *paideia* should have most relevance in early letters, Libanius's praises were lukewarm, and he mostly pointed to Hyperechius's moral traits. In a letter, for example, he mentions his "goodness" (*aretē*), a quality that did not refer to academic excellence and does not appear in other recommendations.[145] In the same year, 361, Libanius mentioned Hyperechius's first interview. The interviewer, he said, would understand immediately, just by looking at him, the sort of young man he was: he did not applaud or shout when Libanius gave a declamation but sat down and admired in silence (**110**). This may not have been a quality in which the interviewer was interested. The years passed, and Hyperechius became increasingly frustrated, to the point of doubting whether Libanius was exerting himself to the fullest on his behalf, since he did not receive correspondence (**112**). In a letter from 363, Libanius mentioned that the powerful Modestus was interested in the young man, "first prompted by me and later after his own *peira*," yet Hyperchius was not hired.[146] In the same year, Libanius wrote to Hyperechius urging him not to be disappointed: he was going to give him a letter for Caesarius, an eminent financial officer in Ancyra, and he advised him on how he should behave in the interview. "Try to show yourself a man of sense when he tests you. He is very good at telling a lion from its claw."[147] In the letter

---

[142] On Procopius's revolt, see Lenski 2002, 68–115. Ammianus (26.8.4–5) reports that Hyperechius got this position as a friend of Procopius but was actually in charge of supplies (*ventris minister et gutturis*).

[143] Pack 1935, 37.

[144] Festugière 1959, 149; on pp. 142–53, he provides a French translation of most of the correspondence involving this student. Petit (1956a, 162–65) thought that Hyperechius was unlucky, but also ventured a doubt on his real worth.

[145] See *Ep.* 298.4 (B99). Cf. **63** to the grandfather of Diophantus, where *aretē* refers to a wise and fair character and good discipline. A clear typology of excellence unfortunately does not resurface from the letters.

[146] *Ep.* 810.7 (N99).

[147] *Ep.* 1441 (N117).

to Caesarius, we catch Libanius as the author (at least once) of one of those inflated recommendations that abound nowadays. A surfeit of commendatory *loci* packs this letter with breathless rhetoric: family merits, talent for rhetoric, self-control, the zeal typical of an old man, the unusual affection he inspired in his teacher, practical ability in managing affairs, good sense, a flowing tongue, family wealth, and honesty. At the end of the letter, Libanius exhorted Caesarius to harness this "colt to his chariot."[148] It did not happen: Caesarius was probably in need of a lion.

RHETORIC: A PASSPORT TO OFFICE?

Libanius's burning passion for the *logoi* and his high standards of excellence explain why he sometimes gave his approval with reservation. If the characteristics of a working evaluation system include that it should permit meaningful distinctions among students, be fair to them, and provide the recipients with needed information, most letters of Libanius do not appear to be much off the mark, once the evidence is contextualized. His high academic status and his addressees' familiarity with his methods of evaluation may have given his statements the credibility that is often lacking in modern letters. But one also wonders about the import of full marks in rhetoric in obtaining a post. The combination of a youth's personality, status, and background in addition to some education must have been compelling. In this regard, the letters that did not praise the academic qualifications of Libanius's former students might also be taken as attestations of the possession of some rhetorical skills. Every student was to some degree a partaker of *paideia*, had gone through some taxing educational experience (whatever its length), and had developed useful working tools, and possibly some sense of responsibility, dependability, and tenacity as well. Far from being a private, insignificant component,[149] schooling did matter in assuring a career, but the short path to rhetoric worked equally well when someone possessed other ingredients for success. The general attainments of *paideia* had to combine with an ability to use various other skills. Posts in the administration did not require very specialized skills; when they did, these could be learned on the job. But a candidate had to show a range of generalized qualifications in addition to sophisticated verbal skills.

Libanius was acutely aware of the social background of the system in which he operated, even though he occasionally attempted to swim against the current. He proclaimed a firm disinterest in wealth and exerted

---

[148] He often referred to his students and former students as "colts"; see, e.g., *Ep.* 154.
[149] As Pedersen (1976) maintains.

himself unsparingly on behalf of students from less-privileged families. In the recommendations, he mentioned family prominence and affluence mostly when these were the principal claims to eligibility. These qualifications sometimes served to give the final touch to the portrait of a candidate. He had to admit that *eudaimonia* ("success") depended on a combination of factors, as he wrote to a former student, Themistius, who became a governor at a very young age.[150] Themistius had shown some discomfort at school, where, in his view, much energy was spent on useless pursuits. The "weapons" he acquired, however, became useful, because "a governor needs the *logoi* as much as sailors need oars." Themistius had an obligation to be a good governor because he had enjoyed all the advantages: family, education, a "wide-awake" nature, and the ability to tell good from bad.

Measuring the actual relationship between degrees of education and social and political success is difficult, because the evidence is mostly one-sided.[151] Some progress can be made, however, by trying to determine the impact of cultural attainments on the careers of those who reached governorships and higher offices.[152] It is to be expected that sophists such as Himerius and Libanius, who had a vested interest in education, emphasized rhetoric as the chief qualification of a good governor. Though Himerius considered justice to be a fundamental virtue of the proconsul of Achaea Cervonius, he hailed his *paideia* and did the same for the governor Hermogenes, "a shoot and offspring of the Muses."[153] Libanius had uneven relations with governors, which mostly depended on their appreciation for his rhetoric, and he presented as an ignoramus every official who did not attend his speeches and had a passion for the theater and the hippodrome. In his tirades against these "bad" governors, he attacked their lack of *paideia* from the outset. When his relations with a governor he had previously presented as cultivated turned sour, he hastened to play down and ridicule the latter's cultural attainments.[154] The governors of which he approved had all received an excellent education, and their effectiveness in office was a function of it.[155] Through Libanius's eyes, we also glimpse the widespread expectation that a rhetorical education provided a passport to office. He presented the success story of the humble and unschooled Heliodorus as the result of the fact that "people believed that

[150] Themistius 2/iii; cf. above, *Ep.* 309. Cf. *Or.* 62.55.

[151] Brown 1992, 38–39.

[152] On the power of governors, see the papers in *Figures du pouvoir: Gouverneurs et évêques, Antiquité Tardive* 7 (1999). See also Cribiore forthcoming a.

[153] Cervonius (*PLRE* I, p. 199; *Or.* 38.9). Hermogenes 9; justice and the Muses permeate the entire *Or.* 48.

[154] See, e.g., *Or.* 33.3, 42.11–13 and 40. On diminishing the *paideia* of Icarius 2, see the contrast between *Or.* 1.255 and 28.2.

[155] See, e.g., Strategius Musonianus (*PLRE* I, pp. 611–12).

he had been through the mill of oratory"; speeches that he had bought on the market conferred an educational aura upon another fellow, who was able to enter the Imperial service because of that.[156]

Epigrams celebrating governors and inscribed in public places put into perspective the evidence considered above, which directly reflects the interests of the sophists.[157] These Late Antique metrical inscriptions distinguish themselves from analogous Roman compositions that were in prose. They testify to a predilection for poetry that was typical of the age and show a poetic ability that was not unusual.[158] Governors must have appreciated these gifts of *paideia,* through which they could be associated with the Muses. These epigrams, however, are not a direct testimonial to the higher education of these officials.[159] They are fundamentally different from sophistic commendations because of their exclusive emphasis on two virtues: respect of justice, and promotion of building activities. The theme of a governor's justice, which is also paramount in the writings of sophists, corresponded to an ideal rather than to reality, since accusations in the literary and legislative sources prove that respect for the law and personal integrity were not customary marks of office.[160] The inscriptions also celebrate the building projects of governors, such as the construction of walls, fountains, aqueducts, and baths, for which the cities were grateful, but which Libanius considered with a mixture of suspicion and admiration.[161] *Paideia,* however, is generally not mentioned in the metrical inscriptions, suggesting that it was neither a prerequisite for office nor a proud attainment of those who held it.

The ideal of the educated governor steeped in eloquence appears only in the works of sophists, and not invariably even there. Libanius certainly would have liked to lock his students into the process of *paideia* forever and, like the teacher of the long road in Lucian, count "not by days and months but by whole Olympic cycles."[162] However, he was not always a firm believer in the objective power of the *logoi* to groom people for high office. As the years passed, he must have come to the realization that although a veneer of rhetoric was important, and a youth needed command of the language and the ability to grasp certain literary references

---

[156] *Or.* 62.46–48 and 63–69.

[157] See Robert 1948.

[158] Cameron 2004b, 346. Cf. Chapter Five.

[159] Brown (1992, 35), however, asserts that they "combine justice with devotion to the Muses."

[160] On the theme of justice in Libanius, see Cabouret 2002, 193–97. Cf. Robert 1948, 108. Gregory of Nazianzus also pointed to integrity as the main quality of a governor, *Ep.* 140.

[161] He extolled this aspect of governorship in **119**, *Ep.* 852, and *Or.* 11.193, but did not approve of it in *Or.* 46.44; *Or.* 10; and **130**.

[162] Lucian *Rhetorum praeceptor* 9.

to show that he belonged to the same world as an official whose entourage he sought to enter, the "long road" was only an option that did not guarantee success. Libanius's personal allegiance to rhetoric seems to have remained always unshaken, but the direct connection between rhetoric and success appears consistently only in his earlier works.[163] The *logoi* were double-edged weapons, for and against governors. They conferred on one the ability "to overcome the irrational impulses of governors by dint of rational argument,"[164] but they also gave governors the verbal sophistication and polished appearance necessary in their daily conduct.[165] "Our governor is nourished in the art of Hermes," Libanius wrote to his student Albanius, "and calls this to mind in front of speakers and confesses to be a slave only of this pleasure" (**8**). In another letter to the same student, he asserts that rhetoric "is a source of strength for those who truly possess it and can say to those who disdain it: 'I am still strong'" (**7**). In his early years of teaching, Libanius's message was more powerful because it had the assurance of success: rhetoric was wealth, beauty, and nobility all together, at least in his words.[166] The *encomion* of rhetoric within the larger *encomion* of Antioch, for example, upheld the strong tie between eloquence and the freedom and dignity of the city.[167]

But twenty years later, in the 380s and afterward, challenges from other disciplines, personal criticism, and the difficulties experienced by some students made Libanius doubt the equivalence of rhetoric and success. When he objected to those critics who remarked on the paucity of the students who had obtained provincial governorship, he was forced to admit that although good governors needed rhetoric, it was possible to obtain office without it. There was not a direct correlation between rhetoric and power (*Or.* 62.50). In those times, he said, those who did not have a chance to display it and had to remain silent lamented as well as those who used it and reproached themselves for breaking the silence. Rhetoric, Libanius regretted, "used to flash like lightning," but was then "under a cloud."[168] Yet, in spite of Libanius's disappointed hopes to groom generations of highly cultivated officials, rhetoric—by itself or in combination with other disciplines—was still able to provide some adequate, functional training.

---

[163] The praise of rhetoric in *Or.* 23.21 sounds like a mechanical, wishful refrain.

[164] See *Or.* 31.7 and 1.2.

[165] Governors in Antioch needed to acquire the favor of the local *principales*; see Cabouret 2004.

[166] See letter **123**. Cf. also **157** and the advice to Calycius, **187** and **189**.

[167] *Or.* 11.139–41. See Milazzo 1996.

[168] See *Or.* 49.32 and 2.43.

CONCLUSION

Words and Silence

> Unfeeling silence is a grave disease; while the warm,
> sympathetic word is health. Silence is shadow and night, the
> word is daylight. The word is truth, life, immortality. Let us
> speak, let us speak—silence does not suit us.
> —C. P. *Cavafy*, "The Word and Silence"

WHEN HE WAS STUDYING IN ATHENS, Libanius was not beguiled by the blustering applause that accompanied his professors' declamations; he listened in silence. In his opinion, those teachers were little better than students (*Or.* 1.17). His attitude toward Athens never changed, and he continued to consider that school with some disdain, wishing at the same time that Antioch could challenge its educational standing. I have shown that his hopes never really materialized. Besides Athens, there was a network of schools of rhetoric on which his students could rely, so that Libanius's school remained for many only a step on the path that would take them to other schools, to different studies, or to various careers. His pupils truly were like those merchants "sailing from port to port, from one that offers small gains to one that is competitive in trade," that he evoked in a letter to Themistius (**117**).

After delivering his own declamations, competing against others, and becoming Antioch's official sophist, Libanius had ample opportunities to experience how necessary overt approval was to the orator and to the teacher. Many aspects of Late Antique life were as resonant as in the Classical period. Horse races and festivals in Antioch were boisterous performances,[1] and the popular, silent pantomime dances went on amid the loud acclaim of the various claques.[2] Reading was often done aloud both in private and in public, and included favorable letters reporting on students (which were shared with many) and letters important for their content or their elegance, which were recited in public gatherings where "no one could stand and listen in silence."[3] Rhetors like Libanius mea-

---

[1] For excessive noise at the Olympia, see *Or.* 10.6. In the latter category, Julian included sacrifices and loud acclamation in the theater. See *Ep.* 811 (N100).
[2] See *Or.* 41.6–9; Festugière 1959, 227–28.
[3] See *Ep.* 779 (B107). See also, e.g., *Ep.* 1259 (B51).

sured their success by the length of the applause, and even philosophers like Themistius, who reproached his hearers for "turning assemblies into theatrical occasions," savored the enthusiastic reception.[4] Themistius disapproved of "singing" sophists who beguiled their hearers with their music, but sophists like Himerius continued to charm their vast followings.[5] Christian writers, who had loved the *logoi* as students, later perceived the vanity of "words" and wished to teach the value of silence to others.[6] Speaking of oneself (as Libanius did in the narrative of his life and as Gregory did in long autobiographical poems) was a sign of pride for Gregory of Nazianzus, who asked his pen to "write down the words of silence."[7] Yet, it was with words that he so often labored.

In the chapters above, we have listened to Libanius and his students as they taught, read, and declaimed. From the moment these young men applied to his school until years after they left, Libanius's voice rang aloud in letters he wrote to them and their families and in speeches he delivered to support or reproach them. Let us now measure the silence, which also is a tangible presence in his work.[8] People who were themselves blameless could be reduced to silence by the bad reputation of their families, and Libanius was proud not to be one of them (*Or.* 1.7). Silence was the additional penalty in prison for Socrates, who was forbidden to talk to his friends; together with those friends, a young Libanius besought Socrates in a declamation to go on speaking even after death.[9] Silence was a punishment equivalent to death for a defeated orator, whose tongue and memory became tied; with mist covering his eyes, he left in shame and in a frenzy of incoherent words.[10] As an orator, Libanius enjoyed ample approval, but it was his performance as a teacher that was often unfairly gauged by the material success his students achieved after leaving him—something for which he did not bear full responsibility. Physical pain and mental anguish at the disgrace or death of beloved ones could force silence and utter breakdown upon one. In the first part of his life, Libanius's voice resounded in innumerable triumphs. The deaths of friends and relatives and the demise of Julian affected him deeply, but he was able to overcome

---

[4] See Libanius *Or.* 25.50, and Themistius *Or.* 23.282–83.

[5] Themistius *Or.* 24.301a.

[6] Gregory of Nazianzus *Ep.* 110.

[7] Gregory of Nazianzus *Carm.* 2.1, 11.106–10; 2.1, 34.1–2.

[8] For the meanings of silence in Archaic and Classical Greece, see Montiglio 2000.

[9] Libanius *Declamation* 2; Foerster (1903–27, 5:123 n. 1) attributed it to Libanius in his youth. See Russell 1996, 58–66; Calder (1960) suggested that this declamation should be read as a protest against the encroachment of Christian teaching upon pagan teaching, a contrived interpretation when one considers the heavy presence of silence in all of the works of Libanius.

[10] See *Or.* 1.50 and 256.

his difficulties with time. Silence, then, mostly visited his enemies and competitors whom his *logoi* left undone.

Yet with the passing of the years, as Libanius's voice became more querulous and discontented, silence began to creep in more and more. New subjects, such as Roman law, threatened the value of his discipline, so that students who dared to rely only on rhetoric ran the risk of being isolated and becoming mute (**51**). Illness and depression paralyzed Libanius for longer intervals.[11] He showed his orations to an ever more restricted audience, and he punished his students with silence for their tepid attachment to the *paideia* he offered and for embracing other studies. Silence opened many of his speeches. Everything that was articulated in an oration already existed in the silence that came before, but the *topos* of the speaker forced to break silence under necessity, which opens many of his orations,[12] became in one of his last speeches a justification of his refusal to deliver the pivotal declamation at the closure of the school year (*Or.* 3). He could not tolerate the silence of his former students and took as a personal defeat their failure to speak in the Council and deliver orations. There were indubitable difficulties that crippled him as the years advanced, and he became more intolerant of words, asked for silence, and hoped to alleviate his silence as a teacher with the help of former students with whom he would (quite exceptionally) share the burden of the school.[13] But I hope to have shown that genre also conditioned his work to some degree. The harsh reality of Libanius's last fifteen or so years of life and teaching (which is well in view in his late orations and in the second part of his *Autobiography*) is tempered by the continuous good relations he maintained with many of his students and by the passion—revealed throughout his correspondence—he kept alive for his profession. We need to keep in sight both sides of Libanius if we want him to continue to speak to us.

---

[11] See *Or.* 34.20; 1.203 and 245.

[12] See, e.g., *Or.* 31, 42, and 62.

[13] See, e.g., *Ep.* 1001 (N175), which dates to the year 391; Libanius begs his supporter to stay silent and not to defend him against his detractors. His own son should stop desiring forbidden success and be content with "fields, trees, and bees." See also *Ep.* 909 (N159), in which he said that he would be dumb without the help of his assistant Eusebius.

APPENDIX ONE

Dossiers of Students

THIS APPENDIX contains my translations of about 200 of Libanius's 1,544 extant letters. The letters that I have selected specifically concern his teaching activity. When several letters concerning a particular student are extant, I call the collection a dossier; if there is a single letter, I preface that letter only with the student's name. The number in bold that distinguishes a letter is the number in this collection; the number after F refers to Foerster's numbering.

DOSSIER OF THE SON OF ACHILLIUS II

1 *F355 (year 358): To Parnasius*
[*Parnasius ii of Ancyra was a fellow student of Libanius, like Achillius. The latter was the uncle of the student Albanius.*]
   1. I have your son (as I wished), and he is fit to receive the teaching he came for. When I examined this young man and tested his nature, I found it quick to grasp the principles of rhetoric. 2. And I told Achillius—he is a man from Ancyra who has fulfilled his duties to his city, and is here visiting the only son he has—I told him: "Parnasius because of us will be the father of a good orator." 3. You brought back memories talking of the schools we went to and rhetoric in Ancyra, but even before reading your letter, I had talked about these things with your son. He said that what he heard was written in the letter. 4. I have such fond memories of those people who drank from the same bowl, and particularly of the Galatians, whom I always regard more fondly. And so you are sending your loved ones from one home to another, and there is no more need for you to urge me to take care of what is yours than for me to urge you to do so.

2 *F139 (year 359/60): To Achillius*
[*On many letters perceived as few, see* Ep. 1443.1.]
   1. If you say that your one letter is many, I would not have received this one only, but you are good even if you lie, for you recognize what you should have done. 2. We are now taking especial care of your child, because we think that we owe him what is yours. He is the best of his

group, probably because of his natural talent. But his pedagogue's role is not insignificant: he threatens, urges, rouses the boy, works hard with him, and for your sake performs a less demanding task than would befit him. 3. What you disclose about Albanius pleases me a great deal and is what I had hoped for. I was afraid that he would choose to stay silent; but now that he is willing to speak, I can feel confident.

3 F767 (year 362): To Maximus
[*Maximus 19/vi was governor of Galatia at this time. Other letters to him are 9, 12, 40, 128, and 169.*]

1. The bearer, Achillius, went to school with me, and I teach his son, who has an alert nature and knows how to work hard. To characterize Achillius, it is enough to show how he did not increase his property in a dishonest way but reduced quite substantial holdings to small ones because of his expenses on behalf of the city. 2. Now he is going to do some public service, but he has arrived here to see his son. He has two pressing concerns: his son and his city. In my opinion, the care he has for his son is part of his concern for his city. Those who foster their sons' intelligence serve their cities better than when they perform public services splendidly. 3. You, therefore, respecting the one thing, praising the other, and keeping in mind my interests, make sure that his burden is light.

DOSSIER OF AGATHIUS II
[*Arion is this student's father, and the older Agathius is his renowned grandfather.*]

4 F728 (year 362): To Arion

1. I was pleased to see your sons, the one who is coming for the sake of rhetoric and the other who is taking his brother to a school of rhetoric. This is nice for everyone, I think, but in your case it is even necessary, if guarding the good name that you have acquired thanks to the wisdom of Agathius is fitting but losing it is a sin. 2. Because of Ancyra, to which I am most grateful, and because of you and the uncle of this young man, I will make every effort, and I will encourage him in every way. Your son must be one of those students who stimulate me rather than needing stimulation. 3. I am convinced that he will be an eager student. The times that did not permit admiration of rhetoric are passed, and for this boy, his name is stronger than any exhortation.

5 F1165 (year 364): To Arion
1. So that you are not unaware when you meet him, know that your son is strong in rhetoric, and his character is such that I wish the gods would give me ten like him, not to conquer an enemy city, but so that our *chorus* might be adorned by the able young men brought up in it.[1] 2. Agathius has never to this day caused trouble either for his teachers[2] or for his fellow students, but has so often delighted so many of them that the former consider him a son and the latter a brother. By his actions he is acquiring a good reputation, since he does not fight if someone fails to praise him. And yet, he is strong, and if he wished to, he could inspire fear by it, but, in spite of that, he loves to live in peace, more than others who are weaker than him. 3. Therefore, I am glad when he comes to class, and I enjoy it when he declaims. Some students are not bad at declaiming but have such peevish characters and take such pride in bringing trouble that I curse my profession when they show up.

AGROECIUS I

6 F294 (year 359/60): To Eusebius x
[*Eusebius x, a school fellow of Libanius, was from Armenia, like Agroecius, who was too poor to undergo public service.*]
1. We take refuge in the same Athena for the same reasons. Lately you snatched a young man out of fire for us and took the trouble as one would for a son. The same trouble and equal (or rather much greater) goodwill are necessary. 2. The bearer, Agroecius, is no different from a son to me, and to this very day I have continued to sustain this family of many brothers, all poor. 3. But those who thoughtlessly write decrees wish to show that I would not be able to help my friends in any way but by joining in their prayers. And yet I defended them against your anger not with prayers but with facts, and I stilled the waters, but they remember this favor as much as Agamemnon returns a kindness.[3] 4. Let them learn, therefore, that your power is both mine and yours, and that I will very hardly suffer evil as long as you are strong. It is for Agroecius to inform you about the situation, but it depends on your courage that this man not be swept away.

---

[1] Cf. *Iliad* 2.372 and letter 30.
[2] Libanius uses the term *hēgemōn*, "leader, guide," only here.
[3] A proverb about ungrateful people, see *Suda* A2637; cf. *Epp.* 194 and 1433.

DOSSIER OF ALBANIUS (AND STRATEGIUS II)

[*Strategius and Albanius are the sons of Agesilaus of Ancyra, and the student Eusebius xx is their nephew; cf.* **75**. *They are favorite students in spite of their relatively brief attendance (Festugière 1959, 153–59).*]

7 F63 (year 359/60): To Albanius

1. Even though you do not have everything you desired, at least you have half. You love our city and have no small part of her since you have noble Priscianus.[4] He took an interest in your work; you heard him proposing subjects for argument; and when you pronounced the panegyric of Modestus,[5] he bestowed honor upon what you said. 2. Repay this man with praises and inform dearest Ancyra of his eloquence and the nature of his character; a good orator is an utter godsend for them. 3. I think that you would again engage in your beloved pursuits (*paidika*) if you learned the reason for his journey: the emperor was seized with longing for his tongue. To prevail in those contests is a great thing in itself, and the origin of greater things. 4. Seeing this, let no one consider rhetoric out of favor; for it is a source of strength for those who truly possess it and can say to those who disdain it: "I am still strong."[6]

8 F140 (year 359/60): To Albanius

1. Now you really gave me my repayment, not gold and silver—this is what most people bring and what most enjoy—but that for the sake of which I also left my patrimonial possessions: a good reputation. 2. You gave it to me by showing that I am not only a wrestler but also a good trainer. You know that those critics who do not dare to find fault with my oratorical power try to bite me in this area, but with your voice you silenced them. 3. Run a shrewd race and choose a way of life that you consider advantageous to you, but be aware that oratory will be useful to you always. There is no type of life that is dishonored by oratory. And consider that your father also begs this of you, and that he is not bereft of this pleasure even though he is dead and buried. 4. Our governor[7] is nourished in the art of Hermes and calls this to mind in front of speakers and confesses to be a slave only of this pleasure. A person of good sense should take advantage of the present opportunity.

---

[4] Priscianus 1/i. Other letters to or concerning him are **92**, **135**, **167**, and **177**.
[5] Domitius Modestus 2. Other letters concerning him are **175** and **184**.
[6] *Iliad* 5.254; *Od.* 21.425.
[7] Hermogenes 3, perhaps.

9 F287 (year 361): To Maximus

[*Maximus 19/vi was then governor of Armenia. Other letters to him are 3, 12, 40, 128, and 169.*]

1. I enjoyed what you wrote. You disclosed what I wished, and the beauty of the letter was so extraordinary that I cried aloud in the square (for I received it there, and as soon as I got it, I read it). "Why are you shouting?" asked Strategius (the one who is in public service, I mean), and, when he knew, he read it and imitated my shout. 2. Come, help this one for us, too, and cherish him since he is my son. You will surely not be cross with me because I call a student this. He was one of the many who studied with me, but was one of the few above reproach, and yet, he was always with me, studying and sharing my table, the afternoon work, and all the other things that befit a young man who is trusted because of his character. 3. His family comes from the people you govern and from the Galatians, but he values the province you govern more and has long since favored Armenia. Although he did not do this before, it is clear that he would now if you showed him the cities that are called the flowers of Samos and the Samian alley.[8]

10 F794 (year 362/63): To Albanius

1. I delight in your letter and much more in the things you do. I hear that you are preserving your property, gladly performing public service, and acquiring the reputation of a good orator. 2. Do not cease, therefore, to benefit yourself and me. Truly what will make you powerful among your fellow citizens will bring their sons to me.

11 F833 (year 363): To Albanius

1. What is this? You sent us money and did us a service though we did you no service, as if you had not already paid off a lot when your father was still alive and not a little after he passed away: you were our host when we traveled up and down the country, not for twenty days, as Oineus with Bellerophon,[9] but once for a whole month, and another time for three. On account of this, it would be right for you to receive something for free from me. 2. So what did you have in mind when you sent the letter? If it is because you prevail because of your eloquence, I owe you payment for that; if it is that Maximus, a righteous man, held his hand over you, again it is I who owe payment to Maximus, and not you to me, since you have received what was due to you. You know the rule that I observe with my students: I behave like a father toward them. 3. It was clever of you not to have mentioned the money in the

---

[8] The "Samian alley" was an alley or bazaar where women sold delicacies.
[9] *Iliad* 7.216.

letter. You knew that I would cry aloud and refuse. Now, your accomplice in this scheme, Ulpianus,[10] gave the money to my servants, before coming in to me, and gave the letter to me. Then, after telling me what you were doing—everything splendid and such as I had hoped for—he left. But as I am walking through the house with the letter, I discover your ruse and thought about sending the money back. But, since I knew that I would distress you, and fearing that it would be rather rude, I left it where it was. I am planning, however, to make restitution in a pleasant and seemly fashion that will not look like restitution.

12 F834 (year 363): To Maximus
[*Maximus 19/vi, then governor of Galatia. Other letters to him are 3, 9, 40, 128, and 169.*]

1. You are adding facts to hopes, noble Maximus, or rather you have surpassed hopes with facts, since, in addition to preserving the property of my companions by watching over it, you have procured them a good reputation for rhetoric. 2. Of Albanius, in any case, you have made both a rhetor and a wealthy man: you did not let him keep silent, but helped him when he spoke, and gave him every honor. So, those who come here bring me two most pleasant pieces of news: the one discloses the efficiency of your administration, the other, Albanius's power, both as it now is, and as it can be forecast, things that come from nowhere else than from your excellence in governing. 3. This is greater to me than Tantalus's talents of money,[11] nor would I take (in addition to those talents) all the land in between Corinth and Sicyon[12] in exchange for being able to hear such news. 4. Please, continue as you have in other matters, too, behaving kindly toward Albanius. If you find him neglecting oratory, be harsh and exact punishment; even if you chain him to the task, I will approve the chains. 5. I ask you to also urge the others to do the same, so that no one may throw the proverb of the one swallow[13] in our face. You have many who can run if they are whipped. If you will spur them on, you will reinforce our work, eliminating the flies' reason to bite us.

13 F1444 (year 363): To Caesarius
[*Caesarius 1/iv in 363 was in Antioch but then moved to Ancyra.*]

1. Albanius, whom my letter wishes to help, is the son of Agesilaus and the brother of Strategius, who took part in an embassy here together with Bosporius. He is my student in the strictest sense of the word,

---
[10] Ulpianus 2.
[11] Tantalus was proverbially wealthy.
[12] The land between Corinth and Sicyon was a proverbially rich plain, cf. **188**.
[13] "A swallow does not make a spring," Cratinus 33.

since he did not come to our teaching from another teacher nor did he have another after us. 2. If his mother's crying and begging had not led him away from his studies before the time was right, he would now do what I do. But he was pulled away and now is bravely and justly engaged in public service, neither frightened nor rapacious. 3. When he appears, I hope that he will get some suitable advice, which befits your nature and which will be better for him, as they say, than the shield of Argos[14] and at the same time an incentive to be better. Such words from such people, when they are directed to young men of such an age, stimulate their souls toward deeds worthy of praise.

ALEXANDER 4/II

14 F456 (year 355/56): To Caecilius
[*Cf. Or. 62.54. Alexander, the son of Caecilius i, became governor of Bithynia in 361.*]
  1. You found a good attendant for your son, the excellent Tatianus, who is very able to urge on the teachers and praise young men's zeal, but also can see and put an end to their idleness. I bid you be of good cheer, since Alexander will not waste even a bit of time while that man keeps his eye and mind on him. 2. I marvel, however, that you put such an excellent person in charge of the young man, but keep the young man himself tied to the wine vats.[15]

AMBROSIUS 2/I

15 F82 (year 359): To Ambrosius
[*Ambrosius had an unknown official post.*]
  1. I am asking you a favor that you are willing to do. Young men like you, when given official posts, enjoy being able to do favors for older men like us; and it brings some pleasure to teachers to ask their students, and to students to be able to do something for their teachers according to their minds. 2. So, Cleobulus the teacher urges me to do what I can through you, and I am asking you to do what you can through your post. Antiphilus is in the forefront among those who work for you and is a relative of Cleobulus. The character he has shown recommended him to me: he does not know how to gain by

---

[14] "Shield of Argos": a golden shield carried in procession by the pure children of the city; cf. Plu. *Paroem.* 1.44; Salzmann 1910, 63.

[15] Perhaps a proverb. It may have meant "in poor condition," or "busy," or "tied to his father."

daring what one should not. Cleobulus testifies to this, and I, trusting him, recommend him. 3. The favor is to look upon him with kindness. He will not use this for his own advantage, but rather in order to have the confidence to inform you about his pressing matters and to assist willingly in whatever you ask.

THE SONS OF AMPHILOCHIUS 2/II

16 *F634 (year 361): To Amphilochius*
[*Amphilochius 2, from Cappadocia, studied with Libanius in Athens. His children are Amphilochius 4/iii, bishop of Iconium, and Euphemius 1/ii; cf. Epp. 670 and 671. The second died when he was 20 years old in 370, so in 361 was only 11. Gregory of Nazianzus wrote nine epitaphs on him: Ant. Pal. 8.121–30.*]

1. If I did not do these things, I would be wrong, but it would not be right for me to be praised for doing them; for if you neglected your sons, you would have some detractors, too, but do not look for someone to admire you because you take care of them. 2. Not a few things make me their father; the most important is that they are well suited by nature for rhetoric.

DOSSIER OF ANATOLIUS V
[*From Armenia, introduced by Leontius 9/iv, pagan teacher of rhetoric. Anatolius's father, Adamantius i, heard rumors initiated by a letter that the sophist Acacius 6 sent to parents in Armenia. The pedagogue Eumathius ii went to Armenia to reassure him.*]

17 *F32 (year 358/59): To Adamantius*
1. It is as if I received a letter from you, even though I did not. In venting your unjust anger against your son and praising things that you previously censured, you were making it clear that you would be happy to write but did not dare. But, my friend, dare to send a letter. 2. Those who sent you a *nice* letter are to blame for this unpleasant situation; or rather, the fact that others deceived them removes the blame from them. We are not unaware of the source of the deceit, but it is preferable to have compassion for it rather than hate. 3. When I consider your son's natural talent and his enjoyment of hard work, I quote the proverb that says: "The plants that are going to bear fruit stand out right away."[16] 4. I would say even more, but I know that I

---
[16] A proverb, *Suda* A4479.3, s.v. *autika*.

will be *commended*, as is a lover who is not believed even when he really says the truth.

18 F41 (likely year 358/59): To Adamantius
1. No small advantage for your son was the presence of his pedagogue, who not only is such in name but really knows how to guide, so that he was the only one who suffered no harm when everyone else was sick. It was necessary, however, to purge your soul of the great deceit inflicted on it by those who work not at making discourses but at slandering those who do. Thus I urged Eumathius to be like a doctor: no one would have escaped his notice by being careless, nor would he have persuaded him with anything but the truth. 2. I was going to drag to court those who wrote that *beautiful* letter, but I refrained in order not to inflict any trouble on you, and at the same time, before going to court, I thought that I would exact punishment on your sons: death itself is more easily bearable for a person who thinks rightly. 3. Let those people slander me and damage themselves, but send Anatolius's attendant back to us as soon as possible and look for that way you defend yourself with him, whenever he refutes the slanderers by facts.

19 F129 (year 359/60): To Adamantius
1. Why are you worried? What reason do you have to believe that your son will be esteemed less, especially when the others praise him and Eumathius does not know how to lie and I honor the truth myself? I have never told fathers that their sons are sharp when they are dull, but I would not even say that those who are wide-awake are sluggish. 2. If you have a son who lets people speak rather well of him, do not be distrustful and do not make slanderers glad by paying attention to what they say. Whenever they learn they are not convincing you, they will stop lying. 3. You could not desire any more than me that Anatolius become one of the best orators: it is in fact from me, and not from you, that the Armenians demand this.

DOSSIER OF APOLINARIUS 2/IV AND GEMELLUS 2/I
[*Apolinarius and Gemellus are always mentioned together. They lived in Cilicia and were the sons of Anatolius 4/ii. They left Libanius after one year to follow their father, who was transferred to Phoenicia. The Ammianus mentioned was probably an official in charge of financial matters.*]

20 F233 (year 360): To Apolinarius and Gemellus
1. It does not at all seem that you have left us, for writing a letter with such skill is not usual for students who are away but rather for those—if I may say so—who are still meeting with me. So, while I was glad

that you wrote to me, I was even more pleased that you were capable of writing in such a fashion. 2. Since I thought that the eunuch who delivered the letter was coming from you, I reproached him when he said that he had remained here. But I immediately acquitted him and put the blame on you when I understood that he remained because you neglected him. 3. Yet, besides your natural talents, he is the main reason why you acquired a good reputation, since he wards off like a dog those who are not good. You enjoyed the fruits of this man's care, but when the time for compensation came, you rejected him. 4. Please, my boys, attend to your pedagogue by recalling him to Cilicia or by sending him something from there. Besides what I have often told you, the man delivering this letter must persuade you to despise wealth. The good Ammianus is included among the soldiers in terms of position, but he is a philosopher in what he does, and imitates Socrates with regard to profit.

21 F211 (year 360?): To Anatolius
[*Libanius alludes to an obscure incident.*]

1. I know that I have rendered very great service to your family, if indeed it is a great benefit for your family that your sons have acquired not a little rhetoric, and in such a short time; but I was so far from wronging you that I have even taught these young men how they will exact sufficient punishment upon the one who caused pain. 2. It is you who wronged me by convincing yourself that I had wronged you. This is like believing that I am bad to my brothers and bad to my children. 3. Work on a speech in defense for this, but you need one that has been carefully thought out if you are not going to be overwhelmed. Rather, I know what you are going to do. You will rest, but you will order your sons to work on a speech for you. This is the only way in which you will conquer me.

22 F304 (year 361): To Apolinarius and Gemellus
[*Magnus 12/iii was an ex-student who needed work. Cf. 42.*]

1. I do not think that even now you are doing anything else but becoming educated, and to be educated (which is the highest attainment of men) is to know how to govern. The father educates his children (a most endearing thing) not by speaking words about the subject, but by teaching how to govern through his actions. 2. Learn those things, therefore, and remember us, and fulfill the hopes of Magnus.

23 F806 (year 363): To Apolinarius and Gemellus

1. No wonder teachers cherish their students even more than fathers their sons, particularly when the students are not bad toward the person who educated them. For they are and certainly they have been

bad. I know this more than others because I toiled for many, but I suffered because of many. 2. You are good, however, and approve the storks rather than the rams.[17] Therefore, I join you in my wishes and prayers for the best. In the present circumstance, the best is what you intend to do. 3. I say this because I know that hesitation often interferes with what is advantageous. But you come from a great city and from such a family. One fears that you would be held back from this course of treatment.

24 F1541 (year 365): To Apolinarius and Gemellus
[*They apparently want to continue their studies.*]
1. Your daring was noble and better than every caution, if loving eloquence is noble; and you proclaimed a longing for it in your letter. 2. In thinking that you partake already of the Muses' pursuits (and god willing you will partake of it), you have acted according to my desire. Young men have many occasions to be close, but the best was receiving a letter from you fledglings. Your eager desire for the trip is praiseworthy, but staying is no less noble: the former is the mark of those who aspire to wisdom, but the latter of those who obey their father.

DOSSIER OF APRINGIUS
[*Apringius was still poor after ten years of practice as an advocate, so he went to Berytus. Cf. Ep. 150 (N62), sent in 358–61; and 1203 (B167).*]

25 F1170 (year 364): To Marius
[*Marius 1, a teacher of rhetoric, became governor of Phoenicia in 363.*]
1. Apringius, as the saying goes, is "back to Pytho,"[18] that is, in school like a young man. He believes that knowledge of the law is also necessary if one wants to be a good advocate. And yet, in the past, an advocate took a legal expert as a partner, and they gained strength through one another. Now, however, one who does not know the law is truly like "a man from Aegium who is of no repute and no account."[19] 2. So, I commend Apringius and consider him blessed. I commend him because he is running where he must, and I think he is blessed because he is setting foot in Phoenicia, a beautiful land that you have made more beautiful. Now that you are putting Phoenicia on the right course, he will enjoy the things he would have, if his father were the

---

[17] Storks feed their parents, but rams butt at those who bring them up—a proverb; Salzmann 1910, 79.

[18] Pytho is a region of Delphi. In Classical times, Athens sent a yearly embassy to Delphi.

[19] Aegium was a city despised like Megara; cf. Plu. *Mor.* 682f.; Salzmann 1910, 35.

leader of this people—actually, he will enjoy them even more. Whereas he would perhaps experience his father as rather harsh, your disposition is entirely calm and gentle. 3. I am sure that you will entrust this youth to his teachers, keep him immune from the usual rough behavior of students, give him entry to you, and show him kindness in other ways.

26 F1171 (year 364): To Domninus
[*Domninus or Domnio 1 taught law in Berytus. Other letters addressed to him are 28, 101, 156, and 175.*]

1. See, you have convinced even grown men to do what young men do! My companion Apringius, after much running because of the tribunal, has come to learn the law, since he can learn it from you. Otherwise, I do not think he would ever engage in this business. 2. If anyone attempts to mock him, he will have an ally in Socrates, who went to a teacher of music in his old age. But please cut your course as short as possible so that he can take advantage for a longer time of what he receives. 3. I would think it worthwhile to say something about the fee (this fellow is good but poor; if he is unable to pay you, he is indeed capable of remembering a favor) if I hadn't long known that this is a *law* that you observe with your students.

DOSSIER OF ARSENIUS 3/III
[*Son of Antiochus ii, school fellow of Libanius, from an important family of Antioch.*]

27 F540 (year 356/57): To Arsenius
1. It would be good if you could take advantage of the usual training right here, but what you do now—not abandoning the training when you are absent—is not bad either. 2. I was pleased that the money came with your letter and that you do the opposite of many students: whereas they avoid those who supervise them, you look for someone to do so and show that you are working hard even now, putting your father in my place. Would that you could nearly resemble him! Being better is impossible.

ARTEMON

28 F533 (year 356): To Domninus
[*Domninus 1/i; other letters to him are 26, 101, 156, and 175.*]

1. The bearer, Artemon, is a fellow citizen of mine but was the student of others—a fact that he forever bemoaned. He happened to study with

others but to be fond of us, though circumstances, fortune, and his imminent departure did not grant him to obtain what he wished. 2. So we number him among our pupils, since he feels for us as do our students. When he came to me and told me where he was going and why, I praised him, wished him luck, and showed him the heaven. 3. I repaid him by sending him to the man he needed. You should teach him what you teach the others, but make sure to be kinder to him than to the others so that everyone will know how much I count with you.

ASTEIUS

29 F820 (year 363): To Atarbius
[*Atarbius was governor of Euphratensis, the province of Asteius. Asteius's father, Marcianus, was a decurion threatened with public service.*]
1. Consider this an embassy of the Muses who would like Asteius, a member of the *chorus*, to spend longer time with them. Asteius came here with no intention of engaging in rhetoric, but when he saw that others were learning it, he wished to learn it, received part of it, and considers it a misfortune not to acquire the rest. 2. If his father Marcianus is freed from his troubles, Asteius will be able to continue to occupy himself with the same pursuits as he does now. But if someone drags the father off,[20] the latter will immediately do the same to his son: he is not unaware of the harm, but is constrained by old age. 3. So let it be your task, noble friend, to let the one live in peace and to help the other toward the art of rhetoric; for not least among the benefits that you give your subjects is the fact that with your help, one of them will be a rhetor. 4. Everyone will know what you'll give, because I will not keep silent and [Asteius] will write about this favor.

BASILIDES II

30 F1408 (year 363): To Basilides
[*Spectatus 1 was a relative of Libanius. Basilides had been a student in Constantinople.*]
1. While talking about Paphlagonia, Spectatus said some nice things, including that he had met the excellent Basilides, who had been my pupil. 2. "Which Basilides are you talking about?" I asked. "The man with a light complexion[21] and a high forehead," he responded, in the

---

[20] "To drag" means "to impose a liturgy," as in *Ep.* 293.1.
[21] Light skin was considered to be a desirable attribute; see, e.g., the handsome "light" student of *Or.* 39.17.

manner of Demosthenes or, if you wish, Homer.[22] He was trying to call this man to my mind through his physical characteristics. Then, since I could not follow him, he passed on to the intellect and said, "I am talking about the fellow whom you trusted the most and who was the head of your *chorus* when you were teaching around the Bosphorus." 3. At this point I recognized you and shouted and, like Agamemnon, wished I could have ten students like you.[23] But I was truly surprised at one thing, how you helped Theophilus through the esteem you have for me but did not dare to write to me in person and recall those times of old, even though you are so skilled at writing elegant letters—at least, if you still possess some of that skill. This is my opinion: you would not merit what Spectatus reported about you. 4. So, write to me now to make up for your wrong, or I will report you to the Muses as a man who is neglecting his father.

DOSSIER OF BASSIANUS 2
[*Bassianus was a relative of Libanius, a Christian. His son Aristaenetus 2/ii might have been pagan. See Bradbury 2004a, 15–18.*]

31 F155 (year 359/60): To Bassianus
1. I knew you would do what you are doing now and that you would not be bad at writing letters. Your good character has long been evident, and you were learning to write letters. When the occasion came for deeds and words, how would you be silent or careless with us? 2. Keep doing this and do not forget the labors of good Cleobulus for you, for I got you when you were fluttering your wings already and then I helped you along, but he was your Phoenix. 3. And now it is also possible for you to learn from Cleobulus what Phoenix did.[24] Pay him back, if you can; but until it is in your power, pray that you secure that power.

32 F231 (year 360?): To Bassianus
1. May you receive many good things, best of young men, for you showed the same concern for your teacher as the laws show for parents in order that their offspring take care of them. I am not unaware of what you write your grandmother about the wonderful Cleobulus, asking that your possessions be open to him. 2. On learning this, I certainly was not going to keep silent about such noble deeds, but the city is full

---

[22] A double reference to Demosthenes *Mid.* 71 and *Odyssey* 4.138–39.
[23] A reference to *Iliad* 2.372. Cf. 5.
[24] The grammarian Cleobulus was a teacher for Bassianus like Phoenix was for Achilles.

of the tale of your munificence, and we have Cleobulus, who surely would have flown away, if you had not been so good. 3. "Therefore, my beloved, aim"[25] to be praised and to live with better hopes. You have received from the Muses a recompense that is not trivial even now. They say that everyone everywhere is devoted to the love of eloquence. This is precisely the gift of the daughters of Mnemosyne.

33 F1293 (year 364): To Bassianus
1. You showed yourself a master in the letter that you have written, but not a blameless man. But the very fact that you are so eloquent has reconciled me to you. Even if you used your wrestling tricks against your trainer, it is great for me that the wrestler has become good. I have put aside my anger and feel toward you as I did before I was angry. 2. I cannot write more than this about the reconciliation. You had to write at length to counter the accusations, but the opposite fits our words.

BASSUS II

34 F693 (year 361/62): To Cromatius ii
[*Cf. also* Ep. *175 (B92). Clematius 1/i, governor of Palestine, was executed by Gallus.*]
1. I have cherished and admired you since Clematius himself (who met an unjust death after a just life), coming here on leaving the office he had by you, praised Palestine exceedingly but defined your talent the chief among its beauties. 2. Hearing of the man's excellence—I am very fond of such men—I felt the urge and intended to write a letter. Then, somehow, the desire passed. Now, however, I pay what is due and indeed, like an old friend, I immediately ask a favor, convincing myself that you will not blame me but will grant it. 3. The bearer, Bassus, who is over twenty years old, a poor man, the son of a poor father, came to me from Phoenicia because of his desire for rhetoric. Knowing how to work hard and shunning pleasures, he acquired something that I hesitate to praise but that perhaps will not seem small to you. 4. A little while ago, he showed himself to his fatherland and to the other Phoenicians and was reckoned a rhetor. But now that he wants to go to Palestine, he thinks that, if he could find safe anchorage by you and go to others with a letter of yours, he would obtain everywhere through your help as much as he would by you. 5. Be a harbor for a man who knows how to speak, to be a friend, and to remember a favor. We will sing

---

[25] *Iliad* 8.281–82.

your praises. Indeed, you do everything for the sake of praise, and because of this your name is illustrious, for many surpass you in abundance of wealth.

DOSSIER OF THE SONS OF CAESARIUS II: EUDOCIUS I AND CAESARIUS III

35 F248 (year 358/59): To Iphicrates
[*The sons of Caesarius ii from Armenia went first to another teacher. Iphicrates, a friend of Caesarius, tried to soothe Libanius. On Iphicrates, cf.* **142** *and* **166**. *In 361, Eudocius quit because of his father's death. Epp. 645 and 646 were written afterward.*]

1. Not even the first time the sons of Caesarius were entrusted to a rhetor was the decision a bad one, and may they now find with me, O Muses, something that will remind them of a certain proverb.[26] You may know what it is, but I better not say it. 2. I laughed at the apology you made, even though nobody was making an accusation, and again I started to laugh when I understood that you feared that these young men would not enjoy all the advantages because they were coming to us from others. If I regarded them as enemies, I would reject them. But since I received them as friends, I would hurt myself if I did not treat them as well as I could. 3. Diomedes would also be ridiculous if he took the horses of Aeneas but, instead of tending them, weakened them, for example, by denying them fodder, reproaching them because they first were Aeneas's. But Zeus, who took care of the horses and gave them birth, would have said, "Son of Tydeus, you ruin what is yours, if you neglect these which belong to you. It is you that they carry and crown with their victories, not Anchises' son."[27]

36 F249 (year 358/59): To Caesarius

1. Your letter has imitated the Lacedaemonians. They went to Marathon after the fact, determined to help, when there was no need of help,[28] and this letter urges me to take good care of your sons, whom we entrusted with the task of taking care of others. 2. Do not be surprised if they have become so able so soon: they are good and love learning. Those who come to me endowed with these qualities are immediately ranked above the others and have my trust. The fact that they are your children is no small advantage to them, for whoever mentions you does so in praise. 3. Would you like me to tell you a

---

[26] The proverb is *deuterōn ameinonōn*, "The second is better"; cf., e.g., *Ep.* 937.
[27] *Iliad* 5.261–67.
[28] Herodotus 6.120.

fourth reason? Their uncle Eusebius went to school with me: I learned this by myself, when I noticed the family resemblance in the younger one.

37 F250 (year 358/59): To Eutherius
[*Eutherius 2 was governor of Armenia and father of Philopatris; cf. 99, 154, 165, and 166.*]

1. The fact that you happen to be governor is sweeter to me than if I had a province myself. I congratulate Caesarius for his character and for his reputation, which is growing because of your influence, but I congratulate him especially because of the fine children he has. So much do they care for decorum and for rhetoric that their father himself might with reason blush with pride before them. 2. I would humor you in anything; even if you ask me to love a lazy student, I will comply, but to tell the truth, their natural talent rather than your letter recommended them. So it is time for you to ask another favor, because this one these young men have granted to themselves.

38 F254 (year 358/59): To Caesarius

1. You are a lucky man not only in your children, who are good and love to study, but also in your son-in-law (for whom both of these things are true). 2. I think that when you decided on this marriage, you did not admire the extent of lands and the weight of gold more than the truly golden soul that you found that he possessed. 3. Your letter was the beginning of my affection for him, but after putting him to the test (*peira*), I do not love him because of you but love you more than before, because of him. 4. What about him isn't fine? Isn't he gentle? Isn't he quick-witted? Isn't he a marvelous speaker? Isn't his judgment sound? Isn't his frenzy for rhetoric fiercer than the Corybantes' frenzy?[29] 5. Do you want me to tell you a secret? Often he came to me when I lay idle and, when he appeared, spurred me on. Leaping up at my first words, he drew my speech to its culmination, so that I was pleased with myself. 6. Sufficient proof of his excellence is the fact that he came to us. What others did not do when spurred by their own brothers, he did for his wife's brothers.

39 F645 (year 361): To Eudocius

It is not an act of daring to write a letter, but to not write is blameworthy. Even if there is nothing urgent, send me greetings; and if something is urgent, write with good courage. I consider both you and your

---

[29] Corybantes were spirits who danced in orgiastic cults.

brother excellent people, and I will not deprive you of my help, if I can do anything.

40 F646 (year 361): To Maximus
[*Maximus 19/vi. Other letters to him are 3, 9, 12, 128, and 169. According to Ep. 814 of the year 363, Eudocius was relieved from his duty.*]
1. They say that Eudocius grieves for his father only a little, and that you are the reason for this, because you diminished his feelings of bereavement with many great deeds. We were able to learn of them no less than those who were present, because the one who was rescued revealed them in a long letter. 2. So this is what you are receiving now from us: applause, praise, and the fact that no one is unaware of these things. But you will rightly have even the greater rewards that the gods usually give good people. 3. Before, I thought that I had to exhort you, but now certainly not. I see in fact that the generals urge on the fighters with their words before action, but then they consider the action itself sufficient to exhort them for what remains. 4. You have been helping this young man for a long time, but now you will see that he shares his father's name and his brother's character.

DOSSIER OF CALLIOPIUS III

41 467 (year 355/56): To Bassus
[*Bassus 5 is Calliopius's father. On Calliopius, cf. Epp. 359 (N28) and 366 (B35).*]
1. We are not unaware of the labors you undertook on our behalf, and you could not find greater repayment from us: we are trying to make your son quite like his grandfather and uncle and such as will bring credit to his father. 2. So let us both be engaged in the same pursuits and always offer each other the most valuable things.

42 F1141 (year 364): To Magnus
[*On Calliopius's death. For Magnus 12/iii, who became an advocate, Libanius wrote many recommendations, Epp. 303, 304, 1270–72. Cf. 22.*]
1. In this respect, too, it is painful to be a teacher: he is necessarily the father of many young men, and it is difficult for a father of many not to mourn. 2. Calliopius has received the honors that I least wanted for him. May the Fates suffer you to reach old age as you imitate his fairness and his contests!

CELSINUS 3

43 F911 (year 388): To Celsinus
[*Celsinus held several offices and was a student in the same way the emperor Julian was. Ep. 949.2 shows that he avidly borrowed books from Libanius.*]
  1. May the daughter of the best father and wife of the best man never cease also making your house greater with her weaving. When I saw the linen tunic, I marveled, but I sent it back, which another would not have done. I said, "Noble Celsinus, at what time were you my student? What tablet full of discourses did you bring me, and what corrections did you get on it that you think you owe me the fee you are sending me?" 2. I declare indeed that you have received more from us than those who spent many years with us, fearing the teacher's eye and the pedagogues' lashes. 3. When you were an *assessor* for those in office and were holding offices yourself, you became a lover of the discourses we made and gave no less attention to those than to your own affairs. Most pleasantly engaged in these beloved pursuits, you became skillful at making discourses and at distinguishing what was better and what worse when another declaimed, so that it was an advantage for those who were not so good that you were not present at the declamations. 4. Because of these things, you owed us a repayment, but, by paying us back, you do not have to pay this. Since you have paid already and do not owe anything, why should you still be giving, as if you owed? 5. So what was that repayment? Applause, praises, jumping up in enthusiasm when mentioning myself and my discourses, and considering real men only those who did the same as you. 6. I say, therefore, that you are my student, since you feed your soul with our works, but since you have fought beside us for our glory, you should no longer look for something else to give. The Athenians, who paid so dearly to be admired, show that this kind of repayment is greater than the other. I trust Demosthenes, when he talks about the Athenians.[30]

THE SON OF CRATINUS

44 F93 (year 359): To Cratinus
[*Cratinus was an unimportant decurion; see Or. 28.24.*]
  1. Neither Helen, who recognized the father of Telemachus in the features of Telemachus, nor Menelaus, who agreed with his wife and com-

---
[30] Dem. *De Cor.* 66.

mented on his hands, feet, eyes, and the other things he mentions, offended the young man himself or his father, but I think that on hearing this, Odysseus would have felt no less joy than when "he sacked the sacred citadel of Troy."[31] You may also know that others consider the likeness of children to their fathers a blessing. 2. What were you thinking when you attacked what I said about the nose? I wrote this to cheer you, but now I am made to appear like someone gauche and rude. 3. See now whether it will be acceptable to you to pass over some of my clumsiness toward your son. Let excellent Cratinus know that I am willing to share what I have if receiving it does not harm the one who takes it.

DOSSIER OF CHRYSOGONUS 2

45 F1208 (year 364): To Marius
[*Marius 1 was governor of Phoenicia in 363. Magnus 7/iv was the famous iatrosophist mentioned by Eunapius and Palladas.*]

1. The bearer, Chrysogonus, is from central Phoenicia. He was rich but became poor because of some fellow citizens who were poor but then became rich. 2. At first he was a student of ours and was not bad at rhetoric. Then he sailed to Egypt intending to learn the art of medicine in a short time. Magnus, who taught this and was a relative of his, had called him there, but, when he arrived, pretended not to know him. He lost heart and fell ill. 3. Therefore, he came back, cursing that man because he had not learned anything, but had actually forgotten much of what he once knew. He occupied his ancestral land when fear forced those unjust men to restrain themselves, but, when their fear subsided, he was driven off again. His only hope of salvation is to become one of your advocates and receive some goodwill. If those people who blame Zeus for making his land small were aware of this, they would leave what belongs to others before the verdict, or, if they were unwilling to do so, they would be forced out by the verdict.

46 F1273 (year 364): To Ulpianus
[*Ulpianus 3/i succeeded Marius 1 as governor of Phoenicia in 364.*]

1. I started to talk to you about Chrysogonus, but, since you were in a hurry, I refrained from speaking and told you that I was going to write. So, I am writing that Chrysogonus the bearer, who was left an orphan, and who suffered a greater misfortune than being orphan, that

---

[31] *Od.* 1.2.

is, dishonest guardians, who made themselves masters of his property and overlooked that he would go hungry. 2. He wished to learn rhetoric and came to us for this reason. He did not learn as much as he wished to, but as much as he could, perhaps, to disclose his tutors' *justice* toward himself. 3. You will then enforce the laws, as you usually do. If, after getting back what is his, he should wish to engage in the practice of law, continue to show him favor in this also.

DADUCHIUS

47 *F1164 (year 364): To Daduchius*
[*Father and son have the same name.*]
 1. Bitter has turned sweet for Daduchius, and he now loves the hard work he used to avoid. It might also have been a god who urged him, but visibly it was the excellent Florentius, who checked everything carefully, grew angry when something was neglected, and urged him to improve the situation, saying that the boy would avoid blame if he became a good student instead of a bad one. Daduchius promised and did not lie, but now he is one of those who get annoyed when we are on holiday.[32] 2. Pray that your son continues to be so eager and be nice to him: now that he has changed, you should change, too.

DOSSIER OF THE NEPHEW OF DEMETRIUS
[*The student in question was the son of the widowed sister of the sophist and governor Demetrius 2/i, the uncle of Calycius. Cf. Ep. 23 (B144), which concerns this youth running away. Genesius is unknown but was probably a relative.*]

48 *F24 (year 358): To Genesius*
 1. How could I not have been pleased to see a young man who is the son of a good mother and the nephew of a man who is a savior of cities and a friend of ours? He ran away from you in a noble flight, the only kind of flight that is praiseworthy. Abandoning one's country in order to possess rhetoric is also good for that country, because the fugitive will be able to make it great with rhetoric. 2. But just as you praise us for the care that the lad found when he came here, so persuade his mother to alleviate his poverty. You will not be able to demand a strict accounting if your own contribution is lacking.

---

[32] On the expression "to be on holiday," cf. *Or.* 43.14.

DIANIUS

49 F376 (year 358): To Themistius
[*Cf. Ep. 374 (B177). Ep. 281 shows that Dianius finally got a position because of his gentlemanly behavior. On Themistius's embassy to Rome in 357, see Penella 2000a, 6.*]

1. Dianius's mother and country you know. He could not disobey his mother when she called him, and his country was dear to him because it was his country, but it was also frightening because of the necessity of undertaking liturgies, poor as he was. 2. Since he had to please his mother and suffer no harm himself, I thought that this man should come to you first, and then from there, after securing the support of Athena, go everywhere else. With the help of this goddess, he would be able to avoid even the Styx.[33] 3. You would be just if you offered him your hand, first of all because more than anyone else, you have helped people in need whose only claim to justice from you was that they were in need; then because one cannot say that our students are not also yours. The third reason (or, if you wish, the first) is that he is a relative of Aristaenetus (and does not put his family to shame),[34] from whom you deserve respect and who deserves it from you. By satisfying him because you love me, also satisfy your goodwill toward him. 4. Besides all the other reasons, you will help a man whom you will find has many of your discourses in his possession (and these not in his backpack or in books, but stored in his memory and soul), particularly those in which you showed that you were an ambassador. 5. Dometius[35] brought us this discourse as if we did not know it, but found that we knew it no less than its father does. I could say that it is my child, too, since it is the brother of my speeches in many ways. I will speak the truth, which does not displease Themistius.

DOSSIER OF DIOGNETUS
[*Cf. also Epp. 859 and 860. In 388, Tatianus made the study of Roman law mandatory for advocates. This law was supposed to come into effect after a period of time, but it was eliminated in 390; cf. Ep. 916 and Or. 48.26.*]

50 F857 (year 388): To Saturninus
[*Saturninus 10 became consul in 383.*]

1. The bearer, Diognetus—a good advocate who has saved the lives and possessions of many but who was forced then to keep silent by

---
[33] The Styx is one of the rivers of the Underworld, *Iliad* 8.369.
[34] Aristaenetus 1, cf. **191**.
[35] Dometius is unknown.

"the law about the time"—considers it a disgrace not to practice his vocation and keeps calling himself a burden on the earth. 2. So he is taking refuge in your good judgment, thinking that the best plan would be to follow your suggestions. Even the emperors complimented themselves for doing so, as did the Lapiths when they took Nestor's advice.[36] 3. Diognetus often told me that his family has benefited from you in not a few matters, so that a benefaction would be nothing new. 4. As I shared in the other favors by which you furthered their interests, I derive no less profit from these if you now give comparable or even greater help. One could show many examples of your past and present concerns for me.

51 F858 (year 388): To Eusebius
[*Eusebius 26/xxvii had an important position at the court of Arcadius.*]
1. When the bearer, Diognetus, born and raised in Samosata, reached the age when one can fall in love with rhetoric, he fell in love with it, came to us, and through continuous hard work attained the things for which he had come. He did not deem it necessary to pay attention to those who urged him toward other pursuits, but invoking Hermes and dedicating himself to pleading in court, he became such that it was essential for those who went to court to have him. 2. He refuted as untruthful those who said that Phoenicia was strictly necessary and that otherwise one had to keep silent. Since you know me well and are not unaware of my situation, you know how important this is for me. I was delighted when he pleaded, but I am distressed now that he does not, and I pray that he will speak again. 3. This is the fruit of the way he chose. He went that way because he trusted me and followed my advice, which you will honor by giving him back to us; if you do not—perish the thought!

DOSSIER OF DIONYSIUS 6/II
[*This unlucky and troubled youth was born in Isauria. Cf. 67.*]

52 F426 (year 355): Addressee is missing
1. Do you know that the fact that we, who are rhetors, dare to write to you, a soldier, also brings you much honor? I think this is a sign that you are harsh with enemies but gentle with friends. It has long been celebrated that a man in your position should be good at doing both things. 2. We look at other commanders from afar and flee when they glance at us. But we approach you more gladly than our parents, and, if you leave, we grieve. The reason is that you are trained in the art of war and in the Muses' pursuits: the former allows one to be victorious

---

[36] *Iliad* 1.273: the Lapiths and their king Peirithoos listened to Nestor.

in war, the latter to win there and to be gentle to those for whom you fight. 3. It would fit your character, therefore, to also lend a hand to this youth, Dionysius, who became an orphan when some robbers murdered his father. After running away because of this misfortune, he incurred great losses at home when his property was snatched away from him, but he applied himself to rhetorical studies, even though he was destitute. 4. Now, however, he has a chance to recover some of his property, because you are in charge of affairs. Pitying the misfortune of this young man and admiring his dedication, alleviate his poverty with your help.

53 F319 (year 357): To Cyrillus
[*Procopius 1/i was possibly governor of Cilicia in 348 and owned properties there and in Euphratensis. Cyrillus is otherwise unknown.*]

1. In urging me to write to you, Dionysius first convinced me that you remember and honor me. So he easily persuaded me, for I wished that Procopius would be good toward these studies, and with some reason I numbered you among his friends, since you have such a relationship with him. 2. Consequently, when I finally dared to write, I did not shrink from asking a favor, particularly because you all had granted that favor long ago, before one asked. Not to speak in riddles, I will be clearer. 3. Procopius did well to show pity for Dionysius when he saw that he was in poverty after the murder of his father. In order that he would not be kept away from rhetoric through lack of livelihood, he ordered the stewards of his properties in Cilicia to send [Dionysius] such and such goods, and he did the same with those of his lands around the Euphrates. 4. He said that the goods from Cilicia should last as long as the letters, but the others should be spent for the matter. Therefore [Dionysius] was supported, and Procopius had a good reputation. Now, however, he is deprived of those goods, too, since the person who always gave them to him does not give them any more, saying that some letters, not from Procopius—he did not dare to lie about this—but from one of his stewards, keep him from doing so. 5. So, persuade the stewards not to care for their master in such a way that they destroy his great reputation for the sake of a small amount of wheat. It makes sense to suspend the aid only in case Dionysius has acted badly toward you, has become rich, does not need it, or his disposition does not deserve to be rewarded. But if he is still in need and his character is the same, and your affairs sail with a fair wind—and I hope they do—do not suspend this aid. 6. Since Dionysius is grateful for your previous help, he will blame Fortune for the present circumstance, but perhaps someone will blame you for not standing

by your previous good decision and because you will miss greater things by pursuing trifles. 7. And if *you* have decided that, where is honor? This change is not worthy of your household. But if Procopius is the same as always, and it is a servant who disturbs his arrangement, let him learn not to transgress his master's orders.

54 F837 *(year 363): To Dionysius*
1. The letter you sent me, which is brimming with such elegance, Dionysius, is more valuable to me than the horses of Tros and Achilles,[37] and even winged Pegasus. 2. They say that you wrote a masterly panegyric for the governor; I believe it because your letter testifies to it. And I have word that you prevailed over your opponents through that knowledge of rhetoric you acquired at the time when they were wronging you. 3. You then reclaimed your land and all that they snatched away; the fact that you possess again what is yours through your own merit has brought me a good reputation. Should you wish to keep the horse, get on it and ride; but if you feel you must send it to me, I will gladly take it because you are sending it in your victory.

55 F1168 *(year 364): To Palladius*
[*Palladius 18, governor of Isauria. Dionysius was guilty of rape or abduction.*]
1. You asked me to judge a case that is not easy. I can neither approve what happened nor could I cast a vote against this young man, since I remember the many long years he studied with us. 2. I have regarded Dionysius as ill-starred since that day when you called him, but he chose his trees and the birds in them over becoming powerful in your retinue. If he had listened and had welcomed Fortune when she approached, he would have fame and wealth as an advocate and would not have had the leisure for the abduction. 3. I blame such a wretched man, but I would not be pleased to see him punished, even if the law would strictly require it. Therefore, I do not write the judge asking him to be humane, but I pray the gods to save for us a companion.

56 F1169 (year 364): To Entrechius
[*Entrechius 1, governor of Pisidia; cf.* **120.** *Julianus xv was another student.*]
1. The noble Palladius sent me what you wrote him about Dionysius and asked me what one must do, showing that even if he wished to do me a favor, he could not because of the laws. 2. I beg you to make the

---
[37] On these horses, see *Iliad* 5.265–68 and 16.148–49.

decision you want without asking me anything. Necessity may dictate that you punish him, but, since I am not constrained by it, perhaps it is not right that I join in attacking a friend in disgrace. The bad luck of Dionysius began a long time ago, when he lost his father and lived in destitution, while his mother and her new husband lived luxuriously. 3. Julianus knows this, and he is the right man to inform you. He took in this young man, shared his funds with him, and made many people think that they were brothers. One was so wealthy that both could have the benefit of it. 4. When Dionysius studied here, his way of life was orderly and chaste: one might as soon have accused the statues of a sexual misconduct as him. When he became a man, he committed the wrongs that he avoided when he was young. 5. The prosecutor says, "Dionysius is guilty," but what I say is: "Fortune is guilty in the case of Dionysius." Whenever the deed does not befit the character of the person who committed it, the wrongdoer should be called ill-starred rather than evil.

57 F1238 (year 364): To Palladius

1. With Athena's influence and help, Herakles escaped from "the dangerous streams of the Styx,"[38] and later Diomedes recovered and became illustrious: "Untiring fire shone from his helmet and shield."[39] 2. You showed us both things in the case of Dionysius: after putting an end to the danger, you are making sure that "he becomes conspicuous among all the Argives"[40] and acquires fame. You gave a lot, but you write little. 3. [Dionysius], however, has informed us sufficiently about the dark clouds from which he was freed and about his present well-being. This deed will be only the prologue, when you have taken over the chair of governorship in Syria. This will not be long, because the gods act justly. 4. Now there is not a student who has not heard about your ready assistance, nor did we simply say whom you succored and in what danger and what honors you granted him, but everyone shares in the hope that you, your child, and your household may be safe, that fortune may be favorable to you, and that your reputation may remain unchanged.

58 F1237 (year 364): To Dionysius

1. I praise your fortune, your attitude, and your letter; the first because it has changed, the second because it knows how to acknowledge a debt, and the third because of its Greek. 2. It is not by letters that one

---

[38] The last labor of Herakles, *Iliad* 8.369.
[39] *Iliad* 5.4.
[40] *Iliad* 5.2–3.

should measure your praise of the man who saved you, but you must compose a discourse of some length on great matters in order that you enjoy good fortune not only because you are pitied by people, but also because you are admired by them.

59 F1470 (year 365): To Palladius
1. Dionysius does not do anything clever by supporting Homer and testifying to the verses in which he says that men are the cause of their own evils. He also testifies to another poet, the wise Sophocles, since he does not know the good that he has in his hands and will recognize it only when it is gone.[41] 2. May Zeus grant you something good for what you wished to do; may he keep the one who chose to tend goats rather than to practice rhetoric at the task of pasturing them; may he never regard the good fame acquired through speaking better than doing that.

DOSSIER OF DIOPHANTUS III
[*This boy's father, Diomedes, and grandfather, Hierax, are unknown. His brother quit his studies with Libanius. In 362 (Ep. 765), Diophantus received an inheritance.*]

60 F465 (year 355/356): To Hierax
1. "To a man God granted one thing, but denied the other,"[42] said someone of a man who wished for two things. You, too, were granted one thing but not the other. Diophantus cares for self-control and rhetoric and is in both areas such as to gladden his father, but the other should not have been born. 2. So do not let the worthlessness of one detract from the excellence of the other, nor should you think that they both have the same qualities, but know that one is good but the other does not wish to be.

61 F600 (year 357): To Diomedes
1. If I noticed any weakness in Diophantus, I would definitely inform you, so that you could correct him and improve his character. By the same token, since he is of the best character and is strong in rhetoric, I am informing you of the fact that he is good in both areas so that you will praise him: because of him you belong to the company of blessed fathers.

---

[41] Cf. *Od.* 1.33; Soph. *Aj.* 964.
[42] *Iliad* 16.250: like Patroclus, Diophantus's brother will succumb in the battle of rhetoric.

62 F601 (year 357): To Hierax
1. Your daughter's son is such as his grandfather would wish: he is a lover of rhetoric but not a lover of bodies; he refrains from insolence and cultivates decorum; he pleases me and is on very good terms with his friends. 2. Noticing this in him, I could not keep silent. I know how to denounce boys who are disorderly, but I also know how to praise those who keep within the rules. 3. Since I found that Diophantus is one of those who do what they should, I thought it was wrong not to also gladden his grandfather's ear.

63 F766 (year 362): To Hierax
1. Such was Diophantus from childhood: wise, fair, willing to work, and dear to the best people. If most of his virtue depends on his blood, both Diophantus and I must be grateful to you, since he received your good traits through his mother. 2. I believe that he is and will be good to me, but let him repay me by trying to declaim, and let him be free from all other concerns.

EPIPHANIUS 3/III

64 F910 (year 388): To Artemius ii
[*Nothing else is known about Artemius, who might have reacted to some misbehavior. According to* PLRE I, *Epiphanius 2 became an imperial courier* (agens in rebus), *but it rather seems he undertook a liturgy. Theotecnus was probably an assistant.*]
1. Know that the good things you have done for the excellent Theotecnus were also done for me, and the things you are doing now are also done for me, and I will also have a share of the things that you will do. I am sending you this letter because I wish to encourage you in this so that you know that by doing this, you benefit not one man but two. 2. Know, however, that you also cause pain to these two men by the decisions that you have made concerning your son. You have taken him from Homer, Demosthenes, and Plato to horses, chariots, and charioteers; but none of these things will make him better and more able when he makes his case before governors. 3. You have the highest regard for Theotecnus as a rhetor, yet you do not consider letting your son become another Theotecnus. But vexed because a boy is a boy, you do not see that you impose great expenses on your house, although there is no need for you to spend the money, thinking that the fact that Epiphanius is of assistance to his city and his fellow citizens is a sufficient gain for us.

DOSSIER OF THE SONS OF EUMATHIUS I

65 F542 (year 356/57): To Eumathius
1. Are you going to avoid my letter, too, and will you throw it away on finding the name of the sender, just as you were happy to see us at first but later avoided us? I would not tell another the reason why you did this, because I am your friend—and it would also cause me some embarrassment. 2. You accuse me, as I hear, of exerting myself as much as possible for my students when I am with my students and neglecting everything else. But I thought that you would call me a bad teacher if I did not do so. The educator who sits on a teaching chair should know that he would incur punishment if he turned to other matters when he is involved with his *chorus*. 3. You would find that the man who is stiff in the classroom knows how to laugh somewhere else. I think that by calling me harsh and difficult, you have not behaved like a gentleman in reproaching me for things you should not have and in leaving without saying goodbye. 4. But you have children, and, imitating their father, they lay claim to rhetoric: perhaps they will come to us. Think, therefore, whether it is to your advantage to launch such accusations against their teacher, or to jest instead of being thoughtful.

66 F1500 (year 365): To Eumathius
1. You have removed ill feeling by an act, a great act, before which everything else pales. Certainly for a father, everything else pales before his sons, because men consider their children's interests more important than their own. 2. For sending these young men, I praise you; for doing it late, I blame you. So now when you should hear that they know rhetoric, you hear that they are going to. 3. The cause of this was that foolish fear that I was going to be bad to your children because of your joke. But neither would I have exacted punishment for a joke nor, even if you were very unjust, would I have punished your children for your own injustice. 4. Now I do not ask for your punishment, but I fear that your children will, when, as they improve, they see more clearly what they lost previously.

67 F1501 (year 365): To Dionysius 6/ii
[*Cf.* the dossier of Dionysius 6.]
1. I was pleased with the length and elegance of your letter: I think that you live not only amidst uproar but also amidst books. You certainly pleaded with the excellent Eumathius enough, but I marvel that, with all your eloquence, you drove out his fear slowly and did not persuade him to be confident right away. 2. Let him know, therefore, that he honored me by what he did and hardly hurt me by what he believed.

But I will definitely hurt him in return by my goodwill toward his children: when they will show improvement, he must become his own accuser.

THE SONS OF EUPATOR

68 F419 (year 355): To Eupator
[*It is not certain who Olympius is.*]

1. Your children are enduring in Daphne the work that ends in summer. They have our permission so that the trees, the waters, and the breezes may make their task more palatable. If someone criticizes them on account of the place, let it be known that he is, in truth, a false accuser. 2. The bearer of this letter will tell you what I think about both of them. I consider both you and your sons blessed because of him: Olympius, the best of men on earth, cares about your family.

DOSSIER OF THE SONS OF EUSEBIUS X

[*Ep. 585, written in 357, shows that Eusebius from Armenia was Libanius's schoolmate, and his two children were his students. From the other letters it appears that there was a bit of a grudge between them, and that Libanius was not joking.*]

69 F584 (year 357): To Eusebius

1. Your children's innate talent is good, and their willingness even better. They have already shown signs that they have [good] ears. It would not be right for me to tell you in detail about this, but it would be disgraceful if they did not. 2. By refraining from giving us instructions concerning them, you showed that you respect me, bearing witness by your silence that they have all that they should.

70 F261 (year 358): To Eusebius

1. You wrote me what a father should write, but I have not become at all better as a result of your letter. Before the letter arrived, I had already done what another would do upon receiving it. One who has already exerted himself and still receives an exhortation cannot humor those who exhort him. 2. If you think of ways to reciprocate, look for something that is appropriate for me, such as saying something nicer about me, if you have ever received anything good from us. If I wished for a lot of money, now I would not have little of it.

71 *F273 (year 358): To Eusebius*
1. It was enough for me to know that you would give something; in the first place, I asked in order to test you, to find out if you would give these things. The mention of the fees due was not the talk of a serious man but of one who enjoyed remembering the teaching. Even if you owed me a lot, you paid me back "three- and fourfold" with deeds greater and more beautiful than the riches of Gyges.[43] 2. So, keep your horse, and do not look for another. Everyone who heard what you promised will also hear what happened and will honor you for sending it and me for refusing it.

EUSEBIUS 15/XII

72 *F437 (year 355): To Eusebius*
[*Eusebius was a Christian; in 355, he was at court. Clematius 1/i.*]
1. I hear that you praise me and you keep on doing it, and it seems to me that you are doing what is just and beneficial to your purpose. One who says that he studied with the best teacher gives back what is due to the teacher, and at the same time glorifies himself by showing the spring from which he benefited. 2. But, in order not to neglect any of the things you can do for me, you should add to the praises a letter. In my opinion, you keep silent because you fear that we would ask a favor of you, and, having received the first, ask for a second, and so you close off the possibility of dealing with you as we should. 3. Refute me, if you say I am wrong. You will refute me, if you write to me. But if you do not write, I will be duped by Clematius, who gave me the news and convinced me to write to you.

DOSSIER OF EUSEBIUS XVII

73 *F305 (year 362 or later): To Pappus*
[*Eusebius was the son of Pappus i from Mesopotamia. Foerster dated this letter to 361 C.E.*]
1. I asked for one and you sent me two. Why? Have you been misled by your son, who said that I needed two, or did you send me two instead of one because you wanted to teach your son to give more than what one is asked? Now, if he duped you, he suffers from love for his studies, but if it is you who sent me more, the father must be rebuked. 2. I did not approve of so much silver spent on the borders. I could not

---

[43] *Iliad* 1.128; Gyges, king of Lydia, was proverbially rich.

wear garments with such elaborate decoration in public and felt it was not right to remove it from your gifts. So, they stay at home. 3. Since you make some requests to us on behalf of Eusebius, perhaps you will also accept our requests on his behalf. But if this makes no sense, think no more about it.

74 F737 (year 362): To Pappus

1. I rejoice at receiving your letter not only because the letter of a friend is a very pleasant thing, but also because it is proof for me that the region is cleared of the enemy. So crucial is Julian[44] when he is expected. Those we saw before him made the foe bolder. 2. The excellent Pappus deserves to enjoy the present security so that the smile that used to bloom on his face may never leave him. 3. The Persians, therefore, will act in such a way as befits men who fight against the gods, who, each taking his own arms, will join in attacking them and teach them to run away. 4. Your son wishes to become a rhetor, and his own natural talent is not unequal to his desire. He also knows how to be modest. The young man who knows this attracts me and receives more than another. 5. So write to him to continue this behavior and you would not need to address any exhortation to us.

DOSSIER OF EUSEBIUS XX

75 F1240 (year 364): To Strategius and Albanius
[*Strategius and Albanius are the uncles of Eusebius xx; cf. their dossier.*]

1. I was pleased with the gift and thought that I was reliving the times your father came and brought you here, one of you to learn rhetoric and the other to observe, although you both would have been capable of learning it. If it is ever possible to shed old age, this would happen when in old age one has something similar to what he had in youth. 2. The image of both your face and your father's never faded from my soul; but when Eusebius came, he made everything much clearer because he carries in himself a part of each of you. 3. Most of the students cried out on learning about the family of this young man and did not need at all to ask, "Where does he come from, what are his city and his parents?"[45] This made that day a feast for us, and it seemed a sign of some great good fortune that another bee should come again from your household to be fed in our hive. 4. You, who may have become

---

[44] This is the emperor Julian.
[45] *Od.* 1.170.

what you are because of our goodwill (and may you always be great), could say to one another that the beekeeper will consider it worthy of his full attention.

76 F1241 (year 364): To Olympius
[*Olympius viii was Eusebius xx's paternal uncle.*]

1. If you had written before, you would not have looked too bold, but would have done something reasonable by writing to a friend when you had the ability to do so; but now we are pleased to receive a young man of good birth and the letter of his excellent uncle. 2. I know that I do not seem to neglect any student who comes to me unless he can find the reason for that. But I value the Galatians' interests so much that I would not even refuse the sweat if, in addition to my own efforts on their behalf, I had to do their share also on behalf of themselves. 3. While this is my general disposition toward the country as a whole, I value Ancyra more than other cities, and your family more than the rest of the people of Ancyra; and in fact, you have surpassed the others in what you have done for us. 4. Do not exhort me, therefore, to take care of Eusebius.

77 F1242 (year 364): To Androcles
[*Androcles was a teacher of rhetoric in Ancyra; Maximus xii was the father of Hyperechius i.*]

1. You sent me a child, my own, who is from that family and has that spirit and whom I often held in my arms together with his brother when I passed through your city. 2. If there is any gain in knowing the mind of more people, Eusebius did well to leave home. But if he thought—and this is what you say—that he was going to find a Phidias,[46] he was deceived by his teacher. I say in fact that the teachings he would have received there would not have been worse than what he will get here now. 3. I trusted, in fact, those who proclaimed that you were a good craftsman of discourses, and I thought that Maximus was attracted by some beautiful thing. By receiving your letter, I know better that those people were telling the truth and that I was right to believe them. Within a little, I saw the whole thing, and none of your meaning eludes me, but I could also tell someone how you are in both areas, when you rouse your mind to invention and your language to expression.

---

[46] Reference to *Od.* 1.3; cf. **206**.

DOSSIER OF EUSEBIUS 25/XXVIII
[*Son of an advocate, adopted by his uncle, Eusebius became a lawyer but wanted to enter the Senate of Constantinople. He was entangled in an obscure affair with a certain Prophetius. On Ellebicus, cf. PLRE I, pp. 277–78: in 388, he was called to Constantinople.*]

78 F884 (year 388): To Ellebicus
1. I care about all those who have studied with me, since I think that I do something that pleases Hermes and the Muses, but I care the most for Eusebius, who partook of our teaching the longest. His effort, talent, and fortune made him an orator of a high standard. 2. I have talked to him, wishing to make him an educator of young men, but he listened to his mother and uncle and went the way he went. He cares much to be a member of the Great Senate, but since much of his wealth has gone in those unfortunate events that resulted from the abuses of Prophetius, he is asking to undertake a public service on the basis not of the popular but of the true estimate of his property. In this way, he can be useful to the city but would not be ruined.

79 F885 (year 388): To Proclus
[*Proclus 6; little is known about Gaius iii.*]
1. I would not need to tell you who is bringing you this letter or from what family and country he is. When in fact I saw you off, I started to tell you about him, but you interrupted what I was saying by talking about Gaius and how cultured he is, and you said that he is the brother of this man's father and that he is his adoptive father. You also added fine promises, saying that you would be very glad to see [Eusebius] when he came, and that you would help him find something suitable, neither overlooking liturgies he could undertake nor putting on him a burden that he could not sustain. 2. Therefore, Eusebius is glad to come, and we are glad to send him because he will soon write to us about what you do on his behalf, and later, when we meet, he will tell us.

80 F886 (year 388): To Eusebius
[*Eusebius 26/xxvii had a high position at the court of Arcadius.*]
1. You were interested to know how we were otherwise, and how our students were, and who the head of the *chorus* was. You may have heard that it is Eusebius, who knows more of the ancients than anyone else and makes discourses similar to theirs: some he memorizes, while others go into his notebook and waxed tablet. 2. On hearing this, you congratulated Eusebius, the *chorus*, and myself. When I impart the teaching, you feel the same pleasure that you would feel were you the

teacher yourself. 3. You also know about Eusebius's family, the intricate situation with Prophetius, and the spears with which he has injured their house: from quite great as it was, he reduced it to small in terms of money, and yet, it still seems wealthy and not completely devastated by this adversity. 4. Now that you know all this, you should become Eusebius's advocate, and not overlook that he undertakes the public service. But we should not talk about this.

81 F887 (year 388): To Palladius
[*Palladius 14/xvi at the time was an influential senator in Constantinople.*]
 1. Eusebius is coming to you because in the present situation he places his hopes especially on you. He has observed that in very many circumstances you have devoted much attention to my things, and that, when you do me a favor, you enjoy it together with the one who receives it. 2. By helping on this occasion, you will help a wellborn and well-brought-up young man who is fair-minded and self-controlled and who has acquired such power of eloquence that, when I was sick, the students did not suffer any damage through his teaching. 3. He would have done quite well had he chosen either my way of life or that of his father. But since he is eager for more splendid things, he is all yours, although he does not have money—it was a lot, but became little. 4. There still would be plenty had not the contentiousness of Prophetius waged war upon it. I am talking about an affair to which there are many witnesses, so that you will not have to work too hard when you plead his cause.

FAUSTINUS

82 F666 (year 361): To Italicianus
[*Latin was the mother tongue of Italicianus, but he also knew Greek. Cf. also Ep. 1, written in 372, in which Libanius recommends Faustinus so that he can enter the Senate of Constantinople.*]
 1. The bearer, Faustinus, is the best of the Pisidians and of our students. You could also learn from others about his family: the distinction of his kin, the splendor of their liturgies, and the fact that his ancestors were and still are like a wall of defense for this city. But I am the one who should tell you about what is going on in our temple of education. 2. Even though he lived among students who were asleep and who believed that rhetoric had no value, as if the soul should be dedicated to other things, he did not entertain these ideas in his soul. Since he is convinced that men who do not partake of education are no better

placed than slaves, he left to others the theaters, the mimes, and the craze for horses. He dedicated his body to work and improved his soul: he was a godsend to willing teachers and a burden for those who were not, since he regarded work itself as a respite from work. 3. From what I have said, you must be aware of the self-control and discipline of his everyday life, for anyone who is so attached to books keeps out of trouble. 4. If either his father had survived him or his grandfather had not yielded to old age, he would have also surpassed his teachers at some future time. Now, however, he must preserve his patrimony, and to his great sorrow he is deprived of achieving more, but he has rhetorical vigor, enough for the law courts and enough to make his fatherland greater. 5. In addition, now there have come some fortunate circumstances. With you as a governor, my companions must be carried by good winds, since Athena is sending a favorable breeze.[47]

THE SON OF FELIX 6/III

83 F1005 (year 391): To Felix
[*Felix was possibly* comes orientis *("count of the East") in 380.*]
   1. Welcome your son, who has acquired the power of rhetoric, since hard work—both his and mine—has been added to his natural qualities. It was a pleasure for me to work with him, because I believed that I also owed him repayment for knowing self-control. He did indeed show self-control, and this, moreover, with such comeliness! This is an advantage for the teacher and could increase the size of the *chorus*. 2. And thus he comes to you. Let him acquire from you what is left, which is inferior to rhetoric, but appears to the common run of men to lead more to success.

THE SON OF FLAVIANUS I

84 F1416 (year 363): To Flavianus
[*Flavianus, from Bithynia, was probably now in Cilicia. In 361, he sent Libanius other gifts, Ep. 655.*]
   1. My word, such a deluge of gifts: sausages, wine, a tunic, a book! At first I was at a loss about the reason for such plenty. But since there was the added clause that I should send Odysseus back to you (the boy has changed his name, and the little weasel[48] is silent), I saw that those

---

[47] Athena sent a wind to help Odysseus, *Od.* 5.385.
[48] The *galē* ("weasel") is the protagonist of several Aesopic fables and of proverbs.

gifts were a ruse of Odysseus who hoped to persuade me by this fee to do what he wanted. He wanted to run to you and go home from there. 2. In other circumstances I would not agree, not even if he surpassed the gifts Agamemnon sent to make amends.[49] But when I asked him if he sacrifices to the gods, I became aware that he rejoices greatly in altars, and therefore I rejoiced to let him go to a city where each day the gods partake in plenty of "drink offerings and the savor of burnt sacrifice."[50] 3. Let him ask *them* for rhetoric, and not only that, but let him be acquainted with hard work, too, remembering the one who says about lazy people that the gods do not do anything for them.[51]

DOSSIER OF GAIUS II
[*Son of Athanasius i of Cilicia, who was a friend of Acacius 7/iii, the father of Titianus (see dossier); Gaius ii's uncle was Gaius i, who composed an* encomium *in verse for Libanius,* Ep. 826, B158).]

85 F781 (year 362): To Athanasius
1. I know what you call the good report about me: it is not thousands of men, tens of thousands, or even double that many, but only the rhetor Acacius and his mouth, which is much better for me than twenty thousand mouths, but it is not beyond suspicion because of his inordinate affection. 2. Gaius, in any case, will enjoy what we have and the same effort on my part as the son of the man who made the report. You are worthy of honor, and Acacius also urges this, for he calls your son his own and also recounts other things: that you love this boy so much and that his mother took him up to the border and parted from him with difficulty. 3. We will always remember this, and you will say that he would receive no more from his own father, if he happened to practice my same art.

86 F782 (year 362): To Gaius i
1. It seems that in Gaius, I have received the son of three fathers: the man who begot him; you, the uncle by the same name; and also the maker of noble discourses, the excellent Acacius, who from the day he came here until the boy arrived, kept on saying that a good son of excellent people would come, a friend from friends, another Titianus. 2. Think now of my position: I am going to do a favor for these great men, but I would not refuse even if only one asked me. Your brother

---

[49] Agamemnon sent countless gifts to make amends with Achilles, e.g., *Iliad* 9.120.
[50] E.g., *Iliad* 4.49.
[51] Hesiod *Op.* 301, 310.

is worthy of our respect, because he is your brother and companion in excellence. You consort with the Muses and are able to commend to them whomever you wish. Is it not risky not to obey to you in everything? 3. As for the power of Acacius with which he is of great service—whatever opinion people would have—who in his right mind would not prefer to others the [young man] he considers like Titianus? 4. Therefore, if you give me a place in the company of fathers, I become the fourth father for Gaius. I consider him blessed on account of the few days when he tasted the mysteries of Acacius.[52] It is clear, in fact, that he participated in the sacred rites.

87 F1371 (year 363): To Gaius i and Athanasius

1. Gaius sailed back unwillingly and kept on blaming his head because it took him away from rhetoric and made him embark. I consoled him, saying that rhetoric was the cause and that his head would be free of these ills. 2. Petition the god with him and persuade him to drive out the pain as soon as possible. I think that you will say that this boy returns with some rhetoric and did not lose time sleeping.

DOSSIER OF GERONTIUS VI AND HIS FATHER GERONTIUS 3/III

[The account in PLRE I, p. 393, is very confused. Gerontius vi was likely the son of Gerontius 3/iii, who was a teacher of rhetoric in Apamea and tried to secure immunities from curial duties; his son, however, had to go back to fulfill his duties. Gerontius 3 became an opponent of Libanius in 380 in Antioch (Or. 1.186–87), but was again his friend in 388 (Ep. 863).]

88 F1391 (year 363): To Gerontius 3

1. Will you still trust those who say that they deceived you, and won't you think that these people are repulsive, that they are your enemies and deserve punishment? And still you have your country and are honored by a country that is beautiful, great, and dear to the gods? 2. I consider you more blessed than the sophists in Athens, since you are awarded a salary at such great public expense and teach your students in peace, and the works of Ares do not intrude upon those of the Muses. I was also pleased that you gave a very skilled speech and that the citizens conferred on you praise out of the ordinary. 3. Judging the future from the present, I see a splendid house, a wife from a wealthy family, and plenty of servants and farming. I do not think that you will pucker your eyebrows,[53] but you will maintain your current modest

---

[52] Acacius may have exposed this youth to some rhetoric and poetry.
[53] That is, put on an air of importance.

demeanor. 4. I would have offered you a salary in kind if I had not thought that you were joking. Why should a man who has prosperous students look somewhere else? But if you are truly asking in all seriousness, I have some objections but will give it to you.

89 F978 (year 390): To Eleusinius
[*The addressee is unknown.*]
1. Gerontius the bearer, the son of a good father, is doing what his father did, has come to me, and has undertaken the same hard work as his father. He is not as good an orator yet, but he will probably reach the same power in the same amount of time. 2. Whether he can be involved in the same studies again depends on you and could happen only with your help. Only you might heal the pain brought by the events that he heard of in a letter. When this grievous letter arrived, he threw down his books in tears and fled, telling us that he would soon come back. 3. I thought this was true not because I took into account this young man's own resources—what resources and from where?—but because of your nature and attitude, since you think it is to your advantage if you can give some help to a man who is being educated so that he acquires eloquence.

GESSIUS 1/I
[*Gessius 1 was a native of Egypt, a pupil of Libanius before 355, an official, and a teacher in Egypt in 388, possibly in Alexandria. His downfall is described by Palladas,* Anth. Pal. 7.681–88.]

90 F892 (year 388): To Gessius
1. I also cherish holy Egypt because it sends me your letters, and such letters! I do not admire them standing in a corner apart from friends and leaning against a wall, but in a group of companions who are able to appreciate such elegance. Then, of course, things follow, applause and comments such as: "Who is this Gessius who feels it necessary not to enrich himself because he wants to teach?" 2. We praise you and blame Fortune because we do not educate your own children the way we once educated you, whereas we are educating others the way we did their fathers. 3. Free yourself of accusations by getting married rather than only thinking about marriage. There are girls on this earth, and it is enough to be willing. I fear, however, lest some eloquent people—those near you directly with words, and those far away by writing—are praising to you the life without wife and children.

THE SON OF GREGORIUS I

91 F1471 (year 365): To Gregorius i
[*Nothing else is known about this family, probably from Cilicia.*]
1. Because of his natural gifts and wish to work, you should feel confident about your son. He is good in both things, and it would be Fortune's task that they bear great fruit. 2. Pray that she will be there, and count the excellent Eustathius among your true friends. He wished to know this young man's standing and thought that, in addition to what he was going to report to you, he had to carry a letter confirming my words. 3. Hearing that report and reading this one, enjoy good hopes.

THE SONS OF HESTIAEUS

92 F144 (year 359/60): To Priscianus
[*Petit (1956a) did not include these students. Priscianus 1/i was Libanius's fellow student. Other letters to or concerning him are 7, 135, 167, and 177.*]
1. I care about the children of Hestiaeus on account both of their uncles, who went to school with me, and of their grandfather, who regarded me as one of his sons. Hestiaeus was not intimate with me but receives my praise. What is most important, these young men are my students and practice modest deportment together with rhetoric. 2. You know the waves of misfortune through which their mother, who has hardly recovered, went: she was freed from the danger but aggravated her previous poverty. 3. There is a man in Kyrus, Mares, who is more destitute than old, and he is quite old. These people are asking for him not to be completely worn out, and I wish this, too, but you have control over it. The old rescript of the emperor, confirmed by Theophilus's letter, will be a pattern for your aid.

DOSSIER OF THE SONS OF HESYCHIUS 4/VI
[*Flavius Asclepiades Hesychius, who became governor of the Thebaid in 390/91, had at least three sons. Two letters, 946 and 995, both dated to 390/91, attest that they were studying with Libanius.*]

93 F894 (year 388): To Hesychius
1. Do not blame us, but only the circumstances that have brought much trouble, and grief and tears in turn. It is not easy to be in such a state and write often to so many friends. 2. Your sons spent the first of two months on both the old writers and myself, and the second just on the

old writers, since it was convenient to do it this way. 3. If Hermes and the other gods grant it, we will have classes this month, too, and on the fourth day of the month we will follow the previous program.

94 F1090 (year 393): To Hesychius
[*Eusebius 32 was a poet, as* Ep. *1089 shows.*]
   1. I am fond both of the son of yours who is studying with me—how could I not be, since he is my student?—and of those who have moved on to other things, because they once were my students. 2. Let a confirmation of that for you be the fact that I ask a favor from their father. The favor is to make the good Eusebius happier with what has been done in regard to the land that he owns. 3. The fruit coming from it [lacuna] will gladden the one who farms more than myself who am writing.

DOSSIER OF THE THREE SONS OF HIERIUS III
[*These students came from Tarsus and had had some rhetoric with Aresius. One of them was Peregrinus.*]

95 F1403 (year 363): To Hierius
   1. I knew that somehow Jealousy was going to catch sight of your sons, as she is naturally prone to see those who are praised. They seemed to distinguish themselves markedly from the other young men in self-control and with respect to rhetoric, so that you were especially blessed among fathers because, of the three children you had with us, it was not that one was good and another was not, but all of them strove for virtue. 2. So the envious god did not tolerate what people said about them and, not having the power to make them base or lazy, threw some trouble and suspicions in their midst and convinced them that they were being wronged by each other. The accusations were lifeless, and when I heard them, I laughed and easily doused them. It was enough for me to bid them love each other, and they did so. And yet they did not neglect to apply themselves to rhetoric and to exercise self-control even when they were in a state of discord, but cared for them even more then, because they wanted to prevail. 3. Now that they are at peace and united, your letter has arrived, bringing discouragement and reviving the war. But I also put a stop to this and did not let it break the treaty. 4. Put no value on slanders and do not come down on Peregrinus like a flood, and let one thing of the accusation (with which you terrified your servant) delight you: that it was stated rhetorically. Let go of what happened entirely and only admonish him about what re-

mains to be done; and, remembering our own youth, let us not be too severe in judging the young.

96 F1539 (year 365): To Hierius

1. Peregrinus is dedicating himself to law, piling weapon on weapon, and from this he has hopes of wealth, offices, and other power. The teacher who expounds the law is good, but even if he would gladly forget the money, he is being constrained by poverty. The fee could seem high, but it is quite small if you figure in the amount of books and the other great things that he procures. 2. Do not, therefore, throw away the gain because you fear the fee, but fix yourself on the one, pay the other, and do as you do with your land: you give the seeds to it and do not blame it after it takes them.

DOSSIER OF HIEROCLES 1/II

[*Cf. Ammianus 29.1.44: he was implicated in an ugly trial with his father, Alypius 4, and hardly escaped death in 372. In 98 there is probably an allusion to breach of moral conduct.*]

97 F324 (year 358): To Alypius

1. Because of the importance of your office, I call you happy, and because of the excellence with which you govern, I praise you. And I say that this is a boon for our city from which you got knowledge of governing (if indeed this comes from eloquence, and your eloquence from this city, and a man who has learned is an ornament to the city that taught him), but her rewards would be much greater if you could take care of her by getting to govern her. 2. But this we will demand of Fortune, and she will grant it, if she does what is just. We are educating for you Hierocles, who is definitely not better than his father but is perhaps his father's equal. Yet this young man's effort is split between language and shorthand, but he is nevertheless equally sharp in both; I tell others about the former, but I hear from others about the latter.

98 F1395 (year 363): To Alypius

1. One could expect anything,[54] as they say, if Hierocles, too, was accused, and moreover by his father, and when he is not a child anymore. When he was a child, he already seemed wiser than old men, and many who rebuked their sons bade them study yours, for thus they would become fathers of good boys. 2. So, has he changed, or has his father

---

[54] A similar expression in Gregory of Nazianzus, *Autobiographical Poems*, Migne's *Patrologia Graeca* 1171.15.

been deceived? If you want me to denounce him falsely, too, he transgressed the laws. But if I am to undo the deceit that an evil man has perpetrated upon you, Hierocles remains well behaved, but you are doing wrong to us and to the proverb, by casting your vote before the defense. 3. And so you accuse Hierocles, but I stand condemned, if on the one hand I was not aware of anything and if on the other, when I became aware of it, I let it go on. Will you not put aside your accusations, my good friend? Will you not consider the liar a foe? Will you not speak in defense of the young man in tears? Will you not hang up votive offerings to the gods in thanks for the virtue of your son? Will you not trust me, the events, the time? Will you not do like Leon the Lacedaemonian?[55] 4. Do not fail to see your blessings, like the one who was blaming his legs in the fable.[56]

DOSSIER OF HIERON
[*Hieron is the son of Hyperechius ii of Armenia, who may himself have been Libanius's student in Constantinople in 340/42. The date 361 of 99 is too late, since Philopatris enrolled in 359/60. Eutherius 2 was the governor of Armenia and father of Philopatris. Letters to him or mentioning him are 37, 154, 165, and 166.*]

99 F262 (year 361?): To Hyperechius
1. If Eutherius did not have a son with us and asked you to write, you would be silent as you were before, in spite of the fact that we taught you to speak. You use this skill in other matters to preserve and increase your property, when it is necessary to speak, but are mute in what concerns us, even though you are faring as I would wish, and your affairs allow you to make a good showing. 2. But I will not exact punishment upon you for the accusations that I can launch. Therefore, I preferred Hieron to many others, and Philopatris will receive what Hieron does, or rather he has already received it, since I think that I gratify you in what I do on behalf of any one of the Armenians.

100 F1475 (year 364?): To Hyperechius
[*Strategius 1/iii was a sophist.*]
1. When I learned that you had asked Strategius to take care of your son, I praised you because you saw full well from whence he would learn rhetoric; I say, in fact, that he is the best among sophists today at conferring the power of speech to young men. But when you

---

[55] On Leon, see Poralla 1985, 83–84. Libanius may allude to Leon's important diplomatic mission in 411 B.C.E.

[56] Cf. Babrius *Fable* 43, on the vain stag.

changed your opinion,[57] started to criticize what you had admired, bade your son leave the man to whom you had entrusted him, and sent letters that were at the end very different from those you sent before, I was troubled for you and your son. Your decision, in fact, is a loss for both of you. 2. Your brother will tell you the charge I leveled against you with him, and if he will bring you pain with his words, he will bring you profit with his censure. By changing your harmful decision, I have served your own better than you have, and by persuading the sophist to bear the insult, I have preserved the interest of the young man. 3. So send a letter asking for forgiveness and consider impious many pedagogues.

HILARINUS

101 F653 (year 361): To Domnio
[*Domnio 1/i, who taught law in Berytus, is sometimes called Domninus; see 26, 28, 156, and 175, and cf. Ep. 652.*]

1. Look, you attracted even Greece! You have convinced young men and those who are almost old to run to Phoenicia. The bearer, Hilarinus, at first wanted to receive some instruction from me but was prevented by Fortune, and now he is coming to partake of yours. 2. You should treat him as I would if he were studying with me. I am not talking of kindness, since you are evidently always kind, but I am saying that he should learn a lot in a short time. Those who come late to learning and are mocked because of this should receive this privilege from their teachers: intensive instruction and eagerness, which instills speed in the art.

DOSSIER OF HONORATUS 3/II
[*Honoratus was the son of Quirinus: PLRE I, pp. 760–61; cf. Epp. 405 (N6) and 359 (N28); 365 (B5), 366 (B35), and 535 (B57); and Festugière 1959, 159–63. Spectatus 1 was Libanius's cousin. Bassus 5 was the head of the corps of notaries. Honoratus was enrolled in this corps when he was a child, and was recalled when he was a convalescing student. Ep. 1346, sent when Honoratus was not in school anymore, shows that he spent time with his old teacher.*]

102 F358 (year 358): To Spectatus
1. Do you remember the words with which I urged you to safeguard what was suitable for Honoratus? So, are you taking into account what

---

[57] The word *kothornos,* a high boot worn by tragic actors that could be worn on either foot, could also be applied to a person who changed his opinion to suit the occasion.

you promised? You readily assented, since you respect the venerable person of Quirinus and since you do not esteem us lightly. But nothing of what we heard do I see accomplished. 2. I accuse you on both counts, if you say that you forgot, or if you remember but are neglecting things you did not forget; the former shows lack of affection, and the latter actual insolence. 3. But even if you did not do this before, now act toward us as you do toward the general run of men—although we perhaps do not deserve to be numbered among the many. We are ready to give if you wish to receive and, if you shun receiving, you will still see that we remember this favor. 4. Let this be done: to us it seems important, though to you it seems a trifle. You know that this is what you told us, that we were asking for something small that did not involve any work. Take care, too, that the present summons does not damage us, for they say that all those who are in the same situation as Honoratus have been summoned right there from everywhere. 5. It is clear that some punishment will be imposed on the person who does not come, but the one who is able to obey and nevertheless remains is in contempt and should be punished. We should have come posthaste, but we have been forced to stay. You are not unaware of the length of this young man's illness; struggling, he has just now reached sure hope, but his nourishment is still limited by the doctors' prescriptions. 6. Let Bassus be informed about this, make this your defense, and preserve the position for this young man who is forced to stay away.

103 F300 (year 361): To Honoratus

1. Now that you seem to be one of the good and great at court, you have handsomely paid my fees. The gold and silver that you sent me were not small—you have outdone the other students in this regard. But, by Herakles, in the things you do now, you show that I have a good son. 2. You have made everyone praise your qualities, and I heard one saying that he was fond of you because of your gentleness, while another loved your ready wit. One praised the orator, another thought that this combination of rhetoric and shorthand was wondrous. 3. Someone who wished to say something worthy of the virtue of your character said, "Which Honoratus do you mean? The old fellow?" Not because what happened to Erginus—white hair at a young age—happened to you,[58] but because you live like older men before leaving your youth. And the greatest thing of all is that, with your mother gone and your father not there, you put yourself under the supervision of a desire for excellence as if it were a pedagogue. 4. I, therefore, cannot

---

[58] Erginus was a young Argonaut who had white hair; cf. Pindar *schol. Ol.* 4.25.

advise you to do anything as if you had overlooked it, but I exhort you in the same way as many tell you, to maintain your present conduct, and to add one more thing: to write to me as you do your parents so that you can master this skill. You will need it when, God willing, you rise from your service in offices and appear ready to govern a province.

104 F310 (year 361): To Honoratus

1. I see that I have achieved my goal for you—that you develop a beautiful epistolary style by writing letters. You are elegant already and in all likelihood will be very elegant. Let me predict, as farmers do, how well the seedling will thrive. Your diction was worthy of admiration, but the virtue of your character surpassed its elegance as purer gold surpasses an alloy. 2. I am pleased that you honor me, but I wish that you neither ignore your greatest possession nor, recognizing it, consider it inferior to another. Your greatest possession is your father, who formed your soul together with us and before us. 3. If a good teacher is an honor for a student, the first you will remember is your father—nor am I ashamed to acknowledge that I am also his student. You will smile, as you usually do, but that's the way it is, and let us persuade my reputation as a teacher to bear it. 4. So, let it be. But remove from your letters to us the things that smack of flattery, which spoil the beauty, although the crowd demands them. 5. But let us not make ourselves part of the crowd; in writing to those people, we should keep their standard, since it is necessary, but in writing to each other, let us maintain our own.

HYPATIUS 1/I

105 F137 (year 358): To Hypatius

[*Hypatius was from Phoenicia, lived in Beroea at the time of this letter, and later became governor of Palestine.*]

1. It is not sending a letter that calls for forgiveness, but if you would not do that, then you would be right to ask for forgiveness. Neither did you labor at rhetoric nor did I labor for you so that you would be silent, but the hope of speaking persuaded us to bear those things. 2. Use what you have acquired in other pursuits and in writing letters. You do this well and will do it even more elegantly if you do not cease doing it. 3. You seem to confirm to myself what I have often said, that you are my son and not only my student. You are listening to Solon[59] and are supporting your father, now that you have left school. 4. But do me a favor in this, too. Run to us not as if you were wasting time,

---

[59] On Solon, see, e.g., Plut. *Sol.* 22.2.

but to please us with your company, and at the same time, you will straighten up anything that may be needed concerning your office. 5. You are not wrong in considering Bacchius a friend.[60] He has come here through this friend and through another friend, too. In fact, I would not wish Evagoras[61] to be better than you in affection, if indeed, running away from his father's hands, he has come from Cilicia looking for you, while you who are free will not move from Beroea.

DOSSIER OF HYPERECHIUS I
[PLRE I, pp. 409–50. Hyperechius was a favorite student from the times of Nicomedia and from 355 in Antioch, and friend of Procopius 4. He was probably just out of school in 360. He was the son of Maximus xii of Ancyra, a wealthy decurion; cf. 77. Other letters: Epp. 298 (B99), 651 (B100), 731 (N87), 732 (B101), 779 (B107), 792 (B180), 804 (B74), 1114 (B48), 1350 (B109), 1441 (N117), 1443 (B45); Festugière 1959, 142–53. Anatolius 3 was an eminent governor.]

106 F311 (year 355): To Anatolius 3/i
1. Hyperechius will see Seleucia under the best of conditions because he will be able to see the noblest of men there. We have become slaves because of this profession, otherwise we would definitely rush to the same place, not because of the attraction of the port or because of what people say are the embellishments of the city, but because you and your manners would persuade us to make haste. Since you are fleeing, in fact, it is left to us to pursue you. 2. And yet, isn't it awful that you come from Italy for love of us, but seek the company of people other than us and bestow more to the countryside than to some other places of this city that you adorned? 3. But Apollo will come again to Delphi. Granting Maximus succor through your letter, grant his son a favor by giving him the letter quickly. The latter, in fact, desires to work more than others desire not to. So, admiring his obedience to his father, shorten his absence.

107 F570 (year 357): To Maximus
[*The son of Himerius is Iamblicus 2, who was probably a student of Libanius.*]
1. It was fitting that you be a friend to Himerius, and your respective children do well to imitate your examples. Your son regards him highly, and Himerius praises him and rejoices, seeing that he has a good reputation and that we take care of him, but he accuses him of one thing only, of wanting to receive few of his many gifts. 2. Praise, therefore, the generosity of the one and the restraint of the other.

---

[60] Bacchius was a man from Tarsus; Seeck 1906, 93–94.
[61] Evagoras 2, a rhetor and philosopher.

108 F224 (year 360): To Hyperechius
[*Gaudentius, also called Heortius, was the father of the student Themistius 2/iii.*]

1. I never felt as much joy or as much sadness as I do now simultaneously. The excellent Gaudentius bore the responsibility for this, and in telling the story he felt as I did. Because of this, he made me love him even more. 2. The first news was that on your return, you immediately drew the city to yourself (many clever people, both young and old) with your fluent tongue and seeming charm. He said that you shrink from strife, contentiousness, and snobbery so that you surpass even the Artemon of the proverb;[62] that other men behave like fathers to you; that your own father is little short of flying, and your mother is called blessed in her son. 3. I heard this and more, and not so briefly but with the details that one naturally adds when he enjoys the story: Gaudentius enjoyed what he announced, and I do not know if he would have enjoyed more speaking about his own son. 4. I felt gratitude to the gods as for nothing else, but his sad countenance suddenly troubled me. "What is it?" I asked. He was silent. I insisted, but he shrank from speaking. 5. But then he was forced to add those terrible and awful events, the two dangers, and the noose that hung ready for your parents. Seeing that I was undone at this news, he quickly applied a remedy, saying that you have recovered and that the fear that your whole city felt is gone. 6. Since Gaudentius was afraid lest he seem to make exaggerated and untrue statements, he looked to someone else and, addressing Romanus, called him as a witness. He came forward and declared that he was unable to say as much as he knew. And because of his words he also was dear to me. 7. So, since the excellent Gaudentius omitted no blessing, I asked him how old his daughter was. On learning that, I said that I would be surprised if one dismissed the young man he praised and looked for another son-in-law. This man, the dearest of all to me, blushed and said nothing, but showed in his face that he did not regard you as beneath his station. 8. So I am watching over your interests although I shrink from such things; I have spread my nets and am trying to deliver to you the daughter of Heortius, even though it is your father who has been living for hunting.

109 F239 (year 360): To Maximus

1. You call Hyperechius my son and, at the same time, say that you are grateful to me for what I do for him. Either the first thing is untrue or the second is nonsensical; rather, since the first is true, the second becomes meaningless, unless he also must be grateful to you for what

---

[62] Artemon, the engineer of Pericles, was called Periphoretus because he was constantly brought about on a stretcher to survey the works: Plut. *Per.* 27.

you do for him. 2. There is nothing extraordinary in doing what you have done for your son—and such a son—and, since I consider him my son in every respect, if I happen to do him any good, I should not ask for any recompense. I will tell you, however, to whom you and I should be grateful for goodwill toward him. 3. The people of sacred Ancyra (it would in fact suit her to hear the epithet with which Homer honors Athens[63]), her inhabitants are my benefactors and yours and deserve crowns and prayers. And indeed, I pray to all the gods and goddesses that their land give them fruit in plenty, that the climate remain moderate, that the women bear offspring similar to their parents, that the city love rhetoric as it does now, and that none of the things that bring happiness be lacking. The reason is that they in fact looked upon me kindly when I passed through and are now honoring me even more by what they did to assure this young man's good reputation. 4. Do not think that I am saying this because they have brought fame to someone who is worthless, but because they did not dismiss the truth on account of envy but were above envy by loving a fellow citizen as citizens. One must be grateful to them for this. 5. This is what I offer to them, vows on their behalf and praises of them, but you also must repay them with deeds. Even if you render every service, do not think that you have paid in full. 6. Know in any case that our city is also grateful to that city: she knows that Ancyra's opinion of him is a testimony to her greater accomplishment. 7. I did not marvel at your munificence toward your son: with good sense you left him as a gift from his father what he would have later by law.[64] I marvel, however, of the fact that while there are many "daughters of the chieftains"[65] who govern the city, you did not take care to soon behold the children of your son. Even though you are called "grandfather" already because of your good deeds, it would be good for you—one would say even better—to be called "grandfather" because of this.

110 F658 (year 361): To Acacius 8
[*Acacius 8 is Marcus's father; see dossier of Marcus.*]

1. You acted wisely, noble friend, on behalf of the truth. It was wise to cut it off and not to waste time, because delays in such matters can generate many openings.[66] 2. Even if I asked you for Arcadia,[67] it does not seem that you would respond, "I will not give it, though I am able

---

[63] *Od.* 11.323.
[64] Maximus gave his son his inheritance.
[65] *Iliad* 9.396.
[66] An unknown allusion.
[67] Cf. the oracle of the Pythia in Hdt. 1.66, when she denied that the Lacedaemonians could have Arcadia.

to." Thus you wish to give everything, and it is clear that you, the giver, enjoy this no less than the recipient. 3. Therefore you will also give the rest to this young man who is coming, and by the same you will do me (though I am away) a favor. The rest consists of continuous goodwill and showing that you enjoy it when he comes and blame him when he hesitates. 4. This and similar things will make him great in the eyes of his fellow citizens and great in the eyes of his parents. I desire that he seem able to aid his father rather than to have need of him. To be able to have recourse to one son's power is sweet to a father and a thing for which one prays. 5. You will support a man who is not worthless but has some good sense and knows how to remember a favor. Putting him to the test, you will say to others about him what you now hear and will not say that I was foolish in exerting myself so much. 6. I think that by looking at him, you will know what sort of young man he is. He distinguished himself among the audience when we declaimed. He sat down and admired in silence, for shouts were not permitted; perhaps not a few times you saw Hyperechius expressing his praises in full and becomingly. 7. Therefore, remembering those things, thinking of what you just did, and believing that you should be consistent with yourself, be for him as I would be myself, if I were governor of Galatia.

111 F777 (year 362): To Hyperechius
[*Sulpicius is unknown.*]

1. I approved your decision to remain at home now. The journey did not offer the opportunity when, as the old saying advises, one should say and do everything.[68] 2. The famine, with which you would have wrestled during the trip, advised you to overcome your desire rather than see me entangled in such misery. If I regarded my own interest, I would rebuke you for choosing not to run through fire. But now, since I do not consider your interests second to mine, I approve of your delay and think that it brings me no less joy than the sight of you because it delivered you from countless woes. 3. But when spring begins to gleam forth, if you see that the land is reconciled with us and the season before summer hints at a good summer, act upon your wish. In your longing, you will see someone who longs for you. 4. I have longed for you since you obtained a victory in oratory; with this you brought a double honor on your father, by being superior to those who tried to seize it and by doing it not with the help of friends, but with your own tongue. 5. Many were those who reported your triumph, but my

---

[68] Salzmann 1910, 73.

favorites were those who announced it with pleasure, Sulpicius and the brothers whom you sent, who thought highly of you and accepted your advice. As a repayment for their news, they have received an increased eagerness on my part in teaching them rhetoric. Thus I think that it is not only you whom I must help, but also those whom I perceive have affection for you. 6. But I am surprised about something, my good friend: why didn't you give a letter to these young men who are so close to you? You could say neither that you are unlearned in this art, nor that the letter would not bring me pleasure, nor that they did not ask for one, nor that it was not proper to give them one before they asked. 7. Do you wish for me to help you and for the accuser to undo the accusation? You thought that it was awful to seem to choose the second course when it was right for you to be with me. So you dismissed that option with the intention of giving me something better.

112 F704 (year 362): To Hyperechius

1. Alas! How many times did you shake your head and tell yourself when you were alone or during the night: "I am neglected, I am despised, everything is changed!" The proof of this was that, while there was a multitude of people running through your country to go to Thrace, no letter from us—either short or long—ever came to you. 2. Many did ask me, but I did not give one to any. I will tell you why. I knew that many would wish to be your guests and fare sumptuously. If you did not receive them, you would appear to do wrong. But if you sat there and entertained "people more numerous than leaves,"[69] it would be a nuisance not so much for the expense but because the land would of necessity be neglected. 3. At the same time, I knew that men eat happily but do not know how to remember hospitality and consider it manly to speak badly about their hosts. 4. The reason for my silence is not that you were out of mind, but that I decided to wait so that I would not become a motif of displeasure or trouble for you. 5. But now, since I have gotten hold of Miccalus—that is, of my very self—I write to dispel the accusation and to remind you of those old predictions, when I forecast that the time for demanding a rendering of accounts and loosening the belts of office would come.[70] 6. It was possible for you not to miss those remarks, and at present there is some possibility. I just wish to know what your opinion is and what you intend to do with yourself.

---

[69] Homer, e.g., *Iliad* 2.468.

[70] The belt (baldric) was the mark of official service. Loosening the baldrics meant making some positions available.

113 F812 (year 363): To Clearchus 1
   1. You should have received my companion from my own hands. But since you were hurrying to the gate and he was not there, remember all that I have told you about him. Honor my letter by showing that it had the same power as if I led the excellent Hyperechius into your friendship with my own hand.

114 F1116 (year 363): To Hyperechius
   1. I believe that you have received the letters and have delivered them to those for whom they were written, and that you are now either on the verge of obtaining something or are hoping for something to happen. 2. If those friends are still sleeping, goad them with these letters, and perhaps they will wake up.

115 F1454 (year 363): To Julianus
[*Julianus viii had a post in the census in Galatia; he was the uncle of the student Calycius.*]
   1. There was an agreement between us that I would write to you about my friends and you would help them, if their demands were just. 2. Begin by helping the bearer, Hyperechius, who has been plagued and harassed for a long time by men who have learned to profit unjustly. This man was a student of mine in that past time of happiness. 3. I call happy the time I spent in Nicomedia, not because it brought me money, but because it gave me virtuous friends, most of whom are dead now. At that time, this man, who is now pinning his hopes on you, came from Ancyra and showed that he was second to none in eloquence and was first in character. Therefore, I love him as parents love the children they have nurtured and, when I see that he is in trouble, I come to his aid myself and appeal to others. 4. If you think that I am acting like a decent man, show by your actions that you approve my intention.

116 F1268 (year 364): To Hyperechius
[*This is the last letter. The student is Eusebius xx.*]
   1. Why did this young man—and especially a relative and the nephew of the husband of your sister—come to us without a letter from you? Are your fields, riding a horse, and hunting everything for you, and don't you take any account of rhetoric and writing? Not that those are bad occupations, but there should be some room for these, too. 2. Did he leave without your knowledge? But since he is from such a family, it is not likely that he escaped the notice of others and, if he did, he certainly would not have escaped your notice. Is it that he did not ask you for a letter? But that is impossible, because he did not ignore my feelings toward you. 3. Is it perhaps that you are again accusing me,

as you did so often, when you were convicted of false accusations? The current situation is more difficult to bear in that then it was possible for me to know what I had to fight, but now I have given up asking myself what the accusation is.

DOSSIER OF JULIANUS 15/VII AND HIS SON
[*Julianus was going to follow Themistius's lessons for some time. He was rather old, since in 364 he sent his own son to Libanius. In that year, he became* comes orientis *("count of the East"). In 361, Libanius recommended him to Clearchus,* Ep. 668 (B79).]

117 F667 (year 361): To Themistius
1. I could not say how distressed at leaving us and at the same time happy about going to you Julianus was, but his pleasure was greater than his sorrow. 2. Just as a merchant who sails from port to port, from one that offers small gains to one that is competitive in trade, does not disparage the first but looks forward to the second, similarly he does not find fault with us but is drawn to your harbor. You are indeed one of those who are learned in every respect, and there is no form of discourse (*logoi*) that he has not grasped. 3. But if you give a rhetorical display, he will applaud; if it is Plato and philosophy, he will be stimulated; if you lecture about the stars, he will show no idleness; and if you examine the poets, he will be serious about these pleasurable subjects (*paidika*). 4. Since I trust that your discussions will progress to other fine matters, I enroll myself as partaker of the pleasure. You will remember me, I am sure. You will say that a certain someone should be there, too, and Julianus will add: "He really should be here."

118 F1296 (year 364): To Themistius
1. The excellent Julianus is a Syrian, but he gladly hastened from us to you. When I marveled at his eagerness to leave home to go to a different place, he said, "Do not be surprised, Themistius is responsible for this change. He attracts and charms by offering great things, and even some poetry." 2. On hearing this, I was full of admiration and thought this was right. The oracle in fact said to the Pelasgian man[71] that every land was his fatherland but, if I am allowed to add something, I would say that any land where Themistius is, is a fatherland to every learned man. And Julianus is in a sense first among learned men: he has mastered our subjects but has also learned Latin, and he can discuss some Plato and some astronomy. As a governor, he dishonored none of these

---

[71] On the expression "Pelasgian man," cf. Salzmann 1910, 63; Zenobius *Corpus paroemiographorum Graecorum* V74; see also Lysias *Or.* 31.6.2.

things, but he also left the Phoenicians (who are experts at becoming rich) as a poor man. 3. Show some books to a man who can see and appreciate the beauty of books.

119 F1261 (year 364): To Scylacius 2/ii
[*Scylacius was a teacher of law in Berytus but met Libanius in Antioch.*]
1. I received the young man you commended and was immediately pleased in noticing his physical resemblance to his father, for this is charming not only for the parents but for all those who see it, and not only in a human being but in a colt, a calf, a bird, and in all living things. 2. When I tested his intellectual capacity, I thought that here also he took after his father, who is ready of wit, since he immediately grasped what I said. The Demosthenes that he has stored up in his soul seems a lot to me, but it is little for his father. No doubt, if it were twice as much, it would still seem little to his father: farmers do not think that the earth yields a lot when it in fact does in plenty, and they complain that it does not yield more. 3. I myself at the same time praise the son but do not blame his father. God willing and with the wind of Fortune blowing astern, I believe that this young man will come to you on a ship laden with eloquence. 4. He will be good and temperate, perhaps with the help of rhetoric, but certainly with the help of the teacher in his own family [home teacher], whom you rightly address as philosopher. Julianus is a man who in his new high office maintains the moral character he had before: he believes that his duty is to render the cities happy; he is pleased if the sword lies idle; he embellishes the cities with buildings, worships the Muses, and in a trial never lets the guilty go unpunished. Is he anything but a philosopher? Since he seems to be one, why should we not rightly call him so? 5. We called him such right from the start because the beauty of his soul shone forth immediately. It may be, however, that it is not the same thing for us as for you to call him by that name, because you recognize the virtue of a soul well suited to high office. 6. I congratulate you for casting your vote fittingly, and I congratulate the household of the excellent Julianus, which is honored by this vote.

DOSSIER OF JULIANUS XV

[*Julianus xv was a student of Libanius in 362/63, but it is uncertain when he joined the school. Libanius asked the governor Entrechius to help him with his family problems. 121 shows that he avoided punishing his mother's murderer personally, and that the city received him with many honors. On Entrechius 1, cf. 56.*]

120 F835 (year 363): To Entrechius 1

1. My dearest Julianus should have gone home to see his mother for other reasons so that she might enjoy her son's excellence in her old age. 2. But now he is going to shed tears on her tomb, mourning the woman who bore him, both because she is dead and because of the way she died. His third misfortune is that in this matter, he is forced to fight those he least wants to: some old tragedy must have come to light. 3. The only consolation in all this is your judgment, your position, and your friendship. Because of all this, I exhorted him to be as confident as if not only his mother but also his father were still alive. 4. You will adjudicate the murder case as the evidence should dictate; but when this is over, please make Julianus great in the city and among his people, imitating Athena's care for Odysseus. You will be not at all ashamed to bring to power someone who is prudent, self-controlled, and an excellent speaker, such as anyone would desire his son to be. 5. I am saying this not because I think that you need any urging—after all, you keep together his home when he is gone. But when I think of Julianus, I can neither say little nor keep silent altogether, since I know so many good things about him. To be sure, I would not hesitate to call him the head of our *chorus*. 6. Do not be surprised, therefore, if I dwell upon this, and also forgive me if often letters come to you. I could prophesy your assistance, but the great affection that I have for him does not allow me to be without worries. 7. If you want to make me as happy as possible in this matter, answer my first letter right away, and do the same with the second. And every time you do something for him, add a letter showing me how you helped, so that he is happy there and I can share in his contentment.

121 F1130 (year 364): To Julianus

1. It is because I predicted this that I urged you to return to your fatherland. You were an excellent orator but a coward. But now you have tested the prophet, and that has convinced you that he did not predict what came to pass without divine inspiration. 2. I praise you because you went hunting but did not kill and therefore both avoided bloodshed and have gained a good reputation. I think yours is a city of good men who honor you like a god. 3. Many other cities are either not aware of the virtue of their citizens or, when they are, resent it; this one, however, recognized your talents, rejoiced, celebrated, and adorned you with honors in the theater. You also behaved like a man fond of giving, but showed yourself superior to pleasures, since you sent money there but remained inside your house. 4. The joy that these events brought you is the same as the joy the things written in your

letter brought me. But besides the facts themselves, the length of the letter and its charm was showing that I am the father of a good child. Your letter is a greater gift to me than if you had sold most of your land and sent me the money. 5. Do many excellent things and write to me when you do them. For me, the greatest repayment is if you are and look the best.

JULIANUS XIX

122 *F1102 (year 393): To Domitianus*
[*Domitianus 5. Nothing is known of this Julianus and his companion.*]
1. The man from whom you receive the letter is my son, one of those still attending school. His sister is also coming with him, and you should consider her my daughter. There is also the young man who married her, another student of mine. 2. Make sure that the bearer, the woman, and Julianus, her husband, are thankful to you and to me: to me for the letter, and to you for what you will do.

JULIUS II

123 *F1335 (year 365): To Julius*
[*This is the only letter about this student, whose family is unknown. He probably left soon.*]
1. When you were here, I both persuaded you and forced you to withstand the labors of rhetoric. I would not be able to do the latter now, since you are away, but I urge you to consider that education is the greatest of goods, and that none of the things that lead to it is heavy to bear. 2. You would do this if you bore in mind the reason why your father governs and elicits admiration. You will find that those things do not derive from great wealth, physical beauty, and noble birth, but are both the gifts of rhetoric.

JULLUS

124 *F1038 (year 392): To Jullus*
[*Jullus of Palestine (PLRE I, p. 485) was a student of Libanius together with Priscio (PLRE I, p. 729). The honor was conferred on Libanius because he was of curial family and Antioch's official sophist; cf. Wiemer 1995b, 114–16. Libanius is grieving the loss of his son Cimon.*]
1. You may have forgotten the honors that you bestowed on me when you were our governor. This is one, I believe. As you were sitting in

the Council chamber, you asked the Council that was deliberating to honor me, as I was teaching the students in school, to have me take part in the deliberations, and to do that on a permanent basis. You do not remember this, but I do, and very well. 2. Besides these, there will be the other favors that you added after you left office, when you were living in private life. They are the following. You have been a tower of strength and a wall of defense for the learned Priscio in everything that you say and do: your work, your efforts, and your standing ovations during his declamations were by no means inferior to those you gave us. 3. We did not learn this in a dream, but he who received these honors informed us in detail. The tale was long, for it could not have been short with so much to say. All this relieved me no less than the words by which he meant to overcome my sorrow. The good reputation of one son dispelled my grief. Priscio's reputation is partly due to his eloquence and partly to his alliance with you: Jullus is a powerful ally, and a man who practices winning. 4. Since I enjoyed what I heard, it would be only fair for me to please you by letting you hear it, too. Know, therefore, that your companion and mine (*hetairos*) shone in the orations he delivered before us, attracted the attention of the crowd gathered for the Olympic Games, and, by the good judgment he received, gladdened those young men who sit in teaching chairs. 5. Hear, moreover, this nice thing for which you have to be grateful to him. He came to a city that, as you know, is mighty and great and is admired on many counts, but he could not find anything more beautiful than in your country. Particularly because of this, he induced the office of which we are part to show him favor, and received here the honors that I think he will receive in your country.

DOSSIER OF LEONTIUS 14/VI
[*Leontius was a student before 388 who became governor of Phoenicia. Libanius recommended pupils to him. He composed beautiful orations.*]

125 F895 (year 388): To Leontius
1. Letters came from you to us, and both I and those who take care of the students with me cried out. What I had told them about you the day before caused the uproar. 2. I was saying that both you and my relative, the son of Bassianus, were wronging me by depriving me of letters when some people came, bringing us a beautiful oration of yours, or, if you wish, of mine. This in fact, as I hear, is what people said in the lecture room where you are, and quite rightly so: it is so similar to those that I composed. 3. This oration was in my hands and under my very eyes for two days, as I read it, approved of it, and admired it: it amply repays what I have done for you. I would not choose all the gold in the world over seeing my son beget such orations.

4. When I thought that there was a good opportunity, I brought this oration to another lecture room, right here, and it was exactly as before: people made the same loud remarks and were equally stirred. Someone even shared the same suspicions that arose among you, that is, that Leontius appropriated what was mine, and that the speech was made here but was delivered there. There is much, in fact, that can deceive. 5. Pleased with you and with myself, I was also pleased with the students who took the papyrus and claimed the oration their property: they wished to get it and own it, and do own it after getting it.

126 F1095 (year 393): To Apollonides
[*Little is known of Apollonides; Seeck 1906, 80.*]

1. Leontius was our student, accomplished in both words and deeds; he has already some gifts of Fortune and will obtain others, I predict, but since he wants to become happier, he wishes to be your son-in-law. When he receives a lot, he will return a lot: he is such a man both at court and in the lecture rooms in accomplishments that originate from rhetoric. 2. So I am your adviser and exhort you to consider this a gift of the gods. Write back to us saying that the adviser is valued for his work of persuasion.

DOSSIER OF LETOIUS IV
[*Letoius iv was a student from Armenia. Letoius iii was his uncle.*]

127 F104 (year 359/60): To Letoius iii

1. When you participated in the meeting concerning important matters that was called in the presence of a friend of ours, you said that your nephew was with us and that you intended to write to him and to me about him, but you did not do either. 2. We, however, are writing and are sending the pedagogue, who does not allow us to write a long letter. If I praised this young man at length, he is the one you would ask if my words were true, so it is better to give my report about these things to him.

128 F285 (year 359/60): To Maximus
[*Maximus 19/vi; other letters to him are 3, 9, 12, 40, and 169. Eusebius x, from Armenia, was a schoolfellow of Libanius.*]

1. His mother brought Letoius, a young man from Armenia, here and entrusted her only son to me. I was pleased with him because he was ready to receive rhetoric—this colt is sharp—but I marveled at the mother, who was not looking for a second marriage, even though she has only one child, and who went on such a journey. She thought that everything would turn out better for him if she were there to take care of things at the beginning. 2. It will be the god's concern and ours that

he belongs to the Greeks,[72] but the preservation of his household will be the concern of his mother, and of Eusebius, too. He lives virtuously and, with the care he has for the divine, has taken upon himself the responsibility for these people, believing that it befits a righteous man to aid an orphan and not to turn him over to those who wish to plunder him. 3. Well, his resolution is noble and should have some effect, if he enjoyed your support. He will enjoy it, I know full well, since you have chosen to further our interests.

DOSSIER OF LETOIUS VI
[Letoius vi came from Pamphylia, where he was a student of the sophist Argeius and stayed one year (cf. Chapter Two). His father, Factinianus, consularis of Pamphylia (PLRE I, p. 323), would have preferred that he study law.]

129 F1011 (year 391): To Argeius
1. In admiring rhetoric and wishing to acquire it, Letoius does well, but I thought that in neglecting the nearby spring, the learned Argeius, and sailing elsewhere, he is behaving more or less like a person who is thirsty but, leaving the spring by his house, runs to the one by the city gate, and ends up drinking the same water. What he would get from us, in fact, is the same as what he would get from you. 2. I thought that from the very letter you personally read to him—if from nothing else—he would see that he should stay and share in the beauty of such discourses. 3. But Letoius missed the point, and this will make him often reproach himself. I delight both in this young man and in your letter and pray that he will not cease to love rhetoric. I fear, however, the ears of his father and those mouths that have learned to sing the praises of Berytus.

130 F1012 (year 391): To Factinianus
1. This fits a man who knows how to govern, not tiles, stones, walls, paintings, and useless colonnades, but encouraging the education of his subjects and having good sense and ability to speak. Such a man—and not the others—should rightly be called father. 2. By giving me this letter and honoring in such a way a man who is your subject,[73] you have awakened those who disregard rhetoric and have made those who do not shrink from it engage with it more. 3. I think that you will send other letters here with the same intent. You are praising us for our students' ability and by saying that our writing is a blessed thing, and

---

[72] "Belongs to the Greeks" with regard to Greek culture and pagan religion.
[73] The man who was his subject was probably Argeius.

this is like shouting to all men: "Fathers, send your dear sons to an old man who still knows how to work hard, and let neither distance nor the sea keep you away." 4. With what you say and do, you glorify both learning and Pamphylia. After accepting Letoius, as you wished and urged, I now accuse the gods who deprived me of children: I would have them, had I not offended Cyprus.[74]

131 F1013 (year 391): To Quirinus
[*Quirinus, probably a Pamphylian, is unknown.*]

1. Your learning and the fact that you are able to prevail because of it sent the first [student] to us and sent the second, too: the first contributed in some way to the coming of the second. This is what reputation does and accomplishes. It carries everywhere word of what is going on: it has denounced one man's idleness and has proclaimed hard work, and this second thing has attracted another crowd. 2. This is how I think Letoius came. He will get what everyone else does—which you embellished with the comparison to the sun. May he keep it when he has it; may he not lose it like those who look at other things and then do not have what they used to.

132 F1014 (year 391): To Palladius
[*Palladius from Tyana in Cappadocia is unknown. His children were sent by Quirinus (cf. Ep. 1013), but brought by Letoius vi.*]

1. Many are the gifts that Letoius gave me, but they are all less valuable than this one. He came and brought to us from the blessed city of Tyana two boys who love rhetoric. In this, they are an honor to their noble father Palladius, who succeeds through his sagacity and self-control and his capacity to administer justice and keep the city safe. 2. But it would be too long to say in a letter all the things that Letoius told us about you. I am urged on first by the natural talent of these young men; second, by the reputation of their father; and third, by Letoius's desire. 3. But there also is a fourth reason, the fact that I went to school with their forebears, who earned great praise from everyone because the beauty of their characters rivaled that of their eloquence. I really trust that your sons will also acquire both, because their preludes permit us to trust.

DOSSIER OF LIBANIUS IV
[*Provenance unknown. Zenodotus was his grandfather, and Antiochus vii his father. The latter had been a student of Libanius but is unaccounted*

---

[74] Cyprus probably as the island of Cypris, an allusion to Libanius's failure to marry and have legitimate children.

by Petit (1956a). He arrived when the school year had started. Another student namesake of Libanius was the son of Paulus iii, Ep. 961.]

133 F1020 (end of year 391): To Zenodotus

1. Albeit late, I finally have the son of Antiochus, whom I long desired and who is named after me because his father honored me, trusting that no one in the family would blame him. 2. My namesake should have learned the principles of rhetoric long ago under my eyes, yet I was glad to see him now. As soon as I saw him I cried out, seeing his father's face in his, and I cried out later, when I heard him saying a few words, because I recognized his father's voice in his. 3. He should have lived to bring his son to us, just as an athlete brings his son to the same trainer. It is important for this young man to have your letters in lieu of his father's, the letters of an old, weak man (you say), but they actually show you a vigorous man in your prime. 4. May the gods, who let you reach this age, allow you to welcome back this young man. How charming a spectacle it would be for the gods themselves: this young man declaiming and attesting the efforts of his grandfather, and the latter unsteady on his feet,[75] delighting in the fruit of his care.

134 F1034 (year 392): To Zenodotus

1. The rest of the wine has arrived, a lot of it; but the first (shipment) was also a lot. You call both shipments small: anything spent on rhetoric seems small to you, even though it is great. 2. May the gods keep you safe and make you write often, since you do it so well. I encouraged Libanius to be acquainted with the letters of the old writers and also with these, and to be nourished by the former and by the latter, too. (This is what he has done.[76]) 3. It is not this [gift] that spurs me on, but the fact that I am honored by it, and what make me even more willing toward him are the man who is alive and the one who no longer is. In fact, I often have the impression that the excellent Antiochus is seated beside me, telling me about his child the sorts of things that a father says about his son.

MACARIUS II

135 F145 (year 359/60): To Priscianus
[The father is Macarius 2, the son Macarius ii. Priscianus 1/i was a rhetor at the time. Other letters mentioning or addressed to him are 7, 92, 135, 167, and 177.]

---

[75] The text needs to be corrected; *astaphos* should not be capitalized. The adjective *astaphos*, "unsteady," occurs in Libanius's *Declamation* 23.32.12.

[76] The text here is corrupted.

1. Macarius the bearer, who is part of your staff, is the father of our student Macarius. Every governor gave him a gift, the gift of time, allowing him to see his son, who is dear to Mnemosyne. 2. In addition to many others, give him this gift, which you would have given him anyway.

MACEDONIUS 4/V

136 *F1071 (year 393): To Aristaenetus*
[*Aristaenetus 2/ii, a relative of Libanius and son of his student Bassianus 2 (see dossier). On this student, cf. PLRE I, pp. 526–27. Macedonius became a philosopher. In Ep. 1325 from the year 365, Macedonius's father Pelagius appears as a cultivated man with an education in rhetoric, poetry, and philosophy.*]

1. The bearer is both Pelagius's son and mine, since the former begot him, but I persuaded him to love rhetoric. He is a skilled speaker, has a good sense of judgment, and is the only one who did not flee from the Council as the others did but bears arms for his country. This is the man whom I wish to be your friend and to fare well, whether words are sufficient or deeds are needed. 2. You will think that you are benefiting only one man, but you will benefit the whole city of Kyrus, which is now small but was great before, and perhaps with your help will be great again.

THE SON OF MARCELLINUS VI

137 *F135 (year 359/60): To Marcellinus*
[*Marcellinus of Apamea was an intimate friend of Libanius. The only other letter is Ep. 1357 (B95), written in 363, when the son was already out of school. Little is known about Mocimus, who appears in other letters.*]

1. I asked others to help Mocimus in the sale to which he is proceeding, but, as it is fit, your son will ask you on our behalf not to omit anything in order that he may find me gentle in memory of this favor, once he joins my school. 2. Show your son this letter and observe his zeal.

MARCIANUS 6/VIII

[*On Marcianus, see also Epp. 1512 and 1513. He was a member of an office under Jovinus II. Decentius (PLRE I, p. 244) in 365 was an important officer, but his title is unknown.*]

138 *F1511 (year 365): To Decentius*
1. Marcianus the bearer is a fellow citizen of mine, a friend, and now at last he is my student, for he considered that it is better to learn late

what is necessary rather than not to learn it at all. But trouble has befallen him and dragged him from the midst of the Muses and brought some anxiety regarding the property of his wife. He married her when he was taking part in the expedition against the Persians, with full knowledge of the emperor; he was happy and even became a father. 2. He is in jeopardy, or rather, the final decision will be good, if you wish and if the laws are not overturned. The experts say, in fact, that as long as the laws are valid, this woman will keep her property, since her first husband and son died, and the husband did so before the child. 3. Therefore, bring help to Marcianus and to the laws and weaken those who are unjust.

DOSSIER OF MARCUS
[*Marcus was son of Acacius 8/i. Another letter concerning him is Ep. 1174 (B102), from the same year. He decided to quit rhetoric and get a minor official post. Palladius 8 is otherwise unknown.*]

139 F1222 (year 364): To Acacius

1. Your most valuable possessions, your good wife and very fine son, are coming to you. We wished to give him more, but we have given him little. He is the reason for this, or rather his uncle is, but perhaps neither of them is, but according to your order (on the ground that it was impossible for him to maintain a good conduct otherwise), he followed the uncle who was going on a long voyage. I do not know whether his character would have become worse by staying here; but this I know, that he definitely would have been better in rhetoric. 2. He will learn it now, though much time has been lost. Great is the art of Hermes in Cappadocia, eloquence flows plentiful, and there is a teacher who is father of many rhetors, the noble Palladius, who received and bequeathed sublime eloquence. 3. Let our Marcus exercise his mind there, turning his eyes a bit away from the belt of office—his own, I mean; he still should look at yours and reason within himself that it is the fruit of rhetoric and that it is his father's rhetoric that also contributes to the post he himself has. If he would reason in this way, he will also be allowed to look at his own post. 4. So you will do this. About the horse,[77] if you bought it, send it. If not, write to us, so that we might adopt the second alternative, that is, those horses that are not more valuable than copper coins. You should not fear that we have some suspicion that you did not wish that. If we hear that it is impossi-

---

[77] Acacius had told Libanius he was going to send him a nice horse. See *Ep.* 1514 (B105), which clarifies that Acacius was forbidden to buy the horse from his provincials.

ble, we will believe it right away. We must believe that neither the gods nor their likes lie.

DOSSIER OF MARIANUS'S SON
[*Marianus and the recipients of the two letters are unknown.*]

140 F875 (year 388): To Theodorus
1. The bearer, the son of the excellent Marianus, is like his father in character but even surpasses him in eloquence, so that he would have become great defending people on trial or great in the same position where I am. Before studying with us, he was enrolled in a branch of court officials and has come now to share its duties. 2. I desire and request from you some words to them on his behalf, making it clear that they will please you personally through their efforts in this matter.

141 F876 (year 388): To Antiochus
1. When this young man was still learning his syllables, his father Marianus made him part of the company of the court officials. He entrusted his son to me, though I did not know this matter, and took such care that he would become a good speaker that he led me to infer that he was asking the gods to be able to look upon him as an educator of young men. 2. Then he approached me and brought to light what was hidden; he blushed, but could not avoid saying that the time had come for his son to go to you and do what he had been selected for in the first place. 3. If another man were involved in this, I would be angry, but Marianus found me so well disposed that he even asked in addition that I should write a letter. I am giving him this and am asking you to make the stay of Marianus's son more pleasant there than here.

MAXIMUS XVII

142 F1003 (year 391): To Heracleius 7/iv
[*Maximus was the son of Iphicrates, a decurion from Armenia. He had previously attended the class of Leontius 9/iv, before becoming a student in 388–90 (cf. Ep. 88 [N45]). On Iphicrates, cf.* **35** *and* **166**. *After Iphicrates' death in 390–91, Heracleius, a rhetor and advocate, helped his widow.*]

1. You think very highly of our letters and are grateful for them. We are grateful to you for your deeds, which began a long time ago and have continued with no interruption to this day. Some of them brought a student of mine to power, and others helped me as I declaimed, by making appear beautiful also what was not beautiful because of a well-

renowned rhetor's standing ovations.[78] 2. Now by what you did for the excellent Maximus and, even more, for all those for whom we labored, you are handing all Armenia to us. 3. By loving the son of Iphicrates, you, who are wise, love someone wise; you, who are just, love someone just; and you, who know how to work hard, love someone who knows hard work. Because of your mutual love, you call him, and he would come even if you did not call. He will soon be with you, since he considers it equally good to see both you and his mother. 4. I also have something good here, because I have your child on my knees with his mother's permission.

THE GRANDSON OF MEGETHIUS

143 F1101 (year 393): To Megethius
[*Megethius 2 was an advocate of Antioch who moved then to Berytus. Libanius also wrote to him about his student Apringius, Ep. 1203 (B167).*]

1. I see you and him, when the son of your son brings me his tablet or recites something he has committed to memory. As he moves his hands and eyes, enters, sits down, gets up and leaves, in each of these actions he recalls his parent and his grandfather. 2. But in his enjoyment [of the toils of rhetoric],[79] he is better than his father and not worse than his grandfather.

DOSSIER OF MENECRATES

144 F720 (year 362): To Diophantus
[*This Diophantus is known only from this letter.*]

1. Receive the finest of our companions and judge his nature from what he presently desires. Although his own rhetorical ability leads him to be an advocate and his family desires so, he judged the beauty of philosophy superior to the power that comes from rhetoric. 2. Since he is inquiring where he may truly learn this discipline, we are pointing to Egypt and Diophantus: the one has nourished the beauty of philosophy as long as men and the Nile have existed, and the other possesses greater wisdom than anyone else. 3. His own passion recommends this young man, but I also recommend him because I believe that he can achieve something with you. With kindly words and glad countenance, give him a share in the mystery that opens heaven to its partakers.

---

[78] The "standing ovations" of Heracleius himself.
[79] A lacuna in the text.

145 F721 (year 362): To Ammonius
[*Ammonius ii or iii, an Egyptian, may have been a grammarian.*]
    1. Menecrates, the bearer, left home with the intention to partake of my teaching on a continuous basis, but numerous illnesses cut his attendance short. This certainly did not diminish our goodwill toward him, and I am ready to help him as far as possible outside of rhetoric. The greatest gift I can give is what I am doing now. This letter, which is assuring your influence, is the beginning of many good things. 2. Since he longed for rhetoric but was prevented from receiving as much of it as he should, sustain him with your help.

DOSSIER OF METERIUS II

146 F472 (year 355/56): To Meterius i
[*Meterius ii was probably from Nicomedia, since Alcimus (PLRE I, pp. 38–39) was his previous teacher. Meterius i is his father.*]
    1. I think you have some anger against your son. But if you are cross because you did not see him for a long time, you give us reason to be happy; if you did not resent this, we would resent that you took it so lightly. In revealing the father by the fact that you are angry because of his absence, you gladden me, but if you have any other complaint, you have been deceived. 2. Let this letter be a proof to you of his good behavior. I was not inclined to neglect your son, nor to ignore the truth when I became aware of it, and it is not in my character to praise one I found not good. 3. So if one who has acquired the very best friends in our school deserves to be punished by his father, let Meterius be punished, for he has them. But if you, too, wished that the whole city felt no worse than his fatherland does toward him, withdraw your accusations and rejoice together with us.

147 F474 (year 355/56): To Alcimus
    1. Meterius hardly escaped the notice of our city when he passed through. Since he had many who loved him, he was watched more than Aristodemus.[80] I also was one of those who wished for him to be here, for he was here because of us. 2. Many things would dispose you well toward him: the rights of his fatherland, your relationship with his family, and the fact that the rhetoric that he possesses is your legacy. Add, if you wish, this young man's regard for us. 3. Bearing all this in mind, persuade his father not to consider his son's popularity here a fault. I would really be grieved if Meterius appeared to have been mis-

---

[80] On Aristodemus, see *Or.* 1.16 and 64.83; he was a *theludrias* ("effeminate person") of Old Comedy: Norman 1992, 1:72.

behaving when he is blameless in every regard, because he admired the Syrians and was admired in return. 4. If he obtains you as an ally, he will find fault rather than being accused. For your knowledge, we are not faring so badly in other respects, but it is not even possible to say how bad our health is.

148 F475 (year 355/56): To Lampetius
[*Lampetius is known only from this letter.*]
1. No blow should have struck your house, but since this seemed right to those who rule human affairs, you do well to bear the misfortune patiently. 2. Meterius the bearer did amuse himself a little here, but for the most part he studied hard: he relished some things with us and enjoyed others with those who oversee the affairs of the city; they often prevented him from going back home. 3. Therefore, he should be praised for the one thing and should not cause resentment for the other. At any rate, even where you are, the elderly do not disdain horse races; it is better for me to say this rather than what I could. 4. So if his father decides not to launch even one accusation, praise his judgment; but if he believes that he has to rebuke, change his mind.

DOSSIER OF OLYMPIUS 4/I
[*Olympius was Libanius's student, probably in Constantinople or Nicomedia. He was a doctor, but he also knew grammar, rhetoric, philosophy, and Latin. Libanius needed him as a Latin teacher. The addressee is the philosopher at Constantinople (PLRE I, p. 894).*]

149 F406 (year 355): To Themistocles
1. The learned Olympius is again with you, and again there are those meetings, conversations, and banquets that deserve to be written about, with a sophist speaking of rhetoric, a grammarian of the poets, and you and Themistius of philosophy. Olympius, flowing abundant and pure on every subject, draws away the guests from the banquet with the beauty of his words and makes listening more pleasant than eating. 2. Perhaps you will mention me, and maybe for the better. So you will praise the absent one and not displease those who are present.

150 F413 (year 355): To Italicianus
[*PLRE I, p. 466; Italicianus was at court.*]
1. I know that my letter makes you happy. You fly to hear us and fly back again from the discourse to your meeting, eagerly seeking the lecture and doing everything while in it. 2. So it was clear that you would not disregard the letter of one whose discourses you value. I repay you by being proud of the fact that you appear noble to the

learned Olympius, who both visits the sick and raises them up and also receives those who seek education with him and fills them up with it. He is such a sure friend that he would even join a friend in an expedition against the Gorgons. 3. You will see him working wonders in his struggles on my behalf, and certainly you will become part of those even if nobody compels you.

151 F534 (year 356): To Olympius

1. As soon as I heard that you had established yourself at Rome, I reckoned you happy because of this, but knowing that there you have a greater reputation and power, I called you even happier. I fear, however, that the fact that her children can acquire fame in other countries will rob our city of what belongs to her. 2. I wish you to obtain praise everywhere, but not to wrong in this way the city that bore you and who asks you through us to come to her: she enjoys the culture you have acquired, but would love to take advantage of that culture you gained. She blames me instead of you, because people believe that you follow my commands, and they reproach me with the fact that you are not coming yet because I do not tell you to. 3. Let Rome be the capital city of the world, but let this not make you forgetful of your friends and nation. Return to the same things we do and share in the tending of the flock, considering it more pleasant to govern them with me than to govern cities. If the ears (of your students) are not on a par with your language, with your language you will improve them. 4. I was pleased with the books that you sent and with those that you said you are collecting. The things you request will also come to you from us in the summer.

152 F539 (year 356/57): To Olympius

1. I wrote to you before to urge you not to scorn your fatherland, and now I urge the same things: to admire Rome but to live in your country. There is a place for you, *choroi* of students, an honorific decree: everything is ready. 2. I have need of your language for what I do. If our students must be strong in court, and this is hard with the other tongue, how can you not be here and shepherd the flock with me? 3. But, my good friend, also become a teacher since you were an excellent student, and come yourself, together with books.

153 F1198 (year 364): To Olympius
[*The drinking and laughing sophist must be Libanius.*]

1. I do not recommend my companion Alexander to you, for you have known and praised each other for a long time: you praise not a few things in him, he, everything about you. But I thought that under the

circumstances it would strike a false note not to write a letter. 2. As I write, the memory comes to me of those dinners and the discourses that flowed from your mouth, and of Themistocles full of pleasure and the sophist drinking. And the latter would say what seemed right to Dionysus, and laugh, and make the others laugh. 3. I think that even now you dine in the same fashion. With the noble Themistius, you are working on a declamation on Plato. But there is also someone who is searching for something more than drinking cups.[81]

THE SONS OF OLYMPIUS IX

154 F270 (year 358): To Olympius ix
[*Olympius was Armenian. On Eutherius, cf. 37, 99, 165, and 166. Ep. 269 mentions that Eutherius 2, the governor of Armenia, will assure Olympius that his children are accepted, for the sake of justice. In that letter, Nemesius 1, who had finished school, arouses Libanius's admiration for his ability.*]
1. Your children will get fair treatment in everything from us, first because that is really just, and because a master who is not bad should do this; then because Eutherius is interceding on their behalf, and because Nemesius brought them, the one an excellent governor and the other a top rhetor. Even if he handed me hostile children, I would still regard them as the sons of a friend, put aside hatred, and love them. 2. Who would not stand in awe of Nemesius's visage, voice, silence? I never saw another man who does everything appropriate to the occasion. But no wonder: he is Armenian. Your country knows how to breed the manly virtues. 3. Make sure to repay the ferryman, nothing that you will give him will settle your debt. I also recognize that I owe these students some repayment, and I will pay it, since it is through them that Nemesius came here, visited us, and is one of my friends.

OPTIMUS AND ROMANUS

155 F1544 (year 374?): To Optimus
[*After leaving school, Optimus became a bishop (PLRE I, p. 650).*]
1. The second thing is better. Why did you have to fight and annoy a man who never annoyed you? You are that most kindly Optimus, whom I was pleased to see when you brought me a discourse, either on the tablet or without it. You are the one who guarded the pure Greek language and gave speeches at home in which I, too, was displayed. 2. I also heard what happened afterward, that the city raised

---

[81] He is alluding to himself.

you to a [bishop's] chair; you tried to avoid it but could not escape either with shouting or with tears. So I was pleased that even now you have occasion to use rhetoric in that place. 3. Make the crowds praise you, and let the rhetor be conspicuous there, too. If you are happy to make me happier, write, and if there is a young man similar to Romanus, send him. Work would not be spent in vain on youths of that sort.

PAEONIUS I

156 F117 *(year 359): To Domninus*
[*On Domninus, see* **21, 28, 101,** *and* **75.** *On Paeonius i, who translated Eutropius's breviary, see Petit 1956a, 24. It is uncertain, however, if this student is Paeanius (PLRE I, p. 657) or Paeonius 2, who taught rhetoric at Tavium.*]

1. Paeonius thought of learning the law in addition; I did not prevent him and showed him from whom he should learn the law. I had to repay him for his fairness, for he gave me neither small nor greater troubles but brought me many small and greater joys. 2. I think that he also honored me by leaving after making me part of his decision; for those who attempt to conceal it offend us insofar as they fear our opposition, if they were to speak in advance. But wishing to be worthy of his father and grandfather and observing the way we are by nature, this [youth] disclosed what he was going to do and is honored by a letter. 3. You should consider this young man not only a student but also a friend, and show all those around you that Paeonius has a greater claim on you.

DOSSIER OF PANDORUS

[*Pandorus's father was Euphronius 2; Celsus 3/i, a former pupil of Libanius, was then governor of Cilicia.*]

157 F743 *(year 362): To Celsus*
1. Pandorus the bearer is a Cilician, the last in terms of wealth but the first in terms of his enthusiasm for rhetoric; he knows full well that those who lack the former must acquire the latter, for the one can also bring the other. 2. Being an eager hunter after rhetoric,[82] he has not divided his attention between countless paths, but has left diversified studies to others and has pursued rhetoric sufficiently: some things he has mastered, and he is not far from others. 3. Now he is coming to

---

[82] The metaphor of the hunter of rhetoric is found in Aristophanes *Clouds* 358.

see his small hometown, be with his father, and present himself to you. Receive this young man kindly and offer him what is right for a youth of his age. If he wishes to give you some display of his ability, offer your ear and lend him a hand.

158 F1394 (year 363): To Euphronius
1. You dared to commit such a great theft and take away the son who is both mine and yours. I have become his father because of what he has received from me. Yet, you should not have called him home, or you should have written to me that you would call. 2. And now, when you think[83] that students already possess the art of rhetoric, you offend those who teach the art. When you believe that Pandorus is able to speak well, you do not do wrong; but if you prevent him from getting better, you wrong yourself, myself, and him. He should not leave when he knows some things but not yet others; rather, he should see you and be seen by you only when he is a strong and elegant speaker. This should happen with the addition of one more year. So be patient and console yourself for the absence of your son with the expectation of what the extra time will bring. You should be grateful because we sent back to you the donkeys whose sale had to provide for Pandorus's living expenses.

DOSSIER OF PARTHENOPAEUS
[PLRE I, p. 668. *Parthenopaeus was from Tyre in Phoenicia and became a rhetor there. The oration mentioned was a panegyric on the consulship of Tatianus 5. Libanius is Parthenopaeus's "father," as Peleus was Achilles's father.*]

159 F996 (year 391): To Parthenopaeus
[*Maxentius 4 was a rhetor who wanted to practice in Tyre.*]
1. The speech you sent came to your father's hands, and the oration of your father also somehow came into the same hands. We called to this banquet those we had to, but did not call those who better stayed away. 2. After the speeches were read, the judges declared that the work of Peleus was inferior to Achilles'. But I, Peleus, was happy of the defeat, and even happier than had I won. 3. So much for the gifts you sent Tatianus. Maxentius, together with his ability in rhetoric, seems to have as his good fortune your own family, which has many friends and would easily procure him many allies.

---

[83] The expression "you think" in the plural refers to all parents with the same expectations.

160 F1009 (year 391): To Parthenopaeus
1. Your speeches came to us, were read among worthy people, and obtained praise, applause, and standing ovations. Some of those who did so called you (the creator) blessed, others called blessed me, the writer's father, and many both of us, and those who voted in this way obtained praise from those who were there. 2. Keep your hand at writing and get many offspring, since you will make them beautiful. The laws, if they are just—and they would be just if they sought to be just to others, too—will pardon those of us who love the beauty of rhetoric and who will grant something to ourselves and something to others, but not all to ourselves.

DOSSIER OF THE SONS OF PHILAGRIUS III
[*Leontius 9/iv of Armenia studied together with Libanius in Antioch and taught these boys in Armenia. Philagrius then sent them to Acacius, but later transferred them to Libanius. Cf. the dossiers of Anatolius v and Maximus xvii.*]

161 F43 (year 358/59): To Leontius
1. I know well that by writing a letter now I incur a charge for not writing before—if indeed now I act justly by writing, and I was wrong then when I did not write. Since I think that writing late is better than not writing at all, I address a fellow student who has forgotten his companion. Or, have I guessed wrong and you remember me well, but shrink back because your nestlings go to others? 2. But, my wonderful friend, do not consider this a hindrance, or believe that my situation is so weak and that other people's loss is mine. It is possible for them to fly somewhere else and for us to be close to one another, since I consider and call the noble Philagrius a friend who has made a decision about his sons that I wish he will never regret.

162 F89 (year 359): To Philagrius
1. It is with joy that I received your sons. What else should I have done, since I consider them my own? It is better to keep silent about your previous decision rather than try to find an excuse and be unable to say anything meaningful. If you were the most amazing of sophists, three times four still makes twelve—even though Philagrius tries to say otherwise. 2. In any case, I will tell and not hide from a friend what I know I suffered because of your decision. I never pursued fleeing students, for I never saw fountains going after those who need to drink, but I believed that goodwill is due to those who come, and one must take no notice of those who take no notice of it. 3. It is on account of

this that I got the reputation of being haughty, because I could never stand pettiness. But when your children turned to another [teacher], I confess that it stung, and I wished that the decision could change, even though those who blamed your decision were more numerous than those who considered it a sign of my inability. 4. So now, since you reckoned that it is better not to abide by your decision, do not believe that you need to exhort us, but rather you should exhort yourself for their sake. Apart from everything else, the very looks of these young men (which remind me of their father's) make me industrious. 5. Eutychius,[84] moreover, is your friend, and he is related to us; I would wrong him if I did not grant him this favor. This man took your children and his own brother to me and showed that he loved the one no more than the others. 6. Therefore, the custom of summer vacation is cancelled for them alone, so that Eutychius may be pleased, and you would obtain what is necessary.

163 F131 (year 359/60): To Philagrius
1. When after a long time I saw Dositheus,[85] he was pale, and I asked him if this was because of an illness. Then I heard that it was not that, but incessant work. He said that he had shut himself in and was writing. 2. I commended him and was happy for you because not even your servant is lazy. Ask him about your sons, too, and "he will not tell a lie."[86]

164 F681 (year 361): To Philagrius
Your children have arrived. Whether they have gained something by working at home I do not know, but right now they are learning: the older one is very willing, and perhaps later we will write the same about the other. I keep on reminding them of their father because I believe that the best exhortation is if they often hear whose sons they are.

DOSSIER OF PHILOPATRIS
[*Philopatris was the son of Eutherius 2/ii, governor of Armenia, who sent him first to the rhetor Acacius 6/ii. On Eutherius, cf. 37, 99, 154, and 166.*]

165 F259 (year 358/59): To Eutherius
1. Love has made you a sycophant, and you consider everyone but me a nobody. But it is equally absurd to praise those who are mediocre

---
[84] Euthychius is unknown.
[85] Dositheus is the boys' pedagogue.
[86] The quote is from *Od.* 3.20.

and not to admire those who are good. By not considering Acacius one of the retinue of Hermes, you cause me, and especially the god, pain. 2. We will certainly not throw away what Philopatris has learned from him, but will try to build on it: the rhetoric he will receive will be the kindred of that he had before.

166 F260 (year 358/59): To Iphicrates
[*Iphicrates, from Armenia, is the father of Maximus xvii, who would become a student in 388. Cf. letters 35 and 142.*]
1. You, who wrestled with us for so long, are saying neither what is true nor what gratifies us. I do not know if there is anything good in our school, but those who wish can enjoy what is there more than they enjoy springs. Of the students, I cherish most the one who makes me work harder. 2. Philopatris will come and bring you things to make you happier if he would convince himself that rhetoric is a noble possession. You have made me happier already by saying that the governor is what he is called.[87] I am grateful to Eutherius because he is good, and to you who bring such news about Eutherius.

POLYBIUS

167 F1250 (year 364): To Priscianus
[*Priscianus 1/i, the father of Polybius and other students, was governor of Palestine at that time. Other letters to or about Priscianus are 7, 92, 135, and 177.*]
1. Polybius came to my house and said, "Write to my father," and then added, "if you wish." The style of the addition is a sign of a soul that is awakened and already exhibits the devices that it will contrive in court. 2. I was amused, laughed, and said, "I wish." I am writing you these few words hoping that they see you and you them and that you enjoy one another for the whole term of your office. Sweet for his children is the father when he returns home after his valuable work and sweet for the father it is to see his children at home after work. None of his preoccupations is heavy to bear any more, so strong is this remedy. May you enjoy it both during and after your service! 3. This is my prayer, but I also have something to predict from the Muses. Since you travel often and widely, you will often recall your children as you do now.

---

[87] The governor is Eutherius; his name could mean "a good catcher, successful in hunting."

DOSSIER OF THE SONS OF POMPEIANUS IV

168 F768 (year 362): To Pompeianus
[*Pompeianus was probably from Galatia, perhaps to be identified with Pompeianus 3.*]

1. If in sending me gold (a large amount of it, of the Colophonian kind) or something more valuable than gold, you would send me the gift without a letter, don't you think that this would be strange and would suggest someone who is a friend but does not have any daring? 2. Know well, therefore, that you are similarly awkward in sending your sons in silence. It would have made more sense to keep them home and write to me according to the custom for recommendations than to hand me your children without daring to add a letter. 3. Look for an excuse; but I believe that you will look for a long time but will not find one. Not receiving a letter, however, will not make me lazier toward them. This is not only because of your city, which I believe I should love no less than my own, but also because they already seem strong in rhetoric and have feasted on some of my discourses before seeing me.

169 F790 (year 362/63): To Maximus
[*Maximus 19/vi was governor of Galatia. Other letters to him are 3, 9, 12, 40, and 128.*]

1. Inscribe upon the roll of our friends the excellent Pompeianus, too, who has long since been well acquainted with me and now also has children with me, who also love their father greatly. 2. This letter represents their work, since they urge and exhort me, fearing lest their father might have less than others, at least in this respect. 3. Praising both—those who exhorted and myself who listened—esteem this man more than before.

170 F1345 (year 363): To Pompeianus

1. Your sons heard from me what I thought about them and will inform you, but nothing can have more authority than a father. 2. Let what you consider useful be done with the assurance that we will be pleased with the one thing but will not fault the other.

DOSSIER OF RHETORIUS

[*Rhetorius was the son of the grammarian Didymus 1; he got an education, probably in Nicomedia, before 355. In Ep. 404, from the year 355, Libanius asks him to visit Antioch.*]

171 F317 (year 357): To Clematius
[*Clematius 2 was governor of Palestine.*]
   1. Rhetorius, the bearer, studied with us, and I used to study with his father: I was able to make the acquaintance of the poets through the latter, while the former met the rhetors through me. He knows what I think about you and how you treat me. He was my pupil in Bithynia and makes completely sure to know everything about me. 2. He is passing through on his way to Egypt, where he will receive a little land through paternal inheritance (that is where his father comes from); but really he was in some way encouraged to take this trip by the fact that you govern Palestine. 3. Since you would have been happy to see him even if you had heard from another source that he was my pupil, how will you rate him now that he is introduced by our letter?

172 F318 (year 357): To Sebastianus
[*Sebastianus 2 had a major military command in Egypt.*]
   1. I grieved with you for the loss of your wife, but was glad that you bore the misfortune nobly: the one thing demonstrates the abuses of Fortune, the other a virtuous character. You will have no small consolation in Rhetorius, the bearer, who has worked through many rhetors and no fewer poets, and is good in both. 2. My letter and the fact that he went to school with your kin will make you friendly to this man; two very important reasons make me well disposed to him: he is my student and is the son of my teacher. You definitely cannot fail to know Didymus, if you know the Great City[88] where he imparted his teaching running day and night. 3. See that he gets hold of his fields for which he has come. They are small but are a source of security for a poor man, and Rhetorius is not rich. You have power in Egypt; others made money through this, but you have acquired a good reputation because of your alliance with justice.

THE SONS OF SABINUS 5/I
[*Sabinus was governor of Syria in 358/59.*]

173 F1309 (year 364): To Sabinus
   1. I saw you in your sons: so many of your physical traits have come to them. But they, like you, are also wide awake and do not dislike working. Presently they have little of what they could have learned and known, but probably it will be a lot if the Muses and Hermes grant much. 2. Even before, I thought you were beloved, but I definitely did not know that your wealth was such as I have now found out: it ap-

---

[88] The "Great City" is Constantinople.

peared much greater than expected. So many people introduced your two sons, and many were sorry that they were not here. Many people ask what they are doing, many join in good wishes, and all, in short, both encourage them and entreat us.

THE SON OF SALVIUS

174 F1464 (year 365): To Aphobius
[*This is the only letter on this student. Aphobius (PLRE I, p. 81) was governor of Palestine.*]
1. I fed with eloquence the son of Salvius, who is welding together a contingent of soldiers near you. As long as he worked at it, he surpassed the lads his age and would have surpassed the older ones, too, if anyone would have brought him to a higher level. 2. Now, all of a sudden, fortune has armed this young man and put him in command of hoplites. But I cannot forget the work I did with him and maintain the attachment I had in those days. 3. Even now, therefore, I act like someone who loves and ask you a favor, to show him every form of kindness.

SILVANUS 3

175 F87 (year 359): To Domninus
[*Domninus is Domnio 1. On Domninus, cf. 26, 28, 101, and 156. Silvanus was the son of the teacher Gaudentius; cf. Or. 38. Modestus 2; other letters concerning him are 7 and 184.*]
1. Your student Silvanus has been inscribed among the advocates since Modestus so kindly admitted him. He will show his knowledge of law when he contends in court, but he has long shown us his good character. I believe that he has been your student also because he partakes not a little of your character, and that, more than the law, is why you praise him. 2. Cherishing you, as one should a teacher, he cherishes myself, for he knows that he is pleasing you in this.

THE SON OF SOPHRONIUS II

176 F199 (year 360/61): To Sophronius
[*Julianus vi, the student's uncle, was* consularis *of Phoenicia, and the family came from there.*]
1. I have your son, as I long desired; late, but I have him. He is almost like his father in everything: appearance, deportment, way of walking, and further he does not shirk and is strong in rhetoric. This he owes

to you. 2. One thing he needs though: Fortune. Let us all pray, you, myself, and the uncle of this young man, who is my friend. I believe that excellent Julianus will appeal to Hermes. He commanded me, but will beseech the god.

DOSSIER OF THE SON OF STRATONICUS
[*Stratonicus was from Euphratensis. He was supported by Theodotus i, who was probably a schoolmate of Libanius, and by an unknown Leontius, a fellow citizen. Seeck (1906, 284) reads the name as Stratonianus.*]

177 F172 (year 359/60): To Stratonicus
1. We number you among those who are in the *choroi* of the Muses, since knowing how to admire those who are educated is also part of education. Acknowledge gratitude to the gods on account of the nature of your son: he has a ready wit and good memory, is one of those who want to learn, and already shows that his voice will become excellent with time. 2. Indeed, his pedagogue is no less than a father in terms of kindness—however much you give him, you will still give little. About my disposition toward my students, your relative and governor[89] is there to tell you; he is as devoted to you as I am.

178 F187 (year 359/60): To Stratonicus
1. This is our reward for coming home: meeting with old schoolmates, telling them and hearing from them about the old days, and feeling that we relive the very events that we remember. 2. This has happened to me with excellent Theodotus: I consider those days holidays, and my affection for him even increased because he loves your household. 3. He began talking with us by quizzing us about your son and did not depart until he had tested this young man by making him wrestle with some verses of Homer. He is coming without delay, and he will tell you the rest himself. He will not deceive you at all, willingly or unwillingly, because he honors the truth and is filled with rhetoric.

179 F201 (year 359/60): To Stratonicus
1. You will remind yourself whether you owe Leontius a repayment for anything else, but I will tell you what I know that you do owe him for. He continued to keep an eye on those with whom your son was, and was not second to the pedagogue in this, nor to a father in what he would have done if he were there by his son. 2. He does not feel that he should ask for anything because he thinks he took care of his

---

[89] This "relative and governor" is Priscianus 1, governor of Euphrateusis in 360/61. Other letters to or concerning him are **7**, **92**, **135**, and **167**.

own son, but it is right for you to give, even though he keeps silent. The compensation is for the matters for which he has come; make sure finally that he gets it as soon as possible.

SCYLACIUS III
[*Scylacius iii was the son of Scylacius 2/ii, professor of law. Severianus 7 was governor of Phoenicia at the time.*]

180 F998 (year 391): To Scylacius
1. The one who ordered gave a good order, and the one who obeyed did well at obeying. But Scylacius, who is afraid to write to us, should be careful not to insult our studies. He was one of those who at the time excelled in them and went through the most difficult material, but now, in writing a letter, he trembles in fear lest he look bad at this. 2. You can show how foolish this is with a letter, by doing the thing well and by showing through your letter how you fare at the bar. I think that you and all the others who presently hold office please the gods by being the best, and you hold office because you please the gods. 3. It is necessary that the cities quickly render service in all things and cooperate in procuring fame for the excellent Severianus, lengthening his term of office through the greatness of his fame.

DOSSIER OF THEMISTIUS 2/III
[*Themistius 2/iii was probably not a good student, but he became governor of Lycia in 361. In 355 he was in need of books (*Ep. 428 [N10]*). See* Ep. 309: *he was restless in school and thought that rhetoric was useless. Cf. also Or. 62.55. On Heortius, this student's father, see Seeck 1906, 171, and cf.* 108.]

181 F547 (year 356/57): To Heortius
1. If I write you something good about Themistius, you will show the letter to many, and not a few will say that you are deceived in that. Praising the students even if they are bad is in fact the custom of teachers. 2. I, however, do not write what I know about this young man, but ask you to come yourself to see the rhetoric he has learned.

182 F579 (year 357): To Heortius
1. We are still writing to you since you are away. You should be with us and see not only in letters your son's discourses, but see how many they are, of all forms. 2. I would pay dearly for you to know the Themistius who has come to our school. You would be so surprised at how I changed him and how he has changed.

THE SONS OF THEODORUS 11/III

183 *F1188 (year 364): To Theodorus*
[*Both Clearchus 1 and his father held many offices. Theodorus 11, who had studied rhetoric in Antioch and Roman law at Berytus, had two sons with Libanius: the younger one is mentioned here, and the older appears in Ep. 339 (B62).*]

1. Clearchus surpassed his father in the administration of Asia. The latter was also good and just and thought for the welfare of his subjects, but the intellect of his son is sharper and more capable to see clearly what makes cities prosper. 2. You accompanied him with the intent of teaching but, in my opinion, you became the student. I consider you fortunate because you share in the glory of the measures devised, although the work was due to Clearchus's intellect. 3. As we take thought for the youth you entrusted to us, we are not even neglecting the son whom we have not met yet, since the noble Julianus informed us of the cruelty of his pedagogue and prevented this fellow, who only knows how to thrash, from doing so. This fellow was deterred by the threat of a beating as soon as he saw the whip brought to Julianus. 4. To me, he looks as if he came from a ship and from the sea, but despite being a bad seaman, he looked to you as if he could be a good pedagogue. That is why this abominable man is so good at beating, because he used to beat the sea with an oar. He does not know, however, that the "back of the sea"[90] and that of a child of free birth are not the same, or rather, he knows now that he fears for his own.

DOSSIER OF THEODORUS IV

[*Theodorus's first teacher was the Spartan Nicocles (PLRE I, p. 630). In 363 he went to Constantinople.*]

184 *F831 (year 363): To Modestus 2*
[*Other letters concerning Modestus are 7 and 175.*]

1. Theodorus, the bearer, was born here but is registered where you are, since he has inherited his father's citizenship. He became my student as soon as I became involved with this occupation and imitated my hard work in rhetoric and his brothers' goodwill toward me. 2. His studies gave us the hope that he was going to be very powerful in the courts and was to make money through his voice. In time he came to honor gold instead of copper, and, becoming better, he ceased overestimating that kind of power: he excelled in wisdom, practiced justice, avoided crowds, and loved peace. 3. Now, however, he is coming to you out of

---

[90] "Back of the sea" is found a few times in Homer, e.g., *Iliad* 2.159.

necessity, to which they say the gods also have yielded.⁹¹ Receive this man with kindness and, as would be right for a fellow citizen of mine and for my student, grant him speedy relief in this affair, and if someone tries to commit injustice, oppose him with the laws. It will be most absurd if neither his father nor I will aid him, especially since we have long been held in esteem by you.

185 F832 (year 363): To Nicocles
1. I do not recommend Theodorus to you because you brought him up yourself, nor am I asking you to cherish him, for you have been cherishing this companion long since, but I am writing to you so that you know that you gratify me with the care you give him. 2. If nobody is insolent, you will make him happy in other respects, but if there are people who do this, you will teach them that injustice flees from where excellent Nicocles is.

DOSSIER OF TITIANUS, CALYCIUS, AND PHILOXENUS
[*These students came from Cilicia. Acacius 7/iii was the father of Titianus and of the girl who married Calycius, the son of Hierocles 3/i. Acacius was related to Philoxenus. Iamblichus 2 was another student. Cf. Festugière 1959, 164–79.*]

186 F569 (year 357): To Hierocles
1. Iamblichus himself will tell you why he has come. Evaluate his intention, and if you find it good, help, but if not, change it; for whatever you think will take precedence over his current opinion. This young man is persuaded of two things, that you have a good mind and that you are kindly disposed toward him. Because of both reasons, whatever you consider advantageous will prevail. 2. Calycius is doing one of the things that you asked but could not do the other. He is occupied with the writings of Plato but did not send you any of my speeches; he said that he lacked someone to copy them, but I think that he feared lest any of the things that are unpleasant to us fall into your hands.

187 F346 (year 358): To Hierocles
[*Julianus viii was Calycius's uncle.*]
1. As I was going to school, I met Julianus, who was exhorting Calycius to work hard in rhetoric. He said that he was doing it because you urged him to in a letter. I shared in the admonitions and took part in advice, from which I have never refrained. 2. I believe we are not boil-

---
⁹¹ A proverbial expression, cf. Plato *Prt.* 345d.

ing a stone.⁹² But because he often hears that he is poor because of the righteousness of his father and that rhetoric is the only way to become rich, he must agree with us and obey, and certainly does not need to hear that he must pursue rhetoric. 3. So you must not rebuke him in everything, but you should congratulate him so far as for his eagerness, for this, too, is a charm to promote eagerness.

188 F371 (year 358): To Acacius

1. I really think that you consider me a lover of gold, for you asked Olympius to bring me the money (*statēr*) for the wedding without a letter.⁹³ But he who knew what I feel about gold and about letters and did not receive both handed over the less valuable thing. He brought me, however, something more valuable than any gold: the story of the wedding. It was this, more or less. 2. He said that you were trembling when you were going to show your daughter. This trembling is sweet for a father, and is what he hoped would occur. And when the maiden appeared, she stunned the onlookers especially with the beauty of her eyes, so that there were some who said, "She is like Artemis."⁹⁴ I was pleased when I heard this because her physical beauty rivals that of her soul and because the father of such a maiden is our friend and her husband is our student. 3. When I learned that you were worried about the banquet and because you had promised fish, and that a storm came and from the waves you got more fish than another would from the calm sea, you can imagine how glad I was and how I laughed and said that the groom had received from his mother a land just like that between Corinth and Sicyon,⁹⁵ which did not become the property of the bride because of your generosity. Let Calycius, this Callias,⁹⁶ cease mentioning his poverty now that he owns the best land from either side. 4. "They have chosen both Hera Zygia and Artemis who looses the girdle."⁹⁷ I did not escape a mother's pangs of childbirth mixed with the wedding of the sweetest daughter I have heard of. The offspring (*tiktein*) is a member of my *chorus*, another Herakles, the rival of Titianus. The latter rightly went there to participate in the celebration, but rightly should come back here in order to receive what he did

---

⁹² Cf. Aristophanes *Vesp.* 280.

⁹³ Symmachus 4.14 also testifies to the ancient habit of giving gifts to the guests of a wedding. In *Ep.* 1488, Libanius arranged the marriage of an ex-student; he was like a matchmaker, but he did not want silver, gold, or beautiful clothes—only a letter.

⁹⁴ *Od.* 17.37.

⁹⁵ The coastal plain between Corinth and Sicyon was proverbially fertile, cf. **12**.

⁹⁶ The Athenian Callias, mentioned by Xenophon and Plato, was notorious for his wealth.

⁹⁷ "Hera Zygia": *Orphic Hymns* 36.5.

before. If he has become great in a short time, he will appear greater in a longer time. 5. Do not marvel if I do something novel by seeking after a student, for the nature of this student is novel. Let him hurry back, and let Calycius not tarry, a young man who is going to imitate what his father did; for he will acquire power in the law courts if he applies hard work, which ultimately brings pleasure. 6. He should rightly devote himself to the art; if he obtains first the prize of eloquence, let him hunt eloquence for that at least; one must never acquire it if it is base, but if it is noble, one should always acquire it.

189 F373 (year 358): To Acacius
1. You apologized at length for your anxiety about your daughter, even though I do not believe that anyone reproached you. Olympius did not accuse but announced with pleasure your anxious trembling. 2. May you feel many such fears; may you feel for your sons and son-in-law that fear that you say you often felt for us when we were going to contend in public. 3. I approve your change of mind with regard to the summer. It was not appropriate for Calycius to jump out of the bridal chamber so soon, and Titianus has a teacher close to him, his father himself. 4. You hid the reason for that, but I proclaim it aloud and reject your excuse that spectacles and crowds could be dangerous to a young man. They could perhaps have spoiled another, but Titianus's nature is stronger than the damage that could come from those. 5. But let him stay with good fortune and let him fill himself with the discourses of the ancients, using his father as guide.

190 F380 (year 358): To Hierocles
1. I thought that your silence derived from the fact that you were occupied with something else, and would that it had been so; but now when you mentioned your illness, and your son revealed that it was complicated, I felt totally disheartened. Both of you, however, did well: you wrote, and he said that the danger is avoided. 2. While giving a wife to Calycius, you are wise in wishing to give him rhetoric, too. In this way, he could preserve and increase his patrimony. We have encouraged him to do this and have called him here. And I am asking the Muses to make rhetoric sweet to this young man.

191 F26 (year 358): To Acacius
[*Aristaenetus 1, a friend of Libanius, died in the earthquake and tidal wave of Nicomedia on August 24, 358, together with the father of Calycius. There is a reference to Aristaenetus in* 49.]
1. I am also one of those submerged by that great wave. O Zeus, Aristaenetus is dead, and a second destructive blow befell us, since fate did

not even spare the life of Hierocles. Because of this, we have been and will be silent, at least with the common crowd. My students, in any case, benefit from us in the same way as before. 2. I am pleased that your son and your son-in-law are so enthusiastically occupied with rhetoric and urge on their teacher, without being exhorted; so it will be sufficient for you to write to them the beginning of that verse that says: "Thus now, dear children."[98] I trust that Philoxenus, too, will do what is worthy of his family.

192 F44 (year 358/59): To Acacius

1. I am pleased that you are well and that your Titianus desires to work hard more than others want to be lazy. I do not know whether he partakes of a better teacher than what you were before; but if you say that he must surpass his father's ability, you will soon want your son to grow wings. 2. And he could grow wings like Perseus more easily than surpass his father in rhetoric, for not even that one surpassed Zeus. And this is not a fault of the young man, unless you also indict Hyllus because, even though he was Herakles' son, he did not outshine his father. 3. I also predict the words he will use with you: "I came back with some competence but not your equal, father. If one of those with thick beards and teaching chairs has surpassed your eloquence, punish me for your defeat. But if this is the common plight of those engaged in rhetoric, do not accuse only me among the many who are defeated." 4. If he says these things, "What will we say? What will we tell?" (in the way of Demosthenes, whom you imitate).[99] You, therefore, see what to respond. As for Marcellus, I was convinced right away that he was excellent, for you used to praise him, and with time I found that he proved himself not unworthy of the praises. He follows the young man like a shadow; there is no time when he is not with him. 5. And yet I believe that Titianus would be exactly the same with Marcellus gone as with him present, for I cannot see any difference whether he is constrained by another or by his own will. So the pedagogue would urge on the laziest student, but the love for rhetoric would suffice this lad for a pedagogue. 6. Let Marcellus do what he is doing, and if he does not need to exhort Titianus, still he will praise him. For one who works hard, this is sweeter than honey. 7. I caught a letter of yours in Hermogenes' house in the following way. I entered and stood on his right side; he was reading a letter and was at the end already. I could not see who wrote it, for this was hidden by one of his hands, but fixing my eyes on the shape of the characters, I started to infer that it was

---

[98] *Iliad* 10.192.
[99] Demosthenes *Or.* 8.37.

coming from you. 8. But then he wished to enjoy the letter a second time, and so the name appeared plainly. He made me participate in the reading, and I did so with wonder. When we stopped, Hermogenes turned to a long speech, or rather to a short one, for in relation to your merits its length was short. He was talking about the beginning and growth of your friendship and the rest of the things that one can say about you. He said that he was in grief when you were ill and that he visited you when he could. 9. These are the things that he was saying, and I was listening, and we pleased each other: he pleased me with his story, and I pleased him because I received the story with pleasure.

193 F45 (year 358/59): To Ecdicius ii
[*Ecdicius ii, a Cilician, had been Libanius's schoolmate in Athens and was maternal uncle of Philoxenus.*]

1. I think you are being pressed by your sister, the mother of Philoxenus, to press me. She does the same thing to my uncle through his wife. He urges the same things you write, but in person: that the young man become an orator with us. 2. Tell Philoxenus's mother that, god willing, her son will be such as to satisfy her: he has a willing disposition and a capable nature.

194 F59 (year 359): To Acacius

1. It is a novel kind of theft to announce when one will take away what he is going to steal, and do the stealing afterward. As you are openly grabbing, you say that you are stealing, so that the wrong you do does not seem arbitrary but somewhat cautious. 2. I would keep Titianus no less happily than you summon him, but I am sending him back because everything that you bid must become fact. And I trust that this young man will do that for which he is brought back. You say that you are ill and are robbed of friends, and are looking for consolation from him. 3. He will alleviate your sorrow not only through the pleasure of seeing him—this is common to all sons—but because he brings back some expertise in rhetoric, which you planted but we cultivated. 4. But try to remember the agreement that you have made concerning time, and return the colt to us before summer reaches its end. At all events, pardon us by keeping in mind your own feelings. If you miss your son, we miss a son, too: we both raised him.

195 F60 (year 359): To Acacius

1. Welcome Philoxenus, too, who has shown himself worthy of your family in all respects: he worked very hard and believed that a reputation acquired through good behavior was no less important than one acquired through ability in rhetoric. 2. And yet, when you were think-

ing of sending him to us, you added to the other praises that he would be of the greatest use when it came to fists. But although he confirmed everything else, in this he proved you wrong, since he values peace more than the weak students do. Therefore it is up to you either to punish him for this or to admire this, too.

196 F148 (year 359): To Acacius
1. It was not only Philoxenus who urged on his brother by returning home a better student; Philoxenus's cousin[100] did the same—you know the one I mean, but, even though you know, you do not want to say it. 2. Should Philoxenus and his brother attend your classes because of this second lad, on the assumption that there is nothing so great and good with us as there is with you? And yet Titianus makes progress in rhetoric here, though I see that the treasure he has at home is more beautiful. 3. In any case, tell the mother of the two boys that it is summer here, too, and a moderate wind blows.

197 F121 (year 359): To Acacius
1. You lied, but your son has become better because of the lie, and we see that even in the city of Plato there was room for such a lie.[101] 2. I always yearned to see Titianus but never believed what he said, that in being with his father he was in lesser company, for Machaon would not be, if he were with his father.[102] 3. If I said that this young man's soul has become golden after receiving so many beautiful things, I would be rating gold itself very highly, even, if you wish, gold from Colophon. 4. I wonder what the reading list would have been if summer had given you some breezes, since you accumulated so much in such a stifling heat. When you listed the selections, I was not incredulous, and I have found an improvement in the excellent discourses that Titianus produces. There will be people who will say that they are bad, not a few because of ignorance, but more, I believe, on account of envy.

198 F147 (year 359/60): To Ecdicius ii
1. This young man, Philoxenus, is outstanding in stature, appearance, voice, modesty, and in his pursuit of rhetoric and understanding of how to gain it. 2. When you persuade students to run to us, it is as if you advised them to run to you. You know that, if I look brilliant, you, too, have a good reputation, and if I do not seem too bad a teacher, this would also profit you, in case you choose to teach. People are not

---

[100] "Philoxenus's cousin" refers to Titianus.
[101] Plato *Resp.* 289b.
[102] His father is Asclepius: *Iliad* 4.193–219

unaware of our common studies in Athens. 3. The fact that you actively promote my interests is no wonder, for, since you were young, your life has been advancing the cause of friends. But admitting in a letter that you do this is not in conformity with your timidity but is a work of love, which renders timid people bolder.

199 F190 (year 360): To Acacius
1. Your letter once again was bound to set Titianus in motion, but now it looks as if what they said is true, that you are ill. They said so, but they also said that, god willing, you recovered. You must survive for other reasons, but also because fate blocked many ports to us, and those in which we trust are few. 2. The foremost of these few is the man who is also the foremost in rhetoric. You definitely know who I mean, if you know yourself. 3. Your son has come to relieve you. I sometimes urged him to run, sometimes held him back, the former keeping you in mind and knowing that by appearing he would make you feel more at ease, the latter so that he would learn more. He is one of those who are getting sharpened in the exercises called *meletai* and who have learned a lot in a short time. 4. At any rate, your case prevailed, and I sent you your son as a solace in the present circumstance. He will cure both the father and the teacher in you.

200 F715 (year 362): To Celsus
[*Celsus 3 was a student of Libanius in Nicomedia and had several official posts. Alexander vi was a little-known decurion.*]
1. It is no wonder if one has fallen in love with Attica. The place is by nature very dear to those who have seen it and to those who haven't yet. Fathers think that their sons will bring back from there rhetoric, or at least the reputation of possessing it. 2. Because I respect him, I would praise Acacius even if he should send his son there, but because I love him, I wish he would not send his child. Some of those teachers because of old age would need to sleep peacefully with their bellies full; others would perhaps need teachers themselves to teach them first to settle things with words and not with weapons. 3. Now, however, they hammer out for us soldiers instead of rhetors: I saw many bearing scars from wounds received at the Lyceum. Titianus would probably not be part of them; it is not good for a student to be seen hanging around with those who are in such a frame of mind. 4. Know, therefore, that you are helping both, me and them: me, by not allowing another [teacher] to be honored because of my work; them, if they do not waste a lot of time probably on small details (it is better to put it this way). 5. In addition to preventing that journey, speed up Titianus's journey back to us. Let him come to learn more rhetoric, if he wishes, or, if he

wishes, to use the knowledge he has. The governor will definitely receive this young man with full goodwill. Prudent men, in my view, know how to reap the fruit of an opportunity. 6. Make sure not to overlook this and also free Alexander of a second bond for our sake. Before he has a chance to catch his breath, he is oppressed again; he has just escaped from one wave and he has to wrestle with another. The financial contribution of a man so young is indeed not much lighter than the expenses for the public baths. 7. Assist him in everything, and make sure that this young man is not oppressed by any charge.

201 F719 (year 362): To Acacius
1. You send me messengers who address me orally but have ceased to address me in letters, you especially, who can charm in letters. If you have changed toward me, tell me why; but if you remain the same, do not begrudge me what is better. 2. I know that Titianus will belong to us rather than to those who drink from the spring of Callirhoe,[103] but I just would like to know whether this is your decision or his. He was in tears when he left. This is natural, because he remembers me even when he is with you.

202 F1538 (year 365): To Acacius
1. Titianus wronged two fathers, me and yourself, me by making it appear that I had not written to you even though I did, and you because you did not receive what you should have. 2. He did wrong not only through his carelessness about the letter, but also because he hid what happened. He should not have cured an evil with an evil but with something good. If he had said that the letter had gotten away from him, he would have comforted you with the fact that I had written and would not have made me appear lazy. 3. But his defense will be the saying, "Not to err is divine."[104] The letter that did not come, then, is coming to you now; when you receive it, read little words on important matters.

ZENOBIUS III

203 F170 (year 359/60): To Cyrillus
[*Cyrillus 1 was governor of Palestine. Zenobius iii, a relative of the sophist Zenobius, was from that province.*]
1. Through us, Zenobius beseeches you on behalf of his father. While his father is in Elousa, this young man, who is devoted to friends and

---
[103] Callirhoe is an Athenian spring.
[104] Cf. Dem. *De cor.* 290.1–2.

fierce with enemies, is with us. The care he has for his parents should be a sign to you that he partakes of education. 2. If you hear that he is coming, you will honor his father because of him; but as long as he is away because of rhetoric, do this favor to me.

UNIDENTIFIED STUDENTS

204 F745 (year 362): To Ecdicius
[*Ecdicius ii, cf. 193 and 198. The old man is probably Gaudentius, the father of Silvanus and other children, cf. 165.*]
    1. A friend's children have come to a friend through a friend. Right away I was pleased with them because of their father and also, when some time passed, because of their natural talents. 2. I praise the older for coming late to us, and because he loves you but blames you for not giving him this advice a long time ago. Someone who considers time thrown away a loss will clearly take advantage of the future. 3. Even in this short time he has achieved something, perhaps more than would be expected in the time. Trust me on this, and trust the old man, too. He cares for them no less than his offspring and is a good judge of discourses because he makes them, too. He would not deceive a friend to please a friend.

205 F1245 (year 364): To Zenodorus
[*Zenodorus was governor of Cilicia (*PLRE I, p. 991*).*]
    1. These two young men engaged in rhetoric late and wasted most of the time for rhetoric lying ill in the hands of doctors. They have not yet acquired sufficient rhetorical ability to perform their best in what they have come for. But poverty could force men to do many things. 2. You have the power to relieve it if it should become clear to all that you would not be displeased to see it relieved.

206 F1098 (year 393): Addressee unknown
[*The addressee is not the Jewish Patriarch, because Argeius taught in Pamphylia.*]
    1. Your son has arrived and is able to learn; he had a taste of me even before seeing me through Argeius's rhetorical power. He has not come to anything better, but perhaps seeing many cities has been to his advantage, as it was to Odysseus's.[105] 2. I am asking you to forgive him for running away and not to be angry and leave him without resources. This may bring distress, which we see can be a hindrance even to those who are passionate about rhetoric.

---

[105] A reference to *Od.* 1.3 and 16.63.

APPENDIX TWO

Length of Students' Attendance

I TRY TO VERIFY the attendance only of those students for whom there are some indications in this respect, taking into account all of the students of Libanius, not only those included in Appendix One. In several cases, the length of schooling is uncertain.

THE SON OF ACHILLIUS
He attended for perhaps five years, but one year is not documented.

AGATHIUS
He remained for two years and a few months. He came in the spring of 362 and stayed for that year (362/63) and for the year 363/64, when he left for good.

ALBANIUS AND STRATEGIUS
Albanius remained for two years and Strategius for one because of his father's death.

THE SONS OF AMPHILOCHIUS
In spite of the fact that Amphilochius studied with and was a friend of Libanius, they probably attended for one year only.

ANATOLIUS V
He attended for two years; his father worried he was not learning.

APOLINARIUS AND GEMELLUS
They attended for one year: Libanius says that they stayed for a short time and learned a lot.

ARISTENETUS 2
He had a very short attendance, probably one year, in spite of the fact that he was related to Libanius; cf. *Ep.* 1081.

ARSENIUS
This is a difficult case to judge; perhaps he attended only the two years when he is attested.

BASSUS
He appears to have been with Libanius for only one year. Letter **34** was written not when he left the school, but well afterward.

CAESARIUS III AND EUDOCIUS II
Eudocius left because of his father's death in the course of the third year; his brother stayed, but then must have left at the end of the year.

CALLIOPIUS III
He attended for two and a half years, and then followed his father, who was moving.

CALYCIUS
He attended for three years: in 356/57, and in 357/58; then he got married and arrived late in 358/59. His father died in August. He was there for this third year.

CHRYSOGONUS
He apparently had a very short attendance.

DIONYSIUS II
After three years he was able to write beautiful letters and a panegyric.

DIOPHANTUS III AND HIS BROTHER
The brother dropped out immediately, but Diophantus stayed for at least two years. It is impossible to know if he stayed longer.

THE SONS OF ECDICIUS
They attended for two years. *Ep.* 1419 was written in the fall of the second year.

EPIPHANIUS
He stayed for a little time; we only know that he was still with an assistant when he left.

THE SONS OF EUMATHIUS
They may have remained only one year, since there were difficulties with their father.

THE SONS OF EUSEBIUS X
They remained for one year, two at the maximum.

FAUSTINUS
This student is attested for one year, but he must have had longer training. He was "the best," but he did not stay enough to become a sophist.

Length of Attendance • 325

THE SON OF FLAVIANUS
Libanius thought that he did not stay long enough, but it is impossible to quantify.

GAIUS II
He left after one year because of illness.

GERONTIUS VI
He did not stay long and left in mid-year.

GESSIUS I
He is only mentioned once, in *Ep.* 436 (B29).

THE SONS OF HESYCHIUS
Hesychius had at least three sons of different ages. The two older ones are attested for two years, the other only for one, but perhaps stayed for two.

THE SONS OF HIERIUS
They had a previous instructor. They certainly did not stay for six years, because Libanius never mentioned them in writing to their father. They probably left at a certain point and came back.

HIEROCLES II
Perhaps he remained for five years, but fewer if he quit in between.

HIERON
Strategius iii was a sophist, not Libanius's assistant, so Hieron was probably a student of Libanius for only one year (not for five).

HILARIUS 7
Petit (1956a) calculated two years, but it is impossible to be precise.

HONORATUS II
He studied rhetoric for three years and not four, because he was sick in 357 and 358.

HYPERECHIUS
He was a student in Nicomedia (maybe for a short time), and then in Antioch for six years. His attendance, though, may have been discontinuous.

MARCUS
He stayed less than a year because he wanted a position.

THE SON OF MARCELLINUS
He definitely attended for only one year.

THE SON OF MARIANUS
Petit considers one year of attendance, but he certainly stayed longer, because **141** shows that he took great care for his education.

MENECRATES
He stayed in Antioch for very little time.

METERIUS
He must have withdrawn after one year of attendance, because many letters concerned his application, but then correspondence ceased altogether.

PANDORUS
He remained in Antioch for two years, but his father probably called him back a little before the end of the year without telling Libanius.

THE SONS OF PHILAGRIUS
They did not study with Libanius for four years, as Petit maintains, but only for two. The year 358/59 should not be counted, because in the fall they went to the sophist Acacius, and they came back in the summer. After that, they went home, worked there, and did not attend for 360/61. They came back in the fall of 361.

THE SONS OF PHILIPPUS
They are almost not to be counted as students because they withdrew immediately.

PHILOPATRIS
Petit maintains that he remained for three years, but this is uncertain, because the date of *Ep.* 262 is unsure. He may have attended for less time.

PHILOXENUS
He studied in Antioch for two years only.

THE SONS OF POMPEIANUS
They definitely remained for two years and then left after their father sent a mysterious letter.

SEVERUS 12
He only appears in *Or.* 57. He was withdrawn in the course of the second year.

SOLON
This student is attested in 364 (*Ep.* 1244), when his father pulled him out at the beginning of the year because his brother had died. He probably stayed for a very short time. Libanius says he could have been as good as his brother in rhetoric, but this does not mean that he was there the year before.

THE SON OF STRATONICUS
He must have stayed for one year only, because there are no more letters after those to secure his attendance.

THEMISTIUS III
He studied for two years and was not a good student.

TITIANUS
This student kept going back and forth from Cilicia. If one calculates the time when he was absent, he stayed with Libanius for a little over three years (not five or even eight, as previously calculated).

APPENDIX THREE

Concordance of Letters in Appendix One Translated into English

THE NUMBER after F refers to the numbering of Libanius's letters in Foerster 1903–27. My translations are listed in bold characters with the numbering used in Appendix One. References to translations in Bradbury 2004a (B) are given according to the numbering in that collection.

F24: **48**	F172: **177**	F318: **172**	F579: **182**
F26: **191**	F187: **178**	F319: **53**	F584: **69**
F32: **17**	F190: **199**	F324: **97**	F600: **61**
F41: **18**	F199: **176**	F346: **187**	F601: **62**
F43: **161**	F201: **179**	F355: **1**	F634: **16**
F44: **192**	F211: **21**	F358: **102**	F645: **39**
F45: **193**	F224: **108**	F371: **188**	F646: **40**
F59: **194**	F231: **32**	F373: **189**	F653: **101, B164**
F60: **195**	F233: **20**	F376: **49**	F658: **110**
F63: **7**	F239: **109**	F380: **190**	F666: **82, B77**
F82: **15**	F248: **35**	F406: **149**	F667: **117**
F87: **175**	F249: **36**	F413: **150**	F681: **164**
F89: **162**	F250: **37**	F419: **68**	F693: **34**
F93: **44**	F254: **38**	F426: **52**	F704: **112, B179**
F104: **127**	F259: **165**	F437: **72**	F715: **200, B126**
F117: **156**	F260: **166**	F456: **14**	F719: **201**
F121: **197**	F261: **70**	F465: **60**	F720: **144**
F129: **19**	F262: **99**	F467: **41**	F721: **145**
F131: **163**	F270: **154**	F472: **146**	F728: **4**
F135: **137**	F273: **71**	F474: **147**	F737: **74**
F137: **105**	F285: **128**	F475: **148**	F743: **157**
F139: **2**	F287: **9**	F533: **28, B163**	F745: **204**
F140: **8**	F294: **6**	F534: **151**	F766: **63**
F144: **92**	F300: **103**	F539: **152**	F767: **3**
F145: **135**	F304: **22**	F540: **27**	F768: **168**
F147: **198**	F305: **73**	F542: **65**	F777: **111**
F148: **196**	F310: **104**	F547: **181**	F781: **85**
F155: **31**	F311: **106**	F569: **186**	F782: **86**
F170: **203**	F317: **171**	F570: **107**	F790: **169**

F794: 10
F806: 23
F812: 113
F820: 29
F831: 184
F832: 185
F833: 11
F834: 12
F835: 120
F837: 54
F857: 50
F858: 51
F875: 140
F876: 141
F884: 78
F885: 79
F886: 80
F887: 81
F892: 90
F894: 93
F895: 125
F910: 64
F911: 43

F978: 89
F996: 159
F998: 180
F1003: 142
F1009: 160
F1011: 129
F1012: 130
F1013: 131
F1014: 132
F1020: 133
F1034: 134
F1038: 124
F1071: 136
F1090: 94
F1095: 126
F1098: 206
F1101: 143
F1102: 122
F1105: 83
F1116: 114
F1130: 121
F1141: 42
F1164: 47

F1165: 5, B160
F1168: 55
F1169: 56
F1170: 25, B139
F1171: 26, B166
F1188: 183, B80
F1198: 153
F1208: 45, B140
F1222: 139
F1237: 58
F1238: 57
F1240: 75
F1241: 76
F1242: 77
F1245: 205
F1250: 167
F1261: 119
F1268: 116
F1273: 46
F1293: 33
F1296: 118
F1309: 173
F1335: 123

F1345: 170
F1371: 87
F1391: 88
F1394: 158
F1395: 98
F1403: 95
F1408: 30
F1416: 84
F1444: 13
F1454: 115
F1464: 174
F1470: 59
F1471: 91
F1475: 100
F1500: 66
F1501: 67
F1511: 138
F1538: 202
F1539: 96
F1541: 24
F1544: 155

Select Bibliography

PRIMARY SOURCES

Libanius

Foerster, Richard. 1903–27. *Libanius, Opera.* 12 vols. Leipzig. Reprinted Hildesheim 1963.
Malosse, Pierre-Louis. 2003. *Libanios. Discours LIX.* Paris.
Martin, Jean. 1988. *Libanios: Discours II–X.* Paris.
Martin, Jean, and Paul Petit. 1979. *Libanios Discours Tome I: Autobiographie.* Paris.
Molloy, Margaret E. 1996. *Libanius and the Dancers. Altertumswissenschaftliche Texte und Studien* 31. Hildesheim.
Norman, A. F. 1965. *Libanius' Autobiography (Oration I).* London.
———. 1969–77. *Libanius, Selected Works.* 2 vols. Loeb Classical Library. Cambridge, Mass.
———. 1992. *Libanius: Autobiography and Selected Letters.* 2 vols. Loeb Classical Library. Cambridge, Mass.
Reiske, J. J. 1791. *Libanii sophistae orationes et declamationes.* 4 vols. Altenburg.
Schouler, Bernard. 1973. *Libanios Discours Moraux.* Paris.
Wolf, Joannes Christophorus. 1738. *Libanius, Epistulae.* Amsterdam.

Other Primary Sources

BASIL OF CAESAREA:
Courtonne, Yves. 1957. *Saint Basile, Lettres.* 3 vols. Paris.
Wilson, N. G. 1975. *Saint Basil on Greek Literature.* London. (*Ad adulescentes.*)

JOHN CHRYSOSTOM:
Schatkin, Margaret A. 1990. *Discours sur Babylas. Sources chrétiennes* 362. Paris.

EUNAPIUS OF SARDIS:
Blockley, R. C. 1981–82. *Eunapius, Historiae fragmenta.* In *The Fragmentary Classicising Historians of the Later Roman Empire.* Liverpool.
Giangrande, Giuseppe. 1956. *Vitae sophistarum.* Rome.
Wright, Wilmer C. 1921. *Eunapius, Lives of the Philosophers and Sophists.* Loeb Classical Library. Cambridge, Mass.

GREGORY OF NAZIANZUS:
Bernardi, Jean. 1992. *Grégoire de Nazianze, Discours 42–43.* Paris.
Gallay, Paul. 2003. *Saint Grégoire de Nazianze, Correspondence.* 2 vols. Paris.
Tuilier, André, Guillaume Bady, and Jean Bernardi. 2004. *Saint Grégoire de Nazianze oeuvres poétiques* I. Paris.

White, Carolinne. 1996. *Gregory of Nazianzus, Autobiographical Poems*. Cambridge.

HIMERIUS:
Colonna, Aristide. 1951. *Himerii declamationes et orationes*. Rome.
Dübner, F. 1849. *Himerii sophistae declamationes*. Paris.

JULIAN:
Bidez, J. 1934. *L'empereur Julien, oeuvres completes*. Vol. 1.2. Paris.

IOANNES MALALAS:
Thurn, Ioannes. 2000. *Ioannis Malalae Chronographia*. Berlin.

MARINUS:
Saffrey, H. D., and A.-P. Segonds, eds. 2001. *Vita Procli*. Paris.

SOCRATES SCHOLASTICUS:
Hansen, G. C. 1995. *Sokrates: Kirchengeschichte. Die griechischen christlichen Schriftsteller der ersten Jahrhunderte,* n.s. 1. 2d ed. Berlin.

SOZOMEN:
Bidez, J. 1960. *Sozomenus: Kirchengeschichte. Die griechischen christlichen Schriftsteller der ersten Jahrhunderte*. Rev. G. C. Hansen. *GCS,* n.s. 4, 2d ed. (1995).

THEMISTIUS:
Schenkl, H., G. Downey, and A. F. Norman. 1965–74. *Themistii Orationes quae supersunt*. Leipzig.

Secondary Sources

Adams, J. N. 2003. *Bilingualism and the Latin Language*. Cambridge.
Adams, J. N., Mark Jansen, and Simon Swain, eds. 2002. *Bilingualism in Ancient Society*. Oxford.
Alonso-Núñez, J. M. 1979. "The Emperor Julian's *Misopogon* and the Conflict between Christianity and Paganism." *AncSoc* 10:311–24.
Amelotti, Mario. 1995. "Massime, glosse e compilazioni giuridiche in età tardoantica." In Moreschini 1995, 31–37.
Amirault, Chris. 1995. "The Good Teacher, the Good Student: Identification of a Student Teacher." In Gallop 1995, 64–78.
Anderson, Graham. 1976. "Lucian's Classics: Some Short Cuts to Culture." *BICS* 23:59–68.
———. 1978. "Patterns in Lucian's Quotations." *BICS* 25:97–100.
Athanassiadi, Polymnia. 1981. *Julian and Hellenism: An Intellectual Biography*. Oxford.
———. 1999. *Damascius, the Philosophical History*. Apamea, Greece.

Bagnall, Roger S., ed. Forthcoming. *Egypt in the Byzantine World: A.D. 300–700. Dumbarton Oaks Papers.*
Baldwin, Barry. 1973. *Studies in Lucian.* Toronto.
Balty, Janine. 2004. "Les mosaïques d'Antioche: Style et rayonnement." In Cabouret, Gatier, and Saliou 2004, 257–69.
Balty, Jean C. 1972. "Mosaïques païennes à Apamée de Syrie." *CRAI*: 103–27.
Banchich, T. 1993. "Julian's School Laws: *Cod. Theod.* 13.3.5 and *Ep.* 42." *AncW* 24:5–14.
Baratte, François. 1978. *Catalogue des mosaïques romaines et paléochrétiennes du musée du Louvre.* Paris.
Barnes, T. D. 1973. "More Missing Names (A.D. 260–395)." *Phoenix* 27.2: 135–55.
———. 1987. "Himerius and the Fourth Century." *CP* 82:206–25.
Barr, William. 1981. *Claudian's Panegyric on the Fourth Consulate of Honorius.* Liverpool.
Baslez, Marie-Françoise, Philippe Hoffmann, and Laurent Pernot, eds. 1993. *L'invention de l'autobiographie d'Hésiode à Saint Augustin. Études de litterature ancienne 5.* Paris.
Bassett, Sarah. 2004. *The Urban Image of Late Antique Constantinople.* Cambridge.
Beaucamp, Joëlle. 1990–92. *Le statut de la femme à Byzance.* 2 vols. Paris.
Becker, Carl L. 1959. "What Are Historical Facts?" In Meyerhoff 1959, 120–37.
Behr, Charles A. 1968. *Aelius Aristides and the Sacred Tales.* Amsterdam.
———. 1994. "Studies on the Biography of Aelius Aristedes." In *ANRW* II 34.2:1140–1233.
Benedetti, Isabella. 1981. "Giuliano in Antiochia nell'orazione XVIII di Libanio." *Athenaeum,* n.s. 59:166–79.
Benjamin, Walter. 1992. "The Task of the Translator." In Schulte and Biguenet 1992, 71–82.
Bernardi, Jean. 1984. "Grégoire de Nazianze et le poète comique Anaxilas." *Pallas* 31:157–61.
———. 1990. "Un regard sur la vie étudiante à Athènes au milieu du IVe S. après J.-C." *RÉG* 103:79–94.
Bidez, J. 1919. "Le philosophe Iamblique et son école." *RÉG* 32:29–40.
———. 1965. *La vie de l'empereur Julien.* 2d ed. Paris.
Binns, J. W. 1974. *Latin Literature of the Fourth Century.* London.
Bonner, Campbell. 1932. "Witchcraft in the Lecture Room of Libanius." *TAPhA* 63:34–44.
Bonner, Stanley F. 1977. *Education in Ancient Rome.* Berkeley.
Booth, Alan D. 1979a. "Elementary and Secondary Education in the Roman Empire." *Florilegium* 1:1–14.
———. 1979b. "The Schooling of Slaves in First-Century Rome." *TAPhA* 109:11–19.
———. 1983. À quel age Libanius est-il entré à l'école du rhéteur?" *Byzantion* 53:157–63.
Bouché-Leclercq, A. 1909. *La revue de Paris* (15 June):741–63.
Bouchery, Herman F. 1936. *Themistius in Libanius' Brieven.* Gand.

Bouffartigue, Jean. 1992. *L'Empereur Julien et la culture de son temps*. Paris.
Boulanger, André. 1923. *Aelius Aristide et la sophistique dans la province d'Asie au IIe siècle de notre ère*. Paris. (Reprinted 1968.)
Bouquiaux-Simon, Odette. 1968. *Les lectures homériques de Lucien*. Académie royale de Belgique, Mémoires 59, fasc. 2. Brussels.
Bourdieu, Pierre, and Jean-Claude Passeron. 2000. *Reproduction in Education, Society, and Culture*. London.
Bowersock, Glen W. 1969. *Greek Sophists in the Roman Empire*. Oxford.
———. 1978. *Julian the Apostate*. Cambridge, Mass.
———. 1983. Review of P. Athanassiadi-Fowden: *Julian and Hellenism, an Intellectual Biography*. CR 33:81–83.
———. 1990. *Hellenism in Late Antiquity*. Ann Arbor.
———. 2000a. *Selected Papers on Late Antiquity*. Bari.
———. 2000b. "The Syriac Life of Rabbula and Syrian Hellenism." In Hägg and Rousseau 2000, 255–71.
———. 2002. "Chalcis ad Belum and Anasartha in Byzantine Syria." *TravMém* 14:47–55.
Bowersock, G. W., P. Brown, and O. Grabar. 1999. *Late Antiquity: A Guide to the Postclassical World*. Cambridge, Mass.
Bowie, Ewen L. 1989a. "Greek Sophists and Greek Poetry in the Second Sophistic." *ANRW* II 33.1:209–58.
———. 1989b. "Poetry and Poets in Asia and Achaia." In Walker and Cameron 1989, 198–205.
———. 1990. "Greek Poetry in the Antonine Age." In Russell 1990a, 53–90.
Boyer, Ernest L. 1987. *The Undergraduate Experience in America*. New York.
Bradbury, Scott. 2000. "A Sophistic Prefect: Anatolius of Berytus in the *Letters* of Libanius." *CP* 95.2:172–86.
———. 2004a. *Selected Letters of Libanius from the Age of Constantius and Julian*. Liverpool.
———. 2004b. "Libanius' Letters as Evidence for Travel and Epistolary Networks among Greek Elites in the Fourth Century." In Ellis and Kidner 2004, 73–80.
Branham, R. B. 1989. *Unruly Eloquence: Lucian and the Comedy of Traditions*. Cambridge, Mass.
Bringmann, Klaus. 2004. *Kaiser Julian: Der letzte heidnische Herrscher*. Darmstadt.
Brown, Peter. 1978. *The Making of Late Antiquity*. Cambridge, Mass.
———. 1992. *Power and Persuasion in Late Antiquity*. Madison, Wis.
Browning, Robert. 1997. "Teachers." In Cavallo 1997, 95–116.
Bruggisser, Philippe. 1990. "Libanios, Symmaque et son père Avianius." *AncSoc* 21:17–31.
Brunt, Peter A. 1994. "The Bubble of the Second Sophistic." *BICS* 39:25–52.
Cabouret, Bernadette. 2000. *Libanios: Lettres aux hommes de son temps*. Paris.
———. 2001. "Correspondance et société dans l'empire romain tardif: Libanios au service de ses proches." In Sohn 2001, 15–27.
———. 2002. "Le gouverneur au temps du Libanios, image et réalité." *Pallas* 60:191–204.

———. 2004. "Pouvoir municipal, pouvoir imperial à Antioche au IVe siècle." In Cabouret, Gatier, and Saliou 2004, 117–42.
Cabouret, Bernadette, Pierre-Louis Gatier, and Catherine Saliou. 2004. *Antioche de Syrie: Histoire, images et traces de la ville antique. Topoi*, suppl. 5.
Cadiou, R. 1966. "Le problème des relations scolaires entre Saint Basile et Libanios." *RÉG* 79:89–98.
Calder, William M. III. 1960. "On the Silence of Socrates, an Interpretation." *GRBS* 3:197–202.
Cameron, Alan. 1964. "Palladas and the Fate of Gessius." *ByzZeit* 57:279–92.
———. 1965. "Wandering Poets: A Literary Movement in Byzantine Egypt." *Historia* 14:470–509.
———. 1967a. "Iamblichus at Athens." *Athenaeum* 45:143–53.
———. 1967b. "Two Notes on the Greek Anthology (*Anth. Pal.* ix.474, 395, and 458)." *BICS* 14:58–61.
———. 1982. "The Empress and the Poet." *YCS* 27:217–89.
———. 1995. *Callimachus and His Critics*. Princeton.
———. 2004a. *Greek Mythography in the Roman World*. Oxford.
———. 2004b. "Poetry and Literary Culture in Late Antiquity." In Swain and Edwards 2004, 327–54.
Cameron, Alan, and Jacqueline Long. 1993. *Barbarians and Politics at the Court of Arcadius*. Berkeley.
Cameron, Averil. 1991. *Christianity and the Rhetoric of Empire*. Berkeley.
———. 1993. *The Later Roman Empire*. Cambridge, Mass.
———. 1998. "Education and Literary Culture." In Cameron and Garnsey 1998, 665–707.
Cameron, Averil, and P. Garnsey, eds. 1998. *The Cambridge Ancient History*. Vol. 13, *The Late Empire: 337–425*. Cambridge.
Casana, Jesse. 2004. "The Archaeological Landscape of Late Roman Antioch." In Sandwell and Huskinson 2004, 102–25.
Cavallo, Guglielmo, ed. 1997. *The Byzantines*. Chicago.
Cavallo, Guglielmo, Paolo Fedeli, and Andrea Giardina, eds. 1990. *Lo spazio letterario di Roma antica*. Vol. 3. Rome.
Cecconi, Giovanni Alberto. 2002. *Commento storico al libro II dell'Epistolario di Q. Aurelio Simmaco*. Pisa.
Chausson, François, and Étienne Wolff, eds. 2003. *Consuetudinis amor: Fragments d'histoire romaine (IIe–VIe siècles) offerts à Jean-Pierre Callu*. Rome.
Chéhab, Maurice. 1958–59. *Mosaïques du Liban. Bulletin du Musée de Beyrouth* 14–15. Paris.
Clark, E. 1979. *Jerome, Chrysostom, and Friends*. New York.
Clarke, Martin Lowther. 1971. *Higher Education in the Ancient World*. London.
Collinet, Paul. 1925. *Histoire de l'école de droit de Beyrouth*. Paris.
Colonna, A. 1951. *Himerii declamationes et orationes*. Rome.
Conybeare, Catherine. 2000. *Paulinus Noster: Self and Symbols in the Letters of Paulinus of Nola*. Oxford.
Constable, Giles. 1976. *Letters and Letter-Collections. Typologie des sources du moyen age occidental* 17. Turnhout.

Constantinides, C. N. 2003. "Teachers and Students of Rhetoric in the Late Byzantine Period." In Jeffreys 2003, 39–53.
Cracco Ruggini, Lellia. 1971. "Sofisti Greci nell'Impero Romano." *Athenaeum*, n.s. 49:402–25.
———. 1987. "*Felix temporum reparatio*: Realtà socio-economiche in movimento durante un ventennio di regno (Costanzo II Augusto, 337–361 D.C." *Entretiens sur l'antiquité classique* 34:179–249.
———. 1996. "Libanio e il camaleonte: Politica e magia ad Antiochia sul finire del IV secolo." In Gabba, Desideri, and Roda 1996, 159–66.
———. 2003. "Iatrosofistica pagana, 'filosofia' cristiana e medicina (IV–VI secolo)." In Chausson and Wolff 2003, 189–216.
Cribiore, Raffaella. 1996. *Writing, Students, and Teachers in Greco-Roman Egypt*. Atlanta.
———. 1999. "Greek and Coptic Education in Late Antique Egypt." In *Ägypten und Nubien in spätantiker und christlicher Zeit: Akten des 6. Internationalen Koptologenkongresses*, ed. S. Emmel et al., 2:279–86. Wiesbaden.
———. 2001. *Gymnastics of the Mind: Greek Education in Hellenistic and Roman Egypt*. Princeton.
———. 2003. "Libanius's Letters of Evaluation of Students." *L'épistolographie et la poésie épigrammatique. Actes de la 16e table ronde du XXe Congrès international des Études Byzantines*: 11–20. Paris.
———. 2004. Review of Bradbury 2004a. *BMCR* 2004.7.45.
———. Forthcoming a. "The Value of a Good Education: Libanius and Public Authority." In Rousseau forthcoming.
———. Forthcoming b. "Higher Education in Early Byzantine Egypt: Rhetoric, Latin, and the Law." In Bagnall forthcoming.
———. Forthcoming c. "Spaces for Teaching in Late Antiquity." In Tomasz Derda, Tomasz Markiewicz, and Ewa Wipszycka, eds., *Alexandria: The Auditoria of Kom el-Dikka and Late Antique Education. Journal of Juristic Papyrology* suppl.
———. Forthcoming d. "The School of Alexandria and the Rivalry between Rhetoric and Philosophy." In I. Perczel and R. Forrai, eds., *Late Antique Alexandria*.
———. Forthcoming e. "Latin Literacy." In *Proceedings of the International Symposium on the Ancient Mediterranean, KODAI*.
———. Forthcoming f. "P.Col. inv. 179c2." In *Proceedings of the 24*[th] *International Congress of Papyrology*.
Dagron, Gilbert. 1968. *L'empire romain d'orient au IVè siècle et les traditions politiques de l'hellénisme: Le témoignage de Thémistios. TravMém* 3:1–242.
———. 1969. "Aux origines de la civilization byzantine: Langue de culture et langue d'état." *RHist* 241:23–56.
Dalven, Rae, trans. 1976. *The Complete Poems of Cavafy*. San Diego.
De Vries-Van der Velden, Eva. 2003. "The Letters of Michael Psellos, Historical Knowledge and the Writing of History." In *L'épistolographie et la poésie épigrammatique. Actes de la 16è table ronde du XXè Congrès international des Études Byzantines*, pp. 121–35. Paris.
Demoen, Kristoffel. 1993. "The Attitude towards Greek Poetry in the Verse of Gregory Nazianzen." In Den Boeft and Hilorst 1993, 235–52.

Den Boeft, J, and A. Hilorst, eds. 1993. *Early Christian Poetry: A Collection of Essays.* Leiden.
Dickey, Eleanor. 1996. *Greek Forms of Address.* Oxford.
Downey, Glanville. 1961. *A History of Antioch in Syria: From Seleucus to the Arab Conquest.* Princeton.
———. 1963. *Ancient Antioch.* Princeton.
Dummer, Jürgen, and Meinolf Vielberg, eds. 2003. *Leitbild Wissenschaft?* Wiesbaden.
Edwards, Michael, and Christopher Reid. 2002. "Introduction." In idem, eds., *Oratory in Action*, pp. 1–10. Manchester.
Ellis, Linda, and Frank L. Kidner, eds. 2004. *Travel, Communication and Geography in Late Antiquity.* Burlington, Vt.
Ellis, Simon. 2004. "The Seedier Side of Antioch." In Sandwell and Huskinson 2004, 126–33.
Elm, Susanna. 2001. "Orthodoxy and the True Philosophical Life: Julian and Gregory of Nazianzus." *Studia Patristica* 37:69–85.
Evans-Grubbs, Judith. 1989. "Abduction Marriage in Antiquity: A Law of Constantine (*CTh* IX.24.1) and Its Social Context." *JRS* 79:59–83.
Fabricius, Caius. 1962. *Zu den Jugendschriften des Johannes Chrysostomos. Untersuchungen zum Klassizismus des vierten Jahrhunderts.* Lund.
Fargues, Pierre. 1933. *Claudien: Études sur sa poésie et son temps.* Paris.
Fatouros, G., and T. Krischer. 1980. *Libanios, Briefe.* Munich.
———, eds. 1983. *Libanios.* Darmstadt.
Fedwick, P. J., ed. 1981a. *Basil of Caesarea: Christian, Humanist, Ascetic: A Sixteen-Hundredth Anniversary Symposium.* 2 vols. Toronto.
———. 1981b. "A Chronology of the Life and Works of Basil of Caesarea." In Fedwick 1981a, 1:3–19.
Festugière, A. J. 1959. *Antioche païenne et chrétienne.* Paris.
Foerster, Richard. 1897. "Antiochia am Orontes." *Jahrbuch des kaiserlichen deutschen Archäologischen Instituts* 12:103–49.
Fögen, Thorsten. 2000. *Patrii sermonis egestas: Einstellungen lateinischer Autoren zu ihrer Muttersprache. Ein Beitrag zum Sprachbewusstsein in der römischen Antike.* Beiträge zur Altertumskunde 150. Munich.
Foss, C. 1977. "Late Antique and Byzantine Ankara." *DOP* 31:29–87.
Fowden, Garth. 1977. "The Platonist Philosopher and His Circle in Late Antiquity." *Philosophia* 7: 359–83.
———. 1982. "The Pagan Holy Man in Late Antique Society." *JHS* 102:33–59.
Fowler, A. 1982. *Kinds of Literature: An Introduction to the Theory of Genres and Modes.* Oxford.
Frantz, Alison. 1988. *Late Antiquity: A.D. 267–700. The Athenian Agora* 24. Princeton.
Gabba, Emilio, Paolo Desideri, and Sergio Roda, eds. 1996. *Italia sul Baetis: Studi di storia romana in memoria di Fernando Gascó.* Turin.
Gallay, Paul. 1943. *La vie de Saint Grégoire de Nazianze.* Lyon.
Gallop, Jane, ed. 1995. *Pedagogy: The Question of Impersonation.* Bloomington, Ind.

Garzya, Antonio, and Denis Roques. 2000. *Synésios de Cyrène: Correspondance.* Paris.
Giangrande, Giuseppe. 1953–54. "On the 'Recensio Lacapeniana' of Eunapius' *Vitae sophistarum.*" *Bulletin of the John Rylands Library* 36:386–94.
———. 1956. "Caratteri stilistici delle *Vitae sophistarum* di Eunapio." *Bollettino del Comitato per la preparazione dell'edizione nazionale dei classici greci e latini* 4:59–70.
Gibbon, Edward. 1946. *The Decline and Fall of the Roman Empire.* Ed. J. B. Bury. 3 vols. New York.
Gibson, Craig A. 1999. "The Agenda of Libanius' Hypotheses to Demosthenes." *GRBS* 40:171–202.
Gill, Christopher, Norman Postlethwaite, and Richard Seaford, eds. 1998. *Reciprocity in Ancient Greece.* Oxford.
Gleason, Maud W. 1986. "Festive Satire: Julian's *Misopogon* and the New Year at Antioch." *JRS* 76:106–119.
Goltz, Andreas, Andreas Luther, and Heinrich Schlange-Schöningen. 2002. *Gelehrte in der Antike.* Köln.
Gonzalez Galvez, Angel. 2005. *Libanio, Cartas, libros I–V.* Madrid.
Gould, Stephen Jay. 1981. *The Mismeasure of Man.* New York.
Goulet, Richard. 2000. "Prohérésius le païen et quelques remarques sur la chronologie d'Eunape de Sardes." *Antiquité Tardive* 8:209–22.
Graff, Gerald. 2003. *Clueless in Academy.* New Haven, Ct.
Gregorian, Vartan. 2004. "Colleges Must Reconstruct the Unity of Knowledge." *The Chronicle of Higher Education* (June 4): B12–14.
Gruenbart, Michael. 2005. *Formen der Anrede im byzantinischen Brief vom 6. bis zum 12. Jahrhundert.* Wiener byzantinische Studien 25. Vienna.
Hägg, Tomas, and Philip Rousseau, eds. 2000. *Greek Biography and Panegyric in Late Antiquity.* Berkeley.
Halporn, Barbara, C. 2000. *The Correspondence of Johann Amerbach.* Ann Arbor.
Hanfmann, George M.A. 1951. "Socrates and Christ." *HSCP* 60:205–33.
Harries, Jill D. 1999. *Law and Empire in Late Antiquity.* Cambridge.
Haubold, Johannes, and Richard Miles. 2004. "Communality and Theatre in Libanius's Oration LXIV." In Sandwell and Huskinson 2004, 24–34.
Hauschild, W.-D. 1993. *Basilius von Caesarea: Briefe, Dritter Teil.* Bibliothek der griechischen Literatur, Abteilung Patristik 37. Stuttgart.
Haverling, Gerd. 1988. *Studies on Symmachus' Language and Style.* Göteborg.
Heath, Malcolm. 1995. *Hermogenes on Issues: Strategies of Argument in Later Greek Rhetoric.* Oxford.
———. 2002a. *Interpreting Classical Texts.* London.
———. 2002b. "Practical Advocacy in Roman Egypt." In Michael Edwards and Christopher Reid, eds., *Oratory in Action*, pp. 62–82. Manchester.
———. 2002–3. "Theon and the History of the Progymnasmata." *GRBS* 43: 129–60.
———. 2003. "Pseudo-Dionysius *Art of Rhetoric* 8–11: Figured Speech, Declamation, and Criticism." *AJP* 124:81–105.
———. 2004. *Menander: A Rhetor in Context.* Oxford.

Heather, Peter. 1998. "Themistius: A Political Philosopher." In Whitby 1998, 125–50.
Heather, Peter, and David Moncur. 2001. *Politics, Philosophy, and Empire in the Fourth Century: Select Orations of Themistius.* Liverpool.
Heitsch, E. 1961. *Die griechischen Dichterfragmente der römischen Kaiserzeit.* Göttingen.
Hembold, William C., and Edward N. O'Neil. 1959. *Plutarch's Quotations.* American Philological Association Monographs. Atlanta.
Henck, Nick. 2001. "Constantius' *Paideia*, Intellectual Milieu and Promotion of the Liberal Arts." *PCPS* 47:172–87.
Henry, René. 1960. *Photius, Bibliothèque.* Paris.
Hernadi, Paul. 1972. *Beyond Genre: New Directions in Literary Classification.* Ithaca, N.Y.
Hezser, Catherine. 2001. *Jewish Literacy in Roman Palestine.* Tübingen.
Householder, Fred Walter. 1941. *Literary Quotation and Allusion in Lucian.* New York.
Hunt, David. 1998. "Julian." In Cameron and Garnsey 1998, 44–77.
Hunter, David G. 1988. "Borrowings from Libanius in the *Comparatio Regis et Monachi* of St John Chrysostom." *JThS* 39:525–31.
Hunger, Herbert. 1981. "The Classical Tradition in Byzantine Literature: The Importance of Rhetoric." In Mullett and Scott 1981, 35–47.
Huskinson, Janet. 2004. "Surveying the Scene: Antioch Mosaic Pavements as a Source of Historical Evidence." In Sandwell and Huskinson 2004, 134–52.
Imber, Margaret. 2001. "Practised Speech: Oral and Written Conventions in Roman Declamation." In Watson 2001, 199–216.
Innes, Doreen, and Michael Winterbottom. 1988. *Sopatros the Rhetor. BICS,* suppl. 48.
Izenberg, Gerald N. 1993. "Text, Context, and Psychology in Intellectual History." In Kozicki 1993, 40–62.
Jolowicz, H. J. 1952. *Historical Introduction to the Study of Roman Law.* Cambridge.
Jauss, Hans Robert. 1971. "Literary History as a Challenge to Literary Theory." *New Literary History* 2:7–37.
Jeffreys, Elizabeth, ed. 2003. *Rhetoric in Byzantium.* Burlington, Vt.
Jones, A.H.M. 1949. "The Roman Civil Service (Clerical and Sub-Clerical Grades)." *JRS* 39:38–55.
———. 1973. *The Later Roman Empire, 284–602.* Oxford.
Jones, A.H.M., J. R. Martindale, and J. Morris. 1971. *The Prosopography of the Later Roman Empire.* Vol. 1. Cambridge. (Abbreviated as *PLRE* I.)
Jones, C. P. 1986. *Culture and Society in Lucian.* Cambridge, Mass.
Jones Hall, Linda. 2004. *Roman Berytus: Beirut in Late Antiquity.* London.
Karlin-Hayter, Patricia. 1992. "Further Notes on Byzantine Marriage: *Raptus*—ἁρπαγή or μνηστεῖαι?" *DOP* 46:133–51.
Kaster, R. A. 1983. "The Salaries of Libanius." *Chiron* 13:37–59.
———. 1988. *Guardians of Language: The Grammarian and Society in Late Antiquity.* Berkeley.
———. 1995. *C. Suetonius Tranquillus De grammaticis et rhetoribus.* Oxford.

Kelly, Christopher. 2004. *Ruling the Later Roman Empire*. Cambridge, Mass.
Kelly, J.N.D. 1995. *Golden Mouth: The Story of John Chrysostom—Ascetic, Preacher, Bishop*. Ithaca, N.Y.
Kennedy, George A. 1972. *The Art of Rhetoric in the Roman World*. Princeton.
———. 1981. "The Classical Tradition in Rhetoric." In Mullett and Scott 1981, 20–34.
———. 1983. *Greek Rhetoric under Christian Emperors*. Princeton.
———. 2000. *Progymnasmata: Greek Textbooks of Prose Composition Introductory to the Study of Rhetoric*. Fort Collins, Colo.
———. 2003. "Some Recent Controversies in the Study of Later Greek Rhetoric." *AJP* 124:295–301.
Kindstrand, Jan Fredrik. 1973. *Homer in der Zweiten Sophistik*. Uppsala.
Kondoleon, Christine, ed. 2000a. *Antioch the Lost Ancient City*. Princeton.
———. 2000b. "Mosaics of Antioch." In Kondoleon 2000a, 63–77.
Konstan, David. 1996. "Greek Friendship." *AJP* 117:71–94.
———. 1997. *Friendship in the Classical World*. Cambridge.
Kozicki, Henry, ed. 1993. *Developments in Modern Historiography*. New York.
Kugener, M. A., ed. 1903. Zacharias Scholasticus, *Vita Severi*. Patrologia Orientalis II fasc. 1. Paris.
Lassus, Jean. 1977. "La ville d'Antioche à l'époque romaine d'après l'archéologie." *ANWR* II.8:54–102.
Labriola, Isabella. 1974. "I due autoritratti di Giuliano imperatore." *Belfagor* 29:547–60.
Laube, A. 1913. "De litterarum Libanii et Basilii commercio." Diss., Breslau.
Lemerle, Paul. 1986. *Byzantine Humanism*. Trans. Helen Lindsay and Ann Moffatt. Canberra.
Lenski, Noel. 2002. *Failure of Empire: Valens and the Roman State in the Fourth Century A.D.* Berkeley.
Leonhardt, David. 2004. "As Wealthy Fill Top Colleges, Concerns Grow over Fairness." *The New York Times*, April 22: A1 and 21.
Levi, Doro. 1947. *Antioch Mosaic Pavements*. Princeton.
Levine, Lee I., ed. 1992. *The Galilee in Late Antiquity*. Cambridge, Mass.
Liebeschuetz, J.H.W.G. 1972. *Antioch: City and Imperial Administration in the Later Roman Empire*. Oxford.
———. 1990. *Barbarians and Bishops: Army, Church, and State in the Age of Arcadius and Chrysostom*. Oxford.
———. 2004. "Malalas on Antioch." In Cabouret, Gatier, and Saliou 2004, 143–53.
Lieu, Samuel N.C. 2004. "Libanius and Higher Education at Antioch." In Sandwell and Huskinson 2004, 13–23.
Lizzi, Rita. 1990. "La memoria selettiva." In Cavallo, Fedeli, and Giardina 1990, 647–76.
Long, Jacqueline. 1996. *In Eutropium: Or, How, When, and Why to Slander a Eunuch*. Chapel Hill, N.C.
Luchner, Katharina. 2004. *Philiatroi. Studien zum Thema der Krankheit in der griechischen Literatur der Kaiserzeit*. Hypomnemata 156. Gottingen.

Maas, Michael. 2000. "People and Identity in Roman Antioch." In Kondoleon 2000a, 13–21.
MacCoull, L.S.B. 2004. "Phaëthon in Dioscorus of Aphrodito." *GRBS* 44: 93–106.
MacMullen, Ramsay. 1990. *Changes in the Roman Empire*. Princeton.
Malherbe, Abraham, J. 1988. *Ancient Epistolary Theorists*. Atlanta.
Malosse, Pierre-Louis. 2000. "Sans mentir (ou presque): La dissimulation des faits gênants dans la rhétorique de l'éloge, d'après l'example des discourse royaux de Libanios." *Rhetorica* 18:243–63.
———. 2004. "Antioche et le kappa." In Cabouret, Gatier, and Saliou 2004, 77–96.
Maltomini, Franco. 2004. "Libanio, il camaleonte, un papiro e altri testi." *ZPE* 147:147–53.
Maraval, P. 1990. *Grégoire de Nysse: Lettres*. SChr. 363. Paris.
Marinescu, Constantin A., Sarah E. Cox, and Rudolf Wachter. 2005. "Walking and Talking among Us: Personifications in a Group of Late Antique Mosaics." In Hélène Morlier, ed., *La Mosaïque Gréco-Romaine*, 2:1269–76. Rome.
Markopoulos, Athanasios. 2000. *Anonymi professoris epistulae*. Berlin.
Marrou, H. I. 1975. *Histoire de l'éducation dans l'antiquité*. 7th ed. Paris.
Martindale, J. R. 1980. *The Prosopography of the Later Roman Empire*. Vol. 2. Cambridge. (Abbreviated as *PLRE* II.)
Massa Positano, Lidia. 1962. *Enea di Gaza: Epistole*. 2d ed. Naples.
Matthews, John. 1974. "The Letters of Symmachus." In Binns 1974, 58–99.
———. 1989. *The Roman Empire of Ammianus*. London.
McCloskey, Deirdre. 2002. "The Random Insanity of Letters of Recommendation." *The Chronicle of Higher Education* (March 1): B14–15.
McLynn, Neil. Forthcoming. "Disciplines of Discipleship in Late Antique Education: Augustine and Gregory Nazianzen."
McNamee, Kathleen. 1998. "Another Chapter in the History of Scholia." *CQ* 48:269–88.
Merkelbach, Reinhold, and Josef Stauber. 1998–2002. *Steinepigramme aus dem griechischen Osten*, vols. 1–4. München.
Meredith, Anthony. 1995. *The Cappadocians*. London.
Meyerhoff, Hans, ed. 1959. *The Philosophy of History in Our Time*. New York.
Michaels, Walter Benn. 2004. "Diversity's False Solace." *The New York Times Magazine* (April 11): 12 and 14.
Milazzo, Antonino M. 1996. "L'elogio della retorica nell'*Antiochicus* di Libanio." *Cassiodorus* 2:73–97.
Millar, Fergus. 1971. "Paul of Samosata, Zenobia and Aurelian: The Church, Local Culture, and Political Allegiance in Third-Century Syria." *JRS* 61:1–17.
Miller, Rodney K., and Gregory J. Van Rybroek. 1988. "Internship Letters of Recommendation: Where Are the Other 90%?" *Professional Psychology: Research and Practice* 19:115–17.
Mitchell, S. 1993. *Anatolia: Land, Men, and Gods in Asia Minor*. Oxford.
Mommsen, T., and P. Krueger, eds. 1985. *The Digest of Justinian*. Philadelphia.
Montiglio, Silvia. 2000. *Silence in the Land of Logos*. Princeton.

Moreschini, Claudio. 1994. "Elio Aristide tra retorica e filosofia." *ANRW* II 34.2:1234–43.

———, ed. 1995. *Esegesi, parafrasi e compilazione in età tardoantica.* Naples.

Morgan, Teresa. 1998. *Literate Education in the Hellenistic and Roman Worlds.* Cambridge.

Morrisson, Cécile. 2004. *Le monde byzantin.* Vol. 1, *L'Empire romain d'Orient, 330–641.* Paris.

Most, Glenn W. 2003. "Violets in Crucibles: Translating, Traducing, Transmuting." *TAPhA* 133.2:381–90.

Mullett, Margaret. 1981. "The Classical Tradition in the Byzantine Letter." In Mullett and Scott 1981, 75–93.

———. 1992. "The Madness of Genre." *DOP* 46:233–43

———. 1997. *Theophylact of Ochrid: Reading the Letters of a Byzantine Archbishop.* Birmingham.

Mullett, Margaret, and Roger Scott, eds. 1981. *Byzantium and the Classical Tradition.* Birmingham.

Norden, Eduard. 1958. *Die antike Kunstprosa.* 5th ed. Darmstadt. (Originally published 1915.)

Norman, A. F. 1960. "The Book Trade in Fourth-Century Antioch." *JHS* 80: 122–26.

———. 1964. "The Library of Libanius." *RhM* 107:158–75.

———. 1983. "Libanius: The Teacher in an Age of Violence." In Fatouros and Krischer 1983, 150–69.

———. 2000. *Antioch as a Centre of Hellenic Culture as Observed by Libanius.* Liverpool.

North, Helen. 1952. "The Use of Poetry in the Training of the Ancient Orator." *Traditio* 8:1–33.

Oberg, Eberhard. 1969. *Amphilochii Iconiensis Iambi ad Seleucum.* Berlin.

Orth, Emil. 1928. *Photiana.* Leipzig.

Pachoud, F., ed. 1986. *Symmaque.* Paris.

Pack, Roger Ambrose. 1933. "The Medical History and Mental Health of Libanius." *TAPhA* 64:53–54.

———. 1935. *Studies in Libanius and Antiochene Society under Theodosius.* Menasha, Wis.

———. 1948. "Two Sophists and Two Emperors." *CP* 42:17–20.

Patillon, Michel. 1988. *La théorie du discours chez Hermogène le rhéteur.* Paris.

Patillon, Michel, and Giancarlo Bolognesi. 1997. *Aelius Théon Progymnasmata.* Paris.

Peachin, Michael, ed. 2001. *Aspects of Friendship in the Graeco-Roman World.* Portsmouth, R.I.

Pedersen, Fritz Saaby. 1976. *Late Roman Public Professionalism.* Odense.

Penella, Robert J. 1990. *Greek Philosophers and Sophists in the Fourth Century A.D.: Studies in Eunapius of Sardis.* Leeds.

———. 2000a. *Private Orations of Themistius.* Berkeley.

———. 2000b. "The Rhetoric of Praise in the Private Orations of Themistius." In Hägg and Rousseau 2000, 194–208.

Pernot, Laurent. 1993. *La rhétorique de l'éloge dans le monde gréco-romain.* Paris.
Petit, L. 1866. *Essai sur la vie et la correspondence du sophiste Libanius.* Paris.
Petit, Paul. 1955. *Libanius et la vie municipale à Antioche au IV siècle après J. C.* Paris.
———. 1956a. *Les étudiants de Libanius.* Paris.
———. 1956b. "Recherches sur la publication et la diffusion des discours de Libanius." *Historia* 5:479–509.
———. 1957. "Les Sénateurs de Constantinople dans l'oeuvre de Libanios." *AntCl* 26:347–82.
———. 1983. "Zur Datierung des Antiochikos (Or. 11) des Libanios." In Fatouros and Krischer 1983, 129–49.
———. 1994. *Les Fonctionnaires dans l'oeuvre de Libanius.* Paris.
Pinker, Steven. 2002. *The Blank Slate.* New York.
Pinto, Mario. 1974. "La scuola di Libanio nel quadro del IV secolo dopo Cristo." *Rendiconto Istituto Lombardo* 108:146–79.
Poralla, Paul. 1985. *A Prosopography of Lacedaemonians.* 2d ed. Chicago.
Pouchet, R. 1992. *Basile le Grand et son univers d'amis d'après sa correspondence. Une stratégie de communion. Studia Ephemeridis "Augustinianum"* 36. Rome.
Puech, Bernadette. 2002. *Orateurs et sophistes grecs dans les inscriptions d'époque impériale.* Paris.
Rashdall, Hastings. 1987. *Universities of Europe in the Middle Ages.* Ed. F. M. Povicke and A. B. Emden. 3 vols. Oxford.
Remie Constable, Olivia. 2003. *Housing the Stranger in the Mediterranean World: Lodging, Trade, and Travel in Late Antiquity.* Cambridge.
Rhodes, Frank H.T. 2001. *The Creation of the Future: The Role of the American University.* Ithaca, N.Y.
Ridley, Matt. 2003. *Genes, Experience, and What Makes Us Human.* New York.
Robert, Louis. 1948. "Epigrammes relatives à des gouverneurs." *Hellenica* 4: 35–114.
———. 1989. *Opera Minora Selecta.* Vol. 6. Amsterdam.
Rochette, Bruno. 1997. *Le latin dans le monde grec.* Brussels.
Roda, Sergio. 1981. *Commento storico al libro IX dell'epistolario di Q. Aurelio Simmaco.* Pisa.
———. 1986. "Polifunzionalità della lettera commendaticia: Teoria e prassi nell'epistolario simmachiano." In Pachoud 1986, 177–202.
Rosovsky, Henry, and Matthew Hartley. 2002. *Evaluation and the Academy: Are We Doing the Right Thing?* Cambridge, Mass.
Roueché, Charlotte. 1989. *Aphrodisias in Late Antiquity.* London.
———. 1998. "The Functions of the Governor in Late Antiquity: Some Observations." *Antiquité Tardive* 6:31–36.
Rougé, J., ed. 1966. *Expositio Totius Mundi et Gentium.* Paris.
Rousseau, Philip. 1994. *Basil of Caesarea.* Berkeley.
———, ed. Forthcoming. *The Blackwell Companion to Late Antiquity.* London.
Ruether, Radford Rosemary. 1969. *Gregory of Nazianzus, Rhetor and Philosopher.* Oxford.

Russell, D. A. 1983. *Greek Declamation*. Cambridge.
———. 1990a. *Antonine Literature*. Oxford.
———. 1990b. "Aristides and the Prose Hymn." In Russell 1990a, 199–219.
———. 1996. *Libanius: Imaginary Speeches*. London.
Russell, D. A., and N. G. Wilson. 1981. *Menander Rhetor*. Oxford.
Russell, James. 2000. "Household Furnishing." In Kondoleon 2000a, 79–89.
Rutherford, Ian. 1998. *Canons of Style in the Antonine Age: Idea-Theory in Its Literary Context*. Oxford.
Ryan, Michael, and David L. Martinson. 2000. "Perceived Effects of Exaggeration in Recommendation Letters." *Journalism and Mass Communication Educator* 55 (Spring): 40–52.
Sacks, Peter. 2003. "Class Rules: The Fiction of Egalitarian Higher Education." *The Chronicle of Higher Education* (July 25): B7–B9.
Said, Suzanne, ed. 1991. *Hellenismos: Quelques jalons pour une histoire de l'identité grecque. Actes du Colloque de Strasbourg*. Leiden.
Salzmann, Ernst. 1910. *Sprichwörter und sprichwörtliche Redensarten bei Libanios*. Tübingen.
Sandwell, Isabella, and Janet Huskinson, eds. 2004. *Culture and Society in Later Roman Antioch*. Oxford.
Scheltema, H. J. 1970. *L'enseignement de droit des antécesseurs*. Leiden.
Schemmel, Fritz. [1907] 1983. "Der sophist Libanios als Schüler und Lehrer." In Fatouros and Krischer 1983, 3–25. (Originally published in *Neue Jahrbücher für das klassische Altertum und für Pädagogik* 20:52–69.)
———. 1908. "Die Hochschule von Konstantinopel im IV. Jahrhundert P.Ch.N." *Neue Jahrbücher für klassische Altertum* 22:147–68
———. 1923. "Die Schule von Berytus." *Philologische Wochenschrift* 43: 236–40.
Schenkl, Heinrich. 1917–18. "Zur Biographie des Rhetors Himerios." *RhM* 72:34–40.
Schindel, Ulrich. 2003. "Der Beruf des Grammaticus in der Spätantike." In Dummer and Vielberg 2003, 173–89.
Schouler, Bernard. 1980. "Dépasser le père." *RÉG* 93:1–24.
———. 1984. *La tradition hellénique chez Libanios*. 2 vols. Paris.
———. 1985. "Hommages de Libanios aux femmes de son temps." *Pallas* 32:123–48.
———. 1991. "Hellénisme et humanisme chez Libanios." In Said 1991, 267–85.
———. 1993. "Libanios et l'autobiographie tragique." In Baslez, Hoffmann, and Pernot 1993, 305–23.
———. 2002. "Libanios en son temps, Libanios aujourd'hui." *Pallas* 60:151–64.
———. 2004. "Le role politique de l'école au temps de Libanios." In Cabouret, Gatier, and Saliou 2004, 97–115.
Schubert, Paul. 1995. "Philostrate et les sophistes d'Alexandrie." *Mnemosyne* 48:178–88.
Schuller, Wolfgang. 2003. "Das römische Recht as Leitbild fur die Spätantike." In Dummer and Vielberg 2003, 191–204.
Schulte, Rainer, and John Biguenet. 1992. *Theories of Translation*. Chicago.
Schulz, Fritz. 1953. *History of Roman Legal Science*. 2d ed. Oxford. (Originally published 1946.)

Schwartz, Barry. 2004. "The Tyranny of Choice." *The Chronicle of Higher Education* (January 23): B6–B8.
Seeck, Otto. 1906. *Die Briefe des Libanius*. Leipzig.
Sievers, G. R. 1868. *Das Leben des Libanius*. Berlin.
Silomon, Hans. 1909. "De Libanii epistularum libris i–vi." Diss., Gottingen.
Simon, Roger I. 1995. "Face to Face with Alterity: Postmodern Jewish Identity and the Eros of Pedagogy." In Gallop 1995, 90–105.
Smith, R.R.R. 1990. "Late Roman Philosopher Portraits from Aphrodisias." *JRS* 80:127–55.
Smith, Robert W. 1974. *The Art of Rhetoric in Alexandria: Its Theory and Practice in the Ancient World*. The Hague.
Sohn, Anne-Marie. 2001. *La correspondance, un document pour l'histoire*. *Cahiers du GRHIS* 12. Rouen.
Steinberg, Jacques. 2003. *The Gatekeepers: Inside the Admission Process of a Premier College*. New York.
Stone, Elizabeth. 2004. "Liberal Arts: Vocation vs. Vocational." *The Chronicle of Higher Education* (November 12): B5.
Struthers, Lester B. 1919. "The Rhetorical Structure of the Encomia of Claudius Claudian." *HSCP* 30:49–87.
Swain, Simon. 1996. *Hellenism and Empire*. Oxford.
———. 2004. "Sophists and Emperors: The Case of Libanius." In Swain and Edwards 2004, 355–400.
Swain, Simon, and Mark Edwards, eds. 2004. *Approaching Late Antiquity: The Transformation from Early to Late Empire*. Oxford.
Tavernini, N. 1953. *Dal libro decimo dell' Institutio Oratoria alle fonti tecnico-metodologiche di Quintiliano*. Università di Torino, Pubblicazioni della facoltà di lettere e filosofia 5.4. Turin.
Taylor, David G.K. 2002. "Bilingualism and Diglossia in Late Antique Syria and Mesopotamia." In Adams, Jansen, and Swain 2002, 298–331.
Thraede, Klaus. 1970. *Grundzüge griechisch-römischer Brieftopik*. *Zetemata* 48. Munich.
Too, Yun Lee, ed. 2001. *Education in Greek and Roman Antiquity*. Leiden.
Trapp, Michael. 2003. *Greek and Latin Letters: An Anthology with Translation*. Cambridge.
Troncoso, Victor Alonso. 2001. "Paideia und Philia in der Hofgesellschaft der hellenistischen Zeit." In Peachin 2001, 81–87.
Van Dam, Raymond. 2002. *Kingdom of Snow: Roman Rule and Greek Culture in Cappadocia*. Philadelphia.
———. 2003a. *Families and Friends in Late Roman Cappadocia*. Philadelphia.
———. 2003b. *Becoming Christian*. Philadelphia.
Vanderspoel, John. 1995. *Themistius and the Imperial Court: Oratory, Civic Duty, and Paideia from Constantius to Theodosius*. Ann Arbor.
Van Rossum-Steenbeek, Monique. 1998. *Greek Readers' Digests? Studies on a Selection of Subliterary Papyri*. Leiden.
Van Wees, Hans. 1998. "The Law of Gratitude: Reciprocity in Anthropological Theory." In Gill, Postlethwaite, and Seaford 1998, 13–49.
Vérilhac, Anne-Marie. 1982. *ΠΑΙΔΕΣ ΑΩΡΟΙ*: Poésie funéraire. Athens.
Vickers, Brian, ed. 1982. *Rhetoric Revalued*. Binghamton, N.Y.

Völker, Harald. 2002. "Spätantike Professoren und ihre Schüler." In Goltz, Luther, and Schlange-Schöningen 2002, 169–85.
———. 2003. *Himerios, Reden und Fragmente. Serta Graeca* 17. Wiesbaden.
Volgers, Annelie, and Claudio Zamagni, eds. 2004. *Erotapokriseis: Early Christian Question-and-Answer Literature in Context.* Leuven.
von Christs, Wilhelm, Wilhelm Schmid, and Otto Stählin. 1924. *Geschichte der griechischen Litteratur. Handbook der Altertumwissenschaft* VII 2.2. Munich.
Vössing, Konrad. 1997. *Schule und Bildung im Nordafrica der Römischen Kaiserzeit.* Brussels.
Walden, J.W.H. 1912. *The Universities of Ancient Greece.* New York.
Walker, Susan, and Averil Cameron, eds. 1989. *The Greek Renaissance in the Roman Empire. BICS,* suppl. 55.
Watson, J., ed. 2001. *Speaking Volumes: Orality and Literacy in the Greek and Roman World. Mnemosyne,* suppl. 218. Leiden.
Watts, Edward. 2004. "Student Travel to Intellectual Centers: What Was the Attraction?" In Ellis and Kidner 2004, 13–23.
———. 2006. "City and School in Late Antique Athens and Alexandria." Berkeley, Calif.
Webb, Ruth. 1994. "A Slavish Art? Language and Grammar in Late Byzantine Education and Society." *Dialogos* 1:81–103.
———. 2001. "The *Progymnasmata* as Practice." In Too 2001, 289–316.
Whitby, Mary, ed. 1998. *The Propaganda of Power: The Role of Panegyric in Late Antiquity.* Leiden.
White, Carolinne. 1992. *Christian Friendship in the Late Fourth Century.* Cambridge.
White, Hayden. 1971. "Literary History: The Point of It All." *New Literary History* 2:173–85.
Whitmarsh, Tim. 2001. *Greek Literature and the Roman Empire.* Oxford.
Wiemer, H.-U. 1995a. *Libanios und Julian: Studien zum Verhältnis von Rhetorik und Politik im vierten Jahrhundert n. Chr. Vestigia. Beitrage zu alten Geschichte* 46. Munich.
———. 1995b. "Die Rangstellung der Sophisten Libanios unter den Kaisern Julian, Valens und Thodosius. Mit einem Anhang über Abfassung und Verbreitung von Libanios' Rede Für die Tempel (Or. 30)." *Chiron* 25:89–130.
———. 1996. "War der 13. brief des Libanios an den späteren Kaiser Julian gerichtet?" *Rheinisches Museum* 139:83–95.
Winterbottom, Michael. 1982. "Schoolroom and Courtroom." In Vickers 1982, 59–70.
Wintjes, Jorit. 2005. *Das Leben des Libanius. Historische Studien der Universität Würzburg* 2. Rahden. Westfalia.
Wolf, Peter. 1952. *Vom Schulwesen der Spätantike. Studien zu Libanius.* Baden.
———. 1967. *Libanius. Autobiographische Schriften.* Zurich.

Index Locorum

This index mostly concerns texts that were quoted or commented on. Abbreviations for classical texts follow the *Oxford Classical Dictionary* and Liddell-Scott-Jones, *Greek-English Lexicon*.

Aeneas of Gaza
  Ep.
    12: 23
Ammianus Marcellinus
  15.1.3: 4
  16.5.3: 170
  16.5.7: 208
  22.10.6: 90
  22.15–22: 78
  22.16.16: 78
  23.2.3: 83
  24.1.9: 74
Anth. Pal.
  7.747: 164
  9.174: 185
  9.451–80: 163
Aristides
  Or.
    31.10: 146
    47.37–39: 150
    51.421.10: 156
  Sarapis
    45: 161
Aristophanes
  Vesp.
    280: 134
Aristotle
  Eth. Nic.
    8.5.3, 1157b23–25
    8.11, 1161a16–19
    8.12, 1161b35–1162a15: 109

Basil of Caesarea
  Epp.
    20: 167
    335–38, 336: 101
    337–38: 102

Cicero
  Att.
    14.7, 14.16, 15.16: 124

  Fam.
    12.16, 16.21: 124
Cod. Theod.
  6.21.1: 44
  13.3.5: 90
  13.3.6: 44
  14.9.1: 31, 213
  14.9.3: 44, 154
  15.1.53: 44

Demetrius
  On Style
    230–32: 8
Demosthenes
  De Cor.
    66: 251
  Mid.
    71: 243
  Or.
    8.37: 317
Dio Chrysostom
  Or.
    18:158
Dio of Prusa
  Or.
    32.68: 53
Dionysius of Halicarnassus
  De imit.
    2: 158

Eunapius
  VS
    43: 52
    457: 40, 72
    458, 460: 74
    462–64: 50, 96
    481: 52
    482–85: 49
    483: 44, 139, 201
    483–85: 51, 92
    484–93: 52
    485: 175

    487: 51, 52, 190
    488:51
    488–90: 53
    490: 190
    491: 52
    492: 52, 54
    493: 58, 79, 162
    493–4: 52, 55, 217
    495: 62
    495–6: 14, 53
    496: 20, 53, 152
    497: 40, 62
    497–99: 79
    502: 52, 156
    504–5: 71
  Hist
    fr. 43: 58
Euripides
  Orestes
    1155–57: 108
Eusebius
  Hist. Eccl.
    7.29.2: 38

Gregory of Nazianzus
  Or.
    4.100–109: 167
    5.23: 128
    43.14: 89
    43.15–24: 166
  Epp.
    7: 167
    10: 167
    11: 166
    14: 208
    30: 89, 95
    38: 167
    52: 171–72
    67: 167
    71: 168
    110: 230
    140: 227
    156: 168

157: 207
173: 208
178: 166
224: 166
Carm.
2.1.1–11, 96–98: 150
106–10: 230
121–210: 175
254–64: 166
308–21: 175
2.1.34.1–2: 230
Gregory of Nyssa
Ep.
13: 100
Gregory Thaumaturgus
Or. in Origenem
5. 57–62: 210

Hermogenes
Peri ideōn
2. 10–12: 158
Herodotus
6.120: 248
Hesiod
Op.
30, 310: 269
Himerius
Or.
4.9
8: 57
18: 193
19: 92, 194
22: 58
26: 193
35: 156, 168, 193, 195
38: 56, 58
39.5: 156
39.8: 58
40.1: 56
48.3: 58
54.1: 45, 109, 194
54.2: 195
54.3: 169
59.1: 56
60.4: 168
62.2: 168
64: 45, 115
65: 193
66: 57, 168, 194
67: 58
68: 115, 169, 195
68 prologue: 56

68.11: 169
69: 58, 169
Homer
Il.
1.128: 263
1.273: 255
2.159: 313
2.298: 85
2.372: 246
2.468: 283
3.22: 29
4.49: 269
5.2–3, 4: 258
5.254: 236
5.261–67: 248
7.216: 237
8.281–82: 247
8.369: 254
8.369: 258
9.396: 281
10.192: 317
14.233: 27
16.250: 259
18.79: 93
Od.
1.2: 252
1.3: 265, 322
1.33: 259
1.170: 264
3.20: 306
4.138–39: 245–6
5.385: 268
11.323: 281
13.399, 431: 78
16.63: 322
17.37: 315
21.425: 236

Isocrates
C.soph.
12: 130
14–18: 130
Antid.
87: 177
180–92: 130
224: 177
Evagoras
8–11: 169

Jerome
Chron.
242–3: 54

de Vir. ill.
71: 38
John Chrysostom
Adversus oppugnatores
47. 368. 8–14: 138
On Babylas
1, 140
John of Sardis
Prog.
144
Julian
Ep.
8: 208
61: 84
Misopogon
359c: 16
Julius Victor
Ars Rhet.
27: 170, 221

Libanius
Epp.: Lib. -Bas
1, 2: 101
3: 102
4: 40, 102
18: 34, 62, 81
23: 68, 190
25: 28, 117, 154
33: 107
62: 64, 65, 222
68: 34
71: 223
80: 190
81: 182, 190
86: 65
88: 37
91: 65
108: 76
113: 181
119: 107
127: 68, 153, 163
136: 207
137: 69
154: 213–14
171: 79
175: 220
176: 120
185: 105
203: 221, 223
206: 60, 61
209: 212
235: 165

Index Locorum • 349

241: 62, 64
243: 150
244: 207
251: 15
255: 57, 165
263: 25
275: 54
269: 221
279: 73
283: 150
288: 216
293: 214, 216
298: 224
299: 76
301: 63, 77, 223
302: 214, 221
303: 220
309: 136
316: 19
331: 153
340: 112, 115, 132
345: 51, 125, 153, 157
347: 80
351: 17
352: 21
357: 36
361: 34
362: 180
363: 210
364: 34
366: 68, 180
368: 34, 63, 64, 65
376: 65
399: 61
405: 21, 63, 96, 119,
  149, 164, 191, 200
428: 123, 170, 188
430: 163
433: 75, 212
434: 64
436: 51
441: 141
444: 7, 182, 200
450: 192
453: 77
454: 33, 36
461: 71
462: 17
469: 54
476: 63
487: 80
501: 100–101

503: 29
517: 69
518: 64
527: 60
529: 17
536: 182
543: 35
546: 76
551: 64
552: 190
554: 96
555: 193
558: 105
559: 171
560: 220
561: 171
571: 128
572: 184
574: 223
575: 63
604: 105
606: 68
617: 18, 213
625: 34, 35
640: 36
646: 216
647: 100–101, 120
648: 40
650: 105
655: 189
664: 68
668: 210
670: 70
674: 106
678: 35
696: 163
704: 125
716: 143
722: 20, 165, 193
733: 106, 113
734: 30, 118, 132
735: 69, 116, 146
742: 55
747: 77
749: 35, 73
754: 17
758: 143
769: 113
771: 30
779: 229
783: 41
793: 64

796: 150
802: 104
807: 214
809: 69
810: 224
811: 229
814: 216
818: 63
819: 77
825: 78
826: 163
828: 164
838: 83, 88–89, 156
843: 16
852: 227
862: 68
863: 74
879: 106
904–908: 36
904: 37
907: 37
909: 231
911: 201
912: 212
916: 212
921: 71, 98
929: 207
951: 211
952: 216
953: 216
956: 66, 77
959: 16
960: 36, 141
961: 80
969: 77
974: 212
980: 106
985: 142
990: 165
993: 106
1001: 25, 231
1002: 106
1004: 151, 215
1008: 68
1014: 69
1015: 71
1016: 78
1026: 16
1032: 212
1035: 78, 170–71
1036: 210
1051: 36

1052: 61
1053: 77
1061: 61
1063: 16, 36
1064: 22, 36, 170
1065: 59–60
1066: 165
1080: 72
1081: 221
1106: 24
1111: 24
1112: 60
1117: 79
1119: 61
1131: 181, 218
1145: 41
1174: 180
1177: 79
1186: 63
1203: 188
1223: 4, 70, 103
1224: 91
1228: 223
1230: 79
1233: 91
1245: 220
1257: 181
1259: 57
1265: 135
1270: 220
1271: 220
1272: 220
1283: 171
1330: 181
1332: 189
1342: 115
1347: 163
1352: 181
1353: 40, 68
1355: 40
1357: 184
1361: 40
1368: 61
1374: 164
1389: 74
1396: 74
1399: 180
1415: 36
1425: 163
1427: 70, 163
1430: 63
1431: 75

1435: 199
1440: 88
1441: 213, 224
1443: 15
1455: 63
1456: 4
1458: 48
1466: 25, 57
1473: 132
1477: 53, 64, 65
1487: 61
1489: 38, 154
1495: 64
1508: 18
1517: 164
1523: 30, 187
1534: 23

Epp. in Appendix One
1: 86, 113, 114, 116, 117, 120, 121
2: 118, 123, 200
3: 120
4: 113, 117, 121
5: 7, 127, 127–28, 200
7: 18, 146, 164, 152
8: 88, 180, 182, 183, 228
16: 31, 69–70, 139
17: 128
18: 40, 118
19: 118, 135, 219
20: 118, 173
23: 140
26: 181, 188, 212
27: 7, 138, 181, 188
28: 75, 212, 218
29: 181
30: 173, 178, 200
31: 34, 172
33: 172
34: 220
35: 95, 114, 180
36: 117, 120, 180, 200
37: 180
38: 121
40: 180
41: 117
42: 140
43: 189
44: 121
45: 80, 135, 153, 212
46: 212

47: 118, 129
48: 68, 113
49: 65, 152, 220
50: 212
51: 129, 212, 231
52: 180, 203
53: 106, 185, 190
54: 173, 189
55: 216
56: 190, 217
58: 173
60: 127, 134
61: 126, 200
62: 126, 127, 181
63: 132, 183
64: 150, 165, 181
65: 18–19, 105
67: 106, 170
68: 27, 126
69: 152
71: 187
72: 148
73: 189
74: 127
75: 7, 113, 115
76: 115, 117
77: 71, 115, 147, 171
78: 178
80: 201
81: 178
82: 7, 180, 201
83: 128
84: 129, 189
85: 114
86: 114, 117, 120
87: 29, 180
88: 49, 74
89: 170, 181
90: 140
91: 120, 125, 126
92: 116, 207
93: 123, 152
96: 188, 212
97: 207
98: 181
99: 105, 180
100: 41, 118
101: 75, 181, 212, 218
103: 118, 128, 170, 183, 207
104: 68, 171, 218
105: 173

Index Locorum • 351

107:120
108: 86, 140
109: 86, 139, 224
110: 222, 224
111: 113, 114
112: 224
116: 113, 114
117: 66, 151, 164, 212, 229
118: 66, 151, 164, 210, 212
119: 75, 115, 121, 122, 132, 138, 227
120: 178, 180
121: 86, 173, 183
123: 135, 228
124: 40, 138, 141
125: 142, 152, 183
126: 140
127: 126
128: 113, 121
129: 68, 103, 115, 116, 147, 177, 222
130: 16, 68, 103, 114, 227
131: 103, 153, 218
132: 113
133: 115, 116, 172
134: 172, 189
135: 120
136: 139
137: 98
138: 31
139: 70, 103, 180, 189
140: 221
143: 120, 126, 132
144: 217
145: 176, 180, 217, 220
146: 127
147: 7, 127, 180
148: 127
149: 51, 63, 94
151: 210
152: 210
153: 19, 51, 63, 94
154: 113
156: 75, 212, 218
157: 179, 228
158: 179, 189
159: 40, 75, 102, 142
160: 40, 75, 102, 142

161: 73
162: 113, 148, 193, 194
163: 17, 118, 119
165: 39, 114, 180
166: 148, 180
167: 181
168: 113, 152, 180, 200
170: 126
171: 32
172: 32
173: 120
174: 181, 200
175: 75, 181, 212
176: 116, 120, 132, 180, 200
177: 57, 118, 120, 131, 135, 176
179: 120
180: 173
181: 120, 124, 125, 135
182: 120, 124
183: 188
184: 128–29
186: 151
187: 120, 134, 228
188: 141
189: 151, 228
190: 57, 187
192: 118, 125
193: 123
194: 139
195: 123, 127
196: 26
197: 151
198: 48, 110, 123
199: 125, 153
200: 47, 65, 81
201: 148
202: 139
204: 35, 110, 117, 123, 181
205: 180, 181
206: 27, 68, 76, 152
Oration 1
2: 228
3: 214
4: 15
5: 16
8: 16, 38

11: 49, 181
12: 118, 218
14–15: 175
16: 51, 192
16–17: 47–48
17: 229, 230
19: 190
20: 192, 201
23: 32, 139
26: 17, 85
27: 86
27–28: 108
29: 86
30: 60
31: 60, 96
34: 14, 108
35: 60
38: 92, 100, 156
42: 89
44: 33, 92, 93
45–47: 89
47: 60
49–50: 72
50: 230
51: 108
53: 48
53–55: 96
54: 15, 156
56: 108
62–70: 72
65: 190
66: 89
68: 72
72: 89
75: 93
75–76: 61
76: 18, 96
77: 212
80: 90
85: 51
86–89: 86–87
90: 156
94: 58
96: 93
101–2: 30
101–4: 37
104: 30, 93, 96, 200
105: 93
109: 92
117: 15
125: 214
142: 18

352 • Index Locorum

155: 152
203: 231
216: 23
221–24: 24
233: 96
237: 153
241: 127
241–42: 191
245: 231
255: 226
256: 230
258: 36
278: 16
Orations:
  2.10: 18
  10–11: 214
  14: 43, 78, 91
  19–20: 41
  20: 20
  24: 150–51
  26: 25
  43: 228
  44: 210
  57: 181
Or. 3: 97, 231
  3: 133
  6: 183, 185, 188
  10: 140
  11: 20
  17: 118
  18: 151
  24: 191
  27–33: 96
Or. 4: 98
  9: 38
  11: 98
  14: 104
  16–17: 187
  18: 133, 188
Or. 5.13–15: 21
  28: 16
  43–53: 154
  45–52: 44
  46: 201
Or. 8.7, 12–13: 108
Or. 9.16–17: 185
  17: 187
Or. 10: 227
  6: 229
Or. 11: 23–5
  1: 3
  8: 25

20–21: 37
32: 96
37: 21
89–90: 202
93: 227
128: 16
133–49: 25
133–52: 29
134–35: 28
139: 29
139–41: 229
141: 29
150: 25
167–68: 27
180: 208
181–92: 29
188: 25
218–20: 28
253–54: 25
266: 26
266–67: 28
Or. 12.63: 22
  92: 155, 164
  92–94: 208
  94: 28, 156
Or. 13.13: 65
  52: 173
Or. 15.6: 143
  27–28: 65
  67–68, 77–78: 143
Or. 16.16: 143
Or. 18.12–15: 142
  12, 14: 61
  14: 192
  16: 207
  29: 143
  29–30: 128
  158–60: 90
  282: 19
  208–9: 133
  284: 22
  288: 90
Or. 19.6, 51: 25
Or. 22.31: 44
Or. 23: 98
  16–18, 22: 97
  20: 21, 170
  26–27: 181
  204: 65
  294: 30
Or. 25: 134–35
  46–50: 206

47: 135
48: 203
50: 230
50–51: 202
Or. 27: 81
  339a: 213
  339: 218
Or. 28.2: 226
  342a: 87
Or. 30: 23
  8: 17
Or. 31: 23, 30–31, 35, 37, 185
  7: 27
  10: 27
  21: 203
  25: 186, 188
  29–32: 186
  30: 84, 204
  42: 76, 77
Or. 33.3: 179, 226
  4: 198
  8: 18
Or. 34: 118–19, 154
  2: 17–18
  10: 29
  12: 17
  14: 96
  15: 144, 148, 165
  16: 201
  20: 99, 191, 231
  27: 29, 148
  27–28: 154
  29: 118
Or. 35.3: 215
  7: 15
  9: 29
  12: 188
  13: 128, 153
  13–14: 28, 181
  16: 148
  20: 204
  21: 148
  22: 201
Or. 36: 41
  8: 203
  9: 186
  10–11: 38
  10–13: 19
  13: 191
Or. 38: 35
  2: 133, 187

Index Locorum • 353

6: 17, 211
8–12: 181
9: 193
15: 21
Or. 39.16–17: 41
Or. 40.22: 65
5: 206
5–6: 211
6: 209
7: 153
Or. 41.6–9: 181, 229
Or. 42.3: 18
9: 65, 138
11–13: 226
13: 128
21–22: 151
31: 27
40: 226
43: 18
Or. 43: 41, 95, 191, 192
3: 193
5: 211
6: 184
6–7, 13: 186
7: 187
8: 109, 191
9: 21, 119
10: 133
15: 220
16: 205
Or. 44.2–3: 152
Or. 45.11: 7
20–21: 28
Or. 46.44: 227
Or. 48.22: 211
Or. 49.23: 134
27–28: 85
32: 155, 228
Or. 50.31: 25
Or. 52.21: 74
Or. 54.16–18: 185
17: 185
17–18: 188
52: 36
34: 85
48: 74
Or. 55: 77
1: 170
6–8: 94
10: 92, 94–95
14: 180
21, 26: 185

23: 1, 92
28: 120
32: 85
32–33: 205
34: 85, 146
Or. 57: 211
3: 187
3–6: 147
Or. 58.6: 127
25: 127
29–31: 181
30–31: 211
33: 104
38: 127
Or. 59.34: 204
Or. 60: 140
Or. 61: 23
Or. 62: 98–99, 102
6: 117, 204
12: 165
15: 49
16: 207
21: 188
21–23: 218
25: 181, 191
27–28: 99
29–30, 32: 206
35: 36, 206
37: 182
38: 215
46–48: 227
50: 228
61: 95
63–69: 227
Or. 64: 23, 132–33
47: 133
48: 181
99: 17
106: 17
Decl.
2: 230
27.6–11: 20
28.13: 2
Progymnasmata
Diēgēmata 27: 26
Encomia 3: 144–45
Psogoi 1: 144–45
Peri euphyias: 40
Lucian
Demon.
12: 53
Lex.

2: 160
Merc.Cond.
11: 200
Nigr.
pref.: 15
Rh.Pr.
6: 156
8: 175
9: 174, 227
10: 196
19: 53
26: 175
Somn.
15: 87
16: 95
Lysias
20.11: 109

Nicolaus
30–34: 149
47: 146

Orphic Hymns
36.5: 315

Philostratus
VS
492: 53
507: 1
539: 160
589: 53
590: 188
604: 45, 118
620: 53
Photius
Bibl. Cod.
90: 55–56
161: 50
165: 55
Plato
Ap.
31b-c: 186
Ti.
22b: 140
Prt.
308b-c: 186
Resp.
289b: 319
377b: 130
Pliny the Younger
Ep.
9.9: 170

Plutarch
  Mor.
    736d: 202
  Per.
    27: 280
  Quaest. conv.
    622d: 156
P.Oxy.
    I.40, I.58: 198
    IV.724: 207
    XVII.2084: 146
    XVIII.2190: 32
P.Tebt.
    II.291: 198
Procopius of Gaza
  Epp.
    35, 61, 94: 23
Ps.-Plutarch
  De liberis educandis
    1c, 2c, 4a-5c: 131

Quintilian
  Pr. 26–27: 131
  1.1.1–3: 131
  1.1.1–8: 131
  1.2.8: 131
  1.3.1: 122
  2.1: 144
  2.1: 160
  2.2.9–12: 202
  2.2.9–13: 154
  2.5.1–17: 158
  2.5.6: 165
  2.8: 131
  2.8.1–3: 122
  10.1: 158

Socrates
  Hist. Eccl.
    2. 46.2: 73
    4. 26: 55, 100
Sophocles
  Aj.
    964: 259
Sozomen
  Hist. Eccl.
    6.17: 55
Suda
    1009, 1010: 47
    A 1128: 79
    E 3407: 76
    λ 486: 53
Suetonius
  Gram.
    10: 154
Symmachus
  Epp.
    1.44: 222
    1.72: 222
  2.16: 222
  7.1: 171–72

Themistius
  Or.
    6.71: 113
    6.71c-d: 208
    8.105: 208
    9.126b: 208
    20.238: 56
    21.246: 56
    23.249c-d: 186
    23.280–92: 189
    23.285–86: 56
    24.282–83: 230
    24.301a: 230
    26.317–18: 56
    27: 177–78
    27.332d–33b: 73
    31.352: 56
Thucydides
    2.39: 27

Xenophon
  Mem.
    2.4.7: 109

Zosimus
    3.34.6: 164

Index

Numbers in bold refer to the letters in Appendix One and are gathered at the end of each entry.

Ablabius 2: 71, 98
Abureius: 78
Acacius 6: 17, 20, 21, 38–40, 75, 93, 180, 192–93
Acacius 7: 68–69, 114, 120, 125, 163; **188, 190, 191, 192, 194, 195, 196, 197, 199, 201, 202**
Acacius 8: 103; **110, 139**
Achilles: 88, 144–45
advocate: 212–13
Aedesius 1: 138
Aeneas of Gaza: 81
Aesop: 194
Aetius ii: 106
Albanius (student): 17, 146, 182, 183, 228
Alcimus: 72, 101; **147**
Alexander 5: 83–84, 88–89
Alexander 8: 79
Alexandra: 30n101, 132
Alexandria: 27, 32, 44, 78
alumni: 104–7
Ameinias: 72
Amerbach, Johann: 9, 32, 119–20, 125, 175, 176
Ammianus: 78, 90, 170, 208
Amphilochius 2: 70
Amphilochius 4: 70, 110, 139, 161
Anatolius 3 (Eunapian): 52
Anatolius 3 (Libanian): 190, 219; **106**
Anaxentius (student): 85, 94–95
Ancyra: 71, 79, 86, 117, 164
Androcles: 71, 115, 171
Andromachus 2: 50, 72
Anon. Lond. professor: 9, 95, 172n197, 175, 185n65, 193n113, 200–201
Antioch: 1, 15, 24–29, 84, 87–88, 161, 203, 208, 209, 210, 219, 229, and passim; climate of, 26; population of, 27; preeminence of, 177, 212
Apamea: 47
Aphobius: **174**
Aphrodisias: 46, 67
Aphrodite: 16

Aphthonius: 59–60
Apolinarius (and Gemellus, students): 182–83
Apollinarius of Laodicea (father and son): 73
Apollo: 57, 194
Apollonius Rhodius: 159
appointment (to position): 197–99
Apronianus: 59
Apsines 1: 50
Apsines 2: 50, 51, 139
Aramaic: 27
Aratus: 159, 162
Aresius: 115–16
Argeius: 68, 115–16, 152
Aristaenetus 1: **136**
Aristaenetus 2 (student): 170, 221
Aristides Aelius: 17, 134, 146, 151, 161; and Libanius, 6, 23
Aristotle: 8, 109
Armenia: 180
Artemis: 21, 154
assistants of Libanius: 19, 35–37, 185, 200, 203
Asterius 2: 69
Athens: 15, 27, 31, 42, 84–86, 89, 100, 124, 171, 175–76, 229, and passim; school of, 47–60, 80–82, 143, 166, 168, 177, 192, 193, 201, 204, 211; school accommodations in, 44–45
attendance: 174–75, 191, 197, 227–28; long, 176–79, 195–96, 205–206; short, 49, 179–83, 196
Atticus: 124
auditoria: 44
Autobiography (of Libanius): 6, 13–14, 39, 60, 87–88, 92–93, 108, 152, 156, 184, 231, and passim

Basil of Caesarea: 2, 52, 55, 69, 73, 100–101, 167, 175; and correspondence with Libanius, 100–104
Basilides (student): 173

Bassianus (student): 172
Belaeus: 77
Bemarchius: 60
Bentley: 14
Berytus: 44, 75, 162, 209, 211, 212, 218
Bonus: 77–78, 170–71
books: 153, 188
brothers: 32

Caesarea (Cappadocia): 69–70, 100
Caesarea (Palestine): 39, 76–77
Caesarius 1: 199, 224–25
Caesarius 2: 167
Caesarius ii: 114
Callimachus: 159, 168
Callinicus: 49, 50
Calliopius 3: 33–35
Calliopius 4: 36
Calliopius iii (student): 180
Cameron, Alan: 161
carriers of letters. *See under* letters
Castricius 2: 78–79
Celsus 2: 210
Celsus 3: 20, 41, 55, 65, 101, 146; **157**, 200
chariot races: 18, 27–28
chorus: 9, 30, 35, 84, 148; head of. *See koryphaios*
Christian: 2, 25, 54, 70, 110, 166, 167, 168, 230
Chrysantius of Sardis: 67, 71
Chrysogonus (student): 80
Chrysostom John: 2, 28, 138, 140, 143
Cicero: 124–25, 135, 209
Cimon: 15–16, 34–35, 98, 118, 140–41
civil service. *See* liturgy
Claudian: 161–62
Clearchus 1: **113**
Clematius 2: **171**
Cleobulus 1: 33–34, 65
competence: of officials, 198–99; of sophists, 87, 202–205; of students, 200–201
Constans (emperor): 204, 219
Constantinople: 15, 27, 30, 48, 56, 86, 87, 88, 90, 92–93, 96, 100, 141, 142, 213; school of, 60–66, 81, 184; Senate of, 18, 213
Constantinus (emperor): 204
Constantius (emperor): 69, 86, 143, 204, 207, 219
copybook: 4
Cornutus: 72

cost of education: 183–91; fees, 183–87; financial aid, 189–91; gifts, 188–89
Crispinus: 86, 108
curriculum. *See* school of Libanius

Daduchius (student): 135
Daphne: 26–27, 126
Decentius: **138**
declamation: 20, 154, 201–2, 230, 231
decurions (*curiales*): 31n102, 186
defections: 19, 80, 95, 109, 191–96, 205
Demetrius 2: 68, 149–50, 190
Demosthenes: 6, 122, 149–51, 152, 153, 157, 159, 165, 167, 172, 174, 195
Dianius (student): 65, 152
dictation: 4
Dio Chrysostom: 158
Diocletian: 72
Diogenes (student): 20
Dionysius 5: 80
Dionysius 6: 106, 173, 190, 216–17
Dionysius of Halicarnassus: 158, 159
Diophantus: 51, 52, 217
Diophantus (student): 126–27
dokimasia: 25n70, 84–88, 110
Domitianus 5: **122**
Domninus 5: 74
Domnio 1 (Domninus): 75, 212, 218; **26, 28, 101, 156, 175**
Dorotheos 4: 164

Ecdicius ii: 80, 110
educated people (*pepaideumenoi*): 85, 87
education: 112, 122, 137, 155; continuity vs. change of, 5; of girls, 30–31; in Late Antiquity, 175; length of (*see* attendance); modern, 112, 122, 147–48, 155; vs. nature, 129–34
Egypt: 147, 159, 161, 162, 208
Ellebicus: **78**
encomium: 94, 144–46
Entrechius 1: **56, 120**
Epagathus: 50
epigrams: 163, 227
Epiphanius 1: 51, 52
Eudaemon 2: 33–34
Eudaemon 3: 76, 163, 165
Eudoxius 1: 70
Eudoxius 2: 70
eugeneia (nobility): 116, 214, 216
Eunapius: 14, 42–43, 44, 49, 50, 51, 52, 58, 62, 67, 79, 92, 139, 175, and pas-

sim; and Acacius 6, 40; and Himerius, 55; and Iamblichus, 73–74; and Libanius, 14, 20, 40, 48, 53, 153, 192; and Prohaeresius, 14, 52–53, 55
Eupeithius: 67
Euripides: 165
Eusebius 12: 79
Eusebius 15: **72**
Eusebius 24: 36–37, 178
Eusebius 25: 178, 221
Eusebius 26: 51, 80
Eusebius xx (student): 71, 115
Eustathius 6: 152, 188
Eustephius: 67
Eustochius 2: 69
Eustochius 5: 70–71
Eutherius 2: 37, **154**, 165
Eutropius 3: 187
Eutropius 4: 59–60
examination. *See* testing
Expositio totius mundi et gentium: 44, 78

Factinianus: 16, 106–107; **130**
Fathers: 97, 114, 131–32, 205; as teachers, 138
Felix 6: **83**
fights: 139–40
financial aid. *See* cost of education
Firmianus: 72
Flavianus: 189; **84**
Fortunatianus: 163
friendship: 42, 107–10; in letters, 8

Gaius 1: 163
Gaius (student): 28–29
Gallus (emperor): 208
Gaudentius 2: 21, 35, 73, 187
Gaza: 77, 94
Genethlius: 50
genre: 6–8, 24, 48, 231
Gerontius: 49, 74
Gessius 1: 79; **90**
Gibbon: 14, 16
Gorgias: 53, 57
Gorgonius 4: 54
governors: 27–28, 88–91, 214, 226–28
grammarian: 31, 116, 156–57, 160
gratitude: 183–84, 188
Gregory of Nazianzus: 46, 47, 52, 55, 69–70, 71, 76, 85, 89, 100, 128, 137–38, 150, 171–72, 175, 190, 195, 208, 230; love for *logoi* of, 165–69

Gregory of Nyssa: 69, 100, 137
Gregory Thaumaturgus: 210
Gymnasius 1: 75

hamilla: 149–50
Harpocration: 33–34, 65
Hecebolius 1: 61, 142, 192
Helicon: 58, 194
Hellespontius: 71
Helpidius 3: 76–77
Hephaestion 1: 51, 190
Heracleius (student): 106
Heracles: 57
Herculius: 59
Hermes: 57, 79, 131
Hermogenes of Tarsus: 6, 59, 151, 155, 158–60
Hermopolis: 75
Herodianus 2: 36
Hesiod: 57–58, 159, 163
Hesychius 4: 152; **93**, **94**
hetairos: 82, 108–109
Hilarius 8: 77
Himerius 2: 43, 45, 46, 53, 54–58, 59, 72, 92, 109, 115, 139, 153, 226, 230; and students' unrest, 193–95; and poetry, 168–69
Homer: 120, 159, 163, 165, 168
Honoratus (student): 170, 171, 207
Hyginus: 145
Hypatius 1: 173; **105**
Hyperechius (student): 15, 86, 113, 125, 213, 223–25

Iamblichus 1: 50, 73–74
Iamblichus 2: 50
iatrosophist: 16, 79–80
illness: **18**, **81**, **87**, **102**, **108**, **145**, **205**
imitation: 142–43, 172
inscriptions: 27, 43, 59, 67, 69, 72, 161; for governors, 227
interview: 217, 222–25
Isocrates: 63, 129–31, 175, 177
Italicianus: **82**, **150**

Jewish Patriarch: 76
John of Sardis: 144
Jovinus 1: 96
Julian (emperor): 14, 19, 22, 28, 48, 55, 61, 63, 67, 83, 90–91, 103, 128, 156, 158–59, 164, 167, 192, 207, 208, 214, 219; edict of, 54, 90; and Prohaeresius,

53–54; as student of Libanius, 142–43, 170, 173, 176
Julianus 5: 44, 49, 50, 51, 52, 55
Julianus 15 (student): 66, 138, 151, 164, 217
Julianus xv (student): 86, 173
Julianus xxi: 40
Julius 1: 33
Jullus: **124**

koryphaios (head of *chorus*): 200–201

Latin: 6, 17, 34, 81, 82, 181, 182, 191, 206–12
law, Roman: 6, 75, 81, 82, 191, 206–12, 218, 231; cost of studies of, 187–88
Leontius 9: 73, 180; **161**
Leontius 10: 69
Leontius 14: **125**
Leontius xvi: 29–30
Letoius vi (student): 71
letters: 3–4, 8, 229; of application (*see under* school of Libanius); Byzantine, 5, 8; carriers of, 116, 125–26, 136; classification of, 111; dossiers, 10; lack of privacy of, 116
letters of Libanius: 1–2, 4–8, 123, 136, 212; addressees of, 213; to alumni, 104–105; and attendance, 97–99, 176–77, 191; audience of, 7; on education, 5, 7–8, 10, 111–12; vs. orations, 6–8, 24, 119, 187, 192, 207, 212; of recommendation (*see* recommendation); subscriptions of, 4; topics of, 4–5; and letter writing in school, 169–73
Libanius: and Athens, 37, 47–49, 81, 83, 102, 108, 152, 179, 194; character of, 6; and Constantinople, 60–61; contradictions of, 1, 6, 107, 207; duplicity of, 8, 24 ; education of, 31, 159 ; family of, 15–16, 214; as foster father, 37, 114, 137–41; and governors, 24, 88–91, 214, 226–28; health of, 6, 22–23, 230–31; and Himerius, 55; humor in, 19–21; invective in, 24; early life of, 13–19, 84–88, 200; love for rhetoric of, 15, 16, 18; old age of, 24, 106–107, 140, 231; and poetry, 163–65; and Prohaeresius, 53–54; salary of, 184–85; son of (*see* Cimon); style of, 13–14, 21–22; as teacher, 5–6, 18–20, 231; and women, 15, 123, 132, 141; works of, 3n10, 152

liturgy: 94n49, 181, 215–16
logoi: 164, 170
love: for rhetoric, 155–56; between teachers and students, 139–40
Lucian: 55, 87, 160, 174, 175, 195–96, 200, 227
Lysias:107

Magnus 7: 16, 79–80
Magnus (student): 220
Majorinus (student): 220
Malchion: 38
Malchus: 41
Marcellinus: 98
Marcus (student): 70, 103, 180
Marius 1: 40; **25, 45**
Marrou: 160
Maximus 10: 68
Maximus 19: 79; **3, 9, 12, 40, 128, 169**
Maximus 21: 67
Meleager: 1
meletē: 150, 153
Menander: 161
Menecrates (student): 217
metaphor: agricultural, 138, 141–42; erotic, 156; liquid, 29, 148, 193
Modestus 2: 18, 41, 146, 213–14, 216, 224; **184**
monks: 17
mosaics: 25, 46–47
Muses: 57–58, 131, 194–95
Musonius 2: 58
myth: 57–58, 162

nature (*physis*): 129–34
New Year: 19, 185
Nicobulus: 70, 170
Nicocles: 60–61, 96; **185**
Nicolaus: 146
Nicomedia: 15, 48, 54, 72, 96, 100, 108, 176, 192
noise: 154, 229–30
Nymphidianus: 67

oath: 61, 94, 142, 191–92
Olympianus 1: 38
Olympius 4: 63, 210; **151, 152, 153**
Onesimus: 50
Origen: 76

Paeonius 2: 71–72
paganism: 2

Palladius 8: 70, 103, 180
Palladius 14: **81**
Palladius 18: 173; **55, 57, 59**
panegyric: 219
Panegyrius: 77
Parnasius: 52
Parthenopaeus: 75
Paulus of Lycopolis: 50
Paulus iii: 80
pedagogue: 17, 104, 118–20, 122, 126, 129, 136, 148, 165, 191
Petit, Paul: 9–10, 33, 103
Phalerius: 71–72
Phidias, 56
Philagrius 3: 89
philia. *See* friendship
Philippus 3: 70, 103, 163
philosophy: 62, 64, 65, 66, 217
Philostratus: 43, 45, 160, 188
Philoxenus (student): 123
Philumenus: 40
Photius: 50, 55–56
Pindar: 46, 167, 168
Plato: 130, 133, 140, 151, 174, 195
Plutarch: 202
Plutarchus 2 (*PLRE* II): 59
Plutarchus 5: 45
poetry: in Late Antiquity, 161–63, 227; in rhetorical schools, 122, 145, 157, 159–65, 167–69
portraits: 18, 23
Priscio: 77
Priscianus 1: **135, 167**
Proclus 4 (*PLRE* II): 45
Proclus 5 (*PLRE* II): 67
Proclus 6: 18, 24; **79**
Procopius 1: **53**
Procopius 4: 223
Procopius 10: 71
Procopius of Cilicia: 106
Progymnasmata: 143–47
Prohaeresius: 43, 44, 49, 50, 51, 52–54, 55, 79, 168, 190
Protagoras: 54, 186
Ps.-Demetrius: 8, 111
Ps.-Libanius: 111
Ps.-Plutarch: 129–31, 141
punishment: 195

Quintianus: 58
Quintilian: 121–22, 129, 131, 133, 141, 144, 154, 158–59, 165, 177, 202, 218

Quirinus: 68
quotations, literary: 158–59

reading: 149, 152, 153, 157, 229; reading lists, 158
recommendation: for admission, 112–17; characteristics of, 116–17, 216, 218–19; modern, 219, 220; for positions, 197–98, 199, 212, 213–22, 225; lack of privacy of, 116, 222; from teachers, 114–16
recruitment: 42, 83–110; geographical, 97–100
reports: 122–27, 200; addressees of, 123; components of, 127–29; veracity of, 134–36
rhetor: vs. sophist: 37
rhetoric: 90, and passim; in Antioch, 29, 81–82; Byzantine, 196; decline of, 6, 66, 78, 165, 186, 201, 206, 228; and poetry, 53; and power, 18, 197, 225–28; roads to (*see* attendance); theory of, 153, 155; tradition of, 5–6
Riot of the Statues: 17, 21, 96, 98
Rome: 27, 85, 210, 211, 213
Rufinus 18: 24

Sarapion: 69
Saturninius Salutius: 91
Saturninus 5: 38
Saturninus 10: **50**
school of Libanius: 30–37, 148, and passim; application to, 112–17; curriculum of, 147–55; location of, 30, 43–44; size of, 30, 88, 95–97, 204
schools: 37, 43–47
Scylacius 2: 75, 173; **119**
Sebastianus 2: **172**
Sebastianus 3: 75, 218
Second Sophistic: 1, 6, 156
Seleucus 1: 18, 132
Severinus: 106
Severus 9: 67–68
Severus 14 (student): 147, 187
Severus of Alexandria: 102
shorthand: 6, 206–207
Sievers: 13
Silanus 1: 75, 212
silence: 214, 228, 229–31; of Libanius, 90, 231, **191**; of students, 15, 153, 221, 224; **2, 12, 50, 51, 72, 99, 105, 110, 154**
Silvanus 3 (student): 17, 181–82, 187

Siricius: 50
sleep: 28–29
Socrates: 56–57, 61, 186, 195, 230
Sopater 1: 50, 74
Sopater 2 (*PLRE* I): 50
Sopater 2 (*PLRE* II): 58–59, 155
sophists: 42–43, 66; in Antioch, 37–41, 180, 205; in Arabia and Egypt, 77–80, 91; in Athens, 47–60, 91; in Bithynia, Paphlagonia, and Armenia, 72–73, 180; in Cappadocia, 69–71; in Constantinople, 60–66; in Galatia, 71–72; in Lidia and Caria, 67; in Lycia, Pamphilia, and Cilicia, 67–69; mobility of, 81; official, 1, 25, 30, 43, 60, 112, 184, 185; in Palestine, 76–77; in Syria and Phoenicia, 73–75; warfare of, 91–95
Sopolis: 52
spectacles: 27–28
Spectatus 1: 153; **102**
Stagirius: 70–71
statues (of sophists): 43, 54, 59
Strategius 1: 41, 75
Strategius 3: 69
Strategius (student): 182
Strategius Musonianus: 48–49, 51
students: 7–8; age of, 31, 154, 181; from Antioch, 91, 97–99, 177; behavior of, 17, 96, 127–28, 181; from Cappadocia, 101–104; careers of, 29, 49, 178, 206, 214, 218, 228; dull, 133–34; fat, 17; lodging for, 117–18; mobility of, 82, 191; sleeping, 133; status of, 31, 183
style: Asianic, 53; singing, 53, 55–56
Suda lexicon: 15, 43, 50, and passim
Suetonius: 144
Symmachus: 171–72; letters of, 215, 222
Synesius: 59, 81
Syrianus: 45

Tatianus 5: 165
testing: 85; diagnostic, 120–22, 200, 223; of students, 199–202, 205; of teachers, 88, 202–205

Thalassius: 18, 151, 207
theatron: 45, 47
Themistius 1: 41, 43, 53, 54, 56, 68, 70, 73, 76, 81, 152, 164, 167, 177–78, 185–86, 189, 208, 217, 223, 229, 230; **49, 117, 118**; and Libanius, 61–66, 152
Themistius 2 (student): 123–24, 135–36, 139, 151, 179, 226
Themistocles: 51, 63; **149**
Theodorus 7: 80
Theodorus 10: 40
Theodorus 11: 23
Theodosius (emperor): 97
Theon 1: 75
Theon of Alexandria: 144, 149, 151
Theotecnus: 150
Thespesius 2: 76
Thucydides: 160
Titianus (student): 125, 146, 151, 153
Tlepolemus: 49
Tuscianus: 51

Ulpianus 1: 38, 51, 53, 73, 83
university: of Basel, 32, 176; of Paris, 32, 119, 176
Uranius: 35–36

vacations: 25, 153
Valens (emperor): 91
Valentinian (emperor): 31
Vergil: 209
Victor, Julius: 4, 170, 221

wealth: 214, 225–26

Zacharias Scholasticus: 67
Zenobius: 34, 35, 37, 38–39, 73, 88, 93, 97, 102
Zenodorus: **202**
Zenon 2: 79
Zenon 7: 61

GPSR Authorized Representative: Easy Access System Europe - Mustamäe tee 50, 10621 Tallinn, Estonia, gpsr.requests@easproject.com